MUNDANE ASTROLOGY

by

MICHAEL BAIGENT
NICHOLAS CAMPION
CHARLES HARVEY

THE AQUARIAN PRESS
Wellingborough, Northamptonshire

First published 1984

British Library Cataloguing in Publication Data

Baigent, Michael
    Mundane Astrology.
    1. Astrology
    I. Title   II. Campion, Nicholas
    III. Harvey, Charles
    133.5'3   BF1708.1

    ISBN 0-85030-302-8

The Aquarian Press is part of the Thorsons Publishing Group

Printed and bound in Great Britain

DEDICATION

To the memory of Charles Carter and John Addey — with grateful thanks.

CONTENTS

ACKNOWLEDGEMENTS

The authors would like to give thanks to their many colleagues who both directly and indirectly gave them help and encouragement with this work. For assistance with specific points we would like to thank Derek Appleby, Geoffrey Cornelius, Patrick Curry, Ronald C. Davison, Dr Liz Greene, Chester Kemp, Christine Ramsdale, Leyla Rael-Rudhyar, and Mike Startup. André Barbault as the greatest living mundane astrologer has our particular gratitude. His many works and his excellent journal *L'Astrologue* have proved a touchstone of clarity and reason in a hitherto often confused and disjointed area of astrology. We owe an especial debt to the Astrological Association for the continual access provided to their Research Section Library with its unique multi-lingual collection of astrological books and periodicals. Grateful appreciation goes to our publishers and our editors Michael Cox and Simon Franklin for their patience and co-operation in working with three authors at the same time — no small task! Finally for Suzi Lilley-Harvey for all her help with the illustrations, proof reading, and her endless support, and inspiration C.H. cannot yet find adequate words but is working on it!

M.B., N.C., C.H.

Then he showed me the river of the water of life bright as crystal, flowing from the throne of God and of the Lamb through the middle of the city; also, on either side of the river, *the tree of life with its twelve kinds of fruit, yielding its fruit each month; and the leaves of the tree were for the healing of the nations.*

Revelation 22, 1-2

INTRODUCTION

Astrology in Tomorrow's World

Perhaps the most pressing need in the modern world, both for individuals and nations is for a greater perspective of the destiny and purpose of the human race in the scheme of the universe. In spite of the seductions of nihilistic materialism, most of us have a deep sense that life would make more sense if we could perceive all its manifestations as a single unity rather than as a series of separate and randomly organized parts. That there is such a need is clearly shown by the proliferation of esoteric groups and religious cults in the West to a greater extent than at any time since the Reformation.

Until the late Renaissance, about three hundred years ago, there was a general acceptance of the universe as a single organism, in which no part could be understood in isolation from the whole. This general assumption formed the basis of all education through the three interconnected studies of theology, philosophy and astrology. Of these philosophy has progressively, over the last three centuries, abdicated all responsibility for any matters above the level of semantics, whilst theology has for the most part been content to become a mere adjunct to social concern and the fashionable causes of the time. Only astrology retains its ancient roots in the philosophy of the universe as a single unity in which, in the words of the Platonists, the heavenly bodies were 'the first born thoughts of God'.

It was no doubt with this in mind that Dr L. Cunibert Mohlberg of the Vatican wrote in his 'Candi's Letters to Tscu' that:

If we look ahead it is already possible to say that Astrology seems this is in essence the great and noble role which mundane, or 'pure', astrology is called to serve once again. We say 'once again', because from earliest recorded times until three hundred years ago in Europe, the study of cosmic patterns was the very core of all attempts to understand collective behaviour. In every community, from the smallest city-state to the largest empire, and from the earliest days of Mesopotamia to the nation states of the seventeenth century, the most important task of the astrologer was to explain and forecast the vicissitudes in collective fortunes.

Astrologers themselves must share the responsibility for the exclusion of astrology from its former spheres of influence, for the amount of time devoted to mundane astrology in this century is minute compared to the time dedicated to natal astrology. Astrologers have been seduced by the over analytical and materialist concerns of the age. They have been drawn into a reductionist, technological, society which has replaced astro-meteorology with 'scientific' weather forecasting, medical astrology with drugs, and agricultural astrology with chemical sprays. Yet if we look at the achievements of these modern alternatives we cannot be impressed: the modern weather forecaster for all his billions of pounds worth of satellites and computers is incapable of making any but the most obvious predictions; despite the undoubted dedication and brilliant research of many physicians, thousands develop serious disease and hundreds die as a result of modern medical methods; agricultural 'experts' destroy the productive capacity of large areas of land with their chemical treatments. In other fields university economists are virtually incapable of making a single correct prediction about economic trends, while the global systems they analyse destroy whole societies and pollute the land we rely on for our survival. Even politicians of goodwill seem unable to do little apart from cobble together *ad hoc* responses to emergency situations, while the political machinery they control appears fit for little apart from war, repression and confrontation. In the absence of a guiding philisophy the potential of nuclear energy has become perverted into the threat of nuclear holocaust, while in the midst of a technological revolution the rich get richer and the poor get poorer. It is time for us to recognize the massive failure of the modern world to organize itself in any reasonable way, a difficult step to make if we live in the prosperous areas of the west, but an essential one if we are to have sufficient determination to re-create a meaningful mundane astrology.

The importance of mundane astrology for the individual lies in the doctrine of 'subsumption', which states that the individual is subsumed, or contained, within the mass. Thus the natal chart is contained within the mundane and it is therefore not possible ultimately to give a judgment on a nativity without considering the relevant mundane horoscopes. Charles Carter summed up the issue succinctly:

> Could the nativities of the victims of Hiroshima all have indicated the death and ruin that overtook them on that fateful day of August 1945? Perhaps, and yet, the horoscope of that city, could it have been studied, would surely have been helpful in judging them. [2]

All experience indicates that Carter's intuition was right, and that mundane charts drawn for cities, organization, nations and events such as the outbreaks of peace and war, can indicate the collective fates of individuals when their nativities are far less clear.

In a sense the natal horoscope may be seen as the map of an individual's drive for self-development and self-fulfilment, whether successful or frustrated. In contrast the mundane chart indicates the needs and demands of the mass, which are therefore likely to be opposed to the strivings of the individual. Mundane astrology therefore provides the philosophical link between the destiny of the individual and that of the mass, as well as that between all the different concerns of the collective.

All of us, even the most remote and solitary hermits, are members of a group, whether family, village, city, nation, or religion, which to a greater or lesser degree exerts pressure on us as individuals. These groups intertwine to form overlapping hierarchies, and none of us is free of their influence. Ultimately mankind's transformation and perfection depends upon the full infoldment of each one of us, a work in which natal astrology can greatly assist. But it is to mundane astrology that we must look to complete the picture of humanity transformed, at peace with itself, with the Cosmos, and with the Unity of all Unities.

References

1 Mohlberg, C.L. *Candi's Letters to Tscu.*
2 Carter, C. *An Introduction to Political Astrology.*

PART ONE:
THE BACKGROUND

1.

THE DEVELOPMENT OF MUNDANE ASTROLOGY FROM THE BABYLONIANS TO THE ARABS

Michael Baigent

Astrology as we have inherited it in the West emerged originally from the mythology of ancient Mesopotamia. From those once great imperial cities, today buried beneath the Iraqi sands, came the rudiments of our modern study. Their ancient astrology was barely separable from the prevailing mythology. The characters of the gods were the characters of the planets. The actions of these gods, as recorded in the great epics, provided the blueprint for the omens which were drawn from planetary movements. It seems that originally the planets were seen to be the gods themselves, not just representatives of the gods, for many of the omens are derived in a surprisingly *literal* way. The Mesopotamian astrologers would see a conjunction between two planets as the two gods competing for the same space in heaven. This conflict in heaven foreshadowed conflict on earth, for they believed that all which happened above was reflected faithfully below. Astrology was in some way a method of drawing upon the mythology in a daily, practical way. It was a method for understanding the actions and desires of the gods who ruled over earth and mankind. This is not so far removed from the modern world — today millions pray daily for the salvation of their souls. The Babylonians instead divined daily for the salvation of their State. Only the approach to the gods has changed.

Astrology, derived from myth, has itself given birth to an entire mythology, especially regarding its own history. Despite the recent publication of numerous well-researched books, both scholarly and popular, explaining the current level of knowledge, there remain many false conceptions about the origins of astrology. Much of the blame for this must fall upon those works which derive more from intuition than from fact and are essentially concerned with matters of faith or religion embracing astrology as part of their eclectic approach to the sacred. Astrology is seen in these works as part of an ancient wisdom tradition, handed down from on high by suprahuman 'masters'. They thus attribute to the study, a hoary antiquity which is unsupported by the known facts. The history of astrology must firstly be disentangled from mystical speculation however well meant and however psychologically useful. It is then perhaps best, at the beginning, to summarize the current position regarding the history of astrology. We can say with a reasonable degree of confidence that:

1.   Astrology, as we know it in the West, developed in the Mesopotamian empires of Babylon and Assyria. The earliest known records, issuing from a set discipline based upon a standard codification of omens derived from planetary phenomena, date from the time of the Babylonian king Ammisaduqa, circa 1700 BC.

2.   The discipline of astrology is not the product of a vast antiquity, stretching back into the past for hundreds of thousands of years, as certain of the Greek writers appeared to believe. Neither did it arrive, fully fashioned, in Mesopotamia, carried in from some unknown external source. Rather, from its beginnings in the first dynasty of Babylon (1950-1651 BC) a development period can be intermittently traced through the subsequent half millenium. This period culminated *circa* 1000 BC with the compilation of a standard astrological text called the *Enuma Anu Enlil.*

3.   Mathematical astrology using a regular zodiac subdivided into degrees did not appear until some time after 400 BC — most likely under the influence of the Persian invasion of Mesopotamia a century earlier.

4.   Despite the assertions by Herodotus, there is still no proof that the Egyptians practised any form of astrological divination until the invasion of their country by the Greeks in 331 BC. The latter brought with them Babylonian astrological conceptions. The Zodiac of Denderah, often ascribed a date of great antiquity in popular

literature, dates from the late Ptolemaic times — 100-30 BC.[1]

5. The first known astrology was, on an official level at least, exclusively mundane astrology — concerned only with the welfare of the king and the State. Individual natal horoscopes are not to be found until the fifth century BC. The earliest known example dates from 410 BC.

Until the nineteenth century little was known about the origins of astrology beyond the writings of the classical writers who all ascribed a vast antiquity to the study. One early writer, Epigenes, is reported as saying that 'the Babylonians have a series of observations on the stars for a period of 720,000 years, inscribed on baked bricks . . .'[2] Ptolemy though, writing in the second century AD, was more realistic when he described having access to eclipse records back to only 747 BC. His conception of astrology's age has found support from modern archeological discoveries.

Huge mounds scattered about the desert regions of Iraq hide the crumbled remains of ancient temples and palaces. During the mid-nineteenth century these mounds began to be opened and explored in a rudimentary manner. One such great mound was that of Kuyunjik, across the river Tigris from the modern town of Mosul. Exploratory digging had been undertaken by the pioneering English archeologist, Austin Henry Layard, but he departed in 1852 having found nothing of consequence. A local expert, Hormuzd Rassam, was left as the British representative. He felt sure that the mound of Kuyunjik contained secrets yet to be revealed and so determined to excavate. Unfortunately the right to dig in the most promising part of the mound had been granted to the French archeologist, Victor Place. Rassam, not one to respect such gentlemen's agreements, began digging at night in the French zone. Late in December 1853, on the third night of his secret work, Rassam's team broke into a large gallery. The walls were lined with the now famous lion-hunt reliefs which are displayed in the British Museum. As his workers cleared the room they discovered, stacked in the middle, thousands of small clay tablets. These were all inscribed in the intricate triangular writing now called *cuneiform* (from the Latin, *cuneus*, wedge). The language was known in ancient times, and now, as *Akkadian* — a semitic tongue of which Babylonian and Assyrian were two dialects.

Rassam and his men had found Nineveh, the royal palace of the Assyrian king Ashurbanipal who had ruled from 668-631 BC. The room they had first sombled upon was his royal library, untouched since the destruction of his palace so long before. The tablets were all shipped back to London where they were gradually deciphered. From them came the basis of our history of ancient Mesopotamia and those sciences which had their birth in those regions. Unfortunately, due to the primitive nature of early excavations and the lack of knowledge of how to ship and preserve these tablets properly, many were broken or lost. As a result, despite many later discoveries of archives, our knowledge of the Mesopotamian empires still contains many gaps and uncertainties.

The tablets revealed that the ancient Mesopotamians had been specialists in the many forms of divination. A dominant part of the intellectual tradition was concerned with attempting to see into the future using omens drawn from a great variety of sources — the shape of a flock of birds, the actions of animals at a city's gates, or the pattern of blood vessels on the liver of a sacrificed sheep. The reason for such effort was simple. Man, they said, was created to toil for the gods that the latter might rest. [3] It was of vital importance that the will of the gods be known on the earth. Divination was the reading of the omens through which the gods revealed their desires. The diviners, the *baru*-priests who formed an important social class, were attached to the temples and to the royal courts. Many functioned as advisors to the king, informing him of the decisions which the gods had revealed.

Among the tablets found in the library of Nineveh were the standard texts of the various divinatory techniques. Each had its *canon* of literature to which all occurrences were referred. Astrology was no exception. The library held tablets containing the standard astrological work of the period, called, from its opening lines, the *Enuma Anu Enlil* — 'When the gods Anu and Enlil . . .' Although the library undoubtedly contained the complete work the vagaries of nineteenth century archeology have meant that certain of the tablets are missing or so fragmented that it has so far proved impossible to reconstruct them. However, sufficient have been identified to enable the series to be rebuilt. [4] It was a collection of either 68 or 70 tablets — depending upon the edition — containing several thousand omens derived from celestial and meteorological phenomena. For *everything* which occured above the earth, whether in the sky or in the heavens, was considered as the proper concern of astrology.

The first twenty-two tablets of the *Enuma Anu Enlil* consist of omens derived from the Moon. Concern shifts to the Sun with tablet 23 and remains there until tablet 41, which begins to omens drawn from meteorological occurrences. From tablet 50 onwards the omens are all drawn from the stars, the constellations and the planets. Only six tablets remain to be identified, but from the numerous fragments in existence the contents of these missing sections can be inferred. It would appear that they all dealt with certain of the planets and constellations. Further, astronomical evidence contained within the series has made it possible to date its final form to around 1000 BC.[5] It is, however, quite plain that this was preceded by an extended period of development. It is though that traditions from various schools of divination were combined to complete the series.

Tablet 63 of the *Enuma Anu Enlil,* a simple set of omens drawn from the appearance and disappearance of Venus, can be dated to around 1700 BC.[6] This compilation is the famous 'Venus tablet of Ammisaduqa', a complete example of which can be seen in the British Museum. This tablet is proof that the basis of the *Enuma Anu Enlil* was laid as early as the first dynasty of Babylon, which lasted from 1950 BC until 1651 BC.

In month Shabati, fifteenth day, Venus disappeared in the West for three days. Then on the eighteenth day Venus became visible in the East. Springs will flow, Adad will bring his rain and Ea his floods. King will send messages of reconciliation to king.[7]

That development continued from this early date is demonstrated by tablets found subsequent to the opening of Ashurbanipal's library. In 1927 the Hittite settlement of Katna was excavated by the French and amongst the tablets found was one forming part of the lunar section of the *Enuma Anu Enlil.*[8] As Katna was finally destroyed around 1360 BC, this indicates that certain at least of the omens had been codified by this date. Other Hittite settlements too have revealed astrological tablets, one apparently an introduction to the *Enuma Anu Enlil.*[9] The Hittite civilization met its end some two centuries before the accepted date for the compilation of the standard astrological work, thus this discovery is another indication of the development period which preceded the completion of the work.

By the time of king Ashurbanipal this treatise was available in many copies, varying in length according to the scribal school which produced it. An expert on the series, the late Professor Ernst Weidner, reports that copies have been found in several of the ancient cities of Babylonia and Assyria: Babylon, Borsippa, Assur, Calah, Nineveh, Uruk and Dilbat. Obviously a widespread reference work, a copy was probably to be found in every major library.

Even after the series' codification around the turn of the millenium, work still continued on it. This can be proved by the existence within the later tablets not only of astronomical data from around 1000 BC but also data from a more recent astronomical work called the *Mul apin*. We have a copy of this text on tablets dating from 687 BC. This latter work classifies the known stars and constellations into three paths — those of Anu, Enlil and Ea. These paths were not however conceived as being bands in the sky parallel to the celestial equator, rather they were seen as sections of the eastern horizon. [10] The central section was the path, or perhaps 'gate', of Anu, the northern that of Enlil and the southern, Ea. The constellations Aquarius, Scorpio, Sagittarius and Capricorn were placed in the path of Ea. Pisces, Aries, Taurus and the Pleiades were among those assigned to Anu. Enlil, in part, held Cancer, Leo and Ursa Major.

Within this library too were the reports from official diviners living in the many cities of the empire. It is clear that there was in existence, at least by the time of king Ashurbanipal, an imperial network of astrological centres, all reporting regularly back to the king. These reports concerned observations of planetary movements which were often, but not always, coupled with relevant quotations drawn from the *Enuma Anu Enlil* — although it must be said that sometimes the astrological advice proffered was stated as being not from any series but 'from the mouth of the people'. [11] Other reports make it clear that the king had himself solicited advice about a coming celestial event:

> The king gave me a command, saying, 'Keep my watch and whatever arises report'. Now everything, that has been clear and manifest in my sight I have dutifully sent to the king my lord, twice or thrice . . . [12]

The main purpose of these reports was to supply the king with advice drawn from whatever statements in the canonical series were pertinent to the phenomena observed. These reports, some 600 of which are now available, seem in the main to emanate not from isolated individual astrologers, but from the leader and teacher of a team of ten or more scholars working probably in a temple school. Certainly the laborious work of continual observation would have necessitated a well organized group of observers.

The evidence from these reports allows us to conclude that by the seventh century BC, astrology had become the main form of official divination. For, despite the existence in the library of large numbers of tablets devoted to the many other forms of divination, also arranged in canonical series, in the reports astrology greatly predominates. What is apparent though, is that the *baru*-priests were not exclusively astrologers but were proficient in many other forms of divination as well. It seems in fact that the 'discipline' in which they were trained included all varieties except that of divining from the livers of sacrificed sheep. The latter was the exclusive concern of a separate group of specialists, seemingly less eclectic in their approach to omens.

While we can express a certain confidence in our brief survey of ancient astrology we cannot afford to become dogmatic in our statements about the ancient techniques. There are numerous problems not only in the interpretation of texts but also in the true weight to be given them. We must in fact view all the extant information with great caution. For one thing, virtually every text we have pertinent to astrology is almost certainly based upon an earlier, now lost, original. Additionally, new discoveries are continually requiring us to modify our conception of the past and our view of the abilities of ancient peoples. However, most importantly for the subject of astrology, as the late Leo Oppenheim points out, the great library of Nineveh was a specialist library, aimed specifically at the requirements of the State astrologers and other diviners. [13] It tells us nothing of the beliefs or the practices of the average citizen of the time. Did they too use astrology? The library gives us no indication. Did they hold identical beliefs to those of the priests or were the 'popular' traditions markedly different? Again, we have no way of telling.

Certainly there must have been a strong oral tradition, most of which has now been lost. The existence of differing beliefs is shown in the early biblical stories of the patriarch Abraham. He was initially a high court official in the Babylonian city of Ur, before he and his family left, developing their religion of monotheism. Abraham is long renowned in Hebrew tradition as a competent astrologer.

It would seem likely that there was in existence some form of astrology available to the average man or woman. Perhaps also there was some form of astrology which used individual birth charts long before the official astrology accepted the practice. But as a birth chart necessitates a sophisticated knowledge of the stars, the calendar and time, this may be a less likely supposition. The clay cuneiform tablets were very much the 'official' records containing that informtion which the king needed daily or which he was quite deliberately leaving for posterity. On the other hand for the greater part of the first millenium BC more and more writing — records of a 'popular' kind — was on a more perishable substance, usually wax tablets or papyrus. The Persian conquerors of the sixth century BC made Aramaic the State language and this was never written in cuneiform but in ink on papyrus. Eventually most legal and commercial documents were written in Aramaic on papyrus and this probably included most astrological documents of a 'popular' type.

As papyrus is highly perishable, many documents must have been consumed by the fires which raged through the ancient buildings while invaders sacked them. Those which survived this destruction have still been lost over the centuries by the gradual rising of the water table in the area. Thus it would seem probable that any astrology in common, rather than official use, would have been recorded upon papyrus and so now be lost forever. Oppenheim suggests that this use of Aramaic and papyrus might have begun earlier, perhaps as far back as the turn of the millenium.

We must then allow the possibility that all our conclusions regarding Babylonian astrology are in fact conclusions about only *royal* Babylonian astrology, which naturally expresses a concern with the king and the State.

That a simple, non-horoscopic, yet individual popular form of astrology existed would seem to be the case. Evidence has been found in excavations at Sultantepe of an individually-oriented divination technique not included in the standard omen texts, yet predating them by hundreds of years. [14] This tradition continued to exist within the official religious framework, so it is not truly 'popular' in the widest sense of the word. In this variety a querent would ask a priest to perform a ritual after which omens would be expected. After the rituals which involved the constellation Ursa Major, astrological omens would be sought, there derived from the various directions taken by the next shooting star.

The major difference between this form and the official royal astrology is that this form was done on request for the private individual. The answers were always simple, being primarily of the yes-no type. This variety of divination is attested from as far back as the first dynasty of Babylon, and thus is contemporary with the 'Venus tablet of Ammisaduqa'. The interesting question of whether, that far back in history, it comprised part of the 'official' technique, and whether the 'official' technique developed from such simple omen ritual cannot yet be answered. The evidence simply does not exist.

There is though an interesting point raised concerning the later appearance of individual birth charts in Mesopotamia. Could the appearance of these charts reflect or suggest a weakening of the central government, such that individuals other than the king were becoming sufficiently important to be the object of interest for official diviners? Or could it be simply that with the ending of royal patronage in the sixth century BC under the Persians, the *baru*-priests had to begin working commercially, for anyone who might hire them?

Although the Hittite use of Babylonian astrology attests to the spread of this knowledge beyond the imperial cities, archeological evidence of this has not been found further afield than the adjoining nations. The Elamites to the east were aware of this Babylonian science. Tablets containing sections of the *Enuma Anu Enlil* were found in their capital, Susa, by an expedition in 1897.[15]

If, however, we can include non-archeological evidence then it is possible to find indications that the knowledge of Babylonian astrology was beginning to spread further afield by the mid-first millenium BC. Some time after 550 BC the Greek philosopher Pythagoras emerged, proclaiming a radically new philosphy founded upon a conception of the universe as a musical harmony. If the later Greek writers can be believed, and there is no good reason why they should not, Pythagoras, after a period of study in ancient Egypt, made his way to Babylon where he stayed for some eight years receiving instruction in their stellar wisdom. It was probably here that he received the basis of his later teachings. Even those critics who remain sceptical of his visits east admit that his philosophical system accords well with Mesopotamian astrological theory. In this way, then, via Pythagoras during the sixth century BC, the fundamentals of Mesopotamian astrology apparently first entered the Greek world. An interesting, if speculative thought, is just how much of Pythagoras' teachings were derived from the Babylonians. Pythagoras taught reincarnation for example and maintained a strict vegetarian diet. Could these ideas also have been current amongst the *baru*-priests of Babylon? Perhaps we need to look again at the Babylonian ideas of fate and destiny, *shimtu* and *ishtaru*. [16]

What is important for this present study is that Pythagoras, drawing from Babylonian astrology (a study which, as far as we can tell, deals exclusively with man as a fated being) arrived at a conception of man as a free individual. Pythagoras gave the Greeks a system primarily concerned with man as an eternally existent creature, containing in his soul the potential for true self-consciousness. He taught men to strive for the supreme experience — direct knowledge of the divine. Pythagoras wanted men to become gods, not remain their sevants. The Babylonian creation epic, the *Enuma elish* states that mankind was created from a fallen god (a curious foreshadowing of both Hebrew and Manichean thought) and a natural consequence of this, though not stated in the epic, would be that man could regain this primal godhood. Perhaps there was some secret mystical tradition running unnoticed through the Babylonian tradition which taught men to rediscover their true relationship with the gods? Certainly no age seems to have a monopoly on mysticism and it would be strange indeed if there was no Babylonian mystics. The ancient 'tree of life', later a supremely mystical symbol for Judaism, frequently appears carved in relief in huge panels. Those from Nineveh are on display at the British Museum, others are at the Louvre in Paris. Could these represent part of an as yet unknown teaching? It seems likely. Certainly a secret writing has been discovered on some Babylonian tablets which no one has yet deciphered. Certainly, if any esoteric Babylonian teachings existed they are more likely to be found in secondary sources of varying degrees of adulteration. Despite the handicaps it may eventually prove possible to tease out much of the truth.

Pythagoras can be usefully seen as ending a period which began with the first attempt at codifying the celestial omens, progressed through the formulation of a standard omen text — concerned

exclusively with what the heavens revealed of the future of the State
— and ended with the growing recognition of the individual. This
change in attitude was to inaugurate a major change in astrology.

The Persian invasion of Mesopotamia in 538 BC, and their
subsequent rule over the empires of Babylon and Assyria, can be
seen as initiating a second great period in the history of astrology.
This invasion changed the life of the area in many ways. One major
change was that they broke the dominance of the temple over the
country, and in the process diluted the immense power previously
held by the *baru*-priests. The importance of this change cannot be
over-emphasized. For the stars could now officially be studied without
having to subscribe to any religious doctrine. Slowly, during this
second period, the study of astrology was *secularized*. Rational theories
began to be advanced to account for the observed planetary
movements, which previously had been seen simply as divine whim.
Early in this proto-scientific period the nineteen-year calendar cycle
was developed by both the Babylonians and the Athenian, Meton,
in 432 BC. About this time also another Greek, Euktemon,
established the solstice and equinoctial points, discovering that the
seasons were of unequal length. Euktemon constructed a tropical
calendar based upon the summer solstice, placing this point at 1°
Cancer. Later, the regular zodiac was to appear. Previously all
references to the 'signs' related to the constellations. Lastly, and most
importantly, the individual birth chart appeared. The earliest
example, now in the Bodlean Library, Oxford, has been dated to
410 BC. [17] However, in this example, it is still not clear whether the
regular zodiac or the constellations are spoken of — though the latter
seems most likely.

It could be that even in this early period, Greek influence was
already beginning to change Babylonian astrology. The Greeks were
concerned with the individual rather than the State. It seems probable
that this attitude, when combined with Babylonian astrology, resulted
in the original concept of the natal chart. In this respect it is interesting
to note that some time around 450 BC the Greek philosopher Plato
was in touch with Mesopotamian thought. One of the papyrii found
in the ruins of Herculaneum records that late in his life Plato was
instructed in the art of astrology by a Babylonian priest who had
come to Athens. [18] Perhaps these roving priests took the Greek concept

of man back to Babylon. Certainly Plato's works contain much astrology. His ideal State was one in which everybody was in harmony with the universe. His *Timaeus,* for example, presents a world view which holds that there exists a close correspondence between the macrocosm and the microcosm. It presents, too, the idea of man having a divine and immortal soul which returns to the earth in successive incarnations. Again we can ask whether reincarnation could have formed part of Babylonian thought. The *Epinomis* too is founded upon this eastern thought. Cumont calls this work 'the first gospel preached to the Hellenes of the stellar religion of Asia.' [19] It is quite possible to see in this work the beginnings of the synthesis of Greek and Mesopotamian thought, foreshadowing the great intellectual syncretic movements in the Greek empire during the last few centuries BC. It was during this second period of astrology's development that the studies of mundane and natal astrology were differentiated for the first time, though of course both types would have been practised by the same individuals.

The peak of this second period came when both Mesopotamia and Egypt were under Greek rule. In 331 BC, Alexander the Great invaded the Middle East and initiated what was to prove an era of extraordinary scholarship and scientific achievement. The initial centre of this renaissance was to be the city he founded on the Nile delta — Alexandria.

Finally, the combination of mathematics and astrology led to the invention of regular zodiacal degrees, and later, the ascendant — the sign and degree rising at the moment the chart is cast. The ascendant does seem to appear much later. Of the six cuneiform natal charts which we possess, the earliest which uses regular degrees and minutes of the zodiacal signs was found at Uruk and has been dated to 263 BC. [20] This chart does not mention the ascendant, nor do any of the others. Neither do any of the original Greek charts until one of 4 BC. [21] It would appear to be a very late development. However, as we have only two papyrus charts from before this date we cannot assume that they are truly representative. Literary sources suggest a much earlier time for the introduction of the ascendant. One has been found for a birth on 27 December 72 BC. This chart has Gemini rising. However, the data was computed around 22 BC, so we must take this date as being the earliest certain mention of the ascendant. [22]

The Greek invasion of Babylonia lead to the emergence of many scholars who flourished under this dual influence. One whose name has survived was Kidinnu, a hellenized Babylonian known to the later Greeks as Cidenas. Around 315 BC he founded an astrological school in Babylon which was still apparently in operation some 200 years later.[23] This school represented a pioneering attempt to teach Babylonian astrology to the many Greek students who had come into Mesopotamia in the years following Alexander's invasion. Unlike Euktemon, Kidinnu placed the equinoxes and solstices at the eighth degree of the zodiacal signs. It is obvious then that perhaps with Euktemon, and certainly with Kidinnu, there was in use the regular zodiacal circle divided into 360 degrees. Thus we can say that its invention and use most certainly predates the cuneiform tablet found at Uruk by at least 50 years. The current opinion amongst scholars is that the regular zodiac dates from the late Persian period of Mesopotamia, that is, from the fourth century BC.

Some time after 281 BC[24] another hellenized Babylonian, Berosus, a priest from the temple of Marduk in Babylon, set up an astrology school on the Greek island of Kos. This was the first such school to be established within the borders of Greece itself. Kos was probably chosen for its strategic location, being an important crossing point for the trade routes connecting Greece with Egypt and Mesopotamia. He doubtless carried with him Greek translations of the *Enuma Anu Enlil* — not a single example of which has survived the ravages of Christians and time. Berosus reflects the intellectual changes taking place, the shift in attitude from an acceptance of religious explanations of stellar motion to a demand for scientific theory. He is credited by Vitruvius with one of the earliest known theories to account for the phases of the Moon. Pliny records that Berosus achieved such fame that the Athenians built a statue in his honour.

The earliest known planetary ephemeris, inscribed in cuneiform, dates from Babylon under Greek rule. It records the celestial position for each year beginning in 308 BC. As the first few lines have been broken off the emphemeris may well have begun with the planetary positions of the first year of the Greek (*Seleucid*) kingdom of Babylonia, 312 BC.[25] Similarly from Babylon comes the earliest extant astronomical 'diary', dating from a few years later, 274 BC. In total, seven of these diaries have so far been discovered, all from excavations at Babylon. They are evidence for an early attempt at empirically correlating celestial and earthly events. They seem to be concerned with establishing a data base from which to improve existing astrological theory. If this explanation is indeed correct then these diaries would be a good example of the Greco-Babylonian scholastic movement. Perhaps these diaries are evidence too of a dissatisfaction with the traditional astrology. Were the astrologers of the day indeed intending to revise the *Enuma Anu Enlil*? It must certainly have been coming under close scrutiny at the time, if only for the vagueness of its astronomy and its lack of any mathematical theory.

Each of these diaries covers half a year, divided into monthly sections. Within each section there is firstly a day-by-day record of astronomical and meteorological phenomena, followed by a record of the commodity prices for that month, the varying height of the river, the zodiacal signs of the planets and any notable political or religious event.[26] The very late formulation of these diaries makes it probable that another astrological tradition is without foundation, i.e., that the ancient Babylonians recorded observations over thousands of years and that the tenets of astrology emerged out of this vast accumulation of data. As has been explained, the ancient omen systems was codified long before the empirical attitude which produced these diaries. We are though no closer to understanding exactly how the various interpretations were evolved. The fact that some of the ancient interpretations still remain valid today would suggest either an empirical attitude or a highly developed intuition on the part of generations of astrologers. The suggestion has been advanced that over a long period of time the 'signal' will tend to differentiate itself from the 'noise'. In other words, the parts of astrology which were valid, and remain so today, would tend to predominate, letting the invalid parts gradually fade from sight. Whatever the explanation we must remain certain that future discoveries will modify or change our views. As a hint of what could be awaiting archeologists in some as yet undiscovered archive is the record of at least one previously accessible data collection from long before the writing of the diaries. Ptolemy, in his astronomical work the *Almagest,* speaks of having available eclipse records from very ancient times, the first dating from 747 BC. We should then be prepared for more discoveries in this field.

The last three centuries of the pre-Christian era saw a remarkable acceleration of learning, based initially about the cities of Alexandria and Athens. Its impetus, especially in the East, was stimulated by the first two Ptolemaic kings of Egypt who built the famous museum and library as adjuncts to the royal complex within the city of Alexandria. Scholars could live there for as long as they wished, supported by royal funds. The library was vast, eventually numbering around 500,000 manuscript rolls at a time when just 500 was considered impressive. Euclid, famous for his geometry, was among the first great scientists to work there, as were the two astronomers Aristyllos and Timocharis, whose observations, recorded and stored in the library, were to prove so important in the future. During the same period, but working in Athens, was the astronomer Aristarchos. He produced a treatise suggesting that the Moon received its light from the Sun, a remarkable thesis for the time, especially since it was so superior to the thesis of Berosus, who was then just opening his school on Kos. It is evidence that Greek abilities in astronomy and astrology could equal those of the Babylonians. Aristarchos also produced a study of the relative sizes and distances of the Earth, Moon and Sun. The fact that his results were grossly inaccurate need not condemn him unduly — the importance of his work lies in the soundness of his method. A further indication that the astrological zodiac predates the Uruk tablet of 263 BC is that Aristarchos used a regular zodiac in his work, divided into the 360 degrees.

Later in his life Aristarchos produced the revolutionary theory that the Earth revolved around the Sun. Eighteen hundred years before Copernicus he had formulated the first heliocentric theory of planetary motion. Unfortunately a later astronomer was to reject this view and return to the ancient geocentric model. Vested interests were obviously at stake; indeed, even at the time Aristarchos was accused of impiety for suggesting such a theory.

Astrological ideas were not simply part of a specialist milieu, they were topics of prime concern to any man of education in the classical world. A prime reason for this was the support given to astrology by the Stoic philosophers. Stoicism was first taught by the Athenian, Zeno, whose life spanned the years of the first two Ptolemies (Zeno died around 264 BC). He stressed a belief in providence and a submission to one's destiny as the way to bring one's life into harmony with the cosmos. The Stoics then all supported and used astrology: the Babylonian conception of a correspondence between heaven and earth found an easy home in this movement. Zeno's successor, Cleanthes, taught a truly mystical view: the universe was a living being, God was its soul and its heart the Sun.

One of Zeno's friends in Athens was the astrologer and poet Aratos. He wrote two astronomical and astrological poems which gained wide popularity amongst the citizens of the Greek kingdoms. He was responsible for making the ideas accessible to the great majority of people, who learned his poems by heart and in this way became aware of the stars, the constellations and the zodiac.

The latter half of the third century BC saw the astrologer Apollonius working in Alexandria. He was concerned (as were all astrologers and astronomers in those days) with producing a theory which could account for all the planetary movements, including that of planetary retrogradation. Apollonius, drawing upon earlier work, especially that done by Heracleides, produced a refined planetary theory which was later taken up first by Hipparchus and later by Ptolemy. They adopted it as their basic model of planetary movement.

Hipparchus — also an influence on Ptolemy — worked a century later than Apollonius, but still in the great centre of Alexandria, ending his life around 127 BC. He firmly rejected the heliocentric theory postulated by Aristarchos and put all his effort into the geocentric view, using the theory of movement as explained by Apollonius. Hipparchus was then responsible for the loss of the correct heliocentric view of the heavens until the time of Copernicus. It is perhaps worth asking just how much Hipparchus' rejection of the heliocentric view reflected his belief in astrology: that he was a practising astrologer is beyond doubt, and astrology does strongly suggest a geocentric view of the universe.

Hipparchus discovered, so it is said, the precession of the equinoxes and produced an accurate measurement of this movement. He continued to remain however, unaware of its true cause. His measurements were surprisingly accurate. He determined the annual precession to be about 46 seconds of arc — the true value being close to 50 seconds.

This knowledge of the precession allowed Hipparchus to draw a distinction between the sidereal year — the time between returns of the Sun to a given star, originally Aldebaran — and the short tropical year — the time between the Sun's returns to the ever retrograde equinoctial point. Hence, in this way, each tropical year grows progressively shorter, progressively out of harmony with the sidereal year. By the twentieth century this discrepancy amounts to about 24½ degrees. Following this discovery, around 139 BC

Hipparchus proceeded to make an accurate measurement of the tropical year, inventing the modern form of the tropical zodiac. The beginning of the new year in spring, which Kidinnu had placed at 8° Aries, Hipparchus changed to 0° Aries — the system we have used ever since in the West, admittedly primarily through the influence of Ptolemy who adopted this system.

From the very earliest times the Italian peninsula had seen an indigenous development of divination, apparently independent from that of the Middle East. The ancient Etruscans, for example, were renowned for their divinatory abilities, in particular using meteorological phenomena, although a simplistic astrology did exist. Early Roman society continued this practice of including divination in the process of making any important decisions. The major methods used involved reading the entrails of sacrificed animals or consulting oracles. Astrology seems to have played a relatively minor role in early Rome, being confined to such simple and infrequent events as comets or eclipses. In fact, a sophisticated astrology did not emerge until contact was later made with the Mesopotamian world. It was near the turn of the last century BC that mathematical astrology began to enter Roman life in sufficient strength as to wield a cultural influence.

To the Romans, astrologers were collectively known as 'Chaldeans' from an old name for Mesopotamia. It was derived from the ancient tribe of the *Kaldu,* source of the Chaldean dynasty which ruled over Babylon from 612-539 BC. This name would suggest that most of the astrologers in Rome at this early time were foreigners, Babylonians or Syrians who had travelled to Rome as scholars or who had perhaps been brought as captives or attendants in the wake of the legions. Pliny supports the latter possibility, stating that astrology, to his knowledge, was first introduced into Italy by the slave Antiochus who had been brought from the east.[27]

By the last century BC the intellectual climate in Rome had become more favourable to astrology, especially through the spread of the Greek Stoic philosophy. One key figure was the great Stoic teacher Posidonius (c.135-51 BC) who headed a school on Rhodes — now second to Alexandria as a scholastic centre — where he taught both philosophy and astrology. Posidonius had a great admiration for the teachings of Plato and Pythagoras and not surprisingly considered the astrological *Timaeus* as central to Platonic thought. Posidonius' enduring fame arises from his combining elements of both the Platonic and the Aristotelean traditions into one philosophy. This synthesis is a crucial element of what later became known as *Neo-Platonism,* the philosophy which now underlies astrology — and, incidently, modern science. Posidonius' Neo-Platonic philosophy was carried to Rome by the young student Nigidius Figulus, later to become a respected astrologer. Nigidius Figulus, and his friend Cicero, studied together in Rhodes.

Posidonius eventually moved to Rome where he became both teacher and friend to Cicero. The latter though, despite his continuing friendship with Nigidius Figulus, eventually became disenchanted with astrology. Around 44 BC, after the death of Posidonius, he produced a scathing work *De Divinatione* in which he refuted all forms of divination, including astrology. The reasons for his hostility appear to lie within the turmoil of the civil war which erupted between Pompey and Caesar in 49 BC. Cicero supported Pompey, and following the latter's defeat, was exiled for a short period. Although Cicero had previously held high government posts he detested Caesar and never actively participated in the new regime. It was during this bitter post-war period that he published *De Divinatione.* Within this often acerbic work he refers to the extravagant promises astrologers had given Pompey:

> I recall a multitude of prophecies which the Chaldeans made to Pompey . . . [28]

> I could give countless (instances) — where the prophecies of soothsayers either were without result or the issue was directly the reverse of the prophecy. Ye gods, how many times they were mistaken in the late civil war! What oracular messages the soothsayers sent from Rome to our Pompeian party then in Greece! What assurances they gave to Pompey. [29]

Cicero had returned to Italy from a post as a provincial governor in Turkey to find his country torn by war. For a time he was undecided over who to support but finally chose Pompey. Could it be then that he chose sides upon the advice of astrologers? Then, when events proved them wrong, was his bitterness sufficient to damn them all? 'What inconceivable madness', he calls astrology, 'For it is not enough to call an opinion "foolishness" when it is utterly devoid of reason?' [30] Despite Cicero's attempted destruction of astrology, his friend Nigidius Figulus was later widely credited with having predicted the outbreak of civil war, if not the eventual victor. [31]

While astrology played a part in the intellectual life of republican Rome, it does not seem to have entered the political arena in any significant way and this despite the fact that most great men of the period had their birth charts drawn up. Julius Caesar does not seem to have had much interest in astrology, or any system. He seemed to delight in acting contrary to the advice of diviners, with no ill effects except for the day of his assassination, which was foretold (apparently) by entrails not planets. Caesar's opponent Pompey received much astrological advice, as did several of the later champions for power. Plutarch records Mark Anthony employing an Egyptian astrologer in his entourage.

Anthony's colleague, and later opponent, Octavian, was similarly no stranger to astrology. Suetonius tells the story of Octavian, in his youth, visiting an astrologer who, upon drawing up the birth chart, threw himself at Octavian's feet such was the remarkable future revealed. Octavian became so confident of his success and of astrology's validity that he had a coin stamped bearing his birth sign. Octavian emerged victorious at the end of the civil wars to become the first emperor of Rome, changing his name to Augustus. The subsequent Imperial era of Rome saw a rapid increase in the use of astrology, especially for political predictions. And it was to be these predictions which would bring great difficulties to Roman astrologers.

Initially astrology remained the preserve of the aristocracy and the intellectuals. Not for some time did it permeate down the ranks of society. When it did, it was primarily through the influence of the eastern religions which were spreading throughout the empire. Many such cults — like those of Cybele, Isis, Baal or Mithras for example — contained within their teachings varying degrees of astrology, especially the cult of Mithras, the unconquered Sun, whose underground temples were decorated with astrological symbols.

The first emperors became strong supporters of the eastern ways of thought, drawn particularly by those doctrines which held the earthly ruler to be god incarnate. This aspect of the teachings was not lost on the Caesars, who, during the first century AD, gradually deified themselves. Given this climate of thought it is not surprising that astrology increasingly became part of Roman daily life.

The last few years of Octavian's reign saw the completion of Manilius' *Astronomica,* one of the more readily accessible works of Roman astrology. This work, in five long poems, offers in poetic hexameters, everything from chart construction to lists of stellar magnitudes. It is a work of some ingenuity if not clarity. It contains an exposition of mundane astrology which quite obviously owes its theory to the Babylonians, proof that Manilius had access to translations or summations of the ancient tablets.

Manilius uses one technique however which has not, so far, been found in any Babylonian text. This is a method of relating certain mundane events to the individual. It involves the use of a movable circle of houses based upon the 'Part of Fortune'. The house in the natal chart which holds the 'Part of Fortune' is considered to be house one, the next eleven houses being placed anti-clockwise around the chart. This overlaid pattern was called the circle of the twelve *Athla* and is quite different from the normal twelve houses or 'temples' of the chart.

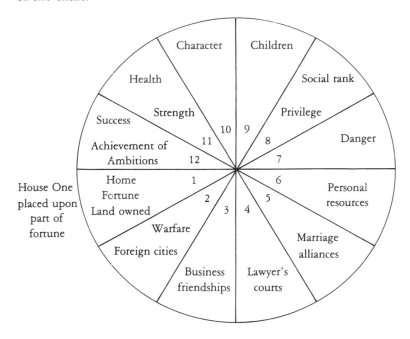

Figure 1.1   The Circle of the 12 Athla.

Certain of the attributions seem to correlate with those in use today. Of the twelve houses, four at least — houses 2, 3, 4 and 7 — are purely mundane. Our modern mundane interpretation of the seventh house includes 'enemies' which is perhaps a reflection of this early attribution of 'danger'. Our modern third house rules business and trade as does this early Roman example. There are though inconsistencies with modern usage — the twelfth house today is not seen as ruling wordly success, rather the opposite.

That Manilius is working firmly within the Mesopotamian tradition is clearly demonstrated by his use of a curious and specifically Babylonian technique of the micro-zodiac, each sign being subdivided into twelve 2 ½ ° segments.[32] Manilius' detailed explanation of the system's intricacies prove it to be identical to the system explained on a series of tablets found by archeologists in the ruins of Uruk.[33] They have been dated to the era of Seleucid king Antiochus I, who ruled Babylon from 281-261 BC. As it is most unlikely that Manilius could read cuneiform we must assume that the information on these tablets had been translated into Greek or Latin and was available to scholars in Rome. Berosus had put into circulation Greek translations of all the contents of the Babylonian tablets. That Manilius was a member of a Greek intellectual circle in Rome is perhaps an indication that even at the beginning of the modern era, Greek was still the purveyor of the astrological tradition.

Like many early astrologers Manilius developed further the Babylonian teaching that areas of the earth fell under specific astrological rulership. While the early system was very simple — Saturn as ruler of the kingdom of Akkad, for example — Manilius' was much more complex. The important point was no longer ruling planets but ruling zodiacal signs. Manilius saw racial differences as being due to differences in the astrological rulership of the national homelands. He considered too that the incompatability of certain nations was a specific reflection of the incompatability of their ruling signs. He claimed that his system should enable Romans to choose more wisely the land in which they should live or the country with which they should trade:

So must every man shun or seek a place to live in, so hope for loyalty or be forewarned of peril according to the character which has come down . . .[34]

Naturally an ominous occurrence, such as an eclipse, would promise disruption within those countries ruled by the same sign as the eclipse. This idea is of course still with us today.

The reasoning behind Manilius' attributions is not entirely clear although he does provide an explanation of sorts for his primary attributions. He divides the world into three continents — Libya, Asia and Europe. The first, Libya, the land of defeated Carthage, of serpents and 'creatures which feed on death', he places under the overall rulership of Scorpio. The second, Asia, which he describes as a land of riches surrounded by sparkling waters and filled with aromatic woods, he places under Taurus. These do have a certain logic. The third, Europe, is less clearly defined. He describes the continent as one filled with heroes and artists, a land of wealth and power. He gives no overall ruler for it but divides the continent up under separate signs: Capricorn ruling over Germany, Gaul and Spain; Libra over Rome; Virgo over Greece and so on. There does not appear to be any real theory behind these rulerships apart from the supposed links between the signs and the physical characteristics of the different regions. There are certain cases where the attribution is derived from the local religion — Phrygia for example is placed

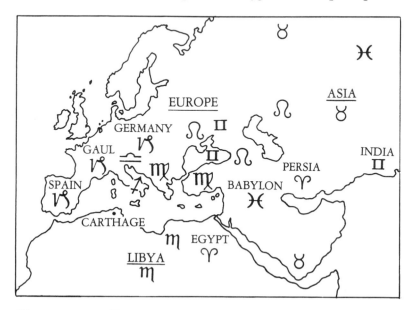

Figure 1.2 Manilius' map of the World showing his astrological attributions.

under Leo because that land is the home of the worship of Cybele whose animal is the lion — but this reasoning does not seem to have been generally applied.

All the Roman emperors of the first century AD had close links with astrologers; some even mastered the art themselves. A measure of the growing seriousness with which they viewed astrology can be seen in the increasing number of edicts published which either forbade astrologers to practice, exiled them, or in some extreme cases, sentenced them to death. Astrology was not a subject one studied lightly in Rome.

The pattern was set by Tiberius, heir to Octavian and emperor from AD 14 until his death in AD 37. His reign witnessed the emergence of an 'official' astrologer, a member of the Imperial court, wielding considerable power due to his influence over the emperor. Parallel to this rise in status for the favoured astrologers grew the systematic persecution of all others. The emperors, it is clear, demanded a monopoly over the art.

Before his accession to power, Tiberius, while visiting Rhodes, had been so impressed by the skill of an astrologer Thrasyllus, that he employed him as court astrologer until the end of his reign. From Thrasyllus, Tiberius learned sufficient astrology to read charts himself. The method by which Tiberius tested the astrologers or Rhodes was simple and brutal. Whenever he wanted astrological advice he would go with the astrologer and a strong servant to a part of the villa which overlooked a high cliff. If, after having received Tiberius' confidential enquiries the astrologer seemed in any way lacking in skill, the servant simply pushed him over the cliff on the way down from the villa. Thrasyllus inevitably found himself called to Tiberius' villa, but such was the astrologer's skill that he greatly impressed his client. However, by way of what seems to have been a macabre final test Tiberius suggested that Thrasyllus look at his own chart for the day. Thrasyllus drew up what appears to have been a horary and immediately expressed great alarm. A great danger was imminent, he cried. Tiberius took the shaking astrologer in his arms and praised his skill. Unlike his predecessors Thrasyllus survived the journey down the cliff. [35] However, if Thrasyllus knew anything of the fate of the earlier astrologers then it would take no great understanding of astrology to foresee imminent personal danger when a guest of Tiberius. Whatever Thrasyllus' true reading of the situation his host was sufficiently impressed to add the astrologer to his immediate entourage and take him back to Rome. Suetonius records that Thrasyllus, as 'official' astrologer, had a calming effect upon the frequently violent emperor. Tiberius feared constantly for his life, and murdered anyone whom he perceived as a possible threat. Thrasyllus, producing his charts, would repeatedly assure the emperor of many more years in power, thus reducing his anxiety and the killing. [36]

Balbillus, the son of Thrasyllus, was astrologer and confidant to to three emperors — Claudius, Nero and Vespasian. He was the product of a much more blood thirsty school of thought. Suetonius gives an example: on the appearance of a comet, supposed to fore-shadow the death of a leader, Balbillus reminded the fearful Nero that in the past kings had managed to deflect the 'wrath of heaven' by executing their most prominent citizens. This is a variation on the ancient Mesopotamian tradition of appointing a substitute king who, hopefully would bear the brunt of fate's ire. Following Balbillus' advice Nero proceeded upon a mass destruction of the Roman nobility. [37] This move was repeated each time such an omen occurred proving, incidentally, to the people of Rome that the appearance of a comet did indeed presage spilled blood and the death of great men.

In the last decades of the first century Vespasian and his two sons, Titus and Domitian, not only had close working relationships with astrologers, but the younger two men became accomplished astrologers themselves. Unfortunately years of astrology did not temper their actions in any way. Dio Cassius tells us that Domitian had a highly unethical use for astrology. He would cast the charts for all the prominent men in Rome who could possibly be considered as rivals. All those whose charts suggested power or success Domitian immediately had executed, even if they were not evincing any interest in assuming positions of power. [38] For the entire first century then, in Rome at least, astrology remained a tool of power for the emperors who were increasingly trapped by their own fatalism and paranoia.

While the Romans adopted astrology, it was the Greeks who provided the scientific discoveries necessary to advance the subject. No figures compatable to Hipparchus or Aristarchos ever emerged from Rome. This hiatus lasted until the mid-second century AD when another monumental figure emerged: once again a Greek, once again living around Alexandria. This man was Claudius Ptolemy, famous for his two major works. The *Megale syntaxis mathematike,* more commonly known by its Arabic title *Almagest,* appeared shortly after AD 151. This remained the definitive astronomical text until the era of Copernicus and Kepler some 1500 years later.

Some time after the *Almagest* Ptolemy wrote its companion piece, the *Tetrabiblos,* which was a major complication of astrological knowledge. In this work Ptolemy, for the first time, ordered and structured the study of the heavens into clearly defined areas. Astronomy was divided from astrology, while astrology itself was subdivided into mundane and natal concerns. This approach gave greater clarity but unfortunately led to the separation of the two astrological areas which, for Ptolemy, were but different uses of the one subject.

It was Ptolemy, more than any other astrologer, who ensured the survivial of astrology through the poligical and religious upheavels of the first thousand years of the Christian era. His intellectual and scientific stature was such that few critics dared raise their voices against the subject for several hundred years. And the critics abounded, this much is quite clear, for even Ptolemy feels compelled to answer them. The opening section of the *Tetrabiblos* is devoted to a spirited defence of astrology: 'We do not,' wrote Ptolemy, 'discredit that art of the pilot for its many errors'.

Ptolemy is filled with praise for those earlier astrologers., especially Hipparchus and Posidonius, upon whose work he builds. He speaks too of using books which were so ancient that they could barely be read. Indeed, it is impossible when reading his words not to feel saddened that these books are no longer available to us today. Ptolemy must certainly have worked at the great library at Alexandria where he would have had access to the Greek translations of the *Enuma Anu Enil* and kindred works. Records of extreme antiquity were apparently readily available to students, for as mentioned earlier, Ptolemy had the eclipse records dating back to the time of king Nabu-nasir of Babylon, 747 BC.

It is impossible to state definitively the influences upon Ptolemy or the sources of his information apart from those sources which he mentions himself, for the great Alexandrian library is now gone, totally destroyed. Tragically the first major destruction occurred not long after Ptolemy's death. The final blow was dealt by a Christian mob in the late fourth century.

Although much of the ancient fatalistic teaching had continued, the spirit of the times had grown more sceptical. The existence of omens was still accepted but mankind's future was no longer held by all to be fixed. The omens, intellectuals felt, pointed rather at possibilities than at certainties. Pliny, for example, around 77 AD wrote: 'The power of omens is really in our control, and their influence is conditional upon the way we receive them'. [39]

Throughout his *Tetrabiblos* Ptolemy adopts a rational, basically Aristotelian viewpoint. The effects of the planets, he states, are not due to divine intervention but to measurable physical causes. His explanations are non-religious and logical, the explanations of a scientist. We see with Ptolemy a complete break from the traditional Babylonian framework founded upon a fated universe dominated by almost inaccessible gods. In practise, though many of Ptolemy's interpretations of the omens remained unchanged: Scorpio continued to be considered dangerous, Mars stayed warlike and Jupiter still brought benefits to king and State.

Like Manilius, Ptolemy devoted considerable ingenuity establishing astrological rulerships over the world. Unlike Manilius he attempts to provide his system with scientific credibility, an attempt which conspicuously fails. The zodiac, Ptolemy says, is divided by element into four triangles: fire, earth, air and water. To each of these triangles, he continues, can be allocated a geographical direction: fire to north-west, earth to south-east, air to north-east and water to south-west. He does not explain upon what basis these directions are allocated but clearly he does not expect the reader to disagree.

He next states that the inhabited world can similarly be divided into four geographical directions — and few would argue with him here. Therefore, he reasons, the four quarters of the earth must be 'in familiarity' with the four triangles of the zodiac, each geographical quarter being ruled by one of the four elements. An example of such reasoning is: my book has four chapters, my car has four wheels; therefore my book and my car are 'in sympathy'; hence if my book is damaged my car will also be harmed! Despite this spurious argument Ptolemy places the north-west part of the world (Europe) under the rulership of the north-west triangle of elements, i.e., fire. The remaining three-quarters of the world are assigned to the other three elements.

Ptolemy then adds two complicating factors. Firstly, although each geographical quarter is ruled by one element, individual countries within that quarter are ruled by the different signs of that element. For example Libya, the ancient name for Africa, is ruled by the element of water; Carthage, the dominating city of the region, is ruled by Cancer; Mauritania by Scorpio.

Secondly he explains that the countries near to the centre of the earth, to the joining of the four quarters (see Fig. 1.3, below) show additional attributes from the influences which 'leak' in from the quarter diagonally opposite. Greece, for example, while being ruled by fire (because of its location in the north-west quarter) has a sub-rulership of earth derived from its proximity to the south-east quarter.

Ptolemy then demonstrates the working of his system. Europe, the north-west quarter of the earth, is under the rulership of fire. This, he says, is shown by the general characteristics of the people. They are seen to be independent, freedom loving, warlike, magnanimous and, oddly, homosexual — 'without passion for women and better satisfied with men'. He then subdivides Europe: Britain, Gaul and Germany he places under Aries, which he feels makes these nations more warlike and bestial; Italy and Sicily fall under Leo, thus they are considered to be more masterful and

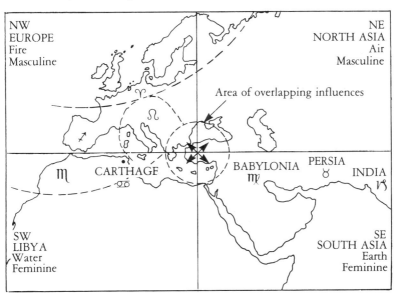

Figure 1.3 Ptolemy's map of the World showing his astrological attributions.

benevolent; Spain is placed under Sagittarius, its people being independent, simple and lovers of cleanliness. Those countries near the centre of the world, such as Greece and Crete, have the additional influence of earth coming from the opposite quarter. Thus their inhabitants are seen as being friendlier and more philosophical.

Even though additions have been made to the Ptolemaic attributions, the basic points remain in circulation amongst astrologers today. Books published on mundane astrology during the last decade continue to repeat them. England and Germany are still given to Aries, Persia to Taurus, Spain to Sagittarius, Africa to Cancer and so on, just as propounded by Ptolemy. As demonstrated, however, there is no justification whatever for retaining Ptolemy's astrological attributions since the reasoning they are based upon is worthless.

The difference between the attributions of Ptolemy and those given by Manilius is intriguing. At the least it is evidence that even two thousand years ago there was little agreement amongst astrologers on these points. The origins of the attributions remains obscure for much early work has now been lost, but the current opinion of scholars is that Ptolemy's attributions derive from the work of Posidonius, the teacher of Cicero and Nigidius Figulus.

How then did Ptolemy use these rulerships in practice? The answer is in much the same way as Manilius — celestial events would affect those areas of the world which fell under the same astrological rulership. Ptolemy does add other methods of circumscribing the effect upon the world of astrological phenomena, especially the effect upon cities. He explains that the Sun, Moon and Ascendant positions in the foundation charts of cities are very sensitive, and any astrological events which happen on these positions should be watched. If the foundation date of a city is not known then Ptolemy advises astrologers to use instead the Midheaven position of the king or ruler at the time.[40] This is an interesting idenfitication of king and city.

With regard to the phenomena themselves, he states that the strongest cause of problems upon the earth are eclipses of the Sun and Moon, followed in importance by the stations of Saturn, Jupiter and Mars. When any of these events are observed the sign it falls within should be noted. Then, any part of the world which also falls under the sign can be confidently expected to be visited by some disaster.

Finally, in a move towards the position of modern psychological astrology, Ptolemy explains that the people who are most afffected by the 'universal ills' are those who, in their own charts, have the luminaries or the angles conjunct or in opposition to the degree of the eclipse or station. Astrologers today would tend to agree with him.

Ptolemy was the last great astrologer to emerge from the empires of Greece and Rome. In the following centuries the focus of astrological research was to shift back to the land of its birth — to the Persian empire of the Sasanians which stretched from Mesopotamia to the Indus valley. Intellectually the West was beginning to decline; its great minds were becoming crippled as they were thrust more and more into the growing problems of Christianity. Astrology was one of the subjects which the Church considered bordered on heresy and its study was discouraged and frequently condemned.

Greek science in general, and astrology in particular, found fertile ground in the East during the third century AD under the Sasanian king Shapur I. He was liberal in the arts and tolerant in his religion: during his reign the gnostic teacher Mani preached openly and even met with the king on occasions. Shapur was a great patron of the Greek philosophers and scholars and with his encouragement many works, amongst them those of Ptolemy, were translated into Persian. Unfortunately the revival of Greek culture was not to last long but the importance of this brief efflorescence was to be apparent some centuries later when the great texts were again translated — this time into Arabic by the Islamic scholars.

Islam, which traditionally dates itself from AD 622, precipitated an expansion not only of empire but also of learning. This learning was eclectic in its source material and embraced a wide range of different cultures. A major contributing group were the Jewish scholars who flourished under the initially tolerant Arab Caliphs — a very different situation from the restrictions Roman and Christian rulers had placed over them. The greatest achievements of learning followed the establishments of the *Abbasid* dynasty in AD 750. The *Abbasid* Caliph left the old Arab capital of Damascus for a new city, Baghdad, which he founded on the west bank of the Tigris in 762. This city was built on geomantic principles: it was circular and bounded by three concentric walls pierced by four gates. Through these gates lead the great highways which connected the central palace with the four corners of the empire. Baghdad became quite literally the focal point of a vast economic network which brought wealth on an unprecedented scale to the city. By the early ninth century Baghdad was probably the largest city in the world with a population nearing one million, at a time when Charlemagne's capital had a few thousand.

The first astrological school in Baghdad was founded in 777 by the Jewish scholar Jacob ben Tarik. A school which became renowned for its writers and translators. Abu Ma'shar, perhaps the most famous of all Arab astrologers, was head of this school in the mid-ninth century. He translated Ptolemy into Arabic and his translations were later themselves put into Latin by European scholars in the West. The schools of Baghdad had available works written in Greek, Syrian, Persian and Indian, a range which embraced all previous scholarship, giving the Arab students a unique opportunity to be at the forefront of learning.

Much of this work found its way to Europe through Arabic Spain where the great city of Cordova — which had a population nearing half a million — was the intellectual centre. Students would travel there from Italy and Gaul to learn under Arab teachers. One such student, Gilbert d'Auvergne, was later to become Pope Sylvester II.

Major Islamic and Jewish astrologers

Latin name	*Arabic name*
Albategnius	al-Battani
Alberuni	al-Biruni
Albumazar	Abu Ma'shar
Alfraganus	al-Farghani
Alhazen	al-Haytham
Alpetragius	al-Bitruji
Anaritius	al-Nayrizi
Avicenna	Ibn Sina
Azarquiel	al-Zarqali
Messahala	Masha allah

While we owe a great debt to the Arab scholars for their translation and preservation of the Greek and Roman astrological texts which were passed on to Europe in the eleventh and twelfth centuries we cannot simply stop at this self-centred appraisal of Islamic astrology. To see the Arab world as merely the transmitter of earlier astrological

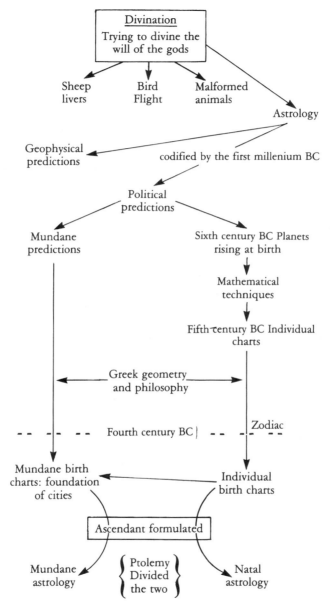

Figure 1.4   The Development of Astrology.

knowledge is to ignore the greater part of its learning. Yet the full value of this learning cannot be comprehended until the huge number of manuscripts on astrology in Arabic, Persian and Turkish are translated; for the moment they lie undisturbed in museum collections around the world. It is tragic to think that even the luminaries are not readily available in translation, let alone the lesser scholars. We can but hope that time will rectify this state of affairs.

References

1   Neugebauer, O. and Parker, R. A. *Egyptian Astronomical Texts,* vol. 3, p71f. However, Herodotus (*Histories*, p. 159) says, 'The Egyptians were also the first to assign each month and each day to a particular deity, and to foretell by the date of a man's birth his character, his fortunes, and the day of his death.'
2   Pliny, *The Natural History,* Book vii, ch.57.
3   *Enuma elish*: tablet vi:8 also see *Atra-Hasis*: tablet i: 191-197.
4   Reiner, E. *Enuma Anu Enlil,* page 23ff.
5   ibid., page 6.
6   Reiner, E. *The Venus Tablet of Ammisaduqa* p.25.
7   ibid., p.29.
8   Virolleaud, C. 'The Syrian town of Katna and the Kingdom of Mitanni', p.313
9   Laroche, E. 'Astrologie', p.94.
10 Reiner, *Enuma Anu Enlil,* p.17.
11 Waterman, L. *Royal Correspondence of the Assyrian Empire,* letter 519.
12 ibid., letter 1006.
13 Oppenheim, A. L. *Ancient Mesopotamia,* p.15ff.
14 Reiner, E. 'Fortune-telling in Mesopotamia', p.27.
15 Scheil, V. 'Un fragment susien du livre *Enuma Anu Ellil*', p.139ff.
16 Oppenheim, op.cit., p.201ff.
17 Sachs, A. 'Babylonian Horoscopes', p.54.
18 Cumont, F. *Astrology and Religion and the Greeks and Romans* p.29.
19 ibid., p.30.
20 Sachs, op.cit., p.57.
21 Neugebauer, O. and Van Hoesen, H. B. *Greek Horoscopes* p.17.
22 ibid., p.76-8.
23 Neugebauer, *Astronomical Cuneiform Texts,* vol. 1, p.22ff.

24 Burstein, S.M. *Babyloniaca,* p.5ff. Burstein, with scholarship
    on his side, identifies Berosus of Kos with Berosus the historian
    in the temple of Marduk, Babylon. The latter's book is dedicated
    to King Antiochus I, who reigned after 281 BC. Thus his leaving
    of the temple for Kos would seem to most likely follow this date.
25 Neugebauer, O. *Astronomical Cuneiform Texts,* vol. 2, p.316;
    vol. 3 p.151ff.
26 Sachs, A. 'A Classification of the Babylonian astronomical tablets
    of the Seleucid period', p.285ff.
27 Pliny, op.cit., xxxv, 17.
28 Cicero, *De Divinatione.*, II, xlvii.
29 ibid., II, xxiv. (my parenthesis).
30 ibid., II, xliii.
31 Lucan, *Pharasalia,* I, 708-46.
32 Manilius, *Astronomica,* Introduction, p.liff.
33 Weidner, E. F. *Gestirn-Darstellungen auf Babylonischen
    Tontafeln,* (esp tablet VAT 7847).
34 Manilius, op.cit., p.289.
35 Tacitus, *The Annals of Imperial Rome* p.210.
36 Suetonius, *The Twelve Caesars,* p.146.
37 ibid., p.234.
38 Dio Cassius, *Roman History,* volume viii, p.355.
39 Pliny. op.cit., xxviii, 17.
40 Ptolemy, *Tetrabiblos,* II, 3 and 5.

Bibliography

Atra-hasis 'The Babylonian Story of the Flood' (trans. W. G. Lambert
    and A. R. Millard) Oxford, 1969.
BURSTEIN S. M. *The Babyloniaca of Berosus* Malibu, 1978.
CICERO *De Divinatione* (trans. W. A. Falconer) London, 1979.
CUMONT, F. *Astrology and Religion among the Greeks and Romans*
    New York, 1960.
DIO CASSIUS *Roman History* (trans. E. Cary) 9 vols, London, 1961.
Enuma elish 'The Babylonian Genesis' (trans. A. Heidel) 2nd edition,
    Chicago, 1963.
HERODOTUS, *The Histories,* (trans. Aubrey de Sélincourt)
    Harmondsworth, 1981.
LAROCHE, E. 'Astrologie' *Revue Hittite et Asianique*, vol. 14 (fasc
    59), 1956.
LUCAN *Pharsalia* (trans. Sir Edward Ridley) 2nd edition, London,
    1905.

MANILIUS *Astronomica* (trans. G. P. Gould) London, 1977.

NEUGEBAUER, O. and VAN HOESEN, H. B. *Greek Horoscopes* Philadelphia, 1959.

NEUGEBAUER, O, *Astronomical Cuneiform Texts* 3 vols, London, 1955.

NEUGEBAUER, O. and PARKER, R. A. *Egyptian Astronomical Texts* 3 vols, London, 1960.

NEUGEBAUER, O. *The Exact Sciences in Antiquity* 2nd edition, New York, 1969.

OPPENHEIM, A. L. 'The position of the intellectual in Mesopotamian society' *Daedalus* spring, 1975.

OPPENHEIM, A. L. *Ancient Mesopotamia* Revised edition, Chicago, 1977.

PLINY *The Natural History* (trans. J. Bostock and H. T. Riley) 6 vols, London, 1855-57.

PLUTARCH *Makers of Rome* (trans. Ian Scott-Kilvert) Harmondsworth, 1980.

PTOLEMY *Tetrabiblos* (trans. W. G. Waddell) London, 1971.

REINER, E. *The Venus Tablet of Ammisaduqa* Malibu, 1975.

REINER, E. *Enuma Anu Enlil, Tablets 50-51* Malibu, 1981.

REINER, E. 'Fortune-telling in Mesopotamia' *Journal of Near Eastern Studies* vol. 19, no.1, January, 1960.

SACHS, A. 'A classification of the Babylonian astronomical tablets of the Seleucid period' *Journal of Cuneiform Studies* vol. 2, no.4, 1948.

SACHS, A. 'Babylonian horoscopes' *Journal of Cuneiform Studies* vol. 6, no.2, 1952.

SCHEIL, V. 'Un fragment susien du livre *Enuma Anu Ellil*' *Revue d'Assyriologie et d'Archéologie orientale* vol. 14, no.3, 1917.

SENECA *Naturales Quaestiones* (trans. T. H. Corcoran) 2 vols, London, 1971.

SUETONIUS *The Twelve Caesars* (trans. Robert Graves) revised edition, Harmondsworth, 1979.

TACITUS *The Annals of Imperial Rome* (trans. Michael Grant) revised edition, Harmondsworth, 1979.

VIROLLEAUD, C. 'The Syrian town of Katna and the Kingdom of Mitanni' *Antiquity* vol. 3, 1929.

WATERMAN, L. *Royal Correspondence of the Assyrian Empire* 4 vols, Michigan, Ann Arbor: 1930.

WEIDNER, E. F. *Gestirn-Darstellungen auf Babylonischen Tontafeln* Wien, 1967.

2.
THE HISTORY OF MUNDANE ASTROLOGY IN EUROPE FROM AD 500 TO THE PRESENT DAY

Nicholas Campion

In the period following the disintegration of the Roman Empire around AD475, there was a gradual regression in intellectual learning in Europe as part of which the study and practice of astrology almost disappeared. This was not a sudden process, but was accelerated by the reluctance of Christian theologians to accept astrology. Two of the major philosophers of the time, Boethius (AD 480-524) and Isidore (c. AD 560-636), accepted the general claims of planetary influence, but their rejection of prediction as un-Christian retarded astrology for the subsequent centuries. [1] The years between 500 and 800 AD represented the nadir or European astrology, during which time the Arabs became the inheritors of Hellenistic wisdom.

The disappearance of astrology was not total, for the ancient learning was to an extent preserved in monastic libraries. Through the works of Boethius and Isidore clerics were aware of the discussion of astrology among the Christian fathers, and through other classical authors, such as Pliny, they were aware of the attribution of various characteristics to the planets. It is possible that more sophisticated astrological texts were preserved, for it was from Iona in northern Britain that Alcuin emerged to become astrology teacher to the Emperor Charlemagne, and instigator of the astrological revival of the ninth century. Astrology at this time was based around a disorganized system of the observance of celestial ph⟨ ⟩ ⟨⟩⟩ — lunar phases, eclipses, and comets — and plane⟨ ⟩ tions with numbers, days of the week, herbs, pla⟨ ⟩ and so on. At a popular level, or in the monasteries, ast⟨ ⟩

one important characteristic — it was mundane, concerned not with the individual but with groups. The earliest practitioner we hear of in England was a certain Pellitus, who was astrologer to King Edwin of Northumbria (*c.* AD 616-32) and whose major task was to supply the king with military advice in his long-standing war with the Celts. [2] Of the scholars of the time the most renowned was the Venerable Bede (AD 671-735) who noted the effects of various comets, including that of AD 729 which he blamed for the death of King Osric of |Northumbria| and the incursion |of the Saracens into Gaul. [3] His interest was clearly in the effect of the planets on the entire world, as would have been the interest of Alcuin, Bede's successor at Iona.

We hear of the continuation of astrology also among the Jews of Marseilles and among the kings of the Jewish kingdom which flourished in northern Spain and southern France in the ninth century. It was from Spain that Pellitus came to serve Edwin of Northumbria, providing evidence of the communication between different parts of Europe at the time, communication enhanced by the links of the Celtic Church via Spain with the Coptic Church in Egypt.

The astrological revival began in Europe under the Emperor Charlemagne, who ruled the Franks from AD 768-814. The revival drew on the strands from both north and south Europe, for Charlemagne was tutored by the English Alcuin (the Emperor himself became a skilled astrologer), [4] while the quest for new texts led to close contacts with the Muslim world. Astrology had flourished in Gaul during the late Roman Empire, so it was fitting that the revival should be centred in the new Frankish Empire, which covered much of what is now France, the Low Countries and West Germany. What was remarkable about this ressurgence of interest in astrology was the speed with which it took hold. Possibly much was due to the prestige of Alcuin, who became the most famous teacher in Europe. From the time of Charlemagne until that of King Robert I (*c.*900), the study of astrology and astronomy was expressly encouraged by councils, bishops and kings, especially to the clergy. [5] The outcome of this, complained Goujet in the eighteenth century, was an enormous increase in the numbers of astrologers. It seems that these astrologers were emerging to fill a demand for, by the reign of Charlemagne's successor, Louis the Pious (814-40), every Carolingian lord had his own astrologer. [6] We find recorded the names of the practitioners: Adalmus, Abbot of Chartres; Odo, teacher at Tournai; Engelbert, monk at Liège; and Gilbert Maminot, Bishop of Lisieux and chaplain and physician to William the Conqueror of England. [7]

Not only was the astrology practised still very much concerned with the prediction of wars, pestilences, catastrophes and revolutions, but only a lord could afford to employ an astrologer. The intellectual and economic conditions were thus set for the domination of mundane astrology over much of astrology's 900-year ascendancy in European culture. This sudden interest created such a demand that when western scholars developed their contracts with Arab learning in the tenth century, astrological texts were among the first to be translated. These texts were to form the basis of the developing sophistication of astrology in European courts and clerical schools.

As far as we know, the earliest translations of Muslim astrological texts were made by Lupitus of Barcelona, who in 984 was contacted by Gerbert, the future Pope Sylvester II, with a request for astrological works translated by him. It seems that Sylvester himself may have studied the work of Julius Firmicus Maternus in Spain prior to 1000 AD. [8] Firmicus Maternus was in fact to be a major influence on European thought before the translation of Ptolemy; he had considerable influence on the writers of Chartres, such as Bernard of Silvester, and a story is told that Gerard, Archbishop of York under Henry I, was refused burial in the cathedral after his death in 1104, after a copy of Maternus was found under his pillow. [9]

By the eleventh century astrology was firmly established, and the first native European texts were produced. The first known work was the *Liber de Planetis et Mundi Climatibus,* which was apparently written sometime in the first quarter of the eleventh century, either by Pope Sylvester, or by another cleric, Adelbold, Bishop of Utrecht from 1010-27. [10] The trickle of translations became a continuous flow in the twelfth century and a flood in the thirteenth. It was in 1138 that Plato of Tivoli published his translation of Ptolemy's *Tetrabiblos,* after which the Europeans had access to the finest astrological mind of the ancient world and were introduced to the techniques of mundane astrology.

Mundane astrology was first distinguished as an entirely separate branch of astrology in European literature in *The Book of the Division of Astronomy and its Four Parts,* written in the 1170s by the English astrologer, Roger of Hereford. [11] The four parts were, of course, Natal, Electional, Horary and Mundane. Roger paid particular attention to the art of mundane astrology, and produced what may be the earliest list of geo-physical rulerships in European astrology, This list is probably derived from Arab works, and displays a concern with the astrological rulership of cultures and religions rather than specific places on the earth's surface. According to Roger, each part of the globe was ruled by a planet and a sign of the zodiac, the two not necessarily being directly related. For example, Spain was ruled by the Moon and by Virgo, while India was ruled by Capricorn and by Mercury. The 'entire land of the Christians' was ruled by Saturn and by the sign of its exaltation, Libra. The complete list given by Roger was as follows:

Aries and Jupiter rule the 'land between babal and herach'
Libra and Saturn rule the 'land of the Christians'
Scorpio and Venus rule the Arabs
Capricorn and Mercury rule India
Leo and Mars rule the Turks
Aquarius and the Sun rule Babylonia
Virgo and the Moon rule Spain.

Other astrologers contemporary with Roger produced variations on this list as follows:

Adelard of Bath (11th-12th centuries)
Saturn rules the Jews
Venus and Mars rule the Arabs
The Sun and Jupiter rule the Christians

Michael Scot (11th-12th centuries)
Saturn rules Pagans and Jews
Jupiter rules Christians

Roger Bacon (13th century)
Mercury rules Christianity
Venus rules Islam

William of Auvergne (13th century)
Saturn rules Jews
Venus rules Islam
The Sun rules Christianity.

There is in some cases a logic to these rulerships; for example Roger Bacon claimed that Mercury rules Christianity because it also rules Virgo, the sign of the Virgin Mary. In other cases the rulerships are quite clearly derived from Muslim cycles as described in Chapter 5, especially those of Abu Ma'shar in the ninth century. For example Abu Ma'shar claimed that Muhammed was born under a cycle known as a 'mighty fardar', ruled by Venus and Gemini. It would seem obvious that such a claim was the basis of the rulership of Islam by Venus in the European texts. These rulerships appear to have been supplanted by others based either on Ptolemy or on the whims of later writers, although they do still crop up in astrological literature. Liz Greene in *Saturn* describes that planet as having a particular affinity with the Jews, to whom she adds the Roman Catholics and Mormons.

Astrology in medieval Europe was considered to consist of two major types: natural astrology and judicial astrology. Natural astrology was regarded as the study of the relationship between celestial phenomena and terrestrial events, so that the observation of planetary cycles, lunar phases, conjunctions and comets could be put to use in understanding general developments in weather, medicine, agriculture and national events such as wars and revolutions, or the growth and decay of religions and civilizations. Judicial astrology was defined as the creation of horoscopes for interpretation either as nativities, horaries or elections. Astrology as a whole formed a central part of European learning, and Robert Grosseteste twelfth-century Bishop of Lincoln, considered it to be the highest intellectual discipline and spiritually second only to divine worship. There was, however, an ideological conflict between Christianity and judicial astrology over the problem of who ruled the human soul — God or the stars. Various compromises were found to this problem, such as that the stars ruled the body while God still ruled the human soul, or that human freedom of choice was able to over-rule the influence of the stars. Yet the conflict remained, and for many scholars judicial astrology was held to be unacceptable and un-Christian. It is this problem which helps to explain the success of mundane astrology, for although it contained elements of judicial astrology, it was based firmly in the realm of natural astrology. It was therefore acceptable to all.

Mundane astrology was to develop as a combination of the two branches of astrology. The scholars in the monasteries and clerical schools were able to philosophize about the evolution of the world in terms of astrological cycles, while at a popular level every major conjunction, eclipse or comet was seen as a possible bringer of upheaval and disaster. This was the 'natural' side of mundane work. Meanwhile at court the astrologers would be called upon to advise in political and military matters for which they would rely far more heavily on judicial astrology, drawing up nativities for the prince, his allies and foes, casting horaries for important decisions and making elections for the beginning of important enterprises.

The theoretical background to the development of mundane astrology was provided by some of the greatest minds of the time, who used as their authorities not only Ptolemy, but also the Scriptures, Plato and, after 1200, Aristotle. Robert Grosseteste (1175-1253), Bishop of Lincoln, and a central figure in the political battles of thirteenth-century England, made a special study of comets,[12] while Albertus Magnus (c.1193-c.1280) Dominican friar, Bishop of Ratisbon and the greatest scholar of his age, discussed at length the influence of the planets over global wars and other upheavals.[13] It was Albert's pupil, St Thomas Aquinas (c.1225-74), the greatest medieval theologian of them all, who first defined the theoretical division between mundane and natal astrology which has been given a new modern importance by the work of Carl Jung.[14] Aquinas argued that individuals are free to make choices, but that people in groups are ruled by their passions. Groups, whether towns, armies or whole nations, are therefore much more easily influenced by the stars, and therefore it is much more easy to make predictions for groups than it is for individuals. This gives rise to the idea that in mundane astrology we may be dealing with events which might be considered to be 'fated'.[15]

As to the use of mundane astrology, this was expanded by the English Franciscan Roger Bacon, considered by many to be the father of scientific thought. Bacon was a much firmer adherent of astrology than was Aquinas and believed that it would be possible to avoid wars through the careful use of mundane astrology. He wrote that the Church should use astrology in order to predict the coming of the Anti-Christ, and to avoid being overcome through the skill of the Tarter astrologers of the Mongol Empire.[16]

Some of these great scholars were also practising astrologers. One of the earliest of the translators of Arab astrology, the twelfth-century scholar John of Spain, is the first to be recorded as an expert practitioner. [17] Adelard of Bath was probably employed in the 1140's as an astrologer by Henry II of England, [18] Henry himself being educated by the astrologer William of Conches. [19] Another early translator, Constantinus Africanus, was employed by the Norman Duke Robert Guiscard of Sicily in the eleventh century, although we cannot be sure what part of his time was taken up by astrology for, like many other royal servants at this time, his literacy made him valuable in many areas of court life. [20] One of the first scholars whom we know was employed as a court astrologer was Michael Scot, who in the early thirteenth century was employed specifically as astrologer to the Holy Roman Emperor Frederick II. [21] Of the existence of private practitioners at this time we have only a few hints. Peter Abelard, the founder of scholastic theology, implies the existence of astrological practice around 1100 by discussing the success rate in prediction, [22] and by the end of the twelfth century there seem to have been astrology practices in the Mediterranean areas of Italy, France and Spain. [23] These would probably have specialized in the other branches of astrology — natal, horary and electional — catering to the merchants and craftsmen of the new towns.

For the most part, however, astrology in the eleventh to fourteenth centuries was practised at court, and except for medical purposes, it had a 'mundane' character. The intellectual work of the scholastic theologians, and the deep interest of many clerics, especially the friars, in the subject, prepared the intellectual ground, and we find astrology taking a crucially important place in the great courts of the Papacy, France and the Holy Roman Empire.

Royal astrological enthusiasts included all the kings of France from Charles IV to Louis XIII, most of the Holy Roman Emperors, including Wenceslaus ('Good King Wenceslaus') and Charles V, Alfonso X of Castile, Richard II, Henry VII and Henry VIII of England and King Matthias of Hungary. Charles V of France actually opened a college at Paris University specifically to encourage the study of astrology. [24] This college was founded with papal confirmation, but the move was perhaps not that necessary, for the original statutes of 1215 had specified astrology as one of the subjects on the university curriculum. [25]

Some astrologers were employed, like the seventh-century Pellitus, for military advice. One of the most successful of the early medieval practitioners was Guido Bonatti, who was born around 1210, and who dominated Italian astrology. Bonatti's book, the *Liber*

Astronomicus, was a basic astrological text until the sixteenth century, and a bound de luxe edition was reputed to be one of the most treasured items in the library of Henry VII of England in the 1500s. The story is told in the Annales of Forli, that in 1282 the town of Forli was being defended by Bonatti's patron, Guido de Montefeltro, against an army commanded by Pope Martin IV. Consulting his charts Bonatti advised his master to lead the papal army into a trap by withdrawing from the town and allowing the Pope to occupy it. This was done, and while the invading army was celebrating its victory, Montefeltro counterattacked. It is recorded that Bonatti received the credit for the resulting defeat of the papal forces. [26]

Most of the new Italian municipalities of the fourteenth and fifteenth centuries employed official astrologers, and one of the most renowned was Blasius of Parma (*c*.1350-1416). Blasius was a leading Italian scholar who was responsible for teaching astrology at several universities, including Bologna. In June 1386 his predictive powers were put to the test during the war between the houses of Carrara and Della Scala. Blasius elected the most favourable time for the Carrara army to attack, and predicted that the Scaliger army would be taken prisoner. The battle at first seemed to be going the way of the Scaliger troops, and the Carrara army was driven back to the town walls. Blasius, who was watching the battle, was mocked by another bystander, but he stuck to his prediction, and was proved right when the rest of the Carrara army attacked the Scaligers in the rear, totally defeating them. [27] Paolo Dagomari, the first Florentine astrologer to compose annual predictions, was credited for the victory of the Pisans over Cascina in 1364. [28]

The general predictions of the time were usually cast in vague terms, prophesying various disasters, famines, pestilences and wars, and unreliability of sources and distance from the evidence makes it difficult to assess the accuracy of astrologers at this time. One of the most remarkable predictions was that made by Cardinal Pierre D'Ailly of France, who not only forecast the Reformation in general terms, but prophesied in 1414 that 1789 would be a year of great upheaval. [29]

It was in the fourteenth century that we find mundane astrology becoming big business, with astrologers seeking lucrative employment at all the courts of Italy, France and Germany. This process was stimulated by the uncertainties of the Hundred Years War, with its never-ending series of treaties, alliances, dynastic marriages, wars, battles, coronations and invasions, all of which required the expert attentions of astrologers. There were numerous claims of successful prediction, many of which centred around the victory of the English over the French at Poitiers in 1356.[30] There was also a fair measure of success claimed in predicting the life and death of Du Guesclin, Constable of France, and one of the outstanding figures of the century.[31] Thomas Brown, a Welsh astrologer, was on hand to record the timing of the important Treaty of Arras, signed by Charles VII of France and Philip of Burgundy in 1435, and gives a more accurate record of the event than other contemporary chroniclers.[32]

The creation of the College de Maitre Gervais in Paris by Charles V guaranteed a concentration of astrological activity in France, and we may take the continuing employment of astrologers as a sign of their success and relevance to the problems of the time.

Many astrologers were employed as diplomats, or in other tasks such as the recovery of ransoms. Arnold of Villanova was employed as a diplomat by Peter III of Aragon (1272-85) and was rewarded for his medical success with a castle,[33] while a noted French astrologer, Angelo Cato de Supini of Benevento, was employed by Charles the Bold of Burgundy and Louis XI of France in the final stages of the Hundred Years War at the end of the fifteenth century. Andelo di Negro, a well-known astrological author, even travelled to Alexius Comnenus, Emperor of Trebizond, as ambassador of Florence.[34]

This expansion of mundane practice in the fourteenth and fifteenth centuries was accompanied by new theoretical work by men such as Peter of Abano, astrologer to the Marquis d'Este around 1300,[35] the English scholar John of Eschenden whose *Summa* (published in 1347) was a major mundane text,[36] and, later, Franciscanus Florentinus (born 1424), who became Dean of the College of Theologians in Florence.[37] These astrologers examined the occurrence of astronomical phenomena — comets, eclipses, conjunctions — and attempted to correlate them with contemporary events. Using their findings they felt that it would be possible to make mundane astrology a little more scientific and use it to gain a deeper understanding of contemporary politics. Pierre D'Ailly's prediction of the Reformation and the upheavals of 1789 were derived from just such an examination of the correlation of political events with astrology. In the fifteenth century Jacobus Angelus produced a major work on comets which methodically examined their supposed effects.[38] For example, he considered that the comet of 1337 was responsible for the outbreak of war between England and France. Using such research astrologers felt much more able to make predictions for the future which would guarantee them a large audience. Astronomical events still had a very immediate and simple appeal for people who knew little of astrology, and could have a profound political effect. The comet of 1402 was hailed in Wales as a favourable omen for the rebellion of Owen Glendower, and was a valuable morale booster. [39] The defence of Mundane astrology by Conrad Heingarter, (1430-1500), court astrologer to John II, Duke of Bourbon, implies that by the fifteenth century there was an educated criticism of mundane astrology, [40] even though the major critics, such as Pico della Mirandola (1463-99), [41] generally accepted the basics of natural astrology. There was thus even more motivation for mundane astrologers to make their art more accurate.

It was inevitable that the popular demand for prophecy, combined with the awe with which comets such as that of 1402 were held, should lead to the popularization of mundane astrology, and in the late fourteenth century astrologers started to address themselves to a mass market. It was in the 1370s that Paolo Dagomari published at Florence the first annual prognostication for the coming year. [42] The first annual prediction which has survived is the *Judgement of the Year 1405* by Blasius de Parma. [43]

In this work Blasius predicted very bad weather, fire, shipwreck, abundance of wine, butter, oil and grain (and inflation in prices), disease among horses, mules and camels, venereal diseases, heart ailments, leprosy, plague amongst humans, illegitimate births, and rebellions by the poor. To complete this pessimistic view he confirmed that the war between Venice and Florence, Milan, Pavia, Genoa and Rome would continue, with the latter four cities suffering most. Following the invention of printing with moveable type around 1450 such predictions began to have a greater and greater circulation, and the first annual almanaks may have been printed as early as 1469. [44]

The sixteenth century witnessed the spread of astrology to new areas of Europe stimulated by the spread of the printed word, Renaissance culture, and the growth of universities in northern and western Europe. The university at Pressburg in Hungary was established by King Matthias Corvinus in 1500 at a time elected by the astrologer Regiomontanus. The university achieved a short-lived reputation for the skill of its astrological masters but was unfortunately forced to close down because of the war with the Turks. [45]

Astrology arrived in the universities and courts of northern Germany, Hungary, Scandinavia, and Poland, but it is its sudden adoption by the English which is perhaps most interesting at this time for it was in England that it became most closely involved with politics. Astrologers were already accustomed to a certain amount of involvement with politics by virtue of the positions which they frequently held. In the twelfth century astrology had been used as the pretext by the political opponents of Archbishop Gerard of York to refuse him burial in the Cathedral, and in 1491 the French court astrologer Simon de Phares was made the scapegoat by the Parlement and the Sorbonne in its battle with Charles VIII. [46] Astrologers also took partisan national standpoints, as did Thomas Brown when he took a pro-English view of the Treaty of Arras, and as did Guillaume Postel who, in the sixteenth century argued that France was astrologically destined to be the centre of universal religion and monarchy. [47] In England, however, astrologers found themselves embroiled in politics from the start.

Astrology arrived in England at the same time as a fundamental shift was taking place in politics away from feudalism and toward a more modern style of administration, a change accompanied by profound economic, social and religious changes. Astrology had existed in England before the sixteenth century mainly as a courtly pursuit encouraged by kings such as Richard II and Henry VI, an adjunct to theology through the medieval scholars or later reformers such as Wyclyf, or as medical astrology. There are hints of astrological practice as early as 1186, [48] although most scholars and practitioners appear, like Thomas Brown or Roger Bacon, to have moved to the more fertile ground of mainland Europe. It is not until 1442 that we can name an astrological consultant in London, [49] but after that date astrology appears to have spread rapidly, with the first almanaks circulating around 1473.

Perhaps the reason that astrology took root in England so rapidly and so firmly was that the English were particularly keen on political prophecy, and many prophecies, including Arthurian ones, formed an important part of the propaganda effort in the century-long dynastic Wars of the Roses. [50] Henry VII, the first monarch of a long line to encourage astrology, deliberately exploited this connection, and his Celtic ancestry, by naming his eldest son Arthur, with the intention that he should reign as King Arthur. That there was a shortage of astrological talent in England at the time is demonstrated by Henry's reliance on the Italian astrologer William Parron, who had earlier established his reputation by predicting the fall of Ludovica Sforza of Milan. [51] Parron established a highly successful business in London offering highly specialized advice to the rich and powerful, and general predictions to the eager masses. Parron opened the first regular English almanak service by 1481, but he fell from grace quickly after he forecast a long and happy life for the Queen shortly before she died.

The political importance of astrology was at first most pronounced in England in the world of court intrigue and conspiratorial politics. The reason for Parron's disgrace was that he lost royal patronage, an essential requirement for public practice at a time when anti-government conspirators were seeking astrological advice. [52] The government was extremely sensitive to the public pronouncements of astrologers, and several were executed at the beginning of the sixteenth century for making indiscreet predictions. One astrologer, Robert Allen, was taken to task by the government because he predicted the early death of King Edward VI, a prediction which ironically came true. [53] Under Henry VIII (1509-47) the central figures of court politics used astrologers, and Cardinal Wolsey, Henry's first Chancellor is said to have had the King's horoscope cast so that his moves could be forecast, and to have used elections to time events. [54] This did not help the Cardinal predict his own subsequent downfall and disgrace. Thomas Cromwell, Henry's third Chancellor and the architect of the English Reformation, used the King's almanak-maker as an ambassador to report on the European attitude to his master. [55] Both royal servants were no doubt deeply interested in the subject as a result of Henry's enthusiasm for it, and during his reign the bishops were ordered not to criticize astrology. Henry employed two astrologers: the German Nicholas Kratzer, and the English astrologer John Robins. Robins went on to serve Henry's successor, Mary I, and no doubt she used him for advice on the plans of her sister and rival Princess Elizabeth, at the same time as Elizabeth was consulting the young John Dee concerning Mary's intentions.

English astrology owed much to continental astrologers, such as Parron and Kratzer, and the visit of Jerome Cardan, the great Italian mathematician, to cast the horoscope of Edward VI, gave the art its major boost. Cardan arrived at the request of Edward's tutor,

John Cheke, himself an astrologer, but his visit was not entirely successful. Cardan was capable of making retrospective judgements — he attributed the Reformation to the conjunction in 1553 of Mercury, Mars and Jupiter in Aries — but made the embarrassing prediction that the King would live a long life shortly before he in fact died. [56] However Cardan's presence was an inspiration because he was one of the greatest all-round scholars of the day, and the young mathematicians John Dee and Leonard Digges were duly impressed. Digges and Dee were the virtual founders of English astrology, and Dee himself, following his advice to Elizabeth during her imprisonment, was to become the royal astrologer. He elected the time for Elizabeth's coronation in 1558, a task we can only assume he performed with outstanding success, and was subsequently employed both by the Queen and her leading administrators as a roving diplomat and spy. Some of his most important work was to facilitate the formulation of foreign policy, especially with regard to the Queen's possible marriage, by casting nativities for European kings and princes. [57]

As with her predecessors, one of Elizabeth's main preoccupations was to restrict the public circulation of unfavourable predictions. As early as the 1530s, Chapuys, the Imperial ambassador, had reported to his astrologically-minded master, Charles V, on the power of prediction to arouse popular feeling in England, and mindful of this the government had banned Nostradamus' gloomy predictions for 1558, lest they cause unrest. Elizabeth herself gained great prestige by ignoring the comet of 1577 which was widely expected to bring violent change. [59] She censored the flow of predictions but did not ban them completely. By 1600 six hundred almanaks had been issued in England, although in 1581 the government had forbidden the discussion of such sensitive matters as the Queen's marriage or the succession to the throne. [60]

By Elizabeth's death in 1603 English society was in the grip of a major social and economic transformation, a transformation whose profound political and ideological consequences were to culminate in the Civil War and the Republic of the 1640s - 50s. Astrology was to play a powerful part in mass politics, and was used at every level — for propaganda, to reinforce theology, to back up political demands, and specifically for advice to all the major political leaders on questions of timing and strategy.

As we have seen, astrology has influenced the course of history in two ways: by influencing the making of political decisions at court; and by affecting public opinion so as to alter the course or events. [61] In other words, regardless of the validity of astrological claims, 'the political role of astrology arose from its self-fulfilling character'. [62] It is worth making an astrological note here that at this time, unknown to contemporary astrologers, Pluto was transiting the ascendant and first house of the English chart — an astrological symbol of profound upheaval.

Astrologers found themselves in demand firstly as advisors to political leaders, and secondly to an enormous number of ordinary people whose lives were disrupted by the war. The foremost astrologer of the time was William Lilly, [63] who was at one time offering advice to both the Royalist and Parliamentary camps. Lilly's fame was based partly on the success of his almanak which in 1649 alone sold 30,000 copies, and his popularity was such that his presence on the side of a Parliamentary army was on at least one occasion credited as a reason for their victory. It was said that he was more use to a Parliamentary army than half a dozen regiments. [64]

Lilly's other claim to fame is that he was the first ever newspaper astrologer. [66] His propaganda talents were such that in March 1649 he was asked to write a column for one of the new newspapers which were starting up in the exciting atmosphere of the time. Some astrologers, including the great physician and herbalist Nicholas Culpepper, took up a defiantly Republican stance, overtly involving themselves in politics and heavily influencing their predictions towards the overthrow of European monarchy. [67] There was little choice but for astrologers of the time to adopt a political colour, and many strongly sympathized with the forces of revolution. Others, such as the English George Wharton, lent their services willingly to the interests of the Crown.

Astrology in England after the restoration of the monarchy in 1660 retained its popularity for a time. Many of the leading intellectual figures were strongly interested in it, and Elias Ashmole was consulted several times by Charles II concerning the timing of important speeches. [68] Indeed, Charles' interest in astrology was such that Louis XIV of France sent an astrologer, the Abbé Pregnon, as his ambassador to Charles in 1669, although Charles was reported to be disappointed when the Abbé failed to predict horse race winners. [69] Charles' brother, James II, was tutored by an astrologer, Anthony Ascham, who was later appointed ambassador to Madrid. [70]

The last English politician known to have consulted an astrologer was probably Sir John Trenchard, Secretary of State to William III.[71] At a popular level the almanaks, containing their mundane predications, sold no less than four million copies in the streets of English towns between 1663 and 1673.

Astrology in the rest of Europe followed a similar course, evolving even from the position of the mid-fifteenth century when it has been said that 'astrologers reigned in many European courts'.[72] The centres of activity were still Italy and France, and Luca Gaurico in the former and Michel Nostradamus in the later held sway over their respective courts. Luca Gaurico in particular achieved an outstanding success by predicting to Alessandro Farnese in 1529 that he would become Pope. When Alessandro succeeded as Pope Paul III he not only rewarded Gaurico with the bishopric of Guffoni, but made the papal court a centre for astrological activity.[73] Gaurico had previously predicted to the fourteen-year-old Giovanni de Medici that he would become Pope, which he did as Leo X in, 1513. He also successfully forecast the death of Paul III in November 1549. Gaurico later tarnished his record by predicting that Henry II of France would live to a 'most happy and green old age'. Unfortunately Henry died young and violently.[74]

More renowned than Gaurico is the figure of Nostradamus, for his predictions are still remembered and discussed today. Like his contemporary, John Dee of England, Nostradamus combined astrology with magic and necromancy, and was employed by the French royal family. He served both the Queen Mother, Catherine de' Medici, and her husband, Henry II, and two of her sons, Francis II, and Charles IX, before his death in 1566. Nostradamus also issued predictions for mass consumption, and the political sensitivity of some of these was such that, as has been mentioned, they were on at least one occasion banned in England. One of his successes was, apparently, a prediction to a humble friar, Felice Peretti, that he would become Pope, a story which may not be true, but is interesting in view of the fact that, as Sixtus V, Felice was responsible for a papal bull forbidding judicial astrology. Catherine employed at least four astrologers at any one time, and consulted both Gaurico and Nostradamus on the same matter. Gaurico had qualified his prediction about Henry II by warning of the danger of blindness or death if the King fought a duel in an enclosed space, with the risk of danger being greatest in the forty-first year. Catherine asked

Nostradamus for a second opinion, but Michel confirmed that the warning should be heeded. It was in his forty-first year that Henry was killed by a head wound during a jousting tournament.[75]

In Italy, and in spite of the traditional clerical reservations about judicial astrology, the papal court finally became a centre for astrology of all kinds. Paul III, Leo X and Adrian VI in the sixteenth century all encouraged astrologers. Alexander VI used astrology to help plan his military campaigns, and Julius II had the time of his coronation chosen astrologically.[76] Innocent VIII consulted horaries concerning his relations with the Duke of Milan, even though horary had been more severely frowned upon natal astrology by strict Christians.[77] This fortunate state of affairs did not last for long, however, and after the Counter Reformation produced popes of a more pious turn of mind, judicial astrology was condemned by papal bull. Supporters of astrology pointed out that these bulls, one by Sixtus V in 1586, and one by Urban VIII in 1631,[78] were directed mainly at prediction, thus leaving natural astrology and ordinary natal astrology intact. There was in fact little that could be done to banish astrologers, for the moment a person fell sick and summoned a physician he was also calling an astrologer, the two professions often being connected. These bulls did restrict the publication of astrological works in Italy, but with the result that many more were published in Germany where papal authority was weak.

About this time a gradual hardening of opinion seems to have started in some quarters against astrology, from religious leaders of both the Reformation, such as Luther and Calvin (although Melanchthon approved of it), and the Counter Reformation. This mood was by no means universal, as we have seen how the Protestant leaders in sixteenth-century England relied as heavily on astrology as they did on the scriptures, but it did find a reflection in intellectual circles. For example at Bologna University, which had for hundreds of years been a thriving centre of astrology, all teaching had ceased by 1572.

This disapproval took some time to affect the world of mundane astrology, and in the fifteenth, sixteenth and seventeenth centuries astrology enjoyed an unbroken popularity at court and in public. At the Imperial court Frederick III was dependent upon the advice of astrologers,[79] and Charles V, the most powerful monarch of his time, consulted astrologers concerning the progress of his war with Saxony.[80] The spread of universities to cities such as Cracow, Vienna and Pressburg took astrology firmly into central Europe, and Germany was to produce two of the most famous mundane astrologers of the sixteenth century — Tycho Brahe and Johannes Kepler. These two men pioneered a new feeling of accuracy in the subject, which balanced the occult leanings of their colleagues in France and England, Nostradamus and John Dee. Both Brahe and Kepler are remembered chiefly for their astronomical observations, but Kepler should be remembered by mundane astrologers for insisting that accurate analysis could only be arrived at if the astrologer were also knowledgeable in political affairs, a point which far too many astrologers have ignored. [81]

The astrological careers of the two were linked in a most interesting fashion. Brahe made a set of predictions on the 'new star' of 1572, whose appearance did so much to undermine the Platonic philosophy of astrology. Brahe's predictions centred around the appearance of a prince from the north who would devastate Germany until 1632. This predication came true in person of King Gustavus Adolphus of Sweden who occupied much of northern Germany and was killed at the Battle of Lutzen in 1632. [82] Gustavus' main opponent was the Count of Wallenstein, a great general who himself employed Kepler, Brahe's colleague, as his astrologer. [83] There is actually no record of Kepler ever performing any useful work for Wallenstein, although Gustavus was so pleased with the predictions which he received from the English astrologer William Lilly, that he sent Lilly a gold chain. Tycho Brahe also made predictions based on the comets of 1577 and 1585. He entered the service of the Danish royal family and cast horoscopes for King Christian IV and his family. For the King himself Tycho predicted death at 56 or 57, some thirteen years before the actual event. [84]

In France the new restrictive attitude of the Papacy was reflected in the banning of astrology at the Sorbonne in May 1619, [85] but patronage at court continued for another half century. Henry IV summoned Larivière to be present at the birth of Louis XIII in 1600 while Jean Baptiste Morin was called to the birth of Louis XIV, the future Sun King. Louis XIII sent two astrologers to the galleys for predicting his death, an indication of the regard with which political predictions were still held, but his son presided over the collapse of French astrology. At the beginning of his long reign Morin was employed by Louis XIV's Secretary of State for diplomatic expeditions, and he received great prestige, being patronized by the

Queen Mother, Marie de' Medici, Cardinal Mazarin (who awarded him a pension), and the Queen of Poland, who helped finance the printing of the *Astrologica Gallica* in 1661. However, Louis refused to name Morin official Royal Astrologer, and resisted his physician's suggestion that Morin be placed at the head of a team of three astrologers on the Royal Council. [86]

In England, France, and all over Europe at this time we find the sudden demise of astrology. It disappeared from court so suddenly that by 1680 the philosopher Pierre Bayle was able to report that the French court was completely cleared of the 'disease' of astrology. [87] The reason for this catastrophe has never been satisfactorily investigated and neither has the role of astrology in the eighteenth century.

We know that astrology was still taught at some universities, notably Salamanca, where classes were not suspended until 1770. This implies that there was still a supply of educated astrologers, yet the philosophical climate of the time was against astrology. [88] The Enlightenment philosophers, and Voltaire in particular, condemned it as irrational superstition, yet then as now there must have been a subculture of astrological practitioners and scholars. There was undoubtedly a demand amongst ordinary people for fortune telling, while at a more scholastic level astrologers such as the English Freemason Ebenezer Sibley passed on their knowledge. It was not unknown for sea captains to take astrological advice for sailing times, [89] and this may have been a widespread practice, but of astrology and politics we have little sign. The political propaganda role of the astrological alamanaks appears to have been negligible, but it is possible that English politicians dabbled in astrology as part of the occult through their membership of decadent aristocratic societies such as the Hell Fire Club.

It is from America that the most interesting rumours come, that certain of the revolutionary leaders, including Washington, Jefferson and Franklin, were astrologers and that the time for the signing of the Declaration of Independence was astrologically arranged. This would seem unlikely in view of the fact that the Enlightenment tradition of which these men were a part was hostile to astrology; yet they were all also Freemasons and consciously selected occult symbols for the American emblem.

In fact it is intriguing that although astrology seems to have no obvious role in politics, European courts still dabbled with the occult, and at the end of the century Cagliostro's 'Egyptian Rite' Freemasonry was popular with decadent aristocrats. This was, after all, the period of the legendary and eternal 'Comte Saint German'. We may not be surprised that the hard-faced politicians of the triumphantly materialistic nineteenth century ignored astrology, but it was during this century that the so-called 'occult revival' occurred, bringing with it groups such as the Theosophists and Rosicrucians. These later two especially combined a view of the relationship between world history and astrology which was to influence Nazi ideology profoundly, although the members of these groups themselves were totally opposed to the Nazis.

The Nazis used astrology both sincerely and for propaganda, but their understanding of it seems to have been limited. Astrology played a central role in the geo-political and racial concepts of the SS and various fascist occult groups. One of the main theorists, Haushofer, revived the ancient theory of periodic destruction of civilization in his theory of the alternating destruction of the earth through ice and fire. It is said that this determinism accounted for Hitler's readiness to destroy Germany at the end of the war, although it is uncertain to what extent he personally was involved in occult beliefs. There is only one convincing account of Hitler using astrology. The story records that during the final weeks of the war Goebbels, the propaganda minister, attempted to raise Hitler's morale. Goebbels produced from his office the horoscope for the German Republic of 1918 and Hitler's own nativity, and is said to have argued that these proved that Germany was destined to win the war. [90] The top Nazis most involved in astrology were Heinrich Himmler, chief of the SS, and Rudolf Hess, Hitler's deputy until his flight to Scotland in 1941. Indeed it was mainly due to Hess that German astrologers came to the notice of the authorities, although the Gestapo had previously taken an interest in astrology because of the possible effect on public opinion of predictions concerning the war. Hess was alleged to have flown to Scotland on the advice of astrologers, and his action resulted in the mass arrest of German astrologers by the Gestapo. Most were released, and only Karl Ernest Krafft, wrongly believed in the UK to have been Hitler's astrologer, died in a concentration camp in 1944.

The British responded to the German interest in astrology by setting up a propaganda campaign which centered mainly around the forgery of German astrological magazines which allied agents would then leave lying around casually in public places in Germany. The magazines would contain predictions designed to weaken German morale, along the lines of: '*April 21* Bad day on the Eastern front; *April 22* Bad day to put to sea, especially if your commander is an Aries'. The British also employed at least one astrologer — a certain Louis de Wohl — on the assumption that if Hitler was using astrologers, it was wise to know what advice he was being given, and are also said to have had more luck from astrological weather forecasting than from more orthodox methods.

Such enterprises have unfortunately not done the reputation of astrology much good, and it would be very rare to find a politician in the western world who would admit to an interest in the art. Some may have had their horoscopes cast, but in much the same way that many people visit a fortune-teller. Ronald Reagan has had his chart drawn up (what Californian filmstar hasn't?) but rumours that he, like Richard Nixon, uses astrology to take political decisions, have no backing.

What is more interesting is that the Israeli secret service, Mossad, one of the most efficient of its kind in the world, has experimented with astrology, and found that the Israeli chart did indeed reflect enterprises which they masterminded, such as the Entebbe airport raid.[91] The Soviet Union is also said to have used astrology for character analysis although such a story is impossible to verify.[92]

Outside Europe and North America the story is different. All politicians in the Indian sub-continent and the non-communist areas of south-east Asia use astrology. The most notable example is Mrs Ghandi, the Prime Minister of India, but a host of less well-known figures also rely on astrologers. Lon Nol, the last Cambodian leader during the Vietnam War, never took a decision without first consulting astrologers, and we can only speculate on the effect astrologers may have had on the outcome of this war. In the Arab world Sultan Qaboos, the leader of Oman, is an astrologer; and Sheik Yamani, the Saudi oil minister and one of the most powerful men in the world, travels nowhere without his astrology books. He is reputed to have even predicted his own death.[93]

It is clear that many politicians in the world today have no thought of ever using astrology, yet equally clear that many others do. It is astonishing that we know so little about those that do use astrology, and the degree to which it affects their lives. It is also said that even those who do use astrology do so with so little good effect. It remains to be seen whether the current interest in astrology will attract attention from more politicians, and whether indeed this is a desirable development. What is apparent is that many of the finer points of political history cannot be understood without a knowledge of the history of astrology.

References

1   Thorndike, L. *A History of Magic and Experimental Science* vol. I, chap. XXVII, pp.617-29.
2   Geoffrey of Monmouth *History of the Kings of Britain,* pp.271-6.
3   Thorndike, op.cit., vol. I, book I, chap. XXVII, pp.634-5.
4   Einhard, *Life of Charlemagne,* p.79.
5   Thorndike, op.cit., vol. I, book III, chap. XXIX, p.672.
6   ibid., vol. I, book III, chap. XXIX, p.673.
7   ibid., vol. I, book III, chap. XXIX, p.673.
8   ibid., vol. I, book III, chap. XXX, p.697.
9   ibid., vol. I, book III, chap. XXIX, p.689.
10 ibid., vol. I, book III, chap. XXX, pp.705-7.
11 ibid., vol. II, book IV, chap. XLII, pp.182-3
12 ibid., vol. II, book V, chap. LV, p.445.
13 ibid., vol. II, book V, chap. LIX, pp.557-92.
14 See below, chapter 3.
15 Thorndike, op.cit., vol II, book V, chap. LX, pp.608-11.
16 ibid., vol. II, book V, chap. LXI, p.674.
17 ibid., vol. II, book IV, chap. XXXVIII, pp.73-8.
18 ibid., vol. II, book IV, chap. XXXVI, p.21.
19 ibid., vol. II, book IV, chap. XXXVII, p.51.
20 ibid., vol. I, book III, chap. XXXII, pp.743-4.
21 ibid., vol. II, book V, chap. LI, p.309.
22 ibid., vol. II, book IV, chap. XXXV, p.6.
23 Thomas, K. *Religion and the Decline of Magic,* p.357.
24 Thorndike, op.cit., vol. III, chap. XXXIV, p.589.
25 Rashdall, H. *The Universities of Europe in the Middle Ages* p.441.
26 Thorndike, op.cit., vol III, book V, chap. LXVII, p.828.
27 ibid., vol. 4, chap. XXXIX, p.66.
28 ibid., vol. 3, chap. XIII, p.206.
29 ibid., vol. 4, chap. XLII, p.108.
30 ibid., vol. 3, chap. XXXIV, p.590.
31 ibid., vol. 3, chap. XXXIV, p.586.

32 ibid., vol. 4, chap. XLI, p.96.
33 ibid., vol. 2, book V, chap. LXVIII, p.843.
34 ibid., vol. 3, chap. XII, pp.191-2.
35 ibid., vol. 2, book V, chap. LXX, pp.879-80.
36 ibid., vol. 3, chap. XXI, p.329.
37 ibid., vol. 4, chap. LII, p.314.
38 ibid., vol. 4, chap. XL, p.87.
39 ibid., vol. 4, chap. XL, p.87.
40 ibid., vol. 4. chap. LIV, pp.366-7.
41 ibid., vol. 4, chap. LXI, pp.529-43.
42 ibid., vol. 3, chap. XIII, p.206.
43 ibid., vol. 4, chap. XXXIX, p.76.
44 Armstrong, J. *An Italian Astrologer at the Court of Henry VII* p.434.
45 Rashdall, op.cit., vol. II, p.297.
46 Thorndike, op.cit., vol. 4, chap. LXII, pp. 544-5.
47 ibid., vol. 7, chap. LXI, p.344.
48 Wedel, T. *The Mediaeval Attitude Towards Astrology, Particularly in England* p.72.
49 Thomas, op.cit., p.357.
50 ibid., pp.471, 494, 506.
51 Armstrong, op.cit., pp.433-4.
52 Camden, C. *Elizabethan Almanaks,* p.88; Armstrong, op.cit., p.436.
53 Thomas, op.cit., p.412; Camden, op.cit., p.88.
54 ibid., p.342.
55 ibid., p.342.
56 ibid., p.400.
57 Deacon, R. *A History of British Espionage,* chap. 2, 3, 4.
58 Camden, op.cit., p.88.
59 Thomas, op.cit., p.354.
60 ibid., p.407.
61 Larkey, S. *'Astrology and politics in the first years of Elizabeth's reign',* p.171.
62 Thomas, op.cit., p.406.
63 Lilly, W. *History of His Life and Times.*
64 ibid., p.406.
65 Culpepper, N. *Catastrophe Magnatum.*
66 Frank, J. *The Beginnings of the English Newspaper 1620-1660* p.177.

67 Thomas, op.cit., p.348.
68 Ashmole, F. *Notes, Correspondence etc.* p.1347.
69 Thomas, op.cit., p.345.
70 Camden, op.cit., p.91.
71 Thomas, op.cit., p.345.
72 Jacob, F. *Italian Renaissance Studies,* p.40.
73 Thorndike, op.cit., vol. 5, chap. XXIII, p.256.
74 ibid., vol. 6, chap. XXXIII, p.101.
75 Campion, N. *An Introduction to the History of Astrology,* pp.48-50.
76 Thorndike, op.cit., vol. 5, chap. XIII, p.252; chap. X, p.175.
77 ibid., vol. 4, chap. LVII, p.434.
78 ibid., vol. 6, book V, chap. XXXIV, pp.156-7.
79 ibid., vol. 4, chap. LVII, p.413.
80 ibid., vol. 6, chap. XXXXIII, p.136.
81 Kepler, J. 'On the more certain fundamentals of astrology', p.103.
82 Campion, op.cit., pp.50-1.
83 Thorndike, op.cit., vol. 7, chap. II, p.22.
84 ibid., vol. 6, book V, chap. XXXII, p.70.
85 ibid., vol. 7, chap. V, p.100.
86 ibid., vol. 7, chap. XVI, p.479-80.
87 ibid., vol. 8, chap. XXXII, p.338-9.
88 ibid., vol. 8, chap. XXXII, p.351.
89 Capp, B. *Astrology and the Popular Press* p.278.
90 Howe. E. *Urania's Children,* part 2; Deacon, op.cit., pp.353-66.
91 Deacon, R. *A History of the Israeli Secret Service.*
92 Personal communication from Richard Deacon to the author.
93 *Daily Express,* 28 May 1981.

Bibliography
ALLEN, D. C. *The Star Crossed Renaissance* London 1941.
ARMSTRONG, J. 'An Italian Astrologer at the Court of Henry VII' in *Italian Renaissance Studies* (ed. Ernest Jacob) London, 1966.
ASHMOLE, E. *Notes, Correspondence etc.* (ed. C. H. Josten) Oxford, 1966.
BONSER, W. *The Medical Background of Anglo-Saxon England* London, 1963.
BOOKER, J. *Black Munday* London, 1651.
BOSANQUET, E. *English Printed Almanaks . . to 1600* London 1930.

BRACKENBRIDGE, J. B. *A Short History of Scientific Astrology* Lawrence University, Wisconsin 1980.

CAMDEN, C. *Elizabethan Almanaks and Prognostications* London, 1931.

CAMPION, N. *An Introduction to the History of Astrology* London, 1982.

CAPP, B. *Astrology and the Popular Press* London, 1979.

CARDEN, J. *The Book of My Life* (trans, Jean Stoner) London, 1931.

COLEY, H. *Clavis Astrologiae* London, 1676.

COOPLAND, G. W. *Nicole Oresme and the Astrologers* Liverpool, 1952.

CULPEPPER, N. *Catastrophe Magnatum* London, 1652.

DEACON, R. *The Book of Fate, Its Origin and Uses* London, 1976.

DEACON, R. *John Dee* London, 1968.

DEACON, R. *A History of the British Secret Service* London, 1969.

DEACON, *A History of the Israeli Secret Service* London, 1977.

DELMAR, S. *Black Boomerang* London 1961.

DREYER, J. *History of the Planetary Systems from Thales to Kepler* London, 190 .

EINHARD. *Life of Charlemagne* (trans. Lewis Thorpe) London, 1969.

FRANK, J. *The Beginnings of the English Newspaper 1620-1660* Cambridge, Massachusetts, 1961.

FRENCH, P. *John Dee* London, 1972.

GARIN, E. *Astrology in the Renaissance* London, 1983.

GEOFFREY OF MONMOUTH, *History of the Kings of Britain* (trans. Lewis Thorpe) London, 1966.

HOWE, E. *Raphael, or the Royal Merlin* London, 1964.

HOWE, E. *Urania's Children* London, 1967.

JACOB, E. 'Introduction' to *Italian Renaissance Studies* London, 1966.

KEPLER, J. 'On the more certain fundamentals of astrology' (trans. Mary Rossi) *Proceedings of the American Philosophical Society* vol. 123, no. 2, 1979.

KOESTLER, A. *The Sleepwalkers* London, 1959.

LARKEY, S. 'Astrology and politics in the first years of Elizabeth's reign' *Bulletin of the Institute of the History of Medicine* vol. III, no. 3, March 1935.

LEMAY, R. *Abu Ma'shar and Latin Aristotlianism in the Twelfth Century* Beirut, 1962.

LILLY, W. *History of his Life and Times* London, 1715.

PANOVSKY, E., SAXL, F. *Saturn and Melancholy* London, 1964.

PARKER, D. *Familiar to All: William Lilly and Astrology in the Seventeenth Century* London, 1975.

RASHDALL, H. *The Universities of Europe in the Middle Ages* vols. I and II, Oxford, 1895.

RAMESEY, W. *Vox Stellarum* London, 1652.

ROWSE, A. L. *Simon Forman* London, 1974.

SHUMAKER, W. *The Occult Sciences in the Renaissance* London, 1972.

SMITH, C. *John Dee* London, 1901.

THOMAS, K. *Religion and the Decline of Magic* London, 1971.

THORNDIKE, L. *A History of Magic and Experimental Science* vols. 1-7, New York, 1923-41.

TILLYARD, E. M. *The Elizabethan World Picture* London, 1944.

WEDEL, *The Mediaeval Attitide Towards Astrology, Particularly in England* London, 1920.

WULFF, W. *Zodiac and Swastika* London, 1973.

YATES, F. *Giordano Bruno and the Hermatic Tradition* London, 1974.

YATES, F. *Occult Philosophy in the Elizabethan Age* London, 1979.

3.

MUNDANE ASTROLOGY AND THE COLLECTIVE

Michael Baigent

'The psychology of the individual is reflected in the psychology of the nation', wrote Carl Jung. [1] The same principles which operate in individuals are seen operating in nations. The inner dynamics of man are paralleled by the outer dynamics of society — the *mass*. And the mass, warns Jung, generally has a profoundly negative influence. Its collective force can encourage a man or woman to act at a lower, less conscious level until the point is reached where the individual no longer acts for him or herself, obeying his or her own conscience, but becomes simply one part of an impersonal mob. Our nightly television news shows us many examples of this process, both local and international. When such mass forces become highly activated a situation can develop where the state itself has a psychotic breakdown, a mental illness. 'Masses,' wrote Jung, 'are always breeding grounds of psychic epidemics.' [2]

Jung viewed the great disasters of 1914 and 1939 as examples of such mass pathology. In his essay 'After the catastrophe', [3] he was concerned with understanding the ruthless forces which burst like an activation of the ancient god Wotan, out of Germany. Without in any way compromising the guilt of the Nazi regime, he opened up a theme which is likely to be unpleasant to most people. The problem was not just Germany, but involved at the least *all* of Europe. The forces unleashed were European forces which found their point of least resistance in the German nation, but, he stresses, the epidemic insanity threatened all of Europe.

I am — and always was — of the opinion that the political mass movements of our time are psychic epidemics, in other words, *mass psychoses* . . . Nations have their own peculiar psychology, and in the same way they also have their own particular kind of psychopathology.[4]

Leaving aside the specific horrors to which he was reacting, Jung's general point is that nations, like individuals, can be described psychologically. Further, a nation can have its illnesses, its psychic dissociations and breakdowns. The nation, the mass, can be viewed as a species of greater individual. This conception is reflected rather well in the term often used for a state — the 'body politic'.

If the mass, the 'body politic', acts as a single entity then astrologers seeking to understand it should be able to construct a birth chart. This chart should remain valid so long as the cohesion of the mass is maintained. Such an astrological chart should provide indications of the internal dynamics of the nation in the same way that a natal chart provides this information about an individual. One would expect though, that the charts may each have to be interpreted in slightly different ways. Furthermore, it would seem possible that the symbolism employed may have to be modified: would, for example, the position of a planet in a nation's chart mean the same as if it were in an individual's?

The implications of this view are important for the study of mundane astrology. For it provides a theoretical framework within which the study can find a grounding. Modern psychological practice has validated natal astrology; let us hope that it can also validate mundane astrology.

If we can clearly construct a working model in this way then we have found limits within which to operate and experiment. For the experimental method demands theory, and the existing non-psychological theories of mundane astrology are less than adqequate. And it is only through experimentation with as many controls as can be built into the method that we can discover the important questions which confront us in mundane astrology: does it work, and if so, under what conditions, and with what degree of accuracy?

A model of the psyche
From the very distant past man has attempted to create working models of the inner and outer worlds — in fact, ever since the two

were separated. Astrologers should all be familiar with the disputes which raged over hundreds of years, arguments concerning various models of the heavenly movements. In the case of Galileo, these disputes cost his life. Similarly the inner world has had its models and today we can see several operating. Most, in the academic world at least, are products of the materialist philosophies which have pandered to man's egotism for the last few hundred years. Thankfully there exists one model of the inner world which can be seen as part of a long, often esoteric, tradition stretching back through the Neo-Platonists at least to the days of Pythagoras. This is the model used by Carl Jung and his colleagues. The basic principles of this model are:

1.   The human psyche is quite as real as the body.
2.   The human psyche is greater than the ego.
3.   The human psyche, at its deepest level, connects to that of all other human beings.

This model sees each individual being, as it were, an outgrowth from a basically unified mankind.

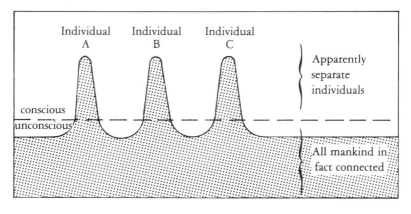

Figure 3.1   A psychological model of Mankind.

Although psychologists of certain persuasions identify the psyche with consciousness itself, Jung considers this a very limited conception. Indeed, it leads to the erroneous conclusion that a child enters this world with an empty psyche which, over time, becomes gradually filled with only that which is gained through experience. Jung's

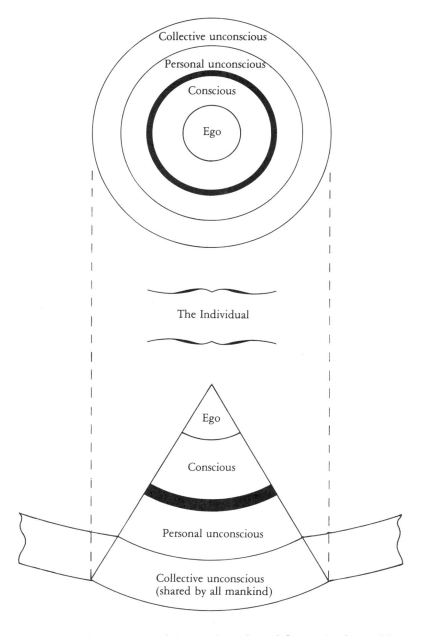

Collective unconscious

Personal unconscious

Conscious

Ego

The Individual

Ego

Conscious

Personal unconscious

Collective unconscious
(shared by all mankind)

Figure 3.2 The structure of the Psyche (adapted from Jolande Jacobi).

research indicated that the psyche is the *total of all psychic occurrence,* both conscious and unconscious. As he explains it, the psyche consists of the spheres of the conscious and the unconscious which are not only complementary but share a compensatory relationship. The *ego,* the centre of the field of personal consciousness, is that side of the psyche which relates to the external world. The ego and the personal conscious float, as it were, on the great sea of the unconscious.

This unconscious is comprised of both the *personal unconscious* and the deeper layer of the mass unconscious, or as the Jungians term it, the *collective unconscious (see Fig. 3.2). The personal unconscious* contains those factors which are unique to the individual. These include all that has been gathered during one's life and which, having been conscious at one time, have vanished as a result of suppression or forgetfulness. The *collective unconscious* on the other hand contains inherited factors which are held in common by all mankind. It is important to stress that every individual has, as a part of the basic structure of his or her psyche, this *collective* or universal component. The *collective unconscious* is the sum total of all psychic contents which do not belong to just one individual, but to all mankind.

The contents of the collective unconscious Jung calls *archetypes.* He defines these as forms which have existed since the very beginning of humanity and which give a definite shape to the contents of the psyche when they emerge. An archetype itself has no definite shape, rather it is a 'pattern of emotional and mental behaviour' which takes on a definite form only when expressed, when *projected* out into the world. An archetype is essentially an unconscious content which is changed by the process of its becoming conscious and apprehended it is changed into a definite form. For example the archetype known as the *anima,* when projected out by a man, can take one of the many forms of the mother image. These could be of a goddess or a witch, an ideal lover or even a devouring sea monster. All these are forms of this 'anima' archetype.

Jung warns that the term 'archetype' is easily misunderstood. It can be used wrongly to indicate the various mythological images and motifs themselves. This is a mistake, for these definite mythological images as found in legend and fairy tale are but conscious representations of the underlying archetype. The archetype itself is not the image but the *tendency to form these images* or representations of a deeper basic motif. These images will be seen

to vary considerably in their details, for there are no set principles
guiding the exact shape an archetype might take. Yet a basic pattern
of expression can be seen:

> Archetypes are like river beds which run dry when the water
> deserts them, but which it can find again at any time. An
> archetype is like and old water course along which the water
> of life has flowed for centuries digging a deep channel for itself.
> The longer it has flowed in this channel the more likely it is
> that sooner or later the water will return to its old bed. [5]

These archetypes generate our myths, religions and philosophies and
these in turn influence, even characterize, entire nations. The
archetypes can emerge into the open via both an individual and a
mass, as both are connected by the collective unconscious.

The psyche of the mass contains complexes, just as the individual
psyche does. These complexes are archetypal images from the
collective unconscious which emerge under the requisite social
conditions. In the mass, many of the collective contents of the
individual are *constellated,* that is, are made manifest in the world.
This archetypal activity can take the form of a national psychosis as
has been seen so many times in the past — and present.

> Hitler's theatrical, obviously hysterical gestures struck all
> foreigners (with a few amazing exceptions) as purely ridiculous.
> When I saw him with my own eyes, he suggested a psychic
> scarecrow (with a broomstick for an outstretched arm) rather
> than a human being. It is also difficult to understand how his
> ranting speeches, delivered in shrill, grating, womanish tones,
> could have made such an impression. But the German people
> would never have been taken in and carried away so completely
> if this figure had not been a reflected image of the collective
> German hysteria. It is not without serious misgivings that one
> ventures to pin the label of 'psychopathic inferiority' on to a
> whole nation, and yet, heaven knows, it is the only explanation
> which could in any way account for the effect this scarecrow
> had on the masses. [6]

And how many such scarecrows lead nations today? Can mundane
astrology show up the latent pathologies which every nation must

hide? For if it can, then perhaps the people may be able to see in advance what sort of creature would aspire to be their demagogue.

It has been clear for some time that astrological symbolism can be linked very easily with the modern, individual-centred, psychological practice and theory. Furthermore, specialized research of a Jungian orientation has shown that while astrology does well to stay fiercely centred upon the individual, the collective can only be ignored with peril. This research, presented initially in the work of Dr Liz Greene, [7] has indicated that the planets can be divided into two symbolic groups: the *personal* and the *transpersonal* planets.

The personal planets, which relate directly to the individual are the Sun, Moon, Mercury, Mars and Venus and Jupiter. The Sun is the symbol of the ego, the others of the powers of the personal unconscious. The transpersonal planets relate to the historical, political and social spheres: they are Uranus, Neptune and Pluto. Saturn is seen as somewhat different. It stands on the division between the personal and the transpersonal planets (see Fig 3.3) and is regarded as the 'dweller on the threshold', symbolic of that shadowed boundary between the personal unconscious and the collective unconscious. [8]

These symbolic divisions will prove useful in the attempt to observe

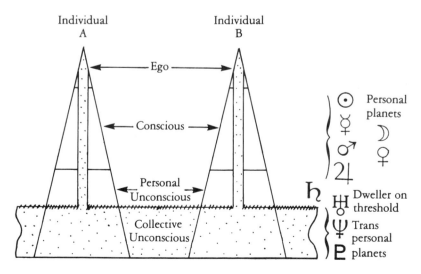

Figure 3.3   Diagram symbolizing the Psyche (from Jolande Jacobi, adapted by Liz Greene).

the effect of planetary placement on the astrological chart of a nation
— a collective entity. Furthermore, as will be seen in Chapter 14,
the transits and cycles of the transpersonal planets are of great
significance to the development of a nation — the cycles especially
can often be seen with great accuracy. This latter effect is one
important point which distinguishes the 'collective's' chart from that
of an individual. A nation, with a life span many times that of an
individual, can often see several of the outer-planet cycles repeated
over hundreds of years.

It will be now be appreciated that from the view of mankind as
a great number of uniquely different and separate individuals, Jung's
theory, while retaining an appreciation of individual uniqueness,
moves towards a view of mankind as a single entity, with individuals,
as it were, being the fingers and toes of a far greater whole. The
stages of unity begin with the collective and finally, on a greater
level, reach the idea of a cosmological unity. Jung himself was soundly
based within the Neo-Platonic tradition which begins with the
principle of the essential unity of the universe. So, while we explore
the parts, we need to keep in mind the whole which embraces them.

The study of astrology itself is not merely a mathematical derivative
from a study of celestial movements but rather a synthesis of both
observation and a cosmological stance. It remains very firmly part
of the Neo-Platonic tradition, a tradition which the rest of science
has regrettably abandoned. Astrology, while dealing on a popular
level primarily with effects, points at a deeper level, towards the
causes or the Cause. It points towards the essential unity of all things
which, while not the stated concern of this book, nevertheless cannot
be passed over. The position of astrology is accurately put by the
late John Addey in his *Astrology Reborn*:

> Astrology belongs inherently to that tradition which sees the
> whole manifested cosmos, and everything in it, as being
> brought forth by a hierarchy of principles, proceeding from
> unity into multiplicity by stages, stages in which each superior
> principle is the parent of a number of effects at a lower
> level . . .[9]

If we regard the studies of psychology and astrology as having
fundamentally similar aims — both are concerned with

understanding humanity in both individual and social spheres — then it is clear that we can make an initial assumption about mundane astrology: that it bears the same relationship to natal astrology as mass psychology does to individual psychology. The principles operating in the mass are the same as those operating in the individual: it is the orientation which differs. Certain psychological factors are dominant in one and subordinate in the other. Freedom of action and spontaneity are greater, for example, in an individual than in a mass. The latter tends towards a motion which is best described as ponderous.

Using the results of psychological observation and experimentation, and having established which factors become dominant in the mass as distinct from the individual, we might expect that the astrological corollaries of these would be usefully emphasized when interpreting the mundane chart. Clarifying these factors — or in astrological terminology clarifying our planetary interpretations from the psychological discoveries — must then be crucial to a pragmatic use of mundane astrology. To simplify this argument we can ask three questions:

1. In what way does the mass change human behaviour and which factors become dominant?
2. How are these factors expressed in astrological symbolism?
3. How does this knowledge alter our interpretation of the astrological symbolism of a nation's chart?

Research into just how mass pressure affect man's attitudes and behaviour has revealed some fundamental principles. It is now clear that a mass develops its own 'norms', its own standards of behaviour. The 'good' members of the mass accept these as their own personal values, despite the fact that previously they may have felt or acted quite differently. An individual's behaviour shifts to harmonize with that of the group. In other words, the mass exerts a pressure on its members towards conformity. [10]

The mass all too often produces an authority figure. In a series of experiments conducted at Yale University, unsuspecting subjects were told to administer ever increasing electric shocks to a second subject — who was in reality a professional actor who produced the symptoms of progressively greater pain (no real electric shocks were used). The object was to find at which point the first subject, the supposed experimenter, would refuse to administer further electric shocks. It was found that the majority continued to give the electric shocks for as long as they were ordered to do so. The rather unsettling conclusion was that most people will do what they are told, no matter what harm they seem to be doing, so long as the order comes from 'legitimate' authority. [11] Through such obedience a mass can become virtually an extension of its leader, whose ideas become the mass ideas, whose commands become the mass commands, whose morals become the mass morals. Here lies another clue for us in mundane astrology. As we shall see, the birth-chart of the leader is often as valid as a national indicator as the birth chart of the nation. It appears that a mass and its leader can become identified for all practical purposes. Astrologers have known this for a great number of years — Ptolemy mentions the use of both in astrological forecasting. [12]

A mass has within it an urge to grow, to expand, to contain all possible members. [13] The particles of the mass, the people, are thus encouraged to seek more members, to increase the size. This then is another factor which bears upon mundane interpretations. A nation is seeking always to expand, which leads inevitably to a desire to capitalize upon perceived weaknesses in surrounding countries. (This idea will be considered further in Chapter 14 when we study the astrology of war.)

To summarize then, we can say that the mass increases an individual's conformity, reduces his flexibility, makes him more predictable and more likely to follow authority blindly. 'A million zeros', said Jung sadly, 'do not, unfortunately, add up to one.' [14]

Lest there be any misunderstanding about this brief view of the mass, it is well to mention the excellent essay by Erich Neuman, 'The group and the great individual', [15] in which he draws the important distinction between the supportive and positive role of the small group and the negative and dehumanizing role of the mass.

The psychological approach to natal astrology sees the birth chart as a map of a man or women's potential for fulfilment, for realization of the self. Natal astrology is thus concerned with the uniqueness of every individual and the necessity for personal freedom. The mundane chart, the chart of the mass, is however quite the opposite. It is in fact a map of those forces which continually move to repress and reduce uniqueness and individuality. It symbolizes those energies which seek to make every man an unconscious particle of a greater mass. We can say then, that in the same way that the individual is the opposite of the mass, there is an opposition in the orientation of the two branches of astrology — natal and mundane.

The chart of the mass, a nation or a state, is a diagram which represents symbolically the ebb and flow of energies within that group. These dynamic forces move through the people who together form this mass. The mass dominates these individuals so that they act primarily as internal transmitting cells for the energies and only secondarily, if at all, as independent human beings.

Paradoxically, growth or change in the development of a mass is dependent upon the individual — upon individual excellence, inventiveness and initiative. Only through the individual is the drive for creation and modification able to find free expression. Yet the fact that the individual alone holds the key to both the full understanding and the revitalizing of the mass must not lead us, in our natural leaning towards the individual's point of view, to regard the mass as somehow irrelevant, unimportant or as unworthy of our attention. The mass is a reality whose pressures confront us at every turn — perhaps more so today in this era of the collective man. The mass demands to be brought into its true relationship with the individual. Mundane astrology, the reflection of the mass, demands to be brought into its true relationship with natal astrology.

What then are the implications for mundane astrology as it seeks to symbolize the collective aspects of those qualities symbolized in their individual aspects by the natal chart. How does the interpretation of a mundane chart differ from that of a natal chart?

The observation has been presented that the mass exacts obedience, requiring conformity from its members with the effect of suppressing individuality. An important conclusion drawn from this is that the mass must be more rigid, more *fixed* than the individual. The mass has lost all ability to act freely. In other words *the mass is more fated than the individual*. The clash between the individual and the mass can be seen in terms of the fatedness of society as opposed to the freedom of the individual. The practical implication then is when reading a state's chart we need to view it as a fated pattern which is limited by its rigid internal power structure, limited by its particular myths and ideals, unlikely to change except by total disintegration followed by rebuilding — a process in a nation which could lead to one national horoscope being replaced by another. Hence we find often in mundane work that a basically pessimistic approach is the most pragmatic as opposed to the optimistic approach most often valid in natal astrology.

This then is the fundamental approach to the reading of the astrological symbols as used in mundane astrology. It is also, in passing, an indication how we might justifiably produce accurate predictions upon the future events likely for a state. Predictions based upon a natal chart which symbolizes that state accurately. Of course the research of such charts must be the most important first step for mundane astrology. Until we have correct charts, all interpretation is useless.

That the psychologists quoted have not appeared in a vacuum, that the ideas which have been the concern of this short essay spring from a long tradition is a point worth remembering. The ideas of natal and mundane astrology put forward here have most certainly been expressed in earlier times, albeit in different terminology.

The distinction between natal and mundane astrology, apparently first delineated by Ptolemy in the second century AD in his *Tetrabiblos,* became important in the hands of later Christian theologians. It allowed them to condemn one part of astrology while approving of another. The early Christian position was that man's mortal body was affected by the planets but the immortal soul always remained free — the intellect being allied to the soul rather than the body. The result was that in general, Christians dismissed natal astrology. The ethic of Christianity, in theory if not in practice, was concerned with man's freedom from fate, from the influence of the planets. Thus natal astrology was condemned by theologians. Mundane astrology, however, was allowed, for they considered that the carnal world was still fated, still ruled by the influence of the planets.

The thirteenth century saw important points made concerning mundane astrology, notably by Thomas Aquinas and the Franciscan, Roger Bacon. Man, pointed out Aquinas, was not only a free intellectual creature with an immortal soul, able to rule over the planetary influences, but also a physical being, driven by sensual desires. It was this sensual side of man, Aquinas claimed, that was still affected by the planets and this in turn affected the ostensibly free intellectual side.

Roger Bacon, also writing in the thirteenth century, echoes this: he argued that the freedom of the will was not compromised when the individual succumbed to those bodily desires inflamed by the celestial forces:

But to a far greater degree are the forces of the heavenly bodies and the strong species of the stars able to influence the body and its organs, and when these have been greatly altered the man will be strongly excited to actions for which he did not previously care . . .[16]

He adds a word of advice to the natal astrologers of the time, advice which is still given today:

The mind is strongly excited to its actions, although it is not under compulsion, and in accordance with this principle the judgement of the astronomer is given, and does not imply infallibility or necessity.[17]

This practical advice for the natal astrologer is an indication of the very pragmatic approach adopted by these two theologians and the latter in particular. For this reason it is to be deplored that Ptolemy has remained such a strong influence over the centuries, for had Roger Bacon attained a similar level of currency amongst astrologers, especially in the nineteenth and early twentieth centuries, the development of the subject would doubtless have been accelerated.

What then are the practical implications for mundane astrology? In what terms did these men see the subject, given their stand that fate did not necessarily rule over mankind? In fact their positions are remarkably similar to those of Canetti and Jung. Aquinas, for example, admits that where the mass is concerned, astrologers are often very accurate. For in the mass the sensual passions of the greater number dominate the intelligence and integrity of the few who can remain free of such celestial influence.[18] Roger Bacon draws similar conclusions, summarized here by Thorndike:

. . . while the individual by an effort of will may resist the force of the stars, in masses of men the power of the constellations usually prevails . . .[19]

Thus the mass is more fated than the individual and hence predictions can be made of sufficient accuracy to justify serious study of mundane astrology. Bacon's support of mundane astrology is never in doubt. He places great value on the study's ability to provide warnings, especially of military conflagrations, for the future. He mentions as an example the great comet of 1264 which he claims was caused by Mars, hence foreshadowing the fighting which broke our after that time all over Europe. Had the leaders read the warnings in the skies, he suggests, the wars might have been averted — proof that Bacon did not believe even the masses to be completely under the spell of the planets.

> Oh, how great an advantage might have been secured to the Church of God, if the characteristics of the heavens in those times had been discerned beforehand by scientists, and understood by prelates and princes, and transferred to a zeal for peace. For so great a slaughter of Christians would not have occurred . . . [20]

In other words the mass passions, symbolized by Mars and the comet, were aroused but these passions could turn to war or to peace. While man naturally inclined to war, wise leadership could direct the masses towards peace. Perhaps Bacon is suggesting that every portent contains its antitheses, which can be recognized by the wise.

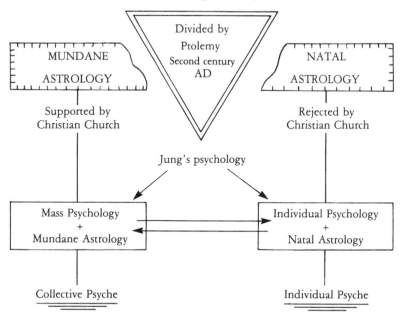

Figure 3.4 The relationship of Natal and Mundane Astrology.

Having based mundane astrology in the collective psyche, by what process can the astrological symbolism best be introduced? In other words how can a birth chart be constructed which accurately symbolizes the collective, the mass? Obviously it must derive from a starting-point, a 'birth'. But how can this be found and what criteria do we use to select the crucial moment from all the available possible foundation incidents? Before any conclusions can emerge the basic terms used must be clarified and defined quite accurately. What, for example, is a state? Is it the same as a nation or a country? Certainly in popular speech little distinction is made between the three. And what of legitimacy — does this have any bearing upon the matter? Would a new *effective* leader who had replaced his 'legitimate' predecessor in a coup take astrological precedence over the deposed or exiled leader? These questions all need to be explored at length when the practical details of mundane astrology are confronted.

We are of course dealing with various levels of social organization. The country is the geographical area, the territory inhabited by the people who comprise the nation. What complicates matters is that the nation usually forms successive states. All of these states can have valid *working* charts drawn for them — each new one generally replaces the earlier — yet none describes the essential *meaning* of the country, the essence of the land and the people in its profoundest sense, a synergism of a nation and its territory captured in the German word *Volkseele* — 'folk-soul', the distillation of a land and its people.

The various state charts relate solely to the people as grouped at that particular moment in history, headed by a particular leader and guided by the image of the future that this leader inspires. The chart of the State then should only continue to operate for so long as that particular expression of the mass or *collective* remains.

The actual 'birth-time' of the state has yet to be defined but the preceding thoughts suggest a basic criterion. The mass of individuals, who in their millions so often share the same aims and desires, myths and history, are all expressing the nation's collective unconscious which finds expression through the various leaders who emerge and focus this energy from the deep psychic well which underlies society. This focusing of the collective is what is entailed in the foundation of a new state, the leader being the point of focus. So the question of which moment constitutes the birth time should really be rephrased as which moment constitutes the reorientation point of the collective expression. For it is at this moment that the focal point is revealed, becomes relevant and effective *in the world*. It is for this moment that the chart for the new state should be set. I would suggest then, that in practical terms, this crucial moment is when *the emergent leadership takes power* — whether that power is granted by a parliament or is assumed through force.

Let us summarize the conclusions reached so far:

1. The mass can act as an individual.
2. The mass is more fated than an individual.
3. Natal and mundane astrology bear the same relationship to each other as do the individual and the mass — they are at opposite ends of the same spectrum.
4. A state is an expression of the mass, usually centred about a leadership.
5. The birth time of a state is that point when the new leadership takes power.

The crucial moment determining the 'birth time' of a state is that of the 'taking of power'. In the past this moment was often the coronation of a king, generally carried out at noon when the Sun, symbolic of the king, was at the mid-heaven, symbolic of rule and earthly power. The great importance of the ceremony was that it mingled the acclamation of the Church and the submission of the nobles and masses. Hence power was effectively focused, materially and spiritually, at the same time. Today of course a coronation is a much less important event and its astrological chart a much less effective symbol of the modern state.

The idea that the assumption of power by an individual or group constitutes the symbolic birth time of a state can lead into a fertile field of speculation: behind the action of seizing or accepting power lies the idea, the latent mental energy, the desire of the leaders. They are harnessing something intrinsic in the people, acting as a lens which can focus the national energy and purpose, the energy born of the collective psyche. This relationship of the leader with the nation or with the new state is often demonstrated astrologically by a close convergence between the chart of the leader and the birth chart of the state he is instrumental in founding. More often than not the two charts prove to be significantly harmonious.

This first desire of the founders can be viewed as a symbolic conception, which is followed by a symbolic gestation period — the necessary planning. The state as it emerges can be viewed as an outgrowth, an expansion of the psyche of the founder. This perhaps can provide some explanation as to why, in the past, the leader's birth chart was held to be of such value in symbolizing the country that he ruled. The King and the state were, in both a symbolic and a real way, inseparable. Ptolemy, for example, when speaking of the necessity of having the birth chart for a city says that when the time of foundation is not known, then the ruling sign for the city will be that which is on the mid-heaven of the ruler. [21]

A state is a man-made entity, as distinct from the land upon which it rests or the people from whom it emerges. All three are significant in understanding the affairs of the world, but only the state can be provided with a birth chart. We are then, in studying mundane astrology, necessarily limited to the most transient and superficial of the three factors. We are seeing only the surface, not plumbing the depths. Hence the conclusions that we draw must necessarily contain great uncertainties, must have lacunae resulting from an inability of the study to reflect those effects which derive from the influence of history, tradition and of course, from the land upon which the people dwell. We can only glean a hint of these effects from the chart of the state, but we cannot allow ourselves to forget that they lie behind every chart we construct.

The land has its own ambience, its own feeling, its own 'gods'. The feeling of Wotan is still strong in Germany as is the sense of the Goddess Arduina in the Ardennes. Further afield the plumed serpent of Central America still emerges in worship and the arts.

> The mystery of the earth is no joke and no paradox. One only needs to see how, in America, the skull and pelvis measurements of all the European races begin to indianize themselves in the second generation of immigrants. That is the mystery of the American earth. The soil of every country holds some such mystery. We have an unconscious reflection of this in the psyche: just as there is a relationship of mind to body, so there is a relationship of body to earth. [22]

In a very real sense, Jung feels, the soil of a land assimilates its conquerors.

This does suggest that we need to exercise care in ascertaining which of the traits we observe or discover from the birth chart come from the state and which are reflections of the national 'folk-soul'. However, it may be impossible for any traits of the 'folk-soul' to be symbolized for it is, strictly speaking, immortal. (For those who accept reincarnation, an analagous situation would be if one attempted to construct a chart for the eternal man rather than for the living individual — difficult, to say the least.)

There is though a hint of an approach towards discovering some of these national qualities. We can draw up and compare the charts for all the states which a nation has formed. Common factors do emerge and these common factors may well reflect part of the 'folk-soul' of the nation.

To speculate even further, if we can view states as successive 'incarnations' of a nation, can we go so far as to suggest the possibility of purpose? Can we ask, what did the nation or the 'folk-soul' *need* to allow such a state to emerge? Did it emerge purely by chance or did it fulfil some function important to the future of the nation? Perhaps a state is what the 'folk-soul' needs at a particular point in time. In other words, it is necessity rather than chance which produces the state, and as a result of these necessary expressions, the 'folk-soul' in some way grows slowly towards whatever future of mass fulfilment might be awaiting.

References
1 Jung, C. G. *Psychological Reflections* p.155.
2 Jung, C. G. *Collected Works* vol. 9, part 1, p.227.
3 Jung, C. G. *Collected Works* vol. 10, pp.194-217.
4 Jung, ibid., pp.465, 466.
5 Jung, ibid., p.395.
6 Jung, ibid., p.419.
7 Greene, L. *Relating*.
8 Greene, ibid., p.29-51
9 Addey, J. *Astrology Reborn* p.12.
10 Cartwright, D. and Lippitt, R. 'Group dynamics and the individual'.
11 Rowan, J. *The Power of the Group* p.19.
12 Ptolemy *Tetrabiblos* II: pp.3-5.
13 Canetti, E. *Crowds and Power* p.29.
14 Jung, C. G. *Collected Works* vol. 10, p.535.
15 Neuman, E. *Origins* pp.421-35.

16 Bacon, R. *The Opus Majus of Roger Bacon: Mathematics* p.271.
17 ibid.,
18 Thorndike, L. *A History of Magic and Experimental Science* vol. II, p.610.
19 ibid., p.671.
20 Bacon, op.cit., p.401.
21 Ptolemy, op.cit., II: p.3.
22 Jung, C. G. *Collected Works* vol. 10, pp.18-19.

Bibliography
ADDEY, J. *Astrology Reborn* London, 1978.
BACON, R. *The Opus Majus of Roger Bacon* (trans. Robert Belle Burke) 2 vols, Philadelphia, 1928.
CANETTI, E. *Crowds and Power* (trans. Carol Stewart) London, 1962.
CARTWRIGHT, D. AND LIPPITT, R. 'Group dynamics and the individual' *Concepts and Controversy in Organizational Behaviour* (ed. Walter Nord) Pacific Palisades, 1972.
GREENE, L. *Relating* London, 1977.
JACOBI, J., *The Psychology of C. G. Jung* London, 1980.
JUNG, C. G. *Collected Works* (trans. R. F. C. Hull) 19 vols, London, 1953-7.
JUNG, C. G. *Psychological Reflections* (ed. Jolande Jacobi) 2nd edition, London, 1971.
NEUMANN, E. *The Origins and History of Consciousness* Princeton, 1973.
PTOLEMY *Tetrabiblos* (trans. W. G. Waddell) London, 1971.
ROWAN, J. *The Power of the Group* London, 1976.
THORNDIKE, L. *A History of Magic and Experimental Science* 8 vols, New York, 1923-34.

4.
THE NATIONAL HOROSCOPE: MUNDANE ASTROLOGY AND POLITICAL THEORY

Nicholas Campion

The historical context

The national horoscope is the basic tool of mundane astrology in the modern world, yet this was not always so. Until recently mundane astrologers have relied almost exclusively on the charts for lunations and ingresses which were made specific to particular locations using techniques such as the zodiacal-geographical rulerships of Ptolemy.[1] The reason why traditional astrology has made no use of the national chart is quite clear, for the state itself is historically a fairly recent creation, being conceived in Europe in the sixteenth to nineteenth centuries, and only becoming the dominant political unit in the world in the twentieth century. It is obvious that if our forebears had no notion of themselves as part of a nation state then they had no reason to draw a horoscope for the state. The concept of nationalism, that mythology which places loyalty to the state above all other feelings, is also relatively recent, and only developed along with the institutional growth of the state which it serves. People in former times were far more likely to identify themselves as part of a geographical area, or as tenants of a particular landlord or as adherents of a religious sect. It was therefore more important for astrologers to cast charts for the landlord, prince, king or emperor, or other leader, and to assess the history and future of great world religions, than to attempt to define a horoscope for the nation itself. It was considered that the king himself embodied the nation, and charts for his birth and coronation were therefore of primary importance. Other matters, such as approaching plagues, droughts and wars would be predicted through the observance of lunations, ingresses and comets and other traditional techniques.

Even today the concept of national 'sovereignty', in which each state is an independent entity, is much overrated, as all states are in fact interdependent, linked to each other through the medium of international law, military alliances and the great economic interests of the multi-national corporations. Yet the nation state remains the basic building block in the global village, and mundane astrology has shifted very much towards the examination of the horoscopes for these states.

This change in political consciousness is perhaps best illustrated with an astrological example taken from the United Kingdom. There are many different possible charts for the UK,[2] but the two most popular are those for the coronation of William the Conqueror as King of England in 1066 and for the legal union of Great Britain and Ireland in 1801. The first horoscope was cast for a moment in which the future of the country was associated solely with the future of the leader, and the second was cast for a constitutional and legal act in which the state was deemed to exist as an entity in itself.

The 'body politic'

In Renaissance political theory the political unit, be it city or state, principality or empire, was often referred to in terms which paralleled the description of the human body. This is not such an unusual concept, for even today we use terms such as the 'organs' of state to describe the branches of government, or the 'head' of state to describe the symbolic leader of the government. The term which the Renaissance philosophers used to describe the political unit was the 'body politic', a phrase perhaps derived itself from the notion of the ruler embodying the entire political unit.

This concept is highly relevant to modern astrology, for in the 'body politic', the political unit was seen as a unified whole in which all the parts were interdependent and reliant on each other for survival. It was the realization of the need to maintain a balance between the different organs and limbs of the body politic which prompted the work of Renaissance philosophers such as Machiavelli (1469-1527) in Italy. The concept that the body politic could indeed become 'sick' is one of the basic metaphors in Shakespeare's great play *Hamlet*, published in 1604. Fulke Grenville, the English poet, brought the human body, the state, the zodiac and the seasons together when he wrote that:

States have degrees as human bodies have
Springs, Summer, Autumne, Winter and the grave.[3]

To Shakespeare and his contemporaries the concept of the state is
an organic whole was inextricably bound up with the astrological
world view in which all aspects of life were but interdependent links
in the 'Great Chain of Being' which linked heaven to earth.

Around the end of the seventeenth century astrology ceased to
be intellectually respectable in Europe, but the concept of the state
as a 'body politic' persisted. The French philosopher Jean Jacques
Rousseau (1712-78) had no known knowledge of astrology, but he
was very much influenced by the old theory. He wrote that: 'As
soon as the multitude is united thus in a single body no one can
injure any of the members without attacking the whole' and 'In
relation to foreign powers the body politic is a single entity, an
individual'.[4]

The theory Rousseau was here describing is the political theory
of mundane astrology. It may indeed be the case that by examining
the works of political philosophers we shall rediscover the theory
of mundane astrology in all its richness, for the political philosophers
themselves have all lived in a world whose intellectual foundations
were laid by astrology.

The theory of the body politic — that there is an analagous
relationship between the individual and the collective — is itself
central to mundane astrology and it is this theory which allows us
to take the rules for the interpretation of the birth chart of an
individual and use those same rules in the birth chart of a nation.
The same assumptions which we apply to psychological processes
in the natal chart can, perhaps, be applied to political processes in
the mundane chart.

The nation
Generally speaking, the modern nation state is a legal entity created
by the nation for the purpose of regulating itself through the means
of a constitution. The nation itself may be considered to be a group
of people who share a common heritage, language and culture, and
who physically occupy a particular geographical location. Obviously
there are many instances of nations who have no state, such as the
Palestinians, the Basques or the Kurds, and of states which contain
more than one nation, such as the Soviet Union and the United States,
but the general pattern holds.

The nation may also be considered to be the physical correlation to the collective unconscious,[5] for the collective unconscious itself provides the cohesive unity of the nation in terms of the common identity of each individual with the past, present and future of the nation. This is by no means a radical suggestion for many political philosophers have postulated that there is an intangible quality, an 'Ideal', 'General Will', or 'National Spirit', which binds a nation together. Indeed such a concept is central to mundane astrology and those modern philosophers who adhere to this notion, such as Hegel in the nineteenth century, do in fact owe a debt to astrology.

Such a theory as this assumes that all the members of a nation share a common fund of thoughts which have been acquired in, and transmitted through, history, and a common will to continue living together as a nation in the future. Therefore, when a nation organizes itself into a state it is expressing the current stage of development of that collective fund of thoughts, memories, hopes, fears and wishes — that is, the collective unconscious.

The national horoscope itself may be defined as the mirror of the collective unconscious of the nation, frozen at a particular and critical stage in its evolution. In fact what we are usually looking at in such a chart is a horoscope for a particular event often, but not always, a legal action involving the seizure or transfer of political power and authority in the nation. This transfer of power is usually enacted through the means of the machinery of the state.

The creation of the State

We may define the state loosely as the system of institutions which a nation adopts for the purpose of regulating its social, economic and political life. A horoscope drawn for the creation of a state will therefore not only show the state of the collective unconscious on a mythological or psychological level but also affairs on the material plane such as public scandals, economic affairs, and foreign relations.

There are two major theories concerning the creation of the state by the nation, and the relationship between the two. We may generally accept that the 'bridge' between the nation and the state is the constitution, that set of rules which sets out to define the correct functioning of the state. A national horoscope is therefore usually cast for a constitutional event, and the horoscopes of most of the world's modern countries are set for such moments.

The first theory claims that a nation decides to write a constitution

— and so create a state — as a conscious act, with the constitution indeed serving as a 'bridge' between nation and state. In such a case we have a clear theoretical basis for taking the constitutional event as the source for the national chart. We may find this theory particularly applicable in the cases of those ex-colonial states in the third world which received legal independence at a precisely-timed moment. We may still have reservations about such charts, however, because the nations which comprise those ex-colonial states had already often been politically organized for many centuries before the arrival of the Europeans. Obviously we must just use the historical data which we do have available and test the resulting horoscopes with transits and progressions to see how far they reflect events in the State's political and economic life.

The second theory is that propounded in modern philosophy by Hegel and Marx, the two pillars of nineteenth-century political science. This theory claims that the State is a fundamental manifestation of human society rather than a conscious creation, and that the constitution arises over a period of time in order to fulfil the needs of the State. According to Hegel the evolving constitution would reflect gradual changes in the 'national spirit', which we can equate with Jung's 'collective unconscious'. This theory is possibly the more relevant to astrology, influenced as it is by Neo-Platonism, the philosophy which represents manifestation on the material plane as a reflection of subtle changes in the 'ideal' plane. The theory may also seem particularly appropriate in those cases in which we have no one satisfactory national chart. The most obvious example in this respect is England, which has experienced 1500 years of independent history, and for which astrologers put forward about half a dozen alternative horoscopes. The problem of finding the 'correct' chart for the country is partly solved if we accept that each of the main contenders is equally valid as a reflection of the gradual evolution of the English collective unconscious. Such a theory may be tested by examining astrological links between the charts. [6]

To the political theorists of the Renaissance, astrology was a generally accepted part of their world view, and the political theorists of today are the intellectual descendants of those Renaissance scholars. It is up to today's mundane astrologers to reestablish the connections between astrology and living political theory.

The hierarchy of charts

Horoscopes tend to be drawn for precise events, such as declarations of independence, coronations and general elections, and sometimes it is difficult to know which exactly is the appropriate horoscope to use. It may help, however, if the charts are arranged in a 'hierarchy' so that one can see which is the most important. Less important charts will always be overshadowed by more important ones, and will tend to have a more specific area of action, and a shorter period of relevance. In addition the importance of each chart may be decided on historical grounds and tested astrologically to see how well different events show up in it. For example a horoscope for the founding of an independent nation state is obviously the most important horoscope for a state, and will be so for as long as that state continues to exist (Note that we have no chart for the nation as such, only for its creation, the state.) Let us suppose that the newly independent state appointed a king, as was the fashion in nineteenth century Europe. The horoscope for this event would describe the existence of the state as a monarchy, but would not be as important as the independence chart, rather being contained within it. At a later date the king might allow a new constitution and the creation of a parliament. The horoscope for this would describe the life of the state as a constitutional monarchy, while the subsequent horoscope for the country's first general election would describe the life of the first democratic government. Meanwhile the chart for the king is, as the focus of national aspirations, operating as a chart for the entire collective in parallel with the independence chart, to be replaced when he dies by the charts for both the birth and coronation of his successor. Let us suppose that the country experiences a revolution in which all previous organs of government are swept away. This presupposes that these organs had failed to keep up with the pace of change in the Collective Unconscious, or National Spirit, and that the physical expression of these — the daily life of the nation — has reached a point of disharmony with the government. A Republican government is declared and all previous horoscopes become invalid except, that is, for the original independence chart. The working charts for the nation would then be the republic and independence charts together, although soon, as a powerful leader again arises, more and more charts would have to be considered.

The previous charts for the monarchical period would still be valid as indicators of the condition of the collective at the time that they were cast, and might even continue to show up particular events by transit or progression. For example, the fate of the royal family in exile, or the future of monarchy in the society might still be indicated in the chart for the creation of the monarchy.

In fact horoscopes are also drawn for events apart from coronations, general elections and other constitutional points, events which are important because they *legitimize* (make legal) the transfer of power in the state. However at certain times, during *coups d'état* or revolutions, power may change hands illegally. Yet even during these times some sort of symbolic action is paramount, for example the execution of a leader, or the storming of a presidential palace by rebels. In such cases the symbolism will be apparent to astrologers, and a chart drawn for such a symbolic moment may well be considered to have the status of a national chart. It is, however, worth noting that even in these circumstances power often changes hands technically through a constitutional act. A prime example of such constitutional change in the midst of chaos may be found in the seizure of power by the Bolsheviks in Russia, when Lenin was careful to legitimize the revolution through constitutional voting procedures. [7] There is also a certain amount of carefully worked out symbolism in the most legalistic transfer of power, and even the town mayor is entrusted with his or her chain of office. Attention to such symbolic points can pinpoint the precise time during the 'taking of power period' which is astrologically significant, for example whether the beginning or end of a *coup d'état* is the most important. It goes without saying that conscientious historical research is absolutely necessary to establish the time at which the events in question happen, and all too often in the past astrologers have failed to appreciate this point.

It might be argued that the coronation for a horoscope or like event is so important because all the hopes and fears and wishes of the collective are focused upon the event. The event therefore becomes the physical manifestation of the collective unconscious at that particular time. Yet this explanation does not suffice in all instances, for while many of the crucial events used to draw up mundane charts do have this element of publicity, some do not. In a *coup d'état*, for example, only the rebel troops are aware of the time at which they seize the presidential palace. Even in certain public constitutional events many inhabitants of the country may be unconcerned or unaware. Who in the north of England in 1066 knew that William was being crowned in London? The answer is that even the collective is manifesting in an unconscious manner, a manner in which it is not necessary for the members of the collective itself to know consciously what is going on.

Often a minority of the population, either the current or the future ruling class, or any other highly-motivated group, manifests the current feelings of the collective on its behalf. Even in cases where the actions of the minority go against the conscious wishes of the majority, the astrology indicates that the collective as a whole is creating its own future in accordance with its unconscious wishes. Many countries in the world today, as in the past, have little democracy in their governmental systems, and some even produce alarmingly repressive phenomena such as Fascism and Communism. Such systems are maintained physically by governments using combinations of fear and military strength, and the mass of the population often appears to have no interest at all in the maintenance of the system. Yet the astrological theory, using the concept of the collective unconscious, would assume that the collective as a whole is responsible for the sorry state of the country, in exactly the same way as the collective in a 'parliamentary democracy' is responsible for the benefits and ills of that system.

The structure of society

We could perhaps compare a model of physical society to Jacobi's model of the psyche (see Chapter 3, p. 79). The pyramidal structure suggests more of the popular conception of the feudal state that the modern, but appears to be relevant astrologically (Fig. 4.1). We may take the class system as our analogy, for this is the major sociological model in use today.

At the summit is the leader, the queen, president, party chairman, or whoever is responsible for receiving, in the medieval style, authority from heaven. The prime minister may also be here. Immediately surrounding this person are the other members of whoever is deemed loosely to constitute the ruling class: aristocrats, politicians, landowners, party officials, capitalists, military leaders and so on. These are the people who are apparently responsible for taking decisions in the society, although the working of astrology indicates that they tend to act as unconsciously as everyone else.

Below the ruling class is the middle class, the group which administers the State on behalf of the ruling class. Here we have

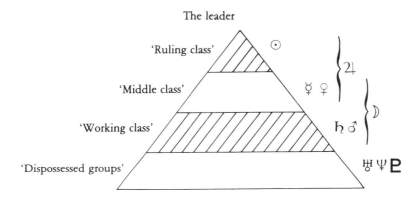

Figure 4.1 The structure of the industrial nation state: a speculative comparison with Jacobi's map of the human psyche with suggested planetary correspondences.

all administrative and professional groups, and white-collar workers. We might speculate that Mercury and Venus are particularly appropriate symbols for this group.

The middle class is responsible for administering the working class, which itself may be seen as a threat by both the ruling and middle class. A parallel here would be the threat that the individual may often feed from unconscious neurosis. The working class consists of all those who perform manual jobs and have usually sold their labour to an employer. Saturn might be seen to have a particular reference to this group, especially as it symbolizes both heavy industry in a mundane chart and often the psychological 'shadow' in a nativity.

At the bottom of the pile are those who have little concern or interest in the nation state. These may be the landless unemployed or disadvantaged national and racial minorities. These people are often considered a threat by the groups above them. When a superior group feels threatened by an inferior one then it will tend to develop authoritarian or totalitarian tendencies such as Fascism. Such philosophies may also be the basis of action by an inferior group against a superior one. It is worth speculating that the transpersonal planets, Uranus, Neptune and Pluto, are perhaps appropriate both to the lowest group in society, bringing as they do various forms of subversion, and to Fascism, the violent eruption of the repressed shadow.

Processes of change in society

In a harmoniously organized society all the varying levels have a common identification in the stability of the State, but in some instances this may not be so. Social and political pressures build up in a society when inferior groups lose their identification with the superior groups. Such a build-up can occur when a national or religious minority loses its identification with the ruling class, which may be of a different nation or religion, or when the middle class feels the ruling class has deprived it of political power, or when the working class feels that the middles class has deprived it of wealth. Such pressures build up when the organization of the State fails to reflect the stage of development of the collective unconscious.

Processes of change in society begin with the gradual evolution of the consciousness of the human race as seen through planetary cycles, particularly the long-term movement of the outer planets through the zodiac, making aspects to each other as they do so, and perhaps through the Platonic Great Year. This change is experienced in the material plane, and will therefore be experienced by different nations in different ways, and even in different ways by members of the same nation. For example the Tibetan tribesman will have a different experience to the urban New Yorker, and the millionaire a different experience to the pauper. This partly depends upon their psychological perspective as seen through the birth chart, but also upon their material experience, for in a famine the rich person still has enough to eat while the poor person starves. When these differences are generalized into the class system, then the peasantry as a whole may be seen to have a different experience to the landlords. Perhaps the landlords buy up the peasants' land and evict them, or perhaps the peasants rise up and seize the landlords' estates. In this way the general change on the Ideal level, or level of the National Spirit or the collective unconscious, has a particular manifestation. A state at any one time will tend to reflect the class interests of the dominant class in society, so that in a 'capitalist' state the interests of the capitalists are protected before all else, and in a 'communist' state the interests of the party élite are protected before all else. When the state fails to adjust to recognize the realities of change in the class structure then revolution occurs. If this is successful, and the state is overthrown, then the collective will have to set about building a new state which will then have a new horoscope. A fact of crucial historical importance is that in such revolutions the new order which so dramatically overthrows the old may in fact come to resemble the old quite closely. For example, after a tumultuous revolution in France the Napoleonic Empire replaced the Bourbon Kingdom, and in Russia the Stalinist state replaced the Czarist regime. In other words, change in the Collective Unconscious of the nation is very gradual and dramatic change occurs in a state when material circumstances have not changed in accordance with the changes in the Collective Unconscious. It is as if several hundred years worth of change in the Collective Unconscious has been blocked and floods through into the material plane all at once.

In some societies the state is organized so as to facilitate gradual social change and political evolution without upsetting the class system, as does the system of Parliamentary democracy. This may be one explanation why there is no definite horoscope for the United Kingdom, where political evolution has been so gradual and so continuous. For the astrologer, to have no revolution is almost as frustrating as to have too many.

In summary we may say that the process of change in a society originates in the evolution of the National Spirit or Collective Unconscious, as read in the changing patterns of the planets and the zodiac. This manifests in the social and economic life of the society, producing changes in the balance between different groups. These changes then produce political changes, and the mundane horoscope is drawn for the moment of political change which itself should combine elements of legality and symbolism. This legitimizes the formal transfer of power which is the final manifestation of the change in the collective unconscious (Fig. 4.2).

We may also take a more overtly materialistic view of the relationship between planetary movements and terrestrial politics, evidence for which may be based principally on the work of Gribbin and Plagemann in their book, *The Jupiter Effect*. [8] In spite of the scientific appearance of such work, and its repetition by many other writers, it should be borne in mind that any such materialistic view of planetary causation is highly speculative.

Essentially Gribbin and Plagemann argue that certain planetary alignments correlate with key geo-physical events on the Earth. This may happen through disturbances of the solar wind, the frequency

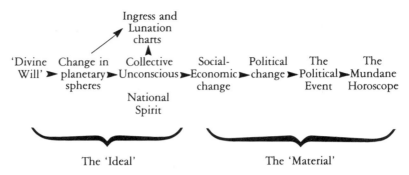

Figure 4.2 The process of change in human society — an astrological model.

of radio waves in the solar system, and the electro-magnetic field of the Earth. This will have two important consequences on the Earth. One may be a direct effect, via possible atmospheric or electro-magnetic conditions, on individual, and consequently collective, human behaviour. The other may be more indirect, with atmospheric conditions disturbing the climate, the climate disturbing agriculture, agricultural fluctuations disturbing the economy, economic changes affecting social conditions which in turn affect political affairs.

An example may be taken from recent history. Gribbin suggests that the eruption of El Chichon, the volcano in southern Mexico, on 28 March and 4 April 1982 was triggered by planetary alignments.[9] It is possible that the ash poured into the atmosphere by this explosion is a cause of the apparent drop in the temperature of the Pacific area by one degree centigrade in 1982-3. It is also possible that this cooling of the Pacific area has exacerbated the drought in Australia and the general climatic conditions which resulted in first massive bushfires and then severe floods in parts of southern Australia in February 1983. The cumulative effect of this may be felt in the huge economic strain put on the important cattle and sheep industry as grazing land is destroyed. We may go further than Gribbin and speculate that such events contributed to the political upsets which brought the Labour Party to power on 6 March 1983.[10]

To accept this series of events as part of a single process we must firstly accept planetary causation in the El Chichon eruption. We must then accept that this eruption was responsible for the cooling of the Pacific region. Indeed, we must accept that such a cooling took place, any measurement of which, taken over such a massive area, over such a brief time and involving such a small drop, must be regarded as highly speculative. We must then accept that this exacerbated the Australian drought which, however, was already serious when the volcano erupted. We must finally try to establish whether the economic conditions produced by the drought were a factor in the defeat of the government of Australia at the general election.

As we can see, scientific and materialist theories are at present as speculative as the theories derived from Neo-Platonism, i.e., change manifesting from a divine consciousness via planetary levels as symbolized in the collective unconscious or national spirit. Nevertheless, the materialistic approach should be taken seriously, and may be represented diagramatically as in Fig. 4.3.

Different nations may have different methods of transferring power, and the diligent astrological researcher should be aware of this, but whatever the society, the event which combines symbolism and legality to the greatest degree is the one to watch out for.

Theories of the State

Political philosophers have always created different theories of exactly how a state works. Astrology has the advantages of combining them all. There are two fundamental views of the origin of society. One is the 'idealist', which views the state as the product of some non-tangible existence, such as Hegel's 'National Spirit'. The other is the 'materialist', which views the state as the result of purely physical demands and needs. Astrology is often identified most closely with the former, but we may equally well see it as the link between the two, for a horoscope is a map of intangible forces and energies which we can scarcely comprehend, enclosed in matter in a particular time, and cast for a particular physical location. We could therefore see the mundane horoscope as the mediator between the ideal and the material conceptions, using a model of the human eye as our example — the eye, after all, is that which allows the mind, the seat of the soul, to perceive visually the outside physical environment (Fig. 4.4).

There are also differing theories concerning the origin of power in a society, which again may be broadly classified under two types. There are those that see power as originating in the leaders, who may receive it from heaven, and may then delegate it to the subordinates; and there are those who see power as residing in the

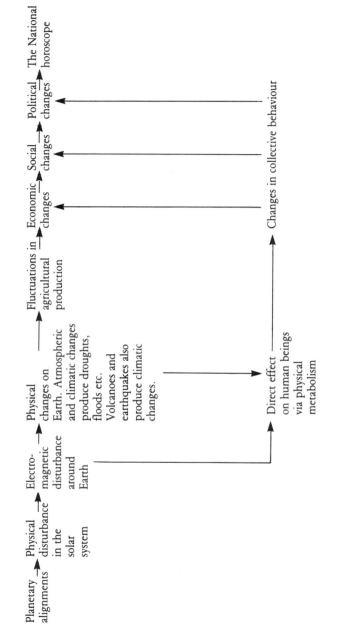

Figure 4.3 A materialist model of planetary and political change.

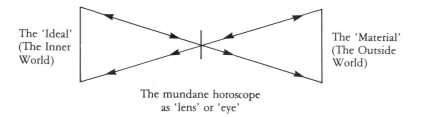

The 'Ideal'
(The Inner
World)

The 'Material'
(The Outside
World)

The mundane horoscope
as 'lens' or 'eye'

Figure 4.4   A model of the mundane horoscope as the mediator between
'material' and 'ideal'.

people, who may then delegate it to their rulers for a limited period. The former theory is essentially that of the high period of feudalism and theocracy in the later medieval period, and is related to Asiatic ideas imported by the Romans. The latter theory relates to the type of 'social contract' theories evolved by those who overthrew the European feudal systems from the sixteenth to nineteenth centuries. The former theory would also seem to be that which most closely fits astrology, especially as some monarchs, such as the Byzantine emperors, drew on astrological symbolism as part of the ritual which placed them second only to God. Astrological evidence would also seem to support this theory, for the birth chart of the leader becomes a working horoscope for the collective, a fact which may easily be tested using transits and progressions. Events which affect the collective may be reflected in, and predicted by, the horoscope of the leader. Obviously the implications of this theory for our view of democracy are enormous. Almost every state in the world, be it a parliamentary democracy or peoples' democracy, propagates the myth that it is indeed a democracy, that the mass of the people is in control, and is in control through taking conscious decisions.

However the theory of the collective unconscious points us in another direction, for this assumes that, albeit unconsciously, the mass of the people is in control, and that leaders only assume power through the consent, albeit unconscious, of the collective. We therefore have a dialectical relationship between ruler and ruled, in which power is flowing in two ways simultaneously. For example in the United Kingdom the effective leader is the prime minister. The prime minister receives power from two sources: first from the collective by virtue of being the leader of the political party with the largest support in parliament; and second from the monarch, who has received authority from God in a religious and symbolic ritual (the coronation) and delegated it to the prime minister. In the United States the president is first elected by the collective, but then has to swear an oath on the Bible that he or she will rule honourably, receiving in the process authority from God also.

The national horoscope in mundane astrology can be a tool to understand these political processes and to raise our consciousness of our political environment. It can become a tool for the creation of greater democracy through greater conscious, rather than unconscious, participation in the decision-making processes of the nation. Mundane astrology, using the national horoscope, can still be a tool for prediction, or for the passive observation of events, but it can become more. It can become a tool for the general improvement of human society, the avoidance of war and tyranny, and the creation of a better future through greater understanding of our political processes.

References

1 See Chapter 1.
2 See Chapter 10.
3 Grenville, F. *Works,* p.78.
4 Rousseau, J-J. *Social Contract* Book 1, Chapter 7.
5 See Chapter 3.
6 See Chapter 10.
7 See Chapter 10.
8 See Gribbon, J. and Plagemann, S. *The Jupiter Effect.* See also Playfair, G. L. and Hill, S. *The Cycles of Heaven;* Gauquelin M. *The Cosmic Clocks;* Tilms, R. *Judgement of Jupiter* and various articles in *Correlation,* the research journal of the Astrological Association.
9 Gribbon, J. interviewed in British Channel 4 News, 3 March 1983.
10 The Australian General Election was held on 6 March 1983, and resulted in a change of government. Interestingly this was predicted in the 1983 Australian edition of *Old Moore's Almanack,* although the Almanack predicted election for February, which was of course when the electioneering took place. For February, 1983 the prediction read 'Electioneering rhetoric dominates the Australian Parliament', and 'Scandals could upset

the government leadership'. It is probable that the basis for these predictions was the transit of Uranus over sensitive points in the Australian federal chart.

Bibliography

BARKER, E. *Principles of Social and Political Theory* Oxford, 1951.

BROWN, J. L. *The Methodus and Facilem Historiarum Cognitionem of Jean Bodin, A Critical Study* Washington, 1935.

CASSIRER, E. *The Individual and the Cosmos in Renaissance Philosophy* New York, 1963.

CASSIRER, E. *The Myth of the State* Yale, 1963.

COLLINGWOOD, R. G. *The Idea of History* Oxford, 1946.

FICHTE, J. *Works, Vol II* (Trans. William Smith) London, 1844.

FRANKLIN, J. *Jean Bodin and the Sixteenth Century Revolution in the Methodology of Law and History* London, 1963.

GAUQUELIN, M. *The Cosmic Clocks* London, 1969.

GRENVILLE, F. *Certain Learned and Elegant Workes of the Right Honourable Fulke, Lord Brooke* London, 1633.

GRIBBIN, J. AND PLAGEMANN, S. *The Jupiter Effect* Glasgow, 1974.

HEGEL, G. *The Philosophy of Right* (Trans T. M. Knox) London, 1952.

LOVEJOY, A. O. *The Great Chain of Being* London, 1933.

MANUEL, F. *Shapes of Philosophical History* London, 1965.

ROUSSEAU, J-J. *The Social Contract* (trans. Maurice Cranston) London, 1968.

ROY, L. L. *Of the Interchangeable Course or Variety of Things in the Whole World* London, 1594.

TILLYARD, E. M. *The Elizabethan World Picture* London, 1944.

TILMS, R. *Judgement of Jupiter* London, 1980.

VICO, G. *The New Science* (Trans. T. Bergin and M. Fisch) New York, 1948.

YATES, F. *Astraea* London.

PART TWO:
THE MATERIAL

5.

THE GREAT YEAR

Nicholas Campion

All life on earth flows in a rhythmic movement, movement which may be described in terms of cycles. Indeed, astrology may be said to be in essence the study of life as a cyclical phenomenon, and the universe as one vast interlocking organism which ebbs and flows in a cosmic pattern almost too vast for us to comprehend. In mundane astrology we find a conscious attempt to understand this awesome pattern on the level at which it manifests in all our lives as we gather together in groups.

We do not know at what time human beings first realized that life moves in a cyclical motion, but this must have coincided with the dawn of conscious thought, as soon as people were able to recognize that night always follows day and day always follows night. The observation of such cycles perhaps at first had a practical significance, for the observation of the seasons with their alternations of hot and cold, dry and wet would have been crucial to all who lived in temperate and cold climtes in prehistoric times. The advent of settled communities dependent on farming would have made the measurement of seasonal changes even more important, and it is perhaps no coincidence that when astrology finally emerged it did so in the fertile Tigris-Euphrates valley.

Astrology evolved as a result of the ability of human beings to equate different cycles, and make correlations between them. Not only were terrestrial cycles linked, providing the origin of vegetation gods, but terrestrial cycles were linked to celestial cycles. Thus, for example, it was apparent that the movement of the Sun was associated

with both diurnal and annual variations. Even before the arrival of
astrology in Greece it was carefully noted which agricultural exercises
should coincide with which planetary and stellar patterns. [1]

Astrology depended for its evolution not just on the assumption
of actual links between cycles (for example the rising of Mars signifying
war) but in the creation of symbolic links between different cycles.
Thus the human life-death cycle was associated with the seasonal
life and death of vegetation, and with the annual and diurnal solar
cycles, which themselves were thus seen as an allegory of human life.
Implicit within this is the concept of 'cycles within cycles' and of
the later theory of 'macrocosm and microcosm', the life of the Sun
representing on a grand scale the life of a human being.

The concern with the measurement of celestial cycles is very ancient,
predating both astrology and settled life. Evidence shows that lunar
phases were being systematically recorded in 6,500 BC, and by the
time of the megalith builders in north-west Europe, as early as 3,000
BC, the measurement of astronomical patterns had reached
unparalleled heights of sophistication. [2] The concern with cycles led
to the postulation, possibly sometime between 4,000 BC and 1,000
BC of greater cycles in the universe. These cycles were similar to
observable cycles, but contained smaller cycles within them. For
example, a Babylonian 'Sar' was equal to 3,600 years, reflecting the
length of the ritual year of 360 days. In such thinking we see the
origin of the notion of the 'Great Year' which was to form an essential
part of early mundane astrology, and which has been reborn today
in the form of the coming 'Age of Aquarius'. Indeed, it seems that
the concept of these great universal cycles may have predated astrology
itself, and astrology may have developed partly as a tool for measuring
and interpreting these cycles which had already been postulated.

Inherent in these theories is the concept of waves or spirals, for
if we combine the flow of linear time to a circular series of events
our circle expands and changes its form (see Fig. 5.1a,b,c). It is
common to think in terms of spirals or waves these days, but the
Babylonians and Greeks believed firmly in a fixed cycle of existence,
ever repeating in a predetermined pattern.

The Assyrian Great Year
The earliest account of a 'Great Year' we have is that of the Assyrians,
mainly perhaps because records of their astrology have survived,
thanks to the Greeks. Assyrian rule began in Mesopotamia around

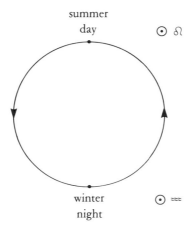

Figure 5.1a   The Cyclical conception of history.

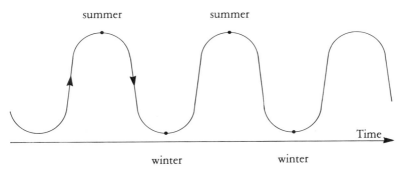

Figure 5.1b   History as a wave.

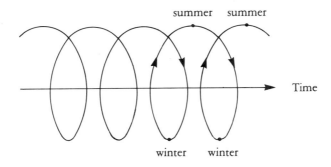

Figure 5.1c   History as a spiral.

900 BC and inherited a 2,000-year-old civilization which had already, prior to 2,000 BC developed a system of mathematics comparable to that of Renaissance Europe.[3] It is on this basis that Assyrian astrology was worked out, and what we know may represent the remains of a system of knowledge common to the civilizations of India, Britain and Mesopotamia in 3,000 BC. However, written records of the time are very scarce and we can only piece together a vague idea of Mesopotamian notions of the Great Year. It is not possible, on the basis of available historical evidence, to attribute a great antiquity to measurements of such historial cycles.

The Assyrians deified time, believing that it was a gift from the gods to measure the life of the soul of the universe. They believed that, like everything on earth, the universe died and was reborn, as winter turns into spring, and night into day. They believed that crucial periods in the life of the universe occurred when there were conjunctions of all seven planets in Cancer or in Capricorn, i.e., at the solstice points.[4] These two points represented the extreme points of the Sun north and south in its annual journey, and therefore points of imbalance. A circle contains within it all possibilities, and the annual revolution of the Sun contains all the possibilities, inherent in life in one year. When an extreme point is reached a state of imbalance occurs and the universe breaks down. At these times civilization would be destroyed; a conjunction in Cancer would produce destruction by fire and one in Capricorn would produce destruction by water. Such a belief clearly formed the basis of the flood myths of Noah and Gilgamesh, and we will see other Assyrian beliefs surfacing through later astrology. The idea that the world must experience a collective death in order to be reborn has, in particular, been a potent one throughout European history. In the alternating destruction in Cancer and its opposite, Capricorn, we see the notion of the world oscillating between two poles, which in China was to develop as the Taoist Yin-Yang theory, and in Europe was to give rise to dualist religion and dialectical thought. As we shall see, the Greeks characterized their Great Year as the story of the inevitable flow of the universe between the poles of two forces — Strife and Love.

The Assyrians also inherited from the Babylonians a complex system of time-keeping which was designed to measure all the manifestations of the sacred and cyclical flow of time from the smallest to the greatest. Although their mathematics was highly sophisticated, their astronomical measurement does not appear to have been so, and as a result their measurement of the Great Year was based on symbolic figures. This measurement was, however, a reflection of the view that all planetary cycles moved in perfect harmony with terrestrial cycles, and it has been argued that their mathematical conclusions were confirmed by reference to musical harmonies.[5] That the Assyrians were concerned with symbol and meaning is demonstrated by their use of the ritual 360-day year, which was also used by other ancient civilizations. Their numerological system was based on the number 6, a figure of vital importance to several cultures. In a sense the importance of this number is derived from the astrologically crucial number 7, this being the number of traditional planets, and one quarter of a lunar phase of 28 days. However the number 6 took on its own importance and, in the Jewish creation myth, the process of creation took six days, with God resting on the seventh. The Pythagoreans rationalized this mathematically, for six was equal not only to the sum of its factors $(1 + 2 + 3 = 6)$, but also to the numbers of the sides of a cube, and therefore descriptive of the secret of the earth. Six describes the creative process, and the union of matter with spirit to create life, and as such it formed the basis of mathematical calculation of planetary cycles and large symbolic periods in Greek, Persian, Arab and Indian astrology until such time as these periods could be measured astronomically. The Babylonian sexagesimal system survives today in our system of days of 24 hours $(24 = 6 \times 4)$, hours of 60 minutes and minutes of 60 seconds.

As it has been re-created by modern historians the Assyrian system of chronology corresponded to the following pattern. The smallest unit was equal to one human breath of four seconds, this being not just a unit of time but a statement of belief that the universe itself is a breathing, living being of which we are a part. From here the system was built up via a four-minute period, a two-hour period, up to one day, and so on through the decan (ten days), the month of 30 days and the year of 360 days. At this point they embarked into the measurement of larger periods, constructed mathematically, which were ultimately designed to measure the life of the universe. The basic period was the Soss of 60 years, but beyond this was the Ner of 600 years and the Sar of 3,600 years (60^2) (see Fig. 5.2). A Great Sar, 216,000 years (60^3) represented one breath, but as the universe must breathe in as well as out the total life of the universe

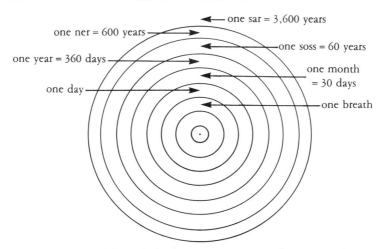

Figure 5.2   The Babylonian-Assyrian view of symbolic time.

was said to be 432,000 years (216,000 × 2). Beyond this is a still greater mythic period of 12,960,000 years (60^4), a period which perhaps delineated the life of the creator. [6] All these figures recur throughout subsequent astrology, and they are remarkable for one further reason: numerologically they all add up to nine (e.g. 4 + 3 + 2 = 9), and the number 9 thus entered astrology as a critical and sacred number.

The Assyrians left one more legacy to astrological thought. They realized that time and space are part of the same interrelated flow of existence. It is generally accepted that they devised a system for measuring the circle in divisions of 360 degrees, a degree of space being symbolically equal to one day of time. [7] They also divided the sky into 36 sectors, grouped in three zones of twelve sectors each, a system perhaps related to the alternative year of three seasons each consisting of 120 days. Such was the foundation of the theory of the astrological ages which the Greeks were to perfect.

The Platonic Great Year

Astrology in Greece would seem to have developed between the seventh and second centuries BC, from the time of Pythagoras to that of Hipparchus. Cyclical thought was much older, however, and a central tenet of the Orphic religion of the vegetation god, Dionysus, was reincarnation of souls on the endless wheel of life. It was the philosopher Plato (428-348 BC) who bequeathed to European astrology the idea of the Great Year of the life of the universe which bears his name. However, he drew heavily on the work of Pythagoras (sixth century BC) and Empedocles (c.495-530 BC) who between them introduced oriental learning into Greece and gave it that peculiar flavour of Greek mathematical logic. It was Pythogoras who provided the mathematical framework, and Empedocles who described the cyclical process, while it was left to Plato to consolidate the whole into a theory of celestial harmony.[8] Plato placed himself firmly within the mystical tradition of Orphism and the Pythagoreans, and was concerned to show how all life on the earth is interrelated and is an intimate part of a universe which is itself alive, and which breathes in and out in a perfect rhythm. As part of each breathing motion all of human civilization first grows to a peak of perfection, and then declines to a point of total collapse only to recover and grow again. This process continues indefinitely and into infinity for as long as God wills it.

To Plato the entire universe, once unity was divided, consisted of two opposing principles — Strife and Love (i.e., negative and positive) — and four elements — fire, earth, air and water — which continually flowed together in a predetermined pattern. As the universe breathed in there was a gradual increase of Strife, and as it breathed out there was an increase in Love. As one increased the other would diminish until a point of imbalance was reached, the four elements unravelled, the world collapsed and human civilization ceased to exist. At this point God would intercede and reverse the process, initiating the rebirth of civilization. This process may be represented as an oscillation between two poles, as a movement through four phases (increase of Love — dissolution — increase of Strife — dissolution), or as part of a cycle. One year of the universe was said to last 36,000 years (a figure obviously derived from the Babylonians, but justified by reference to Pythagoras) and this may be represented as a complete cycle in itself. However a complete breath involves two motions and the complete period of one cycle is 72,000 years, during which time human civilization passes through a complete process from birth to decay (see Fig. 5.3). Plato argued that the value of astrology was that it enabled us to harmonize with these universal rhythms and so help the universe balance itself, and therefore delay the inevitable increase of Strife over Love. For instance, he considered that political life should observe the laws of the passing of time, and that the ideal State would be governed by 360 councillors,

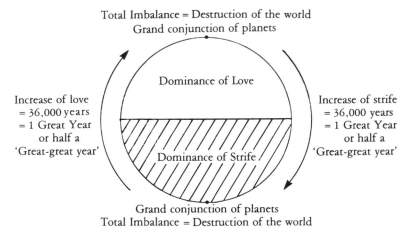

Figure 5.3 The Greek Great Year according to Empedocles and Plato.

divided into twelve groups of 30, each group ruling for one month.[9]

Like the Assyrians, Plato considered that a cycle began and ended when all the planets formed a great conjunction, and he specified that this conjunction must occur at the position which all the planets held at the creation. He does not specify where in the zodiac this point was, but while he was probably aware that the Assyrians regarded conjunctions in Cancer and Capricorn as the two key-points in the Great Year, subsequent commentators have assumed that Plato placed his conjunction at 0° Aries. Thus the cycles of the seven planets and the sphere of the fixed stars taken together represent the sum total of possibilities on earth. When all the planets complete their cycles simultaneously the earth will have experienced every possibility open to it, the purpose of creation will have been fulfilled and civilization will come to an end.

No single astrologer after Plato equalled the beauty and complexity of his vision partly, perhaps, because of the complexity of his writing, although Claudius Ptolemy is said to have been one of the few to understand the meaning of the Platonic Year. Among subsequent Greek and Roman astrologers, however, we find that various Great Years were postulated, such as 18,000 or 15,000 years. Perhaps the most significant suggestion was made by Cicero, who broke with the idea of a universal year and suggested that the length of a Great Year was tied to a particular starting-point, so that different civilizations could have their own cycles. [10] This is an idea which, curiously, is almost unknown to most modern astrologers. The mythic metaphor for the duration of the Great Year is to be found in the Life of the Phoenix, a bird whose life and death cycle was said to parallel that of the world, [11] but we find that very soon myth was to be replaced by astronomy as the basis of the Great Year.

The Great Year in Arabic and Indian astrology

Arab and Indian astrologers appear to have taken much of their knowledge from the Greeks, directly and indirectly, and among their inheritance was the concept of the great 'astrological age'. Both civilizations proceeded to produce their own variations, the Arabs inclining to be more scientific and the Indians more symbolic.

The Arab astrologers, working after AD 800, adopted a Great Year of 360,000 years which they divided into two phases of 180,000 years. It was clear that they derived this number from Plato, but unlike Plato they specified that each phase began with a mean conjunction of all the planets at 0° Aries. [12] The last such conjunction was said to have occurred at midnight on the 17/18 February 3101 BC, at which time the rains of the biblical flood began. Like Plato the Arabs assumed that one phase represented a period of spiritual growth and the other a period of decline, but it is not certain in which period the Arab astrologers thought that they lived.

Being mathematically minded the Arabs, principally Abu Ma'shar (787-886), devised complicated systems of twelve sub-cycles which allowed them to specify the planetary rulerships of precise periods. They combined symbolic philosophy with the study of actual planetary movements, and attempted to reconcile the whole with historical data in order to gain an understanding of the evolution of human history through time. In general the work of the Arabs was to be tremendously influential in subsequent European astrology and history, but in detail their complex chronological systems were not taken up by the Europeans. This may be partly because of the complexity of these systems, but also because European chronology was to be firmly based on the concept of a progression from creation through incarnation to the Day of Judgement. The Indian system of astrological ages, by contrast, has an engaging and mythic simplicity.

Certain evidence indicates that as early as 3,000 BC the Indians may have helped originate the sexagesimal system which the

Babylonians passed on to the Greeks. But it also seems likely that
the Indians benefited from a reintroduction of Greek ideas in the
centuries after Christ, ideas which contribute to the famous system
of Yugas. In describing time the Indians were attempting to describe
eternity, but it is clear that they wished to sum up non-existence
in the same breath as existence. Thus their smallest unit, the *truti*,
was equal to 0.0000074 of a second, while the largest runs into billions
and billions of years. The Babylonian year of 432,000 years is the
basis of the system and is the length of the so called Kali Yuga, the
reign of the Mother Goddess Kali. Like the Arab year, it began at
a grand conjunction of planets at 0° Aries in 3101 BC. Their
fundamental unit of mythic time is the Maha Yuga of 4,320,000
years which is divided into ratios of 4:3:2:1 as follows:

Krtiayuga (Golden Age)	1,728,000 years =	4
Tretayuga (Silver Age)	1,296,000 years =	3
Dvaparayuga (Copper Age)	864,000 years =	2
Kaliyuga (Earthen Age)	432,000 years =	1
	4,320,000	10

This whole cycle represents a period of spiritual and material decline
from the original Golden Age, and as a system is complete within
itself, but also represents a part of an endless series of 'cycles within
cycles' on to infinity. One thousand Maha Yugas represents one
Kalpa, or Day of Brahma: 360 Kalpas equal a Year of Brahma; 1,000
of these is a Life of Brahma; and two Lives of Brahma is a Century
of Brahma. The basic building block in all these figures is the Divine
Year of 360 ordinary years, which, using the passage of the Sun around
the Earth as its metaphor, assumes that 360 years is one year in the
life of a soul. The premiss behind the whole system of Indian
astrological ages is this the unfolding of the human spirit in accordance
with the cycles of the heavens. [13]

European astrological ages

The Great Year in Europe
Little was heard of Great Years in western astrology until
comparatively recently, for most western astrologers were concerned
with planetary cycles, in particular the Jupiter-Saturn cycle, and

interpretations of scriptural chronology.

Such chronology was heavily based on the work of the great Jewish and Arab scholars who pioneered the flowering of Islamic culture. Abu Ma'shar in particular had devised a complicated astrological theory of history which was to be especially influential amongst the medieval and Renaissance Europeans. One of the innovators in Europe in the field of astrological history was a certain Peter of Abano, who lived in Italy at the end of the thirteenth and the beginning of the fourteenth centuries and was regarded as one of the most influential men of learning of his day.

Peter's major historical cycle was the 960-year period based on the complete cycle of the Jupiter-Saturn conjunction. Peter assumed that every 960 years these two planets made a conjunction at the beginning of Aries, a conjunction whose character was determined by whatever third planet combined with Jupiter and Saturn in the conjunction. For example, when the Sun was the third planet, Peter claimed, the Egyptian civilization has started, a civilization whose religion was based on the worship of the Sun. The purpose of such a scheme was to predict the coming of the Anti-Christ, and Peter forecast this event for the period following the conjunction of Jupiter and Saturn with the Moon.

Peter also used a Great Year based on more symbolic assumptions. He argued that, as the life of a human could be divided into seven periods, each ruled by a different planet, so history could be divided into seven similar periods. These planetary periods were calculated to last for 354 years and four lunar months, a figure derived from the 359 days of the lunar year. Each period had particular historical characteristics so that, for example, the period ruled by the Moon was said to include the fall of Sodom and Gomorrah and the migration of the Jews from Egypt. [14]

Peter's thought was influential in later astrology as well in the subsequent development of history as a separate discipline. Pierre D'Ailly, the French Cardinal and a contemporary of Peter's, agreed with his system, giving it ecclesiastical blessing. However, he argued for the existence of four, rather than seven, great historical phases, based on the symbolism of the four seasons and the four ages of man. [15]

Historical epochs and Great Years based on scriptural numerology were very influential with astrologers and historians. These usually took their authority from the apocalyptic passages in the Books of

Daniel and Revelation, which were themselves related to astrological numbers such as the *seven* planets and the *four* seasons. One of the most thorough expositions of such chronology was given by the English astrologer John Booker in 1643.[16] Booker based his historical periods on the number 7, although his reasoning was not based explicitly on the existence of the seven astrological planets. Rather he argued that Christ was baptized at the age of twenty-nine (the Saturn return) and crucified seven years later in his thirty-sixth year. He also used a 245-year period based on the seven angels of Revelation who blew their seven trumpets seven times, an event which Booker assumed occurred symbolically five times (7 × 7 × 5 = 245). Using this system he calculated that the Day of Judgement would occur in 1786 (three years before the French Revolution), a figure which he ammended to 1700. Booker combined these two cycles with a 6,000-year period, working from the six days of the week, and other calculations based on the prophecies in the Book of Daniel.

Such periodization has been extremely influential in the subsequent development of history as a science and art, and modern historians owe an enormous debt to mundane astrology. In medieval and Renaissance Europe historical change was frequently explained by reference to astrological considerations, although since about 1700 the two studies have been as separate as astrology and astronomy. The last book written by an historian which sought to explain history on astrological grounds was published in 1711,[17] since when only a few astrologers with an inadequate knowledge of history have attempted to continue the old link between the two subjects.

Although all explicit references to astrology were dropped by the advocates of the new science of history in the eighteenth and nineteenth centuries, the symbolic division of history into cycles has continued. Oswald Spengler and Arnold Toynbee are the two major advocates of the practice in the twentieth century, but ironically it was Karl Marx, the firm supporter of scientific and materialist history, who did most to ressurrect the old symbolism. The astrologically critical numbers of 3, 4 and 7 all form the basis of Marx's historical system, and hence of the historical thought of all who class themselves as Marxists. For example Marx claimed that there were in history four great class societies, a claim in which he was influenced by Hegel's earlier delineation of four great empires. Hegel himself had taken the number 4, through the medieval historians, from the Book of Daniel where it represented the four fixed signs of the zodiac. Thus, unacknowledged and unrecognized, astrological symbolism stills plays a central role in modern historical studies.[18]

The Precessional Year

The concept of the Great Year has been given fresh impetus in western astrology by the new importance attributed to the phenomenon of the precession of the equinoxes. This precession arises from the fact that, due to a wobble in the Earth's rotation known as 'nutation', the point of the vernal equinox moves in a gradual retrograde motion through the constellations. Thus, since the second century AD the Sun has risen at the spring equinox in the constellation of Pisces, even though in the 'tropical' sign of Aries. The rate of precession is measured at 50.3708 seconds of arc every year. Based on this figure the spring point precesses through one degree every 71.46 years, one sign every 2,144 years and through the entire zodiac in 25,729 years, although most astrologers give different figures. Usually the figures given for precession are one degree every 72 years, one sign every 2,160 years and 25,920 years for an entire cycle. This figure is now known as the length of a Platonic Year, although it would be better known as a 'Precessional Year' to distinguish it from the true Great Year of Plato. The time of precession through one sign is similarly known as a 'Platonic month', or 'astrological age', and we are said now to be moving from the Age of Pisces into that of Aquarius.

Precession was discovered for the modern world by the Greek astronomer Hipparchus in 139 BC although it has been seriously suggested that he was 'rediscovering' an earlier known fact. The evidence for this is largely circumstantial, and whether or not precession was known to the ancients, the fact remains that it is an extremely recent addition to the repertoire of western astrology. There are a handful of vague references to precession as astrologically significant in classical literature (for example, Macrobius in the fourth/fifth centuries[19]), but within the mainstream of European astrology the present authors are unable to find a reference earlier than the 1870s.[20] The important consideration is not whether astrologers knew of precession as an astronomical phenomenon, but whether they considered it significant astrologically. It was not considered important by astrologers, and in this sense the concept of precession has been a part of western astrology for little over a hundred years.

The importance of the Precessional Year was at first pointed out by the Theosophists and Rosicrucians, even though their mentor Madame Blavatsky did not consider it of interest. Unfortunately contemporary astrological views on the meaning of precession still reflect much of the influence of these nineteenth-century writers and their simplistic versions of both astrology and history. The Theosophical version of historical ages is based on a literal interpretation of various classical myths, but also involves a high dose of fantasy and a great deal of historical misinformation. The Theosophists believe that civilization today is descended from the fantastic continents of Atlantis and Lemuria, and consider that the progress of human development moved from an originally spiritual plane down to a physical trough, which we have now passed. They assume that we are now returning to a more spiritual plane of existence, and therefore that the supposed imminent arrival of the Age of Aquarius represents a major step forward in this spiritual renewal.

These preconceptions mean that the Theosophists looked back at earlier ages and saw a golden period stretching into prehistoric antiquity. If this is true then it is not supported by any historical or archeological evidence. For example, the Age of Leo (c.10,000-8,000 BC) is regarded literally as a time of heroes when the Olympian gods walked the earth,[21] Similarly the expectation of a golden age in the future is responsible for the common view that once the Age of Aquarius arrives the world will become a 'better' place.

A major problem with these 'ages' is that no one can agree when they end and when they begin. There seems to be a general expectation that the Age of Aquarius will begin sometime in the twenty-first century but different writers have quoted dates ranging from AD 1762-2658 with cuspal periods of anything up to 700 years on either side.[22] Perhaps the most accurate assessment is AD 2369, a date worked out with reference to the astronomy of Ptolemy's era (second century AD), the time when it is generally agreed that the Sun last rose in the constellation of Aries at the spring equinox.[23]

Since individual character may be seen through the medium of the signs of the zodiac, it is reasonable to assume that collective character may be as well, and the theory of precession states that there would be a gradual evolution of the human psyche through the signs, and reflected in human history. Using AD 2369 as the entry into Aquarius, we might expect a system as follows:

10567 BC	*Age of Leo*	Formation of hierarchies in social groups; individuation; exploration.
8411 BC	*Age of Cancer*	Formation of settled agricultural communities; goddess worship; matriarchy.
6255 BC	*Age of Gemini*	Creation of new means of communication and tools; invention of writing; dualism in thought; migrations.
4099 BC	*Age of Taurus*	Building of cities, walled settlements; fertility cults; bull worship.
1943 BC	*Age of Aries*	Aggressive empires, warrior invasions, magnificence, worship of powerful gods (Zeus, Yahweh).
AD 213	*Age of Pisces*	Spirituality, confusion, breakdown of previous systems, instability.

Our archeology cannot tell us how far these interpretations fit the facts, but it is obvious that they are too generalized to be of much historical use. The most glaringly inappropriate is the Age of Pisces, for however temperamental a sign this may be, it is an introverted sign greatly preferring peace and harmony to the kind of bloody upheaval and materialism which has dominated the present age. Those who argue that the sign has overcompensated from being too tolerant and ethereal into being too Virgoan, i.e., intolerant and materialistic, are avoiding the central problem which is that the characteristics of the signs which rule the historical ages bear only the flimsiest relationship to what we know of the history of the relevant period. This may partly be a result of the apparent failure of some of those who have written on the 'ages' from an astrological point of view to make any more than the most cursory study of history, but there is an astrological problem as well. The astrological problem arises because when we look at the precession of the equinoxes as an astrological phenomenon we are using sidereal signs, yet we are ascribing exactly the same meanings to these signs as we would to those of our conventional tropical zodiac. This confusion raises questions concerning the nature of astrology which are not within the province of this book, but we may find our main criticism of the theory of the precessional age in the study of history itself. A simple knowledge of history demonstrates that a strictly historical interpretation of the 'ages' breaks down, especially when attempted on a more precise level in the analysis of the supposed twelve 'sub-ages', each of about 240 years. [24] The symbols of the signs are too vague and the timing of the 'ages' too loose to translate effectively into a coherent view of history.

We have an alternative, however, which is to examine the process of precession psychologically, in order not to gain an insight into the 'ages' themselves so much as to create a myth through which we may understand how we have arrived at our own situation. [25] Thus we may see that the essential problem in the Age of Pisces has been the dissociation of psychic and physical functions, leading to the repression of the physical and its eruption in various forms of barbarity. Such an interpretation may seem more suitable, but we must face the fact that it only applies to our western culture. There is no universal cycle.

The only convincing evidence concerning the existence of the precessional ages is the coincidence of the entry of the vernal point into Pisces with the foundation of the Christian religion, a religion which is well known for its fish symbolism. However, even this evidence is weak, and based on an exclusively European view of the world, for in Tahiti and Tokyo the people had never heard of Christianity.

The Age of Aquarius and the myths surrounding it also fit firmly into a western concept of apocalyptic millenarianism — the expectation of an imminent catastrophe followed by a new dawn of peace and human happiness. If we look around we may see some justification for this belief at present in view of the destruction of the natural environment, the threat of nuclear holocaust, the encroachment of Uranian technology and Saturnian uniformity on our lives. Yet people in times past have always felt, with equal justification, that they were living in momentous times, embarking on a new era in human history. We look at current changes in the world and assume that we are moving from one astrological great age to another, but this may be nothing more than human vanity. Conveniently the theory of precessional ages has come along to provide the theoretical justification and a whole new astrological view of world history has been born.

Let us approach the problem from a new angle, from the point of the creation of a myth relevant to our present situation regardless of historical considerations. We may see the evolution of human ideas of divinity, using the precession of the ages as a model. Thus in the Age of Cancer the Earth was worshipped as Mother, the unifying spirit, and in the Age of Gemini the duality of spirit and matter was recognized with the worship of twin gods, such as the Egyptian Horus and his brother Set. In the Age of Taurus the physical nature was worshipped in the form of a bull, the Egyptian Apis or the Creton Minotaur; and in the Age of Aries God was anthropomorphized as the father god — Zeus or Jahweh. In the Age of Pisces God came down to earth in the form of Christ — half human, half god — and the Age of Aquarius should mark a progression from this. Perhaps we will recognize the presence of the Divine within us, rather than projecting it outward onto various superhuman gods and goddesses. Human beings will have to acknowledge themselves as the source of both good and evil, and of all other possibilities on earth. Just as the cycle of the planets contains all possibilities, so the circle of the individual nativity contains all individual potential contained within the circle of the collective as represented in the Great Year. However, as the source of potential for collective change lies within the individual, personal change must precede collective change. Change is not predetermined but depends upon individual free will, and the development of the individual capacity to make independent choices. The 'New Age' will therefore come about not as a result of a preordained pattern but as a result of the ability of humanity to realize its full potential.

How can we come to understand this potential? We can perhaps examine the issue in terms of our psychological understanding of mythology. We may also examine the natural phenomena of the world around us in order to understand physical cycles on a material level. That such cycles exist is, of course, now widely appreciated by modern scientists who until recently would have been sceptical of such claims.

A major clue to the natural cycles lies in the mathematics of Pythagoras as expressed in the relationship between the Great Year of Plato, the Precessional Year, and certain scientifically measured natural cycles. The critical number on the Platonic Year is 36, which Plato expressed as 36,000, the Assyrians as 3,600 and the Arabs as 360,000. To Plato this number was the one which contained the secret of change. There is a direct relationship between the mathematics of the Platonic Year and those of precession, a relationship which stems from the fact that the constellations precess over the vernal point by one degree in every 72 years (36 × 2). Perhaps, then, Plato was closer to describing the actualities of astronomical cycles than he realized. Perhaps, as has been suggested, Plato was using the mathematics of earlier philosophers who had in fact measured precession. This is conjecture, but what Plato cannot have known is that many natural cycles do indeed relate mathematically to his speculations. The majority of natural cycles measured by the Foundation for the Study of Cycles in the United States do in fact correlate with the length of the Platonic Year, and by implication, with the Precessional Year.[26] Many of these cycles, measuring phenomena from cotton prices to lynx abundance to Presbyterian Church membership, occur at intervals of 3.5 (36 ÷ 10), 9 (36 ÷ 4) or 18 (36 ÷ 2) years.

Clearly there is a scientifically observable relationship between natural cycles, and the philosophy of Plato, and the phenomena of precession. In this respect it would be as well to mention that Jung preferred to study precession in terms of the precession of the constellations rather than of the sidereal signs, a preference in which he has been followed by certain other astrologers, such as Robert Hand.[27] The precession of the constellations and fixed stars can give a precise system of timing and correlation in addition to supplying the mythological analogy of the signs, and has been used to provide an altogether more satisfactory historical account of precession. For example, in conventional accounts of the Age of Pisces, the Reformation — the greatest upheaval in European history — has no astrological correlation. But when viewed against the background of the constellations the Reformation was seen to occur when the vernal point had just passed the mid-point of the two fishes in the actual constellation of Pisces. Perhaps, then, it will be possible to understand the precessional cycle through a combination of scientific observation and Jung's psychological approach to mythology, generating a truer understanding based on a synthesis of reason and belief.

Summary
Modern astrology, in accepting the concept of Precessional Ages, has revived a belief in Great Years which may even predate the development of Babylonian astrology. But there are three fundamental differences between the Precessional Year and the old Platonic Year. The first is technical: the change from one cycle to

another is no longer dependent on the conjunction of all the planets at the point of creation. The second is theoretical: the concept of a cycle of endless growth and decay in human civilization, repeated to eternity in an infinite progression, has been replaced by the concept of a spiral in which even though we move through the cycle of the zodiac, when we come back to our starting-point we have in fact grown in terms of wisdom and experience. Modern ideas of progress have this intervened. The third difference is that predetermination has been replaced by free will, so that we are no longer chained to a world in which we are fated to repeat the mistakes of our forebears, but we may intervene in the flow of destiny by reforming ourselves, and in so doing affect the course of future cycles. Thus the individual is linked in an *active* sense to the collective, and the integration of natal with mundane astrology becomes a necessity.

References

1   Hesiod, *Works and Days* pp.18-19.
2   See Alexander Thom, *Megalithic Sites in Britain* London, 1971, and Gerald Hawkins, *Stonehenge Decoded* London, 1975.
3   Neugebauer, O. *The Exact Sciences in Antiquity* pp.36-48; Boyer, C. A. *History of Mathematics.*
4   Berossus, *Babyloniaca* book I, chap. 2.
5   McClain, E. G. *The Myth of Invariance* pp.10-14.
6   Cumont, F. *Astrology and Religion Among the Greeks and Romans* p.31; Campbell, J. *The Masks of God* pp.118-121; Lewis. G. C. *An Historical Survey of the Astronomy of the Ancients,* p.401.
7   Neugebauer, op.cit., p.95; McClain, op.cit., p.70; Graves, R. *The White Goddess* p.279.
8   Plato *Timaeus* chap. 21-23, 35-38; Plato *Republic* book VIII, chap. 545-6; Adams, J. *The Nuptial Number of Plato* p.77; Santillana, G. *The Origins of Scientific Thought* p.110.
9   Plato *Laws* book VI, chap. 758.
10 Macrobius *The Dream of Scipio* chap. 2.
11 Lewis, op.cit., pp.282-3.
12 Pingree, D. *The Thousands of Abu Ma'shar* pp.59-64.
13 Muller, M. *Ancient Hundu Astronomy and Chronology* pp.52.
14 Thorndike, L. *History of Magic and Experimental Science* vol. 2, chap. LXX, pp.897-8; vol. 4, chap. LII, pp.319-21.
15 Thorndike, op.cit., vol. 4, chap. XLII, p.108.

134 MUNDANE ASTROLOGY

16 Booker, J. *The Bloody Almanak.*
17 Henri de Boulainvilliers *Histoire de Movement de l'Apogée de Soleil . . .* Paris, 1711.
18 Campion, N. *Astrological Symbolism and Historical Periodization* London, 1983.
19 Macrobius, op.cit., book 2, chap. 11.
20 Pearce, A. J. *The Textbook of Astrology* vol. 1, p.10.
21 Reid, V. *Towards Aquarius* p.15.
22 Cheiro, *Book of World Predictions*, p. 170; *Prediction Annual* 1983, p. 85 David Williams, *AA Journal*, Vol. XX, No. 1; Alice Bailey, *The Externalisation of the Hierarchy*, p. 3-7; John Sturgess, *The Piscean Age and the Aquarian Age*, p. 1; A. Woldben, *After Nostradamus*, p. 24; *Astrologers' Quarterly*, Winter 1983; C. G. Jung, *The Sign of the Fishes*, p. 82; Dane Rudhyar, *The Lunation Cycle*, p. 149; Robert de Luce, *Constellation Astrology according to the Hindu System*; Charles Carter, *Introduction to Political Astrology*, p. 76; Vera Reid, *Towards Aquarius*, p. 8; Paul Councel, *Your Stars of Destiny*; Zip Dobyns, *The Zodiac as a Key to History*, p. 24; Cyril Fagan, *Zodiacs Old and New*, p. 29; Powell and Treadgold, *The Sidereal Zodiac*; Graha Laghav in *Directions in New Age Astrology*, p. 332; Sepharial, *Why the War Will End in 1917*; Sepharial, *The World Horoscope*; B. V. Raman, *A Manual of Hindu Astrology*, p. 51; Max Heindel, *Simplified Scientific Astrology*, p. 134-5; Robert Hand, *Essays on Astrology*; Rupert Gleadow, *Origins of the Zodiac*, p. 171.
23 Fagan. C. *Zodiacs Old and New* pp.18, 25, 27.
24 Carter, C. *An Introduction to Political Astrology* pp.75-87; Pottenger, Z. *The Zodiac as a Key to History* pp.13-17; Rudhyar, D. *Astrological Timing* pp.126-36.
25 Rudhyar, op.cit.; Jung, C. G. *Collected Works* vol. 9, part 11.
26 Dewey, E. *Cycles* pp.191-6.
27 Hand, R. *Essays on Astrology.*

Bibliography
ADAMS, J. *The Republic of Plato* Cambridge, 1902.
ADAMS, J. *The Nuptial Number of Plato* London, 1891.
ARISTOTLE *Politics* (trans, R. H. Rackham) London, 1932.
BEROSSUS *Babyloniaca* Malibu, 1978.
BOOKER, J. *The Bloody Almanak* London, 1643.

BOYER, C. *A History of Mathematics* New York, 1968.

BLAVATSKY, H. *The Secret Doctrine* London, 1893.

BLAVATSKY, H. *The Secret Doctrine of the Archaic Ages* London, 1931.

CAMPBELL, J. *The Masks of God: Oriental Mythology* London, 1973.

CAMPION, N. *The Great Year: Theories of Astrological Ages* London, 1983.

CAMPION, N. *Astrological Symbolism and Historical Periodization* London, 1983.

CAPRA, F. *The Turning Point* London, 1982.

CARTER, C. *An Introduction to Political Astrology* London, 1951.

CHEIRO *The Book of World Predictions* London, 1931.

CICERO *De Divinatione* (ed, E. E. Kellett) Cambridge, 1936.

COLLIN, R. *The Theory of Celestial Influence* London, 1954.

COOPER, J. C. *Yin and Yang* London, 1981.

COSTARD, G. *The Use of Astronomy in History and Chronology Exemplified* London, 1764.

CURTISS, H. A. and CURTISS, F. H. C. *The Message of Aquaria* Albuquerque, 1981; first published 1921.

CUMONT, F. *Astrology and Religion among the Greeks and Romans* New York, 1912.

DEWEY, E. and MANDINO, O. *Cycles: The Mysterious Forces that Trigger Events* London, 1971.

DIODORUS SICULUS *History* (trans. C. H. Oldfellow) London, 1933.

FAGAN, C. *Zodiacs Old and New* London, 1951.

GLEADOW, R. *The Origin of the Zodiac* London, 1968.

GRAVES, R. *The Greek Myths* London, 1953.

GRAVES, R. *The White Goddess* London, 1961.

HAND, R. *Essays on Astrology* Rockport, Mass: 1982.

HEINDEL, M. *Rosicrucian Cosmoconception* California, 1911.

HEINDEL, M. *The Message of the Stars* London, 1918.

HEINDEL, M. *Simplified Scientific Astrology* California, 1919.

HESIOD, *Works and Days* (trans. S. Butler) London, 1923.

JUNG, C. G. *Collected Works* vol. 9, part II, London, 1951.

KEPLER, T. *Dreams of the Future* London, 1963.

LEVI, *The Aquarian Gospel Of Jesus the Christ* London, 1965.

LEWIS, G. C. *An Historical Survey of the Astronomy of the Ancients* London, 1862.

MACROBIUS, *Commentory on the Dream of Scipio* (trans. W. H. Stahl) New York, 1952.

MANUEL, F. *Shapes of Philosophical History* London, 1965.

MASSEY, G. *The Natural Genesis* London, 1883.

MCCLAIN, E. *The Myth of Invariance* London, 1978.

MULLER, M. *Ancient Hindu Astronomy and Chronology* Oxford, 1862.

NEUGEBAUER, O. *The Exact Sciences in Antiquity* Oxford, 1957.

NORELLI-BACHELET, P. *The Gnostic Circle* New York, 1978.

PEARCE, A. J. *The Textbook of Astrology* vol. 1, London, 1879.

PEARCE, A. J. *The Science of the Stars* London, 1881.

PINGREE, D. *The Astrological History of Masha'allah* Cambridge, 1971.

PINGREE, D. *The Thousands of Abu Ma'shar* London, 1968.

PLATO *Laws* (trans. R. G. Bury) London, 1926.

PLATO *Timaeus (trans. R. G. Bury)* London, 1929.

PLATO *Republic* (trans. P. Shorey) London, 1930.

PLUTARCH 'Life of Sulla' in *Lives* (ed, R. M. Hutchins) London, 1957.

POPPER, K. *The Open Society and its Enemies* London, 1945.

POTTENGER, Z. *The Zodiac as a Key to History* Los Angeles, 1968.

PRESTON, E. W. *The Earth and its Cycles* London, 1931.

REID, V. *Towards Aquarius* London, 1944.

RUDHYAR, D. *The Lunation Cycle* California, 1967.

RUDYHAR, D. *Astrological Timing* London, 1969.

RUDYHAR, D. *Occult Preparations for the New Age*

SANTILLANA, G. di. *Hamlets Mill* London, 1969.

SANTILLANA, G. di. *The Origins of Scientific Thought* vol. 1, London, 1961.

SEPHARIAL, *The World Horoscope* London, 1965.

SEPHARIAL, *Why the War will End in 1917* London, 1914.

SPENGLER, O. *The Decline of the West* vols. 1, 2, London, 1934.

THORNDIKE, L. *History of Magic and Experimental Science* 7 vols., New York 1923.

TIPPET, M. *Moving Into Aquarius* London, 1959.

TOYNBEE, A. *A Study of History* abridgement of vols. 1-6, London, 1948.

TREVELYAN, G. *A Vision of the Aquarian Age.*

WINCHELL, A. *Sketches of Creation* London, 1870.

6.
CYCLES IN PRACTICE
Part 1: The Concept of Cycles

Charles Harvey

'Time is the flowing image of Eternity'

Plato

'All astrological effects can be understood in terms of the harmonics
of cosmic periods.'

John Addey

The previous chapters have placed mundane astrology in an historical
and psychological perspective. In this chapter we will look at the
concept of cycles that is now re-emerging at the centre of astrology.
Cycles are described as the means by which the enfolded, infinite
and eternal potentiality of all ideas is unfolded in the dimension
of Time. The different phases of any cycles are seen as representing
the sequence of processes through which any idea passes in its total
unfoldment. We see how 'harmonics', the unified cyclic approach
developed by Addey, promises to allow us systematically to identify
and understand the main ebb and flow of ideas in the collective
unconscious of humanity. By extension such methods are seen to
allow us both an increased understanding of the present dynamics
of nations and groups, and the possibility of a constructive method
of forecasting their future trends and developments based on sound
comprehensive principles. Such types of forecasting are seen as
powerful tools for raising society's consciousness and understanding
of individual and collective life.

We will examine the ways of interpreting and applying these cycles and some of the important first steps which have begun to be made in constructive forecasting by Barbault in France, and explore the significance of cycles for national leaders. A summary is given of the general cultural, social, economic, and political significance of each of the main planetary synods. A brief account of non-astrological cycle studies and of their potential significance for astrology is given at the end of the chapter.

The Great Year re-emerges

Having been almost entirely neglected for several centuries the cyclical view of the world, which seemed so self-evident to the Assyrians and Greeks, and indeed in some form to almost all early cultures, is now reclaiming the attention not only of astrologers but of the whole scientific consciousness of the west. In almost every area of study and research, the value of using 'wave models', rhythms, and cycles to describe the universe has become once again apparent. From biology and ecology to theoretical physics and cosmology scientists have been returning, albeit unconsciously, to this ancient and fundamental conception of the Great Year and all that it implies, to the perception that life, the cosmos, is indeed one vibrating whole. And, though as yet few non-astrologers realize it, the implication must be that it is these circles, cycles, and spirals of the heavens and the heavenly bodies which unfold the eternal music of life within the circle of time on the sphere of space. The planetary cycles are thus the threads of eternity which weave the great tapestry of life in time.

Although in theory astrology has always been the torch-bearer of this grand cyclical view of the universe, we have, since the days of the great Morin de Villefranche, let our torch burn very low. We have allowed a preoccupation with minutiae and with the particulars and fragmentary aspects of our tradition to distract us from the sheer magnitude and power of the vision that astrology offers. In consequence mundane astrology has over the past centuries gradually lost sight of the ancient vision of Plato and his predecessors, with its emphasis upon the collective importance of all the planetary synods taken together.

The result of this neglect is that for all its post-mortem pretensions (which claim retrospectively to an understanding of every aspect of world events from earthquakes to military coups and the price of gold), the success record of astrologers at making intelligible *forecasts* of future trends is, with honourable exceptions, fairly ignominious. A glance at the valiant, conventional attempts to make mundane forecasts which appear in the astrological and popular press, reveals just sufficient rays of sunlight to keep us faithful, but also sufficient to show up the very thickness of the intervening fog! No doubt this is a major reason why so few astrologers have, until recently, been drawn into working in this area.

However the tide is now rapidly turning and, thanks to the pioneering work of a handful of distinguished philospher-astrologers, the central place of cycles in astrology and all that they imply is now beginning to be generally recognized and taught once again. This approach is bringing about a regeneration of astrology in general, as well as promising to make possible the resurrection of mundane astrology in particular. The most outstanding contributions in this field of cyclical astrology have been made by John Addey (1920-82) in Britain, André Barbault (1921-) in France, and by the French-born Dane Rudhyar (1895-) in the USA.

The hierarchy of cycles and their interpretation
The overall picture that is re-emerging is of a universe which is unfolding in time through a great interlocking hierarchy of cycles of Ideas (Ideas in a Platonic sense that is). In this scheme each cycle has its own particular and unique place and purpose. The general significance of some of the cycles is already emerging whilst others still remain to be clearly defined.

The important implication of this picture for mundane astrology is that if we are to understand any one fragment of the picture, for example a particular 'event', we need ideally to see it in the context of its place in the complete tapestry of interweaving cycles, rather than just in terms of one or two cycles as we do at present. Likewise when it comes to attempting any kind of systematic forecasting we are going to need to develop ways of considering the future interweaving of whole hierarchies of cycles and charts rather than treating them in relative isolation as we do at present. How this is done most effectively is one of the great challenges of the next few years. As we shall see later, work on various forms of composite cycles has already begun. No doubt the use of computers with multi-colour graphics will soon prove of enormous value in this work.

Equally this cyclical model implies that we need to develop a far greater clarity as to the essential meaning of each of the planetary principles, their combinations, and cycles. We need to develop a much more precise understanding of what each cycle is describing, so that we can minimize the use of inappropriate tools. As Dennis Elwell so graphically puts it in another context, we can obtain some measure of temperature using a barometer because temperature and pressure are interrelated, but it is much more efficient to use a thermometer. All too often in astrology we are unclear about the appropriate use of any particular tool due to the vast array of charts and techniques from which we can choose. If we can decide what each refers to, and for what it is best used, we will be half way to establishing mundane work on a sound basis.

At this stage it may be useful to look at a brief summary of some of the main cycles currently used and what appears to be their main value and application.

Table A: A summary of some of the cycles used in mundane astrology (For a general overview of mundane astrology this needs to be considered together with Appendix IV, pp.481-2).

	Cycle	Coverage/Application	Comments	See
A	The Hindu Yugas 432,000 years +	Plotting major historical, evolutionary cycles	Theoretical, of unproven value	Chap. 3
B	Plato's Great Year, 36,000 yrs alleged	Plotting major cycles of civilization and culture	Now seen as possible basis for integrated concept (see G)	Chap. 3 Chap.5
C	Precessional Great Year: 25,868 years	Plotting major cycles of civilization and culture	A modern tool unrecorded pre-1870: unproven value	Chap. 5 App. III
D	Cycles between 'collective' planets, Uranus, Neptune, Pluto	Main phases of development in cultures and civilizations (centuries of time)	Suggestive clues encourage further historic study	Chap. 6
E	Declination cycles Uranus, Neptune, Pluto	As D but particulary related to Earth as a whole.	Deserve careful study	Chap. 13
F	Cycles of major planets into and through signs	Changes of social emphasis and dominant values cultivated	Mark major nuances of social/cultural development	Chap. 6
G	Cycles between social and collective planets Jupiter, Saturn and Uranus, Neptune, Pluto	Focusing major economic/ cultural developments to specific decades/years	Promising tool for all forecasting: needs developing	Chap. 6

H	Cyclical Index of Gouchon and Barbault	Plotting critical periods of years from concentration /dispersal of planets	Modern quantification of ancient concept highly promising	Chap. 6
I	'The World Horoscope', so called	Alleged to trace cycle of 'ruling planets' for each year	Non-astronomical: needs to be evaluated systematically	Chap. 13
J	Collective planet cycles in national charts, e.g. USA	Mark critical national periods and possible international repercussions	Barry Lynes shows the importance of USA and Russian cycles for world	Chap. 6
K	Cycles of intermediate Mercury, Venus, Mars	Local 'triggers' focusing timing of changes/crises to periods of days/weeks	Barbault demonstrates their power as timers of slower processes	Chap. 6 Chap. 14
L	Annual cycles of Sun: ingresses and with planets	Focuses timing and location of long-term trends within the year	Valuable 'close-up' tools to use with longer-term cycles	Chap. 9
M	Solar cycles with other planets	Key factor in close timing to a week or so	Barbault demonstrates their great value	Chap. 6 Chap. 14
N	Lunar cycles: New, Full, and Quarter Moons	Fine timing and localizing of social/economic trends to within weeks	Powerful 'fine grain' tools: keep in perspective	Chap. 9
O	Daily cycles of planets and angles	Final timer of precipitation of 'events' in time at given location	Poorly understood: needs integrating with all above	Chap. 6

The hierarchy of cycles used in mundane astrology

The table above gives an outline of the main cyclical techniques that are currently employed in attempting to assess mundane trends and to interrelate cosmic and cultural movements. They are presented in approximate order of 'magnification'. The cycles at the top of the table are like low-powered telescopes giving us a picture of very broad sections of time ('broad' by human standards that is — on a cosmic scale even the largest of these cycles are fairly ephemeral). As we work our way down the list we are, as it were, looking through more and more powerful telescopes at smaller and smaller areas of time. We should not forget that without the broader perspective of the low-powered tools, the fine-grain detail of the high-powered tool, will lack any context and could produce a very misleading picture. Today's headline 'crisis' may not even merit a mention in the annual news round-up!

Whilst all of these cycles have their advocates, very little systematic work has been done to evaluate many of them until recently.

As in natal analysis there are two main and *complementary* ways in which we can approach the interpretation of these cycles. We can reflect upon the celestial harmonies as abstract principles and formal causes, or we can look at them empirically in terms of the effects they are most likely to manifest within a given time, place, and condition, i.e., in terms of a particular nation, society and culture at a particular place on the earth's surface, in a particular period of its development.

The first is the approach of the musical conductor who can 'read music'. This allows us potentially to consider this heavenly music in the abstract, in its pure archetypal potential, without any particular human and social context. In this way we might look at a particular millenium, century, decade, year, quarter, month, week, day, simply in terms of the pure planetary, aspectual, and cyclical *principles* involved in the abstract; as a particular interweaving and unfoldment of cosmic ideas, as pure forms. This is rather like listening to Bach or a piece of eighteenth-century classical music which is appealing in some mysterious way to the abstract ideas within us. The ideal of such an approach awakens the ineffable universal archetypal patterns within us which are beyond words, images or pictures, and beyond the particular effects and 'probable manifestations' of the textbook reading. Whilst this is the more difficult approach to interpretation it is the one which will tend to give us the deeper understanding of a particular situation because it remains, in a real sense, closer to the principles. Even more important, such an approach, in allowing us to see and intuit the abstract potential of a period, enables us to see the deeper potential for good which lies behind even the greatest of seeming catastrophes.

We can look on all such cycles as representing the dynamic aspect of the creative principles of the universe. They are, as it were, the means by which the unific Ideas, represented by the planets, fixed stars, and so on, unfold themselves in time, giving rise to appropriate psychological processes, manifestations, and events within individuals and the collective.

Just as we can consider each planetary principle as representing a creative Idea, so too we can consider each pair of planets as forming a single idea, rather than two separate ones. Thus the 'real' meaning of Neptune-Pluto as a duad, i.e., as one polarity of principle, is not Pluto + Neptune but Pluto/Neptune as one idea which is unfolding from its unity, at conjunction, to its fruition and objectification at the opposition and thence disseminating back into its seed from unity once again.

In general terms we can say that the longer a cycle, the more fundamental, universal and long lasting will be its importance; the shorter the cycle the more it will tell us about particulars and ephemera. However, the shorter cycles also serve to trigger the slower, long-term cycles into manifestation. The importance of this triggering function can be seen in Chapter 14 on cycles during World War Two. Whilst the conjunction phase of each of these cycles is always the key, seed phase, as we shall see shortly, the sub-harmonics, i.e., phases, of each of these cycles is of great importance. Considering the table on pp.140-141 in greater detail we have:

A   The Yugas. These have been discussed in the last chapter and are outside the scope of practical mundane astrology at present!

B   The Ancient Great Year of 36,000 years is perhaps the longest cycle we can usefully take. This might be considered to begin with the total ebb and flow of *all* planets from approximately one point (0° Cancer/Capricorn according to the Chaldeans), expanding and contracting about this point from maximum, 'super conjunction', concentration, to a maximum dispersal of all the planets. This is a theoretical cycle which has yet to be identified in detail. Barbault's modern version of this principle on a smaller timescale is given below (see H).

C   The Great Precessional Age of about 25,000 years. This is said to mark out major shifts of civilizations, though the kind of historical evidence educed for this at present is, as we have seen (Chapter 5 and Appendix III), still very naive and contradictory. Nonetheless the cyclical movement of the earth's poles against the fixed stars would seem an important cycle in theory and ought to have considerable significance with regard to the larger pattern of the earth's evolution. Dr Christine Janis suggests that the very pattern of evolution on earth has been, and presumably is being, dictated by a larger version of this cycle. She shows that vertebrate evolution parallels a twelve-fold zodiacal division of the Great, Great, Great, Great Precessional Year of 518,400,000 earth years. Amongst other things she shows astounding correlations between three of the four major extinction periods, the most well known being that of the dinosaurs and 0° of the cardinal signs in this precessional scheme. [27]

D   The major planetary synods Pluto, Neptune, Uranus, in their dance one with another and all three combined. The cycles of these outer 'collective' planets would seem to be the great shapers of mankind's collective development. The interaction of all three in harmonic (i.e., aspect) patterns and mid-point combinations deserves deep consideration as we shall see later.

E   The planets' declination cycles form the basis of one major 'school' of mundane astrology, that of C. C. Zain (Elbert Benjamin). [9] Since the equator is the plane of the earth's rotation it can be seen to symbolize mankind's collective orientation to the universe as a whole. It thus seems very reasonable to suppose that the moment when a planet crosses the plane of our rotation must mark a very important intersection of ideas. These are discussed in Chapter 13.

F   Despite the negative findings of Gauquelin, Addey et al. in relation to natal astrology, the movement of the outer planets individually around the zodiac and through the signs would appear to be of great importance in 'bringing in' the archetypal zodiacal ideas from the collective, as anyone who keeps their ears atuned to the 'sounds of the time' will rapidly discover (see Chapter 8).

G   The movements of the middle planets Saturn and Jupiter in relation to the outer collective planets, and in their own twenty-year synod with each other and through the cycle of the elements (which last about 860 years) have always been considered to play the crucial role of the Great Chronocrators, the 'rulers of time'.

H   Barbault's 'Little Great Year' of about 498 years. [7] This measures the period between maximum concentrations of the five outer planets (Pluto, Neptune, Uranus, Saturn, Jupiter) within a narrow sector of the zodiac. This occurs within 100 years of each NE-0-PL. Thus following the NE-0-PL of 1891/2 there was the UR-0-PL of 1965/6, and at the present time (1982/3) the concentration of all planets within 72°. The last time such a concentration occurred was in 1485 at the point when the western world began its great voyages of exploration into the physical environment.

I   The World Horoscope, which was elaborated by Sepharial [45] under the name of Hebrew astrology or Kabbalistic astrology is based on a system of rulerships for each year, starting at the Aries ingress of that year. A Great, Precessional Year of 25,920 years, is divided into sixty sub-divisions of 432 years. These in turn are divided into twelve cycles of 36 years each. Each 36-year period is under the main rulership of one planet, in reverse order of the days of the week. Thus the Venus period is said to have began in 1801, the Jupiter in 1837, the Mercury in 1873, the Mars in 1909, the Moon in 1945, and the Sun in 1981, and so on. The rulerships of the individual years start with the main ruler and then follow in the Chaldean Order of the planets: Saturn, Jupiter, Mars, Sun, Venus, Mercury, Moon. These do not of course relate to any kind of astronomical cycle as such but could relate to a natural sequence in the unfoldment of planetary principles. The authors have not studied this cycle. The rulership by Mars of the 36 years from 1909 to spring 1945 almost exactly spanning both world wars is provocative!

J The transit cycles of the outer, collective, planets through the natal chart of a country, and of its leader, are always important for a nation, and are one of the most valuable tools for forecasting the main shifts in national affairs. But no nation is an island unto itself and, as Barry Lynes[31] lucidly shows in his pioneering works *The Next 20 Years, Astroeconomics,* and *Secret Astrology: Russia's Past and Future,* these transits through the USA and Russian charts seem to take on an international significance. We would imagine that major transits through the charts of other leading industrial nations such as the UK, Japan and W. Germany, and strategically important ones such as Israel and Saudi Arabia must reflect clearly in the world at large.

K The shorter cycles of Mars and the inner planets clearly have an important role to play. They appear to act as local 'triggers' to the long-term outer planetary cycles. However, because of retrogradation these cycles can be very complex. For instance, Rudhyar has pointed to the importance of the long stay of Mars in one sign. Recently, the long stay of Mars in early Libra, on the Ascendant of the UK chart was one of the factors that coincided with the Falklands war. Such 'minor' cycles clearly deserve further historic investigation.

L The annual cycles appears to be the key cycle which modulates *all* of the other longer cycles, i.e., it translates them into the terms of our major regulatory rhythm of the seasons and 'earths' them, as it were. This is the cycle of our planet Earth in relation to the Sun. In some senses, the year appears to be mankind's natural maximum 'attention span', our natural unit of planning, preparing, accounting, etc. It is the predominant pulse to the life of mankind as a whole.

M   The Sun's cycle in relation to each of the other planets, and particularly to those from Jupiter outwards is, as we shall see, of great importance in precipitating the effects of the slower cycles. Whilst the -0- of Sun to planet is the most powerful phase of this cycle it also triggers off planetary patterns by other aspects and notably by the hard-angle aspects, -45-, -90-, -135-, -180-.

N   The monthly cycle of the Moon from New to Full and back again marks out the main 'beats' within the annual cycle. It modulates the higher-level energies to our span of consciousness, at a mass and individual level. This is apparent in the menstrual cycle, the cycle of plant growth etc., and would also appear to be an important factor in changes of political mood, movements on commodity markets, etc., though few attempts have been made to quantify these, or other cycles for that matter, on a statistical basis. Though fine-grain refinements, other lunar phases, notably the 'Quarter Moons', will undoubtedly have their place in the overall scheme.

O   The daily cycle turns the Earth through all possible relationships with each of the planets. It sees all planets rise, culminate, set, reach their nadir and rise once more. In so doing it is unfolding the whole unitary idea of each planetary principle. In the sub-harmonic rhythms, the aspects and micro-aspects, of this daily cycle are the final keys to the precise timing and release of ideas and 'events' into the individual and collective.

All cycles are identical in their essential nature
There is an important philosophical and conceptual fact that we may note at this point. If we consider any of these cycles, we will see that there is a sense in which they are all essentially identical. For during each of these complete cycles the *whole* cosmic orchestra is involved. Each cycle sweeps through the whole of the zodiac. It will aspect, i.e., 'look at', every planet, fixed star and sensitive point, from every angle. Thus in a very literal sense each microcosmic cycle unfolds the whole macrocosm, in terms of itself. Each plays out its same processes, at many different octave intervals, all spiralling together in an unfolding dance which is ever the same, yet always different.

Interpreting the cycles: static and dynamic approaches; inner and outer cycles
Any cycle can be interpreted in two ways. In the first static and

'structural' approach, we adopt the techniques of natal astrology and study a cycle in terms of charts set for the precise moment of each phase, e.g. -0-, -180-, 120, -90-, etc. In the second approach we study each cycle as a unitary, dynamic and indeed 'organic' unfolding process. In the first case we 'freeze-frame' a key moment in the continuous cycle of unfoldment and study that moment as we would any birth chart. This chart can thus be seen as the 'birth' of an idea, or as the birth of a particular phase in the unfoldment of that idea. In the second case we simply use the times of each phase to construct a timetable of when the ideas enfolded within the cycle will be unfolded. Later in this chapter we will be looking at the value and application of both of these approaches.

In studying maps set out for the exact phases of each cycle we will be particularly interested in the relationship, i.e., the angular distance, between the cycle planets and the other planets. This will give us some measure of the interaction of this particular idea with all the other planetary, stellar, and zodiacal ideas for the coming phase in the cycle. In the second approach we are simply concerned with the cycle itself, in relative isolation, and with plotting it out on the calendar so as to note when important phases in the unfoldment of this idea will occur.

We should note at this point that this complex interweaving of transit cycles is only half the picture. These 'outer' transits are interacting with countless individual organisms of varying complexity, each of which has its own *inner* life cycles. Thus just as each one of us has our own chart, so too every organism, group, nation, organization of any kind has its own chart. This chart has an inner life of its own. As a microcosm this life is unfolding within itself on its own inner time scale. This inner unfoldment of a group can be studied in exactly the same way as we would human unfoldment i.e., through the various different systems of progressions and directions, the inner cycles of the natal chart.

An informed and constructive forecast of the likely potential for growth and manifestation for a nation or group can thus best be assessed from a consideration of the dynamic interaction between these inner cycles of unfoldment and the outer transit cycles.

Here we should remember that, as in any natal chart, how the organism will respond to particular transit cycles will depend upon its own natal 'tuning'. A chart which contains a strong SA-NE contact will inevitably resonate strongly with the SA-NE cycle as a whole.

A strong JU-UR aspect at birth will 'tune in' a nation to the subsequent phases of all future JU-UR cycles. This will be studied in greater detail later.

Harmonics and the work of John Addey

As we have seen, the idea that all the activities of our manifest, mundane world are ordered and regulated by the cycles of the heavens was a fundamental part of the teaching of Plato and the Neo-Platonists. It was equally the vision that consciously inspired John Addey. His life-work on the harmonic basis of astrology[1] was, in effect, a development and a demonstration of the Neo-Platonist concept that the heavenly bodies are the 'first-born thoughts of God' ('born', that is, in the sense that they are primary lives of the manifested cosmos).[1a] As a philosopher as well as an astrologer, John Addey's abiding concern was to understand by what laws these 'primary lives' unfold themselves throughout space and time. The result of his study and reflection upon a vast array of statistical studies produced his now famous law that: '**All astrological effects can be understood in terms of the harmonics of cosmic periods'**. Addey's insights are so fertile in their implications, and so central to the way in which astrology, in all its branches, is developing, that it would be as well to pause at this point and look briefly at his theory in greater detail.

Addey's law makes five main points:

1. Apart from the heavenly bodies themselves, all the tools that we use in astrology can be seen to be *circles or cycles of relationship*. Thus the circle of the aspects, the houses, the signs, and the various other circles we may choose to use (such as the circle of the equator, or the horizon, or the constellations) are all means by which we are enabled to speak about the relative positions of particular points to one another.
2. The way we employ each of these circles/cycles is identical in its essential features. In each case we are using a circle to measure *relationships* to a given starting-point, e.g., 0° Aries, the ascendant, a nodal point, another heavenly body, etc.
3. The way we express this relationship within each of these circles is in terms of specific *number divisions, i.e. harmonics* of the circle. Thus when we speak of a planet as being in trine (one-third of the circle relationship) aspect to another planet, we are

saying that there is a 'third harmonic' relationship between the two bodies. Likewise we can see that planets in Leo and Sagittarius have a trine, third harmonic, relationship to Aries, and that planets in the corresponding houses, the fifth and ninth, will have a third-harmonic relationship to the ascendant (see 4 below for further details).

4. The essential means by which we establish the qualitative content of these relationships within any of these circles, and can thereby interpret them, is rooted in an understanding of Ideal Numbers. Numbers in this Pythagorean sense represent archetypal processes and powers of unfoldment within the cosmos. Thus, to take the example of the third harmonic in the last paragraph, the number Three is related to the idea of life, vitality and enjoyment, and hence to what motivates us and moves us to action. In harmonic terms we can say that, for example, the trine aspect, the sign Leo, and the fifth house, (which are the sign and house in trine to their starting points), will all share a strong third-harmonic quality. Clearly in the case of the signs and the houses this third-harmonic quality is also overlaid with some element of the number Five. Unfortunately space does not permit a further coverage of these ideas; they can be followed up elsewhere.[1, 21, 22]

Cycles and the concept of time: what is a cycle?

Since astrology is in essence the study of the unfoldment of cycles, it is important that we attempt to get to grips with what it is that a cycle represents. First we must recognize that rhythms and cycles are basic to all life and to our very concepts of time and existence. We find cycles all around us. From our own heart beat and breathing to the cycles of day and night, and the annual seasons, which form the ground base of our lives, to the vast ebb and flow of civilizations, of climate, and of geological and evolutionary epochs, which have shaped our development in prehistoric times, we are confronted by the picture of endless growth and decay, waxing and waning, birth and growth followed by decay and death. What then are cycles and the time in which they manifest? Are time and cycles in some senses one and the same thing?

This is one of the central mysteries of life which has taxed the minds of philosophers since the beginning of time. It is a mystery which lies at the heart of astrology and cycle studies, and therefore demands some consideration, even if no final answer can be given. For the astrologer perhaps the most satisfying solution is that given by Plato who suggested that outside of time, in eternity, all things simply *are* in their pure complete essence. In eternity there is no becoming but only Being, a state in which all that is subsists as pure, pristine Ideas. Plato saw time, as we experience it, as 'the flowing image of eternity', i.e., as both the medium, as it were, through which that which eternally is can become objectively known and manifest and also the necessary product of the process of becoming. Looked at in modern guise we might say that when viewed from the next dimension beyond time, all things are in fact coexistent, 'simultaneous', or simply 'as one'. There is of course considerable evidence for this view both from the experience of mystics, and seers, such as Nostradamus, and more mundanely from reports of those who have come close to the point of death. Such people have repeatedly reported suddenly seeing their *whole life* played before them *in an instant,* something which is clearly impossible within our normal concept of time. Indeed, if time were not in some way related to eternity, and both to the idea of cycles, the very act of attempting to make astrological forecasts would be illusory.

Definition

Bearing this in mind we might define a cycle as the progressive unfoldment and expression in time of some idea or unity which essentially subsits outside of time. A cycle unfolds and expresses its seed potential through a series of phases to its fullest flowering and fruition, and then back, returning through a process of distribution decay into its seed form again. We are all familiar with this idea from the cycle of the seasons and from the growth and decay of plants. Astrologically it is perhaps most familiar from the idea of the lunation cycle with its cycle of change from New Moon to First Quarter, to Full Moon, Last Quarter, and back to New Moon again. Indeed it was the book *The Lunation Cycle* by Dane Rudhyar[43] which was the first attempt in modern times to reawaken the English-speaking world to the concept of cycles in astrology.

To test our understanding of this definition we can consider the following question. Is an acorn the oak tree's way of producing a new oak, or is an oak tree an acorn's way of producing a new acorn? In a sense this paradox holds the key to a fuller understanding of cycles. Upon reflection, it becomes clear that we cannot really understand the unitive meaning of a cycle within our normal perspective of time. For the norm is to be constantly separating out different parts of our circle of experience and placing value judgements on them. We almost inevitably tend to see birth and growth as 'good' and decay and death as 'bad'. In fact they are all part of the acorn-oak tree complete process.

The most powerful implication of this model is that every seed moment contains enfolded within it all that it will subsequently unfold in time. Thus we can see the truth in the dictum 'in our beginning is our end'. Correctly read, the chart for the beginning of any cycle contains within it all that will subsequently unfold in time. This of course must be closely related to the principles at the foundations of horary astrology (see Chapter 13).

Cycles and astrological judgement
Such a cyclical view of astrology and manifestation gives rise to important considerations for us as budding mundane astrologers. For with our own inevitable personal, political and cultural biases, it is only with this larger perspective that we can attempt to see cycles whole. Without such an approach our perception of current affairs and the threads of history will all too readily become even more distorted than need be. I was forcefully reminded of this fact recently when reading a study of the Jupiter-Saturn cycle. To the writer, obviously of strongly Liberal-Democrat persuasion, the Jupiter expansionary, benevolent, social-welfare, aspect of this cycle was essentially 'good' and the Saturn cut-backs, restraints, self-reliance aspects were essentially 'bad' (and by implication part of a big business 'plot'!). This is like saying 'winter bad, spring good', or considering one sign in the zodiacal cycle more worthy than another! All signs and seasons are necessary and essential or they simply would not continue to exist! Seeing cycles in their totality can help us to cultivate an approach which attempts to see things for what they are, and as part of a larger scheme.

Cultivating such an approach can allow us, as we look ahead, to see the kinds of things that the cycles say the world (or a particular group, company, or nation) *needs,* or will be obliged, to be doing at a particular time, rather than seeing either doom-and-gloom, or pie-in-the-sky. As Plotinus observed: 'Those who find fault with the Cosmos make the mistake of considering it in part'; or as Alexander Pope so eloquently expressed it, in what might be part of the astrologer's creed:

All are but parts of one stupendous whole,
Whose body Nature is, and God the soul,
All Nature is but Art, unknown to thee;
All Chance, Direction, which thou canst not see.
All partial evil, Universal Good.

Interpreting the complete aspect cycle

We now need to consider how we can interpret these cycles in practice. We will first look at the dynamic approach, examining in some detail the principles being unfolded at each particular phase of any cycle. Then we will look at the interpretation of the cycles as seen in the charts set for the moment of their exact phase.

A summary of the main phases of the aspect cycle

Whilst some cycles may move so rapidly from seed to flower, from midnight to noon, that the intermediate stages are barely distinguishable, every cycle will go through the same series of stages. By distinguishing these and what processes they represent we can quickly come to at least an abstract understanding of any particular relationship between any two points that we care to consider. And this is of course what the aspects represent: the different formative phases and powers in that cycle, each of which is essential and necessary to the development of the whole, but none of which, in truth, can be taken in isolation.

Before we look at this cycle in detail it will be as well to take a quick overview of the main phases of any cycle.

The first major division of any cycle is into its waxing and waning halves. These can be seen symbolically as starting from mid-winter (0° Capricorn) and from the point of the first stages of fruition in mid-summer (0° Cancer).

1. The waxing phase from 0°-180° relates to the process of growth, development, expansion, moving towards fruition. In terms of the mass psychology when a cycle is in this phase, and particularly when a majority of cycles are in this phase, it produces a sense of optimism, buoyancy, initiative, extravagance, a willingness to take risks, to explore, to begin enterprises.

2. The waning phase from 180°-0° relates to the process of distribution, dissemination, and decay, of the return to the seed form again. When a cycle is in this phase, and particularly when

a majority of cycles are in this phase, it produces within the collective, an increasing sense of caution, withdrawal, pessimism, an emphasis on consolidation, conservation, economy, cutting out of fat and deadwood.

Looking at the sub-divisions of these two phases we can particularly distinguish:

Waxing phase — emphasis on individual initiative:
   0°   A seed idea is initiated. Death and rebirth. New upward and outward movement begins.
  60°   The idea begins to establish itself and work actively in the world. Strong growth.
  90°   A first 'crisis' point as the idea of the cycle begins to manifest, testing and strengthening itself in the world by overcoming challenges and obstacles.
120°   The idea flowers, is accepted, and begins to move and motivate people strongly.
180°   As the fruit sets and is given objective expression in the world, the idea is confronted by a need to reconcile views and possibilities.

Waning phase — emphasis on collective needs:
240°   The motive power of the seed is now seen as fruit and becomes a desirable, and hence motivating, idea in society.
270°   A new challenge to prove its worth demands that the idea justify itself in the eyes of the world, and reassert itself.
300°   The idea consolidates itself in the daily work and rhythms of society.
   0°   Death of the old cycle and a rebirth of the idea in a new guise.

Having familiarized ourselves with this broad outline let us now look at this cycle in detail.

A detailed look at the cycle of aspects in mundane astrology
Most readers will no doubt have a working understanding of the aspects as normally delineated. In the following I have emphasized the interpretation of the aspects as a sequential process. I have also stressed the numerical interpretation of each aspect on the lines pioneered by John Addey[1] and included the fifth and seventh series

of aspects, the quintile and septile. The important ninth harmonic series (40°, 80°, 160°) which seems to be related to different stages of creative fruition (cf. the -120°- phase which is part of this series) has had to be omitted here for reasons of space. (See Harvey[22] for further material on these and other phases.)

The testing ground for all the planetary cycles and their phases is of course both past and contemporary history. However just as so much of history is presented as lists of events so equally the different news media constantly bombard us with lists of 'events' and current happenings. Such analysis as there is by experts and commentators on the causes and significance of these 'events' is inevitably limited to material causes: economic, political, climatic, etc. Astrology on the other hand is concerned with formal causes, with the underlying ideas, principles, and processes which are expressing themselves in the world. The astrologer sees the departure of the Shah of Iran from the oldest empire in the world, and the earthquake that accompanied that event, as all manifestations and expressions, at different levels, of the formative idea of Uranus, of change, shake-up, which was touching off the nation's chart as this time. Such events are signals, signposts, of the ideas at work within the collective.

For the purposes of tracing out the significance of these outer 'events', turning-points, fruition, and crises of a cycle, it is usually quite adequate to look at the conjunction, opposition, trine and square phases in any cycle. These will usually give us a graphic picture and timing of the most significant periods for the manifestation of the idea symbolized in the cycle. But if we wish to understand something of the inner significance of a cycle, and of world events, then some of the so-called 'minor' aspects can, in some senses, be even more instructive. Thus the -45- and -135- aspects always mark significant testing moments within a cycle, for at this point the seed idea is asserting and manifesting itself in the world. Likewise the -30- and -150- aspects, with their ambigious dynamic, often mark periods of passing uncertainty, strain, instability and change. But it is particularly those aspects that are the divisions of the circle by 5, 7 and 9 that indicate something of the deeper creative impulses, inspirational factors, and formative forces which are potentially available to the individual and the collective at any time. In particular the aspects based on 5 and 7 have a great deal to do with the creative and inspirational aspects of life.

It is probably easier to perceive the underlying significance of these lesser-known phases in the case of the six slowest planetary synods (see next section), and especially those of NE-PL, UR-NE, and UR-PL where such aspects can last for many months on end. To give an idea of these I have included some examples of the outward expression of these deeply important phases in the sequence below. These can be omitted until the larger and outwardly more obvious features of a cycle have been grasped, but in the long run these phases are likely to hold the key to a real inner understanding of the significance of world events.

The outgoing aspects
The first half of any cycle, when the faster of a planetary pair is moving out towards the opposition phases, is strongly innovative, outgoing, forward-looking. During this period the ideas, principles, and processes symbolized by the pair of planets involved will be actively working to create and establish themselves in the world. Ganeau, [18] whose work is discussed later, shows that historical periods when the majority of the ten main synods are in this outgoing phase are usually marked by a dominant sense of optimism, enterprise and exploration. The most recent such period was that beginning in 1956 and peaking in 1962. The next will begin in 1983/84 and peak around 1989.

The conjunction: 0°
This is the 'seed idea' of any cycle, and as such needs to be considered very fully, for it contains within itself all that follows. The power and importance of conjunctions has always been recognized in mundane astrology. From the monthly lunations to the Great Conjunctions of the outer planets which mark out the key seed-moments of history, it has long been considered valuable to set up charts for such moments for the leading areas of the world, and to note particularly those areas where such conjunctions culminate or where other planets are placed on angles (see Chapters 9 and 10 for a fuller discussion of these charts). As we shall see later in this chapter, clusters of Great Conjunctions would appear to be associated with important turning-points of history and are one of the most reliable indications of the stability or otherwise of a period.

Because the conjunction represents both the final fulfilment of the preceding cycle and at the same time the birth of the new cycle, it is usually accompanied by some measure of instability and the initiation of new directions and activities. Thus the conjunction aspect has the quality of death and rebirth. Whilst we tend to think of the two principles involved in a conjunction as separate, there is a very important sense in which we need to understand each pair of planets as a dual-unity which expresses the unfoldment of a *single* complex idea. As an example we might consider the most fundamental of all the conjunctions for ancient astrology, that of the two giants Jupiter and Saturn.

Taken separately we can see that Jupiter will represent the sense of self-esteem and well-being of a nation, the desire of a people to seize opportunities, to expand, to increase trade or territory, to take a larger and more optimistic outlook. Or it may represent national 'inflatus' (both psychological and economic), arrogance and a 'holier-than-thou' desire to 'play god' with allies or neighbours (see Chapter 7 for a fuller consideration of Jupiter and the other planets). Saturn on the other hand represents the more conservative and sober elements in social life. It is the 'reality' principle. It shows the ability to produce concrete results and handle material resources. It gives the desire for national security, stability, and long-term structures. Negatively it can relate to ingrained defence mechanisms, habit patterns which no longer serve any useful purpose, phobias and fears which may subtly dominate certain aspects of national life.

The cycle of these two principles when considered as a dual-unity is strongly related to the creation of philosophical, religious and moral codes, laws and long-term social structures. It is the process by which potentialities are related to the means for their accomplishment. It plots out the unfoldment of planned and organized growth, of systematic and methodical development of resources within the group, and their patient and purposeful application to longer-term goals. As such it seems to be particularly related to the sense of group purpose and social responsibility, to the creation of the infrastructure of societies, to the formation of an organized civil service and institutional government. Barbault, [5] not surprisingly in view of the many layers of Eurocrats and bureaucrats, has noted that European culture has been particularly responsive to and dominated by the Jupiter-Saturn cycle! When studying any particular phase of the Jupiter-Saturn cycle we can therefore see it as part of the process of working out of the idea of structured, purposeful, and responsible social growth, of giving substance to possibilities and potentialities, rather than as a conflict between expansion and contraction, optimism and pessimism. As a dual-unity these principles are totally interrelated.

The same basic idea applies to all pairs of planets when considered in terms of their mutual cycle. Thus we always need to reflect on the seed idea of the conjunction aspect when attempting to assess and interpret later aspects in the cycle. This idea will become clearer when we follow through the specific examples of cycles given in the next section.

The semi-sextile: 30° = 1/12 of circle
12 (3 × 4) is very much related to life (= 3) in the terrestrial world (4). This marks the point at which that which was initiated at the conjunction is beginning to make its first discernible impact in the world, so that the ideas and ideals (= 3) inherent in the conjunction begin to really affect (= 4) life. There is often an element of instability and uncertainty about this phase as the aspiration (= 3) and the challenge to effort (4) interact. Ideally such movements offer the opportunity of producing together (3 × 4 = 12) progressive unfoldment in the world. The NE-0-PL of 1891-2 in 9° Gemini, which as we shall see marked the start of what Barbault[7] calls a 'mini-Great Year' of about 500 years, was in its 30° phase from October 1915-July 1918. We can perhaps see the NE-PL synod, the longest of the known planetary cycles, as the process by which mankind's false dreams and illusions are purged and eliminated, by which collective ideals are transformed and regenerated, and by which the collective is sensitized and opened up to a higher purpose and vision of reality. Observe the immense breakthrough of Geminian intellectual and inventive energy which accompanied and followed the conjunction during the 1890s, producing the birth of depth psychology on one level (Freud was born at the incoming 45 of NE-PL), and on another level the motor-car, the wireless, and the seeds of the 'global village'. This process was given the renewed stimulus of large-scale application by World War One. The period greatly accelerated the development of motorized vehicles, aircraft, and international communications generally. Out of the mass purgation rose a new way of looking at the world, the beginning of a new consciousness, and new sensitivity to the world, which will presumably continue to unfold itself through to the close of the twenty-fourth century.

The semi-square: 45° = 1/8 of circle (= 2 × 2 × 2)
8 is related to concrete manifestation and the purposeful application

of the ideas inherent in the conjunction. It relates to justice in the fullest sense and to the precipitation of 'events' through which past and present can be reconciled and worked out. As such the 45° can produce a first 'crisis' point in the cycle. It is, as it were, a test period when a solid basis for what is to follow has to be established. The Neptune-Pluto cycle arrived within 1° orb of 45° in November 1929 immediately following the Great Crash and lasted within orb on-and-off through until early summer 1933. This period saw the publication of Einstein's Unitary Field Theory, the development of the first 'atom smasher', the discover of cosmic radio emissions making possible radio astronomy (1932), the cyclotron, and rapid progress in the commercial development of the airship and airplane.

The septile = 51.26 = 1/7 of circle
7 is related to the inflowing of inspiration, of some kind of 'higher vision' which comes from perceiving the unity, the complete wholeness of the idea behind the parts which are expressing it. It is traditionally associated with religious and mystical experience, and with sacrifice to some higher ideal. As such it is likely to indicate that stage in a cycle when something of the larger meaning and guiding vision of the basic cycle becomes apparent. As a consequence there often seems to be something more obviously 'fated' about the events and circumstances of this phase. The Neptune-Pluto cycle was within 1° of orb on and off from November 1937 through into the summer of 1942. As these aspects are not given in the ephemerides the following were the dates of exactitude: 16/11/38, 5/5/39, 22/10/39, 11/6/40, and 20/9/40. This period saw both positive and negative collective 'inspiration' as the world was precipitated into an ideological struggle to the death. This period coincides exactly with Hitler's fateful decision to plunge into war. Interestingly Hitler was born with NE-0-PL intimately connected with his Sun in the higher harmonics. [22] It is interesting that Churchill's famous 'blood and toil' inspirational rallying speech was made on 13 May 1940 when the Sun was exactly 120° to Neptune, which was by then only four weeks in time, 35' of arc from the exact 1/7 to Pluto. In terms of science and technology, atomic research entered a key phase of breakthroughs during 1940/41. Polythene, a chemical (Neptune) transmutation (Pluto), was invented in 1939, the antibiotic penicillin, a key destructive and regenerative (Pluto) medicine (Neptune), was developed in 1940. It is interesting to note that the first regular trans-

Atlantic flights (by Pan-Am) began on 20/5/39 only two days after the first exact Neptune-Pluto septile. Someone there saw a larger vision of what was to follow!

Sextile = 60 = 1/6 of circle
6 is related to the rhythmic activity of creation, the pulse of life, to systematic and productive work and the implementation and application of ideas. It is the objective expression (2) of the joy of life (3) and is often symbolized by the 'busy bee', methodically creating his hexagonal honeycomb. At this stage in any cycle we normally see the ideas launched under the conjunction being set to work in the world and becoming integrated into the basic pattern of daily life. Remarkably Neptune and Pluto have been in an almost continuous sextile within 1° or 2° since 1948 through to the present time, and will be within 4° orb through into the 1990s. Looking back to the NE-0-PL in Gemini and all that this presaged at a material level, we can see how this long sextile has been putting this root idea to work with astonishingly powerful consequences. For this is surely the background to the vast boom in consumer technology, the all-conquering advance of the motor-car over the past three decades, which has transformed, for better or worse, our towns and villages and countryside, bringing about the creation of unprecedented mileages of new super highways, and a totally transformed way of life. Even more the continuing astonishing developments in air and space travel and in communications technology of all kinds is obviously further outworkings of this same basic theme. At the psycho-spiritual level this long-term aspect seems to be obviously related to the accelerating development of depth and height psychology, of the growth movement and of psychedelics generally. It should not be forgotten that all those born during an aspect literally 'incarnate' that idea and bring it into the world. Thus the 'generation of 1948-90' are likely to have a vital role in actively developing the inner and spiritual aspect of life in practice and establishing the workings of what Quanier[40] refers to as a pneumotocracy, i.e., government of the Spirit.

The quintile: 72° = 1/5 of the circle
5 is related to the conscious application of the will. It has always had particular associations with man as a self-conscious being with the powers of rational thought and the ability to analyse and

conceptualize. As 5 = 1 + 4, it can be seen as man as the artist-soul (1) at work amongst the four elements of Nature. It is also related to the idea of Power in the sense that 'knowledge is power' and he who 'knows what he is doing' is able to take command over his materials or indeed other people. At this stage in a cycle we can expect to find the cycle's root ideas and ideals becoming more consciously articulated in the world and beginning to form part of the thinking of the time. Neptune does not form its quintile with Pluto until way into the twenty-first century. If we extrapolate present communications technology and marry it with a greatly deepened awareness of telepathic communications, we may begin to grasp something of what this period will be about in material terms. We can hope that this will also mark the growth of widespread spiritual development and increased sensitivity and insight into higher levels of reality. Looking back to 1821 we find the major conjunction of Uranus and Neptune in 3° Capricorn. On 27 December of the following year Pasteur was born with his Sun conjunct this UR-0-NE. During 1861, on 27 June, Uranus formed its outgoing quintile with Neptune. It was during this year that Pasteur developed his germ theory of disease, i.e., he was the channel for the conceptualization (5) of an insight and illumination (Uranus) about the agents of disease and decay (Neptune). Here, as with Hitler above, we have the classic case of an individual born at the time of a major configuration becoming a key figure in the unfoldment of that idea.

The square: 90° = 1/4 of the circle
The number 4 is related to manifestation and the Cross of Matter. It represents a striving to manifest, test, and actualize the potential that was inherent in the original conjunction, through a determination to overcome obstacles and meet the challenges of the mundane world. For collectively as well as individually new powers only arise through conscious determination and effort. At this stage in a cycle's unfoldment the developing idea of the cycle will usually be confronted by some kind of crisis which will have to be overcome in order to realize the central ideas and ideals of the cycle so that it can reap the fruits of these efforts and come to flower at the upcoming trine aspect. In terms of plant growth it might be thought of as the final pushing through the earth out into the upper air.

Bi-septile: 102°.51' = 2/7 of the circle
Potentially an immensely creative point in any circle when individually
and collectively a sense of fervour and 'inspiration' may move through
society bringing the root idea of the cycle to consciousness.

The trine: 120° = 1/3 of the circle
The number 3 is related to life and vitality and enjoyment. It
represents the third factor which reconciles opposites producing
harmony and order. It is strongly associated with the heart side of
life and with those things which bring a sense of delight, pleasure
and well-being. Because of its relationship to the pleasure principle
3 also relates strongly to motivation and aspiration. This stage in
a cycle marks the rapid growth of the main plant through to its
flowering stage. There is usually a harmony and ease about this phase
of first flowering, a sense of vitality and happy excitement at the
potential and promise of things — in short all the joy, verve and
aspiration of spring!

The sesquiquadrate: 135° = 3/8 of the circle
This is similar to the *semi-square*. But being 3/8 there is here an
element of additional life and vigour added to the productive quality.
This is analagous to the 'setting' of the fruit of the fertilized flower.
It marks a potential crisis point in the unfolding cycle, a testing period
in the growth process which, if overcome, establishes the foundations
for growth of the future 'crop'.

Biquintile: 144° = 2/5 of the circle
A time of objective (2) understanding (5) of the meaning of the basic
cycle is likely to emerge, with a period of very effective application
of creative ideas and policies expressing its quintessential essence.
This period will merge on into the *quincunx* phase.

Quincunx: 150° = 5/12 of the circle
This is analogous to the *semi-sextile,* but being 5/12, rather than
1/12, there is a growing measure of self-conscious progress and
awareness involved. At this stage the idea that was set moving in
the world at the 1/12, and consciously understood and conceptualized
at the 1/5, is moving towards complete fruition. There is likely to
be an awareness of a sense of enjoyment (3) yet the need to make
some kind of final effort (4) if things are to be brought to the

fulfilment of the opposition. This ambiguity can make this a point of temporary crisis, strain, instability, uncertainty and change, yet also a point of immense forward potential as conscious effort is applied to specific goals.

Tri-septile = 3/7 of the circle
Potentially a phase of intense inspiration and excitement when the 'wholeness' of the idea of the 'dual-unity' of the cycle will become apparent, more particularly in creative works of all kinds. We would also expect this to indicate appropriate 'fads' and 'crazes' sweeping through society.

Opposition: 180° = 1/2 of the circle
If conjunction (1) represents the infinite subjective potential of the seed then the opposition (2) is its objective expression: the fruit. But they oppose each other: thesis and antithesis, parent and know-it-all rebellious child, who is now potentially seed himself. This is usually an extreme crisis point in any cycle, marking as it does the beginning of the incoming phase. This is often characterized by a state of being 'at loggerheads' and 'at daggers drawn', lined up in opposite camps. It can thus produce some of the more dramatic periods in history. A recent classic example here is the SA-180-UR-PL of 1965/66. This marked the beginning of the rapid acceleration into bloody confrontation in Vietnam between the USA (which as we shall see later is strongly associated with the Saturn-Uranus cycle) and China, which resonates with the Saturn-Pluto cycle. The likelihood of such a confrontation was spelt out in 1963, by Andre Barbault, on the basis of this configuration. Likewise in 1966 he predicted that these two opposing ideas would probably have to fight out their conflicting ideologies until 1971/2 when Saturn would move to the 120 of first Pluto and then Uranus.

The incoming phase
As the cycle moves into the descending phase, from its fruition at the opposition back towards the conjunction, the energies of the cycle are turning inwards and downwards. The sap, as it were, is beginning to sink back into the roots. This marks a generally involutionary period of growing reflectiveness, caution, economy, and cut-backs, and the process of decay, dissolution and death ready for the new birth following the next conjunction. Rudhyar calls this

the 'disseminating' half of the cycle, when what is harvested at the opposition is then distributed to the world. During periods in history when the great preponderance of cycles are in this phase there is a general decline in enterprise, an increasing de-stabilization, disruption, and corruption of the existing order. The three outstanding descending periods of this century are: 1910-19, with its steepest descent being from 1914 onwards; 1931-45, with the steepest descent occuring from 1940 onwards; 1967-83 with its steepest fall being from 1977. This last period, which we are at the very end of, is possibly related to the cumulative lack of confidence in the world's banking and economic system which is even now (July 1982) moving towards some kind of crisis. Happily from mid-1983 there will be a rapidly accelerating move into a positive and ascending phase through to 1988!

Tri-septile: in fact 4/7 of the circle
Theoretically this will mark a crystallization of the inspirational impulse within the cycle, and the earthing of some kind of vision.

Quicunx: 7/12 of the circle
The incoming quincunx mirrors the temporary crisis, strains and creative opportunities of the outgoing one, but with the emphasis on more 'starkly objective' and inward-looking solutions. The involvement of the 7, i.e., 7/12 of circle, seems to lend a more obviously 'fated' quality to this phase, which is often associated with the 'death' of some element involved in the cycle.

Bi-quintile: in fact 3/5 of the circle
In its descending phase this is likely to produce a clear, reflective understanding and expression of the basic idea of the cycle. Effective methods of applying theories are likely to be developed.

Sesquiquadrate: 5/8 of the circle
As with the outgoing 135° this marks a secondary period of crisis centred round the precipitation of specific events which have to be dealt with, but which if met can produce lasting results.

Trine
At the incoming 120° 'harvest' phase which sees the fruits of the preceding labours, there is a period of renewed harmony, equilibrium

and more intimate 'good cheer'. A sense of quiet well-being ensues. It will lack the spontaneous enterprise and whole-hearted zest of the outgoing trine but offer possibilities of positive, creative co-operation.

Bi-septile: in fact, 5/7 of the circle
This marks a renewed possibility for some kind of inner vision in relation to the meaning and purpose of the cycle in question.

Square
A point of major crisis, instability and tension in any cycle. There is often a sense of urgency and the desire to actualize the ideas of the cycle through a sheer effort of will. The challenges of this time seem matters of life and death. This is the 'winter' point of the cycle when dead branches fall and all is stripped bare.

Quintile
Potentially a time of 'summing up', drawing conclusions, and 'doing something' about them. It will be a time when theories, ideas and concepts come to maturity in action. The ideas of the cycle will be given a dynamic and commanding power in the world. It is striking that Uranus was within 1° orb of 72° to Pluto from June-September 1938, the period of German mobilization (actually ordered 12 August) and the build-up to the Munich crisis when Hitler, a man whose chart is entirely dominated by quintiles, was beginning to wield and tap the Uranus-Pluto powers of the time with growing confidence. It was again within 1° orb from April-June 1939 in the final build up to World War Two. The Hitler-Mussolini political-military Pact of Steel was signed 22 May.

Sextile
The incoming sextile is a final working out of the central theme of the cycle in daily life. This marks a phase of active cooperation and systematic effort to carry through the ideas represented. The Uranus-Pluto cycle reached within 2° orb of this sextile phase in June 1942 and was almost continuously in orb through most of 1943-44 until, it finally moved beyond 2° orb at the end of March 1945. A somewhat terrifying illustration of the 'institutionalization' of rhythms of mass destruction and transformation Uranus-Pluto in the fabric of daily life throughout this period.

Septile: in fact = 6/7 of the circle

This would seem to be indicative of some kind of manifestation of the 'seed image' and a possibility of seeing the 'whole' both of the cycle that is ending and the new. It sees the vision being put to work in the world. UR-1/7-PL was within orbs of exactitude on and off during the period from May 1946 to April 1948. It was within 1° orb at the time of the announcement (5 June 1947) of the Marshall Plan for the reconstruction of Europe, and at its implementation (31 March 1948). This was indeed an inspired 'building again on the ruins of the old' to use Ebertin's[17] description of Uranus-Pluto. In view of the connections of 7 with both the spiritual impulse and self-sacrifice, it may perhaps be significant that Mahatma Gandhi was assassinated on 20 January 1948 by a Hindu religious (= 7) fanatic when Uranus-Pluto was within 7′ of its exact septile — again the 'fated' quality of 7 revealing itself.

Semi-square: 7/8 of the circle

A period likely to produce events in which past and future are reconciled in some kind of dynamic fusion. This can be a time of friction and tension. This aspect between Uranus-Pluto came exact for the first of three times on 31 May 1949 only nine days and 20′ arc after West Germany came into being — again the manifestation of 'building again on the ruins of the old'. It was exact again on 24 March 1950, only three days after Adenauer advocated an economic union between France and Germany. The Schuman Plan, forerunner of the EEC, was announced on 9 May 1950, when Uranus-Pluto was still within 1° orb.

Semisextile

This is the final phase we can normally consider prior to the conjunction, and must mark the real 'seed' period in preparation for the new cycle, and the final 'tidying up'. Again it is notable that the third Uranus-Pluto came exact on 11 May 1955. On 9 May Germany was admitted as a member of NATO and on 15 May Britain, France, USA and USSR signed the Treaty of Vienna restoring Austria's independence! Somewhat ominously the first UR-30-PL came exact on 26 July 1954, only three days after France's approval of the Indo-China settlement and 6 days after the signing of the Indo-China armistice. As was noted under the Opposition above, the Uranus-Pluto conjunction of 1965/66 was part of the hallmark of the next

Indo-China (i.e., Vietnam-Cambodia-Laos) war.

Conjunction
This marks the final 'death' of the old cycle and the birth of a new one, which begins the whole process over again.

6.
Part 2:
The Planetary Cycles and their Interpretation

Charles Harvey

We now need to consider the way in which the specific planetary cycles unfold eternity here in the realms of time and space. In a sense we could say that each pair of planets, each cycle of the heavens, is responsible for spinning one thread of the tapestry of unfolding creation. But before we look at these separate threads we need first to see whether there is some way in which we can have a global view of all the planets together. For ultimately all the planets are one 'multi-unity' hymning one unitive symphony which only appears fragmented to our limited vision.

The Great Year and the Cyclic Index — The work of André Barbault

Such a global vision is that promulgated by the fine French astrologer André Barbault.[5,6,7] For whilst other individual astrologers have periodically interested themselves in correlating the cycles of history with astrology (e.g. Jayne, [28] Rudhyar[42] the resurrection and systematic reconstruction of mundane astrology on a methodical basis is due almost entirely to the industries of one man, André Barbault. This pioneer is one of the most outstanding astrologers working in Europe today. He has studied and written authoritatively upon almost every aspect of the art, including very considerable work on the depth psychological approach. His well produced quarterly journal *L'Astrologue*[51] ranks alongside the journals of the British[51] or the Austrian[51] Astrological Associations, as one of the finest publications of its kind. But mundane astrology was and is his first and continuing love. His first-ever article was a study of the Spanish

Civil War published in December 1937 when he was only just sixteen! He studied the then current method assiduously with his brother Armand (who was later to become famous as a twentieth-century alchemist) giving considered assessments of the pre-war political situation.

Then dawned September 1939. This was an intellectual bombshell for Barbault. Not only had he, at the ripe old age and experience of eighteen, failed to forsee the possibility of open war but, to his chagrin and dismay, so had his older and supposedly more experienced colleagues. This traumatic blow determined him to get to grips with the problem. As though to redress his oversight, the day after the war broke out he put on record that the USSR, which he considered, as a communist state, to be ruled by Neptune, would become involved in the war on 16 September when the Sun came conjunct Neptune. On 17 September the Soviets invaded eastern Poland! Likewise he suggested that a major offensive by Hitler, an archetypal Uranian, would take place when the Sun came conjunct Uranus on 12 May 1940. The German invasion of the West began in fact on 10 May. These precise forecasts we imagine must have helped him regain some of his adolescent confidence! At any rate, from this point forward Barbault dedicated himself with his characteristic enthusiasm to his self-appointed task, a task which still, over forty years later, continues to absorb him.

From the start Barbault saw the absolute necessity of continuously monitoring methods and approaches by putting them to the test of published prophecy. Thus he has constantly put himself on record in his books[4,5,6,7] and in L'Astrologue with closely-timed and well-argued forecasts.

These have not often been accurate in their particulars but have often been right in terms of overall perspective. Coupled with this concern for the larger vision of historical processes, he has (as we shall see) at the same time developed techniques and skill, through his study of cycles, for assessing the possibilities of particular periods of a few days, as exemplified above.[7a]

With his constant concern for reliable and objective methods and for an approach which would look at world trends in the round, it is not surprising that around 1965 Barbault's attention should have been caught by a neglected study by the French astrologer Henri-Joseph Gouchon, on world prospects for 1946-49. In this study Gouchon had produced a graph indicating that it was unlikely that there would be another major war before 1950/51, a view which he continued to hold during the next years in the face of bleak forecasts from political commentators. As another astrologer disillusioned by astrology's failure to predict the world crisis of the previous five years, Gouchon wanted to try to establish a means of measuring planetary intensity on a neutral basis. In this barely-circulated, mimeographed study that Barbault had happened upon, Gouchon set out a remarkable discovery. He had found that by calculating the total angular separation between each of the pairs of the five outer planets for 21 March for each year from 1880, and then plotting the results on a graph, the resulting curve showed a striking correspondence with the main periods of international crisis and, most impressively, major and sustained 'lows' for the period 1914-18 and 1940-45 (see Fig. 6.1, p.170). This graph has continued to perform remarkably well since. As Gouchon suspected, it predicted a major crisis in 1950/51. The Korean War began as the index began to plunge in 1950. This was accomplanied by the war in Indo-China. The index bottoms out with the Suez Crisis, after which follows the long period of growth through into the early 60s. The graph turns down again with US involvement in Vietnam, turns up briefly following the end of the Vietnam war in 1972, and then in '76 begins its long and precipitate descent which is still not over. Whilst the world has not experienced one all-consuming war duing the last six years, it has been a period when many commentators have spoken of the real possibility of a collapse of the whole world's economic order, and when there has been a general rapid increase in terrorism, urban violence and social decay world-wide. On this basis we can look forward to the next six years, 1984-89, which ought to see a renewed period of growth comparable to the post-war recoveries of 1919- and 1945-.

What Gouchon had hit upon with his planetary index was in fact nothing less than a means of quantifying the ever-changing movements of Plato's Great Year. Here was a direct means of assessing how close the planets are at any given time to their primordial conjunction, or minimum elongation, a time, as was noted in Chapter 5, which Plato related to confusion, chaos, death and dissolution; or by contrast to what extent the planets are moving away from conjunction, initiating a period of optimism, growth and recon-struction.

The construction of the graph in Fig. 6.1, is in fact remarkably

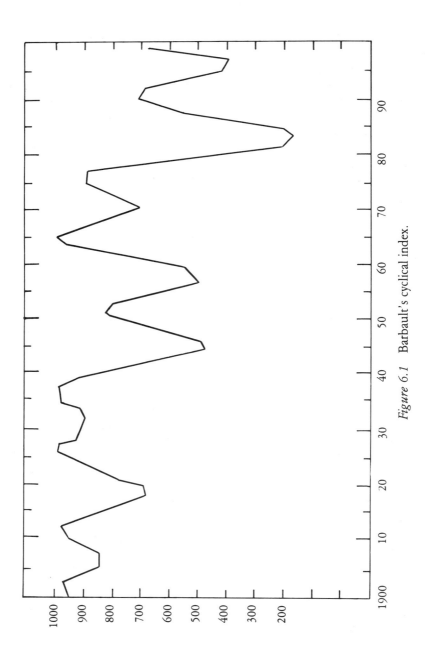

Figure 6.1 Barbault's cyclical index.

simple. It is simply the grand total of the exact angular separations, in rounded degrees, for each of the ten pairs of the outer five planets. Thus, by way of contrast, we have below the figures for January 1979 and January 1983. As we can see, the difference in total angular separation is extremely large. In Plato's terms the world, over the past eight years, has been descending towards chaos and crisis at a dramatic rate. Happily this necessary but unnerving process is about to reverse itself.

Calculation of Barbault's 'Cyclical Index' for 1979 and 1983

1 January 1979			*1 January 1983*		
PL-NE	60		PL-NE	58	
PL-UR	30		PL-UR	38	
PL-SA	35		PL-SA	4	
PL-JU	72		PL-JU	32	
NE-UR	29		NE-UR	20	
NE-SA	95		NE-SA	54	
NE-JU	132		NE-JU	26	
UR-SA	66		UR-SA	34	
UR-JU	103		UR-JU	6	
SA-JU	37		SA-JU	28	
Total	659	= Cyclic Index	Total	300	= Cyclic Index

Barbault set to with alacrity to examine this quantitative technique in greater detail. It was clearly one of the tools for which he had been looking. Through constructing graphs for earlier periods, he soon became convinced that though a technique could not be expected to mark out every detail of world history, by and large it did show the main trends of global tension, of growth and decay, with a fidelity which would no doubt have pleased Plato himself.

Naming it the 'Cyclical Index', Barbault first drew attention to it in 1967 in his major work *Les Astres et L'Histoire* (*The Stars and History*). The publication of this work has stimulated further exploration on these lines by various of his colleagues in the pages of *L'Astrologue*. Notable amongst this work is that of Claude Ganeau[18], who had in fact developed his own variation on this idea in 1947, following a suggestion of Armand Barbault, which was not published. Ganeau's work plots the difference between the total number of degrees of ascending, i.e., outgoing, waxing cycles as

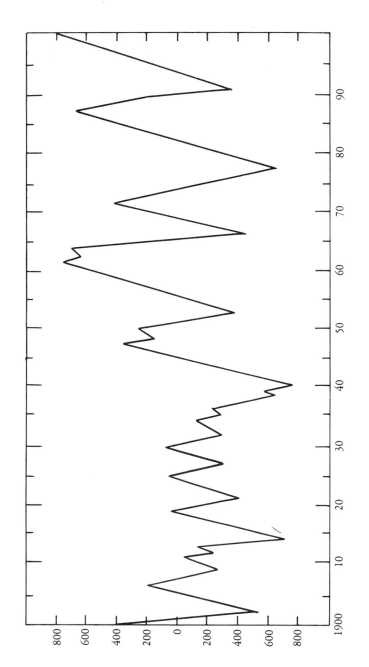

Figure 6.2 Ganeau's index of cyclic equilibrium.

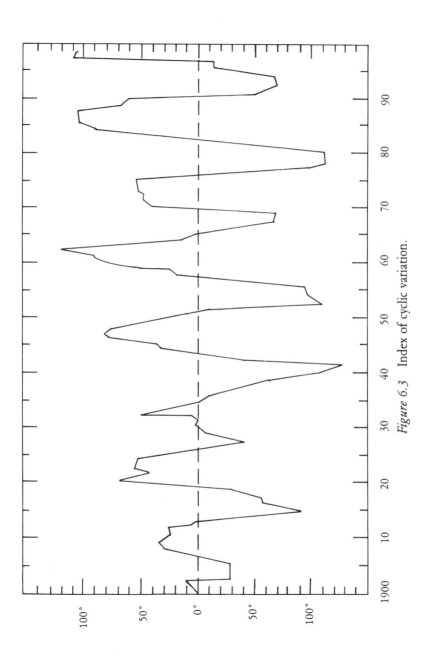

Figure 6.3 Index of cyclic variation.

compared to the total number of degrees of descending, i.e., incoming or waning, cycles. Ganeau calls this the 'Index of Cyclic Equilibrium'. A plot of this for the twentieth century is shown in Fig. 6.2. On the basis of this Ganeau has proposed a 'Law of the Rhythms of Time':

> The stability or instability of the world is directly related to the difference in the sum of the phases of all waxing cycles of the five outer planets, and the sum of the phases of waning cycles of planets. Whilst the resultant figure remains positive, the earth will tend to experience relative stability and a period of evolution; when the resultant figure is negative the earth enters a period of crisis and involution.

Closely parallel in concept to the Equilibrium Index is the 'Index of Cyclical Variation' shown in Fig. 6.3. This plots out the relative movement year on year between the waxing and waning cycles and is a direct reflection of the total number of cycles that are waxing and waning at any particular time. Thus in 1914 only two cycles were waxing compared to eight that were on the wane. Likewise in 1940 only one of the ten cycles was waxing. By contrast, at the height of the graph in 1961/62 we see a period when eight cycles were waxing and only two waning. These variations are of course in fact theoretically purer than the Gouchon curve, though in practice all these methods tend to tell essentially the same story and to complement each other.

Amongst several other variations suggested on this technique is one which proposes the creation of a separate index for the four synods involving Jupiter, i.e., JU-SA, JU-UR, JU-NE, JU-PL, and likewise for each of the four involvements of Saturn, Uranus, Neptune and Pluto. From these it ought to be possible to obtain a potentially valuable general picture of each planet's overall contribution to the stability or otherwise of the time.

Another version proposed by Pierre Julien[29] takes a geometric approach to the index, analogous to the charting techniques employed by certain stockmarket analysts. He draws lines joining up all the peaks in the Cyclic Index and another set of lines joining up all the troughs. He then draws a line exactly mid-way between the peak line and the trough line. This is considered to be the mean line. When the actual Cyclic Index crosses this mean upwards it seems to mark a point of increased optimism, growth and construction.

When it crosses the mean downwards there is a move towards pessimism and destruction. Remarkably the Index crosses the mean downwards in August 1914 and does not cross back up again until the end of World War One. Likewise there is a downward plunge in the autumn of 1939 which does not cross back up again until 1943.

The Great Conjunctions

What the Cyclic Index in its various forms is doing in effect is to measure the degree of 'conjunctionness' of any time. And another way of approaching the question of evaluating the stability or instability of any period is to examine the distribution of the 'Great Conjunctions', i.e., those between Jupiter, Saturn, Uranus, Neptune and Pluto. In accordance with the ancient idea of the Great Year it is found that when several of these occur close to one another this is likely to produce a period of crisis as though too many ideas were going through a radical death and rebirth simultaneously. Barbault[7] points out that periods when multiple conjunctions occur and do not occur during this century make interesting reading.

Thus in the fourteen years from 1900-13, those relatively tranquil Edwardian days, there were only four major conjunctions, JU-SA and JU-UR in 1900 and 1901, JU-PL in 1906, and JU-NE in 1907. The next four conjunctions occured in only five years between 1914-18, followed by two more in the next three years. There was another lull during the seventeen years between 1922 and 1939 when there were only three conjunctions. These all occurred at the time of the great financial crisis with JU-0-UR in 1927/28, JU-0-Pl in 1931, and JU-0-NE in 1932. Then the next six years from 1940-45 saw no less than five conjunctions. During the next nineteen years (1946-64) there were six conjunctions fairly well dispersed. 1965-71 saw four conjunctions and then the next was not until 1981. The four years between 1981-84 see no less than five conjunctions. The next three will follow in 1988-92. Perhaps the most impressive aspect of this is that the eleven years of the two world wars saw no less than nine conjunctions! (A listing of the full details of the major conjunctions throughout recent history, together with other details of the major cycles will be published shortly by ISCWA[25].)

The Ten Major Planetary Cycles

Synods of the five outer planets: Jupiter, Saturn, Uranus, Neptune and Pluto

Against the global picture that emerges from taking all the main outer planets working together, let now us consider the underlying meaning of each of the ten planetary pairs as separate cycles of unfoldment. For it must be with these individual unfoldments of the 'threads of eternity' in themselves, and as modulated through the charts of nations and their leaders, that we can begin to read the meaning and qualities of the time.

In interpreting these synods we can draw on our general understanding of the planetary principles involved, and on observation and experience. Once again André Barbault supplies us with a wealth of information and experience in this area from his many studies and long years of observation. These are summarized in his books *Les Astres et l'Histoire,*[5] *Le Prognostic Experimentale en Astrolgie*[6] and *La Crise Mondiale de 1965.*[4]

A general consideration of all of the planets is given in Chapter 7. Before considering the planetary pairs let us summarize the essential qualities of the five outer planets in terms of their social psychology.

Jupiter   Tends to a relaxed liberalism, tolerance, goodwill and moderation, but also a certain moral certainty and religious intolerance. A desire to 'play God' encourages paternalism, benevolence from a position of authority, *noblesse oblige*. Essentially expansive, optimistic, encourages legislation, or negatively legalistic wranglings and disputes, national inflatus and 'imperialism'.

Saturn   Seeks social order, structure, planning, regulations, controls, material and social security 'from womb to tomb'. Imposes and enforces law and order. Can be strongly disciplinarian, intolerant, extremist, tends to be protectionist, isolationist, and to build 'iron curtains'.

Uranus   Individualistic, independent, self-reliant, encourages free enterprise, also seeks autonomy and is liable to rebellion and revolution. Tends to be right-wing, but equally to the 'facism of the left'. Once in power can be autocratic and totalitarian.

Neptune   Universal and utopian tendencies, collective values, communal, communistic, collectivist, pluralist, left-wing. Can be politically unrealistic, seeking soft options, avoiding confrontation. This can encourage devious, underhand and subversive tactics, 'entryism' and 'fifth column' methods.

Pluto The power of the masses, totalitarian, compulsive collective pressures, forces of elimination, regeneration and resurgence. Relates to emerging nations and nations in a state of renaissance and reconstruction. Also to fanaticism, to an obsession with impersonal, collective ideas and ideals. Can indicate the need to purge the body politic of old, deep-rooted problems. Constellated by a leader it can awaken compulsive instincts for power and dominance.

These can be combined into ten possible pairs. In descending order of cycle length, and hence theoretically in their overall powers as rulers of time, these are:

NE-PL approx. 492 years	SA-PL approx. 33 years
UR-NE approx. 172 years	JU-SA approx. 20 years
UR-PL approx. 127 years	JU-UR approx. 14 years
SA-UR approx. 45 years	JU-NE approx. 13 years
SA-NE approx. 36 years	JU-PL approx. 12 years

A valuable way of thinking about these ten cycles is that devised by Leyla Rael Rudhyar.[44] She divides them into three classes: Class A (NE-PL, UR-NE, UR-PL) she considers 'sound the low-frequency tones of evolutionary epochs, and their cycles develop their transformative themes'; Class B (SA-UR, SA-NE, SA-PL) she sees as 'mid-frequency harmonies — or more often discords — resulting from the interplay or clash of transformative Class A, and conservative or inertial Saturn forces'; Class C (the four Jupiter synods) she sees as 'the higher-frequency melodies of new discoveries, visions, ideals, and social trends unfold ''in sync'' with these Jupiter-based synods'. Against this background we can look briefly at each synod and some of the theoretical ideas and empirical findings associated with each.

Neptune-Pluto
Various writers, including Barbault, Jayne, and Rudhyar, have pointed out the importance of this cycle in terms of major epochs of civilization. Both planets have to do with the deep unconscious/superconscious of the collective, to an opening up to higher,

transcendent collective ideas and ideals. We would suggest that in some sense they relate to the higher ideas and ideals of the time, and to the larger spiritual, cosmic, and human purposes which are coming into manifestation. As noted, this cycle sets the tone of the underlying and compelling aspirations of the time. The current long-term -60- phase, which remains within orb from $c.1941$-2035, can be seen as marking a period when real ideas and ideals can be increasingly set to work in the world. Rudhyar[43] and Rael[44] consider that five such cycles mark out a major 2,500-year period and that a new cycle began with the PL-0-NE of $c.22$ April 579 BC. (Because of cumulative errors in the outer planet orbits the actual dates given for these should be treated with extreme caution!) There can be no question that this period, reinforced by the UR-0-PL of 21 December 577 BC / 1 February 576 BC, and the UR-0-NE of 10 July / 18 October 576 BC and 3 April 575 BC, was one of the most fertile and creative in recorded history. Pythagoras, Deutero-Isaiah, Buddha, and Lao Tze all suddenly sprang to life and light at this time, bringing a new vision and spiritual awareness into the world.

As mentioned above, tables for all the major synods will be available soon. However, for those wishing to consider the possible correlates with this major synod now, the next conjunctions occurred $c.9$ July and $c.14$ October 85 BC and $c.7$ April 84 BC. The next was $c.30$ April 411 AD, which coincided with a UR-90-NE, $c.28$ July 409, 12 September, 29 October 410, and UR-90-PL 9 January, 11 September, 11 November 410, and all joined by a triple JU-0-SA on 29 August and 3 November 411 AD and 12 March 412. This coincided with Alaric's sacking of Rome in August 410 AD and the general collapse of the Roman Empire. The next occurred $c.19$ July and 29 October 904 AD and $c.18$ April 905 AD. The millenarian sentiments at the turn of the fourteenth century were probably accentuated by the conjunction $c.11$ June 1398, and 13 January and 26 February 1399, which was however a period that saw the final flowering of the Middle Ages. The most recent conjunctions were in 1891-2 in 8° and 9° Gemini, considered by many to be the seed time of the present accelerating move towards a global culture.

Uranus-Neptune

Remarking on the importance of this 172-year cycle for the unfoldment of civilizations, Jayne[28] notes that after twenty-one conjunctions, or 3,600 years, that the UR-0-NE returns within 6°

of the first conjunction of the series. If this cycle is divided into six sub-periods of 600 years each, we have the great Chaldean Naros Cycle (see Chapter 5). DeVore goes on to say about this 600-year cycle that 'Naros milestones are marked by the following historical dates: 576 BC, the birth of Buddha (Buddhism), Mahavira (Jainism), Pythagoras, and the activity of Lao-Tze (Taoism); AD 25, the mission of Christ, (Christianity); AD 625, the Hegira of Muhammad; 1225, St Francis (vital for Catholicism); 1825, birth of Bab and Baha'u'llah (co-founders of Bahaism) and of Mary Baker Eddy (Christian Science).'

The last UR-0-NE have occurred in November 1308, three times in 1478/9, in 1650 and in 1821. The next will begin to form up during 1992, being within 2° orb for much of the year, and coming exact on 2 February 1993 in 19CP33. Rael Rudhyar[44] cites Cheryl Martin[32] on this cycle, saying that she (Martin) considers that the recent Uranus-Neptune cycles work closely with the Neptune-Pluto cycles, a view which Barbault[7] has independently voiced. Thus Martin sees the 1478/9-1650 cycle as 'phase one' of the 1398/9 Neptune-Pluto cycle, and relates this combined interaction with the discovery and initial settlement of the Americas, the rise of Humanism, the Renaissance and the Reformation in European culture. She goes on to observe that the Mogul Empire of the Ottoman Turks reached its height during the sixteenth century, as did the Mogul Empire in India. The 'phase two' Neptune-Uranus cycle of 1650-1821 is related by Martin to the period of the Enlightenment and European classicism. In Britain the last cycle could be said to have died with the execution of Charles I on 30 January 1649 and the new to have begun with the establishment of the Commonwealth under Cromwell. This cycle included the American and French Revolutions and ended with the Death of Napoleon in 1821, the independence of Spain and Portugal's former South and Central American colonies, and the acceleration of the Industrial Revolution. The 'phase three' cycle, which we are still in, Martin considers to relate to the transition from industrial to post-industrial society.

Rael Rudhyar indicates that the coming conjunction, and the approach to it, are likely to focus on Central and South America. She also points out that this Capricorn emphasis during the last part of this century is further reinforced by the two JU-0-NE of 1984 and 1997, and the three SA-0-NE of 1989, which all occur in the sign. This she relates to a period of stabilization of governmental institutions, and increasing conservatism.

From an empirical approach Barbault[5] has related the 1821 synod in Europe, beginning in 1821, to the growth of Capitalism, and to the interaction between capital (Uranus) and labour (Neptune), between the forces of authority/conservatism and liberalism, Capitalism and Communism (the development of Communism itself he relates to the Saturn-Neptune cycle, *q.v.*), and to the process of industrialization which was gathering momentum in the western world. This finding is very much in agreement with what H. S. Green[19] had already found at the beginning of this century. The 'good' aspects between these, he says 'produces harmony between rulers and ruler, the higher and lower classes . . . promotes reform and changes in the nation'. About the 'bad' aspect he says 'The rulers and the ruled may be at variance'.

Returning to Barbault, he finds that following through the Uranus-Neptune cycle, each main phase is marked by appropriate interactions between these different interests, groups and ideas. The first decade after 1821 saw the enormous impact of machinery and the emergence of an industrial proletariat as distinct from the growing bourgeoisie and business classes. In 1847, at the -45-, a consciousness of this class divide was crystallized with the publication of the Communist Manifesto. At the -90- phase in 1867-70 antagonism in Europe between liberal and conservative elements culminated in the Franco-Prussian war and the establishment of the German Empire. By the -120- in 1883 Europe had settled down to an amicable stage of détente with generally co-operative relations between capital and labour and improving social legislation. This was not to last and the -180- phase of 1907 saw the repolarization of Europe between the liberal-oriented Russo-Anglo-French alliance against the Central Powers of Germany-Austria-Italy. This polarization was reactivated when Jupiter joined the waning Uranus at the outbreak of World War One. The incoming -120- of 1939-42 saw the astonishing reconciliation of the Stalin-Hitler pact. No sooner had this dissolved in 1941 than the Allies joined with Russia as equally unlikely bedfellows. The -90- of 1952-55 coincided with the polarization of Moscow and Washington and the depth of the Cold War and the McCarthyite witch-hunts in the USA. Again at the incoming -60- during 1965-67 we see a relaxation of east-west tensions and increasing cooperation. On this basis we can perhaps look to the next -0- in 1992/3 as marking the real beginning of the 'New Age Economics' of which Barry Lynes[31] is such an impassioned advocate.

Uranus-Pluto

This 127-year cycle appears to be important for the radical restructuring of peoples and nations. Ebertin[17] describes it as 'building again upon the ruins of the old'. The process is not necessarily as immediately drastic as this would imply. But as was seen on p.164-6, the main incoming phases of this cycle marked out very precisely some of the main destructive and reconstructive phases in the development of Germany between 1938 and 1955 and the main phases of the Vietnamese/S.E. Asian transformations which came to a crisis under the last such conjunction during 1965/66. Barbault has also noted a strong relationship between this cycle and the emergence of Japan.

On the scientific and intellectual plane the 1965/66 conjunction in Virgo correlates closely with the emergence of the electronics, computer, and micro-processor industry. This may well be an indication that this next Uranus-Pluto cycle will focus more on intellectual revolutions than on physical ones. Non-astrological observers now talk of the pre- and post-1965 generations, i.e., those for whom the world of computers is still essentially strange and those who have grown up with electronic wizardry as part of their natural environment. Undoubtedly this Uranus-Pluto generation will provide the systems and linguistic analysts and logicians who will develop artificial intelligence, the next information technology revolution, and all that this implies for mankind's evolution.

Previous recent UR-0-PL occurred during 1598/9, 1710/11, and 1850/1.

Saturn-Uranus

As a result of studies covering 1625 to the present time, Barbault identifies this 45-year cycle as a right-wing and essentially conservative/authoritarian process which emphasizes the politics of Order. He finds it strongly associated with the development of 'imperialist' tendencies and with capitalism. This agrees with astro-economic analysis which points to this cycle as a crucial one in the ebb and flow of investment and production in heavy industry, which has for a long time been dominated by the USA. In broader terms it can also be seen to relate to the practical 'earthing' of brilliant ideas, insights, inventions, reforms, and so on. Thus, for example, we shall see under Jupiter-Uranus below, there was an almost exact SA-120-UR at the time of the launching of the first Sputnik. Likewise

Saturn was just past the incoming -144- phase to UR-0-JU at the moment that Apollo XI was successfully launched to the moon (also exact was SA-135-PL).

The very strong connections between this cycle and the Middle East are dealt with in a forthcoming ISCWA publication.[26] For example Israel was conceived under a SA-0-UR. The Balfour Declaration and Allenby's entry into Jerusalem, and the Palestine mandate all occurred at the -180- phase, the latter within two days of exactitude. Israel was born at the exact septile (see Fig. 15.24, p.459). Most of the crises in her history have occurred close to critical phases of this cycle, and/or the Saturn-Pluto cycle, which is also a dominant one. Likewise Egypt's history correlates closely with this cycle. The 1922 Republic was proclaimed with Saturn rising in an incoming, applying tri-septile to Uranus (cf. Israel's septile). The 1953 Republic was established at the outgoing -90- phase. Sadat was born with SA-180-UR. He was assassinated just five days after the exact incoming SA-45-UR. The last SA-0-UR occurring on 3 May 1942, 1.16pm GMT set for Cairo, is still of great importance in considering the unfoldment of this area.

Saturn-Neptune
Green[19] saw this synod as benefiting democracy, political changes and reforms. Barbault considers this to be the paramount cycle which governs the development of socialism/Communism. He points out that the SA-0-NE 1846 (and UR-45-NE of 1847) was followed by the publication of the *Communist Manifesto,* and that the main phases of this cycle trace the development and the establishment of the main European socialist parties around the 1882 SA-0-NE, and then the Russian Revolution in 1917, immediately following the next SA-0-NE. The SA-0-NE of 1952/3 saw the death of Stalin and the beginning of the expansion of soviet communist influence out into Africa and the Third World. Russia became involved in Afghanistan, now described as 'Russia's Vietnam' at the incoming -90- phase in December 1979 shortly after the Sun came -0-NE and -90-SA, whilst the Polish crisis blew up under this same aspect close to the time that the Sun came -180-NE and -90-SA, and Gierek was obliged to resign. Most recently the SA-60-NE on 14 October 1982 was part of a pattern of factors which can be related to the death of Brehznev. The SA-45-NE occurring on 10 January 1984, and quickly followed by JU-0-NE (another 'socialist' cycle) on 19 January,

is likely to mark the focus of another highly critical period of some months for the Soviet Union. After this the three conjunctions of 1989 in Capricorn are likely to mark another major and crucially important stage in mankind's social development.

Curiously enough it has been observed that the British Royal Family has responded very strongly to this same cycle for at least the past century. This is perhaps indicative of its relationship to self-sacrifice and dedication to higher ideals. Leyla Rael Rudhyar says of this synod: 'The cycle of these two planets refers most positively to the dissolution (Neptune) of whatever has become negatively crystallized (Saturn), and to the ''descent'', as it were, of new, inspiring collective images.' She notes its relationship to Marxism but also to the Baha'i movement which was also founded at the time of the 1846 conjunction, which envisions a global world-order (Saturn) based on revelation (Neptune). Regarding the cycle beginning in 1952/3 she says that this 'can be interpreted as referring to the ''religion'' (Neptune) of paternalistic materialism (Saturn) that has been guiding political, economic, and social development . . . It coincided with the formal conclusion of peace treaties following World War Two, the explosion of the first hydrogen bomb, and the death of Josef Stalin.' To this we may add, in the light of the above remark, that it also coincided with the death of George VI of England, and the accession of Queen Elizabeth II, and the beginning of an important new phase in the evolution of the British monarchy.

Saturn-Pluto

As I write this we are approaching the beginning of a new Saturn-Pluto cycle which began on 8 November 1982. This 33-year cycle appears to have a great deal to do with emerging nations and very deep cultural transformations, purgations and 'resurrections'. In this respect Barbault relates its activities in this century to decolonization and the development of cultural structures. It is a remarkable fact that India and Pakistan gained their independence only days after the last SA-0-PL on 11 August 1947. Here we have ancient peoples (Saturn) entering a deep inner purgation (Pluto). (The Indian subcontinent was plunged into appalling rioting, bloodshed, civil war and sectarian violence as soon as independence came.) This closely parallels the experience of the ancient (Saturn) people of Israel who declared their unilateral independence in 1948 with Moon and Mars bracketing the SA-0-PL in the tenth house (Fig. 15.24, p.459) and were immediately plunged into open war with their Arab compatriots. Israel's history since has closely followed the subsequent phases of this cycle, most recently with the war in Lebanon (1982/3) at the -0- phase. Likewise China under Mao began to emerge during this conjunction though the Republic was not proclaimed until 1 October 1949 (Fig. 15.9, p.449) when Saturn had moved out of orbs.

Leyla Rael Rudhyar points out that since the previous SA-0-PL had occurred in 1914-15 in early Cancer, that this and the 1947 conjunction spanned both world wars. She goes on 'which some historians lump together and call "the second Thirty Year War" '. What is called the first Thirty Year War occurred in Europe between 1618 and 1648, under a Saturn-Pluto cycle which spanned 1617 to 1648.' As she goes on to say such conjunctions do not always portend war. However we can see that the intensely tough, purgative qualities of Saturn-Pluto can indicate periods when there is in some way a need to 'get back to basics', to the 'skeleton' of things as it were. Thus critical phases of the Saturn-Pluto can lead to seeing things in black and white, so that only some kind of drastic action will suffice. In so far as Pluto has to do with collective power the Saturn-Pluto cycle would seem to be related to the unfoldment of the ordered exercise and administration (or imposition) of collective, compulsive, power. Barbault observes that the -90- phase seems to relate to periods of 'crisis of authority'. (A discussion of this point is given under the entry on 'Solar cycles' below.) It is interesting to note that the Brezhnev era ended almost exactly at the SA-0-PL of 8 November 1982, which followed hot on the heels of the SA-60-NE of 14 October 1982, another indication of transformative processes within the Communist world.

Jupiter-Saturn

This cycle, of almost exactly twenty years from conjunction to conjunction, has always been considered of the greatest importance in shaping the course of history. These two planets used to be known as the 'Great Chronocrators', or rulers of the ages. Their cycle can be considered the ground base of human development which marks the interaction between the perception of ideas, potentialities, possibilities (Jupiter) and their manifestation in the concrete material world (Saturn) (cf. the Saturn-Neptune cycle which is related to a similar process at a higher level). As noted under the interpretation of the conjunction this pair has a great deal to do with the development and evolution of social structures and a sense of corporate national identity. Barbault makes a compelling case for the dominance of this cycle in the unfoldment of European history, so that each phase in this cycle, though relatively short, appears to mark out a relatively clear pattern of development year after year. Unfortunately there is not space here to illustrate this because of the background details that would be required to make full sense of this process. It is hoped that Barbault's writings which clearly illustrate these cycles will be made available in English soon.

The Jupiter-Saturn cycle was of course the mainstay of the ancient's cyclical theory of history. Although in itself a relatively short cycle the series of JU-0-SA form an intriguing pattern as the conjunction occurs for approximately 240 years in any one element, so that they complete a cycle of the zodiac in about 960 years. The twenty-year synod was known technically as *Minima* or *Specialis,* their 240-year cycle as *Media* or *Tigonalis* and their full cycle as *Maxima* or *Climacteria.* The transition of the conjunction from one element to another — the 'Mutation Conjunction' — has always been considered to be of particular importance marking a major shift in emphasis and orientation in the world. There was a Great Mutation in Fire on 8 December 1603 in 8° Sagittarius which has been related to the subsequent colonization of America due to religious (Sagittarius) oppression (van Nostrand).[35] The Great Mutation of 26 January 1842, 5.21 am GMT when the conjunction moved into Earth is often related to the development of materialism and mankind's increasing mastery over the material world which has followed. Despite the 'maverick' JU-0-SA in Air in 1981 this -0- is considered to last until the Great Mutation in Air — about AD 2060 (see p.394) for the chart of this conjunction).

Under this cycle mention has to be made of perhaps the most famous alleged cycle correlations — the US 'presidential death cycle'. The facts are that since 1840 every president elected during the year of a JU-0-SA has died in office. The significance of this was in fact pointed out at the time of the assassination of Abraham Lincoln, by an astrologer Dr L. D. Broughton who, it is alleged, having noted that William Henry Harrison (elected in 1840) and Lincoln (elected in 1860) had died in office, then went on to predict that every president elected in a year ending in 0 would die in office, down to 1960. His stated reason for this highly prophetic prediction was that the JU-0-SA would occur in Earth signs every twenty years through until 1960.

In an interesting study by Kelsey Richfield[41] of all eight presidents who have died in office (one, Zachary Taylor, was *not* elected in a 'zero' year) he concludes that the JU-0-SA in Earth is an inadequate explanation for this pattern since in none of the cases does the conjunction actually make any particularly significant contacts with the USA chart. In saying as he does that the JU-0-SA 'were not only no causative of the presidential deaths, but *not even related*' he is probably overstating a position. The study of Kennedy's assassination (on p. 194ff) is indicative that there is at least *some* connection here.

Though Richfield's findings are not directly related to the JU-0-SA his analysis is sufficiently interesting in its own right to be mentioned here. In sum he found that, using the 7GE35 rising US chart rather than the Sagittarius rising chart at present preferred by the writers of this book, in seven out of eight cases there was a square between the president's Mars (3 cases), Saturn (2 cases), SO/SA (1 case), NN (1), Moon (1), to the USA's Mars (2), NN (4) Moon (2). Furthermore he found that in almost every case there was a progressed aspect close to time in the USA chart involving the Moon and Mars. Thus he found progressed MO was -180-US MA (3 cases), -90-MA (1), MA-180-MO (1). Of the other two cases one showed progressed SA-120-MA, but -90- the president's Saturn, and the other showed progressed MO-90-ME and progressed ME-90-MA. He ends with the ominous comment that the US-MO is again -90-MA mid-September 1983. This said it is clear that in astrolgy we are constantly dealing with a whole intermeshing web of such cycles and it would seem in terms of first principles extremely unlikely that any one or two such factors would be adequate. Such events can be expected to echo and resonate through a wide range of charts, as we shall see (p. 194).

Jupiter-Uranus

About fourteen years long, this cycle appears to be very much to do with the growth and awakening of human consciousness, and the purposeful extension and transcendence of horizons. It combines aspiration and effort and as such relates to the possibilities for progress and furthering the evolution of man. It encourages a perception of deeper potentialities, poses questions, opens up opportunities. It encourages a growth of the Promethean spirit of rebellion and self-will, and a spirit of individual and collective optimism and enterprise. This seems to be both one of the key cycles of the 'free-market economy' measuring the buoyancy of the markets. As such Barbault considers it one of the predominantly capitalist-oriented cycles. He also sees it as an important factor for rebellion against the *status quo,* whatever that may be at the time. Writing on the conjunction phase he says: 'This gives rise to power, ambition, audacity, risk-taking, excessively extremist behaviour. In a constructive phase it is a most powerful agent for change and progress. In a society in crisis it can cause highly volatile situations to erupt without warning and an atmosphere of acute tension. In this state it has a particularly dangerous ''war mongering'' potential'. (Further discussion of this cycle is given on pp.205-208.)

Jupiter-Neptune

This cycle has a strongly idealistic, humanitarian and ideological quality about it. It seems to be related to the unfoldment of idealistic and religious belief systems, and as such its hard-angle aspects can often relate to sectarian quarrels, political differences and 'religious wars'. The -90- phase seems to be particularly prone to precipitate action to fight for a particular idea, as for example in the chart for Franco's uprising in Spain, in the last Portuguese revolution, or Ataturk's Turkey. Economically it can produce periods of boom and optimism, but also 'pie in the sky' plans and rampant inflation, if not well earthed.

Barbault relates this particularly to the socialist economies of the Eastern bloc, and more specifically to the destiny of France, which has been locked in step with this synod for many cycles now. Thus the Fourth Republic was born at the conjunction in 1945 and elections gave a stong left-wing majority. At the -45- in 1947 De Gaulle rallies the anti-Communist vote creating a major split and polarization with Communists, the harvests are poor, and a wave of strikes exacerbates the situation. At the -60- in 1948, the Third Force emerges uniting the middle ground producing a brief period of economic stability. The -90- phase in 1949 sees a new economic crisis and the resignation of President Queuille. With the -120- in 1950 there is a general Franco-German rapprochement and the USA pledges 2 billion dollars financial aid. With the -180- in 1951-52 the Communists lose ground to the conservatives but a series of resignations and terrorist violence in Morocco and Tunisia create a new sense of crisis. The -135- in May / June coincides with a ministerial crisis and a general disruption of the nation. At the -120- in 1953 / 54 the economy begins to pick up and Mendes-France ends the war in Indo-China. The -90- from mid-1954 to mid-1955 is a time of insurrection and instability in French North Africa which creates governmental crisis and Mendes-France resigns. The -60- at the end of 1955 sees peace in Morocco and the formation of a relatively stable government. But at the -45- in autumn of 1956 the government splits and there are setbacks over the Suez crisis. With the conjunction of 1958 comes the final crisis, with the threat of civil war over Algeria. General de Gaulle takes over as premier and on 28 September a new Constitution for the Fifth Republic was approved, and inaugurated on 5 October, under the new JU-0-NE!

It should be pointed out that with his insight into the dominance of this cycle, and of the Sun-Jupiter cycle (see below) for France, Barbault was able very much to 'call the changes' during the Fourth Republic often within a few days, and unequivocally predict the final crisis at the end of the cycle. In the same way he was able predict with complete confidence the Soviet crisis with the death of Stalin from his knowledge of the importance of the Saturn-Neptune cycle for the USSR.

Jupiter-Pluto

Barbault relates this twelve-year cycle to the growth of international terrorism. As a cycle it ought to relate to the development of plutocratic as well as political power. Crawford[52] has evidence for its impact on economic cycles. Ebertin relates this combination to the attainment of power of all kinds, be it physical, material, mental or spiritual. The conjunctions in the past century occurred in 1894, 1906, 1918, 1931, 1943, 1955/56, 1968, and 1981.

Solar and other Short-term Cycles — fine timing the major cycles

With the slower-moving cycles, planets may be within even a narrow orb for many weeks at a time. Admitting that the whole period is likely to be strongly coloured by the idea of that cycle and phase, nonetheless there are times when these ideas will come to a head. What is the mechanism which clicks the final 'ward of the combination lock' into place, to use Addey's imagery (see p.193), so that the door can be opened to the precipitation of these long-term energies?

The answer must obviously lie in the shorter cycles of the inner planets Mars, Venus, Mercury, Sun and even the Moon. Alfred Witte, the great German pioneer astrologer who founded the remarkably fertile Hamburg School, and who first developed the systematic use of mid-points and planetary pictures, formulated the rule:

The Sun indicates the day of the event
The Moon indicates the hour of the event
The MC indicates the minute of the event
The AS indicates the place of the event
The MC / AS indicates what is happening 'at this time and place'.

This maxim does appear to be empirically very soundly based, though it should not be taken too literally. Thus André Barbault has also independently come to the same basic conclusion about the importance of the Sun as a timing factor, though he is inclined to allow it orbs of several days either side of exactitude. He also considers th.:t the other inner planets can substitute for Sun as the final 'ward in the lock' to trigger an effect one day rather than another.

The simplest and most classic example of this effect is the annual cycle of the Sun in relation to each of the outer planets. Barbault has made a special study of these and has found that these are remarkably powerful indicators of the dominant trends in world affairs. He has noted that the Sun-Jupiter cycles seems to be particularly related to détente, to treaties, cease-fires, and so on. The SO-0-JU appears to be particularly potent in this respect, but the -60- and -120- also appear to be powerful. Using this simple technique alone Barbault has been able to make some remarkable predictions, including dating within a few days all the main turning-points and final cease-fire agreement in the last year of the Vietnam war.

On the other hand Barbault notes that in the unfoldment of the history of the ill-fated Fourth French Republic that having been born with SO-0-JU on 6 September 1944 that the -0-, -90-, -180-, and incoming -90- of this thirteen-month cycle of these bodies very often marked crisis points for the nation. In fact of the 27 major governmental crises experienced by the Fourth Republic, nine occurred within 15° of a conjunction in its fourteen years of life. This is remarkable in view of the many other factors one must assume were also involved in these crises (cf. the Jupiter-Neptune cycle notes above).

Barbault has found that the SO-0-SA cycle is often related to important high-level international diplomatic moves. In connection

with this Barbault observed that Nixon had visisted Moscow over
31 May 1972 (when SO-0-SA), and that Brezhnev returned the visit
over 18 June 1973 (SO-0-SA). On the basis of this he wondered aloud
in the pages of *L'Astrologue*, 'What will happen around 30 June
1974?' (the next SO-0-SA). Nixon returned to Moscow 27 June 1974
and stayed for five days! In the autumn 1974 issue of *L'Astrologue*
Barbault wonders: 'Would it be pushing it to suggest that another
Brezhnev visit to Washington might take place about 15 July 1975
when SO-0-SA at 22CN?' He adds that this is a doubly important
-0- because it is also an occultation of Saturn. Brezhnev did not visit
the USA. However it was in fact exactly on 15 July that the USA
and USSR launched spacecraft 7 ½ hours apart. These orbited earth
together, docked with one another, the crews shared a meal together,
the link-up being seen on TV throughout the world!

The Sun-Mars cycle can be remarkably precise in timing moments
of international tension and crisis. Barbault[6] notes that the perihelion
-180- which occurs about every fifteen years appears to be particularly
powerful in this respect. Such a perihelion conjunction occurred on
23 July 1939 as the Polish question was coming to a head. This was
quickly followed by another on 10 October 1941 at the very juncture
when Japan was secretly planning its attack on Pearl Harbour. (The
orders were transmitted on 5-7 October.)

These are examples of simple solar / planetary cycles in their own
right. But the principle becomes the more powerful when it is applied
to timing slow-moving configurations. Thus Barbault has noted that
the SA-90-PL seems to bring about periods in the world when there
is some kind of crisis of authority. The SA-0-PL of 1974 serves as
a brilliant illustration of this, and of Barbault's key observation that
it is the transiting Sun which activates these slow-moving
combinations.

During early May Saturn was moving to the incoming -90- of Pluto.
It came exact on 28 May. Is this the date when its impact will be
strongest? Many would say yes. But can we narrow it down? Listing
the fast-moving factors over this SA-90-PL during this general period
we find the following trigger points (on 1 May Saturn is at 1CN06
and Pluto at 4LI34, their mid-point is 17LE50). On 20 April
MA-0-SA; on 24, MA-45-SA/PL; on 28, MA-90-PL. On 7 May the
SO-45-SA; on 8, SO = -90-SA/PL; on 10, SO-135-PL. But Mercury
is also -0- SO at this time so we also find ME-45-SA on 7, -45-SA/PL
on 8, -135-PL on 9 May. In addition Venus is -45- the Sun and Mercury

at this time and she moves -90- SA on 6 May and -180-PL. The theoretical build-up is fairly clear. Were there any 'crises of authority' precipitated at this time? Let us examine the record:

25 April   (MA = -0-SA on 20, = SA/PL on 24, -90-PL on 28). After 42 years Salazar's Portugal falls to an army coup.
6 May   (SO = ME = VE = SA-90-PL on 6-10) Willy Brandt, Chancellor of West Germany, resigns.
8 May   Canadian government falls; same day Irish government falls.
9 May   Chou-en-lai departure from power because of illness.
9 May   Nixon impeachment by Judiciary of House of Representatives begins.

A remarkable catalogue of 'crises of authority' by any standards. What are the chances of such a concatenation of causally unconnected events occurring by chance at one time? But this was not the end of it. On 12 July Mercury stationed exactly -90-PL and 5° orb of -0-SA. Around this time: Peron died in Argentina, Makarios resigned in Cyprus, General Franco handed over power in Spain, Tito fell ill, and the 15-23 July Cyprus war ends the colonels regime in Greece!

Interestingly enough on this occasion the major impact of this configuration seems to have been released either side of exactitude, despite the fact that the Sun came -0-SA and -90-PL near exactitude, which theoretically might have been judged a particularly powerful date. The early May triggering was of course a multiple one.

Further examples of the timings of slow cycles by Sun and Mars transits can be found in Chapter 14, on p.408, where they are used to plot out some of the major focal points of World War Two.

Every cycle has its place in the scheme of things and we should not forget that the ancients, who did not have Uranus, Neptune, and Pluto, considered that the cycles of the seven planets then known, were explanation enough of all that occurred in the mundane realm. The cycles of every planet will no doubt be traced in detail in the coming years. The cycles of Mars with outer planets will obviously be of great importance. One of these which deserves special mention because of its great value in studies of day-to-day political life is the Mars-Jupiter cycle, which could be said to relate to 'legal activity' amongst other things. John Naylor[34] has noted that the -90- and -180- aspects nearly always coincide with periods of crisis and conflict over legislation and legal matters generally, with bills tending to be blocked or giving rise to problems for the government.

Barbault's peace cycle

Happily as we saw with the Sun-Jupiter cycle there are cycles which produce harmony as well as disruption. Perhaps the most powerful of these, and one of Barbault's most consistent observations, [6] is the importance of contacts between Venus-Jupiter and usually the Sun at the time of major peace treaties. Thus for examples we find that at the armistice to end the Franco-Prussian War (28 January 1871) SO 8AQ, VE 20AQ, and JU 16GE, i.e., Jupiter is basically -120- both Sun and Venus. At the armistice on 11 November 1918 which ended World War One we find SO 18SC, VE 15SC, and JU 15CN: an exact -120-. At the Franco-German armistice of 22 June 1940 we find JU 7TA-60-VE 7CN and SO 1CN. The armistice of 8 May 1945 (World War Two) shows VE 17AR -0- ME 21 AR -120- JU 17 VI and SO 17 TA exactly -90-. The armistice with Japan on 2 September 1945 occurred with VE 3LE-60-JU 1LI and SO9VI was not directly involved though applying by 22° to -0-JU. Barbault cites many other examples and shows that to a very considerable exent these aspects signal periods of intensified peace negotiations, treaties, armistices, and agreements.

The daily cycle

The final link in the chain between the major long-term planetary cycles and a specific 'event' is the daily cycle. This is the final trigger which will locate the happening at that particular point rather than any other. There is probably no quicker way of being convinced of the validity of astrological symbolism than to study the charts of closely-timed events (the case of Kennedy's assassination is examined in detail later, see p.194ff in this connection). Almost invariably the 'signature' of the event is written into the moment in a way that cannot be gainsaid. The most telling 'signatures' will almost invariably involve precise aspects to the angles of the chart and/or the MC/AS mid-point.

If this is the case then there must be specific laws at work, though as yet we cannot pretend to understand them. When we see Uranus *exactly* on the MC for Hiroshima, or Saturn *exactly* on *cusp 5* (Koch) for the moment when 145 people, 116 of them, *children*, were crushed to death in a *coal*-tip slide, or Jupiter *exactly* on the MC for the moment that Queen Elizabeth was crowned, or the degree and minute of Princess Diana's natal Sun *exactly* on the MC as she takes her marriage vows, we then know that we are in the presence of a level of order and formal causes which lie outside our normal, commonsense, conception of things.

On the day that Princess Diana went into labour the BBC rang up to ask when the baby would be born. I was in the midst of very urgent work and told Suzi, my wife, to tell them it would obviously be when Jupiter culminated later that day but I did not have time to work it out. In due course Prince William was born at 9.03 pm with Jupiter just 2 degrees past the MC. In some senses this was a lucky, commonsense 'hit', but at another level one wants to know why Jupiter was 2 degrees past the MC and not exactly on it! There must be good and sufficient reason for this. This may well be involved with the intricate laws of astro-genetics for it is a fascinating fact that Prince William's MC and AS are identical within minutes of arc to those of his great-great grandfather Edward VII.

The most important pointer here to unravelling the mysteries of this final daily timing of events is, as we might expect, given by John Addey in the very last pages of that most profound of astrology books *Harmonics in Astrology*. Here he states that the harmonic approach to astrology offers us:

> . . . a more credible view of how the nativity can coincide so precisely with the appropriate symbolic cosmic conditions. The major harmonic (i.e., aspect) patterns, being relatively slow forming, determine the approximate time of birth; the higher frequency harmonics indicate possible appropriate moments of birth of shorter duration but which occur more often, so that in the case of, say, the 100th harmonic of the Ascendant, there will be one hundred moments in the day of *equivalent value* (in relation to that harmonic). Thus one after another the wards of a complex combination lock can engage, as it were, to yield a moment of birth which corresponds symbolically with the pattern of the life to be born.

This is an exciting path which as yet lies relatively untrodden. Undoubtedly explorations in this direction will serve to illuminate the workings of cycles at every level in the chain.

The Phases of Planetary Cycles and National Leaders

Whilst it is convenient to talk of nations as abstract entities we know that in practice a nation's ideals, aspirations, and efforts, or lack of them, at any one time, tend to be personified and expressed through the nation's leadership. This is most obvious in the case of the absolute dictator as is found in the Communist and Facist systems of government. For better or worse absolute leaders like Brezhnev, Franco, Hitler, Mao, Mussolini, Stalin, and Tito directly express and constellate the unconscious development of their people at a particular time. In hereditary monarchies such as, for example, the UK, Belgium, Denmark, Holland, Japan, Norway, Spain, or Sweden, the reigning monarch, in so far as he or she is truly identified with the nation's highest interests, symbolizes the ground base of the nation's attitudes and development during a particular period, whilst the prime ministers, who come and go with changes in popular sentiment, express particular phases in the developing themes of the national consciousness.

In the elective systems of leadership such as adopted in, for example, the USA, France or Israel, the president has a very large measure of power, albeit temporary. Such individuals will tend therefore to be particularly 'products of their time', resonating to the major cycles as they occur in the sky.

We can obtain something of the full force of the interweaving of planetary cycle and catch a hint of what is implied by the cyclical unfoldment of time by studying a specific example. The great subtleties of the way in which we resonate to cycles can be seen in the case of the assassination of President Kennedy.

The well-known alleged connection between the cycle of Jupiter-Saturn conjunctions and the death of US presidents is summarized under the notes on Jupiter-Saturn, and it would therefore seem reasonable to see if there is any connection between the phases of this cycle and the life of Kennedy.

Kennedy (see Fig. 6.4) was in fact himself born with Saturn on the MC with Jupiter in the eighth house applying to the sextile. We will therefore perhaps not be surprised to find that he resonated to the Jupiter-Saturn conjunction which was within 5° of conjunction at his Inauguration on 20 January 1961 (12°.51′.13 EST) (Fig. 6.5) and which actually came exact on his IC at 25CN12 on 19 February 1961. The fact that Saturn is in the tenth, the classic signature of a dramatic fall from grace at some point, and that Jupiter is in the eighth house associated with death seems to link him with the so-called 'presidential death cycle'. What has not been noted before

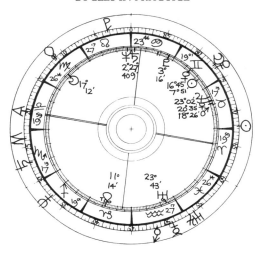

Figure 6.4 J. F. Kennedy's natal chart, 15.00 EST, 29 May 1917, Brookline, Massachusetts, 42N20, 71W08. Data as from mother and birth certificate.

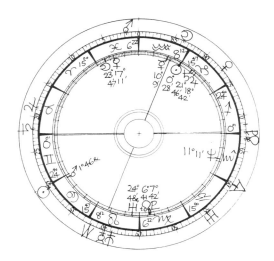

Figure 6.5 J. F. Kennedy's inauguration as President, 17.51.13″ GMT, 20 January 1961, Washington, 38N53°03″, 77W00′06″, mNN 8VI18. Data from Richard Murakami of New York.

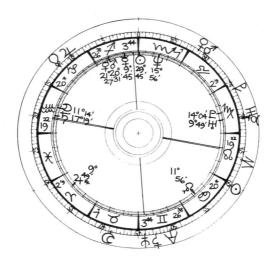

Figure 6.6 The assassination of J. F. Kennedy, 12.30 CST, 22 November 1963, Dallas, Texas, 32N47, 96W49.

is that at the time of his assassination (Fig. 6.6) we find that Jupiter is just forming up a 'fated' outgoing septile with Saturn, which was to come exact on 5 December at Jupiter's station.

Interesting though this is, a closer examination shows that the picture is in fact much more subtle and interesting. If we look at Kennedy's chart we find that he was in fact born with Jupiter and Saturn at crucial phases in two other major cycles. Saturn was just forming up its conjunct with Neptune on his MC, whilst Jupiter was at its exact outgoing square to Uranus 89°.20'. We might wonder what these cycles were doing at these two crucial moments in his life.

At his Inauguration as president we find that Saturn is within 16' of exactitude of its 'power'-oriented quintile to Neptune, which might be translated as 'knowing how to earth visions', and that Jupiter is within 59' of bi-quintile Uranus, 'knowing how to develop personal autocracy'.

At his assassination we find Saturn is just separating (by 1°.23') from the exact outgoing square to Neptune, 'I manifest my sacrifice', and that, as at birth, this Saturn-Neptune contact is closely angular. Perhaps even more striking is the fact that Jupiter is at its exact (0°.0') partile incoming (i.e., eighth-house 'death'), quincunx to Uranus on the very day. Indeed it occurred exactly ten minutes on the clock after the fatal shots were fired! And as though to complete the interlinking we find that Uranus at this time at 9VI49 has just passed the 90 to the USA's natal Uranus at 8GE55 (see p.439) and cf. Uranus was at 10GE22 when Roosevelt suddenly died in April 1945).

We could of course go on to examine many of the other current cycles for this time but space does not permit. Other striking resonances that should be noted in a fuller analysis are that Kennedy was born with an outgoing ME-90-UR. At the time he was shot we find an outgoing ME-90-UR is within an hour or so of exactitude. He was also born with an outgoing MA-90-UR. He died as Mars was closing to the outgoing 'fateful' MA2/7-UR. Born with an almost exact incoming MA-45-PL, we find an outgoing MA-90-PL in the assassination chart.

Thus whilst we normally tend to think of looking at events in terms of transits to natal positions what we are in fact seeing is that far from being separate and isolated from the natal chart, the transits are in fact a pattern of continuing cyclical resonance. Thus, for example, other points not yet noted are that the line of Kennedy's lunar nodes has passed through 1 ½ cycles at the time of the shooting. Thus the natal true NN was at 11CP14, here we find it conjoined by the true SN at 11CP56 and as though to underline the critical importance of this connection we find that the MC/AS of this fatal moment is 11CP33, within 2′ of the exact NN/SN!

Likewise not only do we find the AS of the moment triggering Kennedy's UR-90-MA-JU but we also find that this with Saturn triggers one of the most highly sensitive areas in the USA chart (see Chapter 13). Furthermore we find that the MC of this moment is almost exactly -90- the JU-180-UR position of 8 November 1962 of 3PI33.

These are intriguing interconnections but we must now ask whether there is some way in which these particular cycles could have been located to a particular place on earth. It is here that the drawing up of charts for planetary cycles has a potentially powerful role to play, and it is to this that we shall turn next.

Interpreting the charts of planetary cycles

Most astrologers are used to interpreting charts for specific moments rather than thinking in terms of cyclical processes. This is certainly an important approach which needs to be developed on a systematic basis, for there can be no doubt that the charts for conjunctions and phases of cycles, when properly interrelated with one another, can be deeply illuminating. A detour into astrological theory may help some to get to grips with what it is we are doing when we look at these charts. (Those readers who would prefer to skip the theory are advised to move on four paragraphs.)

The disconcerting thing about these cycle charts is that they must be considered to remain in effect for the full length of their cycle, and to be in a state of constant interaction with every other cycle. Thus, to take an extreme example, the chart for the 1891/2 NE-0-PL must in some senses be sensitive for the following 492 years! This may at first sight seem absurd, especially when we consider the large number of cycles that must therefore be 'in force' at any given moment. Yet in fact if we think about the interrelationship of time and eternity we realize that, in so far as the motions of the heavens are almost totally regular and predictable, we can say that the subsequent unfoldments of time are totally implicit in eternity in the first place. Thus we have to accept that the cosmic conditions in which mankind participates at this moment are an inevitable consequence of it being this moment.

So it is at any point in time. The position of any conjunction is the outgrowth of all the motions that preceded it, and it in turn implies all the relative positions of each subsequent phase and their intermeshings with other cycles. Indeed such total patternings are in a real sense predetermined. We accept this to be the case every time we look into our ephemeris which was probably calculated some years ago. Short of physically shifting the orbits of the planets there is, in one sense, nothing we can do about this. Yet if the physical sequence of processes is preordained, our response to these patterns in time need not be. By raising our level of response we can open ourselves to receive and work with these same preordained patternings at a higher level.

When we set up a chart for a particular phase in a particular cycle, say JU-0-UR, we are, as it were, taking a cross-section through the preordained unfolding 'body' and life processes of the cosmos as a whole. Such charts are in a sense like a hologram of what the cosmos, as a whole is doing at a particular moment in its life. Put another way, our charts for different phases of different cycles are like a series of 'freeze-frames' of a holographic videotape of the cosmos. Each hologram is registering a selected moment in the total process of unfolding time.

Such charts show us exactly where everything is at the moment that our selected synod reaches its exact phase. We thus have both a picture of that moment in time *and a picture of the implications of that moment, for the process of that cycle and the cosmos as a whole*. By examining different threads, different synods, of the cosmic whole at precise moments, we are looking at this same cosmic body from different angles and through different magnification lenses. The views taken through the low-powered, wide-angled lenses (i.e., the slow cycles) give us the large situation that is being unfolded in context, against the broad background. The pictures taken through the close-up lenses zoom in on particular facets of the situation, the particular ideas that are unfolding and enmeshing one with another in particular ways at particular times.

Each phase in a cycle is an expression of a particular numerical archetype. Thus, for example, the *conjunction* phase can show us the unity of the cycle as a whole. The *opposition* reveals something of the objective expression of the idea of the cycle. The *square* will show us the way in which the idea of the cycle will strive to manifest itself and so on. If we understand the meaning of the phase then we can put up a chart for that phase and it will show us how that aspect of the root idea of the cycle will manifest itself during that cycle. By setting such charts for different parts of the world and noting the angles and the MC/AS (and the house cusps if we wish), we can see how that aspect of the idea will resonate with that particular point in space.

We will be concentrating primarily here on the conjunction or unitive phase of cycles on the basis that these should give us something of the essential essence of the meaning of the cycle. But charts for other phases each have their own particular value. Thus the pioneering Canadian astrologer Heinz Antoni[2] has made a specialized study on the -120- phase of cycles, and has come up with some remarkable results. This phase has very much to do with 'flowering' and 'fruition' and enjoyment. Antoni has found that election successes are often best seen reflected in the charts for the preceding SO-120-JU, SO-120-SA, and VE-120-JU, and also ME-120-MA, and ME-120-JU, when these are set for the candidates place of birth. Examining many hundred such charts he has found that 'the candidate from the stronger region always wins'. By stronger he means with appropriate planets angular and traditonally well-configured. Using this method alone, without any reference to the candidate's birth chart or the

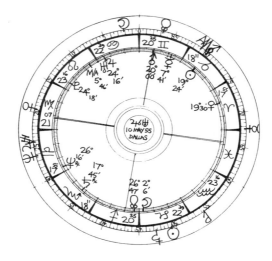

Figure 6.7   The JU-0-UR prior to J.F.K's Assassination, 20.34 GMT, 20 May 1955, set for Dallas, Texas, 32N47, 96W49.

national birth chart, he has been able to make some highly confident predictions, including the last US election when he was able to declare with confidence well ahead of the polls that 'Ronald W. Reagan will be the new president of the US'. Antoni has also noted the importance of trine configurations in world affairs. Thus on 19 April 1948 there was an *exact* Grand Trine of SO-120-MO-120-JU at 28°55' of AR/LE/SG. Calculated for the moment of exactitude Jupiter fell exactly on the MC through Palestine, just twenty-four days later the State of Israel was called into being, under this very meridian.

Returning to our example of Kennedy's assassination, let us look at the pictures we get when we freeze-frame some of the main cycles in which this event took place, and the way that these cycles relate to those of Kennedy and the USA.

The preceding JU-0-UR occurred on 10 May 1955, 20.34 GMT. Fig. 6.7 shows this set for Dallas. We note first that the JU-UR fell exactly on Kennedy's natal MC, thus searchlighting him as a potential key figure in the unfoldement of this cycle. Mercury at 7GE41 is only 10' from Kennedy's Sun indicating perhaps that he can be in some sense a spokesman for what this cycle embodies, whilst the

Sun is exactly with Kennedy's ME-0-MA-45-PL, emphasizing that this cycle will for him focus on his forceful powers of persuasion, debate, and argument. Most dramatically we see that here at Dallas at this moment Mars, ruler of gunshots, was exactly culminating right on the USA's natally difficult Mars at 21GE23-90- US's NE 22VI25 right on the AS, and US NN at 6LE36 right on the MC / AS. Furthermore we find for the moment that the cycle AS = JU/SA 21 V101 = SA/UR 21VI01, whilst the MC = SO/JU 21GE50 = SO/UR 21GE50. These fall with Kennedy's SO/PL 21GE50 = MA/SA 22GR48. Thus whilst the cycle as a whole throws Kennedy into the limelight (JU-0-UR on his MC) when viewed specifically from Dallas we see that it is creating highly tense, potentially violent and destructive combinations both for Kennedy and for the USA chart. If the above pictures are translated literally using Ebertin's[17] COSI they will be found to tell much of the story.

We may now pause and reflect that what we are looking at here are two pictures that were implicit in the structure of the cycle over 8 ½ years prior to their eventual manifestation! But the JU-150-UR which occurred just ten minutes after the shooting is also not without significance. Here we find that the AS has moved to 22AQ41 approaching -180- Kennedy's UR -90 his JU. Thus the JU-150-UR phase (with all its 'death' connotations) picks up his own JU-UR. The MC at 6SG07 is applying to -0-ME and -90- UR at this moment, and -180- Kennedy's SO and -90- Kennedy's MC / AS 6VI52. The resonance is complete. But why did this in fact occur ten minutes earlier? Was it perhaps the fact that at the moment of the shooting the MC at 3SG44 had just formed the manifesting -90- aspect to the position of the 8 October 1962 JU-180-UR at 3PI33, the 'objective expression' of the idea of this cycle, and which had marked the Cuba Crisis? This must we imagine be one of the 'final wards of the combination lock' . . .

Turning to the Saturn-Neptune cycle, since this is clearly of crucial importance, with the -0- occupying Kennedy's natal MC, we find that the preceding SA-0-NE to the Kennedy era occurred three times. The first on 21 November 1952 at 13.22 GMT, the next on 17 May 1953 at 17.22 GMT, and the third on 22 July 1953 at 01.39 GMT. This cycle as we have seen (p.183) is related to the earthing of ideals, or the fear of ideas. Over the past three cycles this seems to be particularly related to Communism and its development. It is

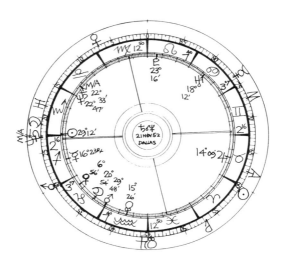

Figure 6.8   The first SA-0-NE prior to J.F.K's Assassination, 13.22 GMT
21 November 1952, set for Dallas, Texas, 32N47, 96W49. The second and
third conjunctions were at 17.22 GMT, 17 May in 21LI38, and 01.39 GMT
22 July 1953 in 21LI12.

intriguing to note that Lee Harvey Oswald, Kennedy's assassin, was
a communist who had been greatly influenced by his visit to the Soviet
Union.

When there is a triple conjunction such as this it is arguable which
one we should take as the beginning of the cycle. In fact all three
will, each in their own way, offer an important perspective on the
enfolded picture, as though we are looking at the same seed from
different angles. We may note first of all that all three conjunctions
fall in the same area of the cardinals as the JU-SA, and JU-UR just
discussed. Thus they fall on Kennedy's AS and -90- his MC. The
first, the only one we have space to illustrate (Fig. 6.8) shows SA-0-NE
at 22LI47 exactly on the MC/AS at 22LI33 at Dallas, in a T-square
with MO-MA, -180-UR. The MA/UR is at 24AR00 with the
conjunction and the MC/AS. The MC is -90-MA/SA and MA/NE
at 11SG17, whilst Pluto is closely -180- Kennedy's UR and -90-JU
— cumulatively a dangerous picture. This is further reinforced by
the second conjunction, at 21LI38, which shows MC 11TA14, AS
16LE50, MC/AS 29GE02, Pluto rises in 20LE51, with the AS this

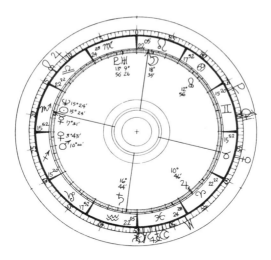

Figure 6.9   The SO-0-NE prior to J.F.K's assassination, 12.58 GMT, 8 November 1963, set for Dallas, Texas, 32N47, 96W49.

time on MA/SA and MA/NE at 16LE31. The MA/UR is at 28GE35 -0- the MC/AS. This dangerous combination falls close to Kennedy's relocation MC for Dallas of 29GE58. The third conjunction, at 21LI12, shows the MC at 19SC55 -180- Kennedy's ME-0-ME, and is -90- PL at 22LE08. The true SN, 3LE18, and DS conjoin Kennedy's NE, whilst a triple conjunction of UR 19CN25, MA 24CN59, and SO 28CN57 falls -90- Kennedy's AS, and -0- MC, and -0- SA respectively.

Having looked at some of the major synods covering this period we now need to do what Barbault advocates (see p.189) and consider how the solar cycle brings this general potential of the time into specific manifestation. Barbault himself does not advocate drawing up such charts but simply uses the solar aspects as timers. However it will be seen that the actual charts for such conjunctions can be a powerful additional tool in our work when used in conjunction with the spectrum of other cycle charts.

Fig. 6.9 shows the beginning of the annual Sun-Neptune cycle on 8 November 1963, 00.57 pm GMT, set for Dallas. Sun-Neptune represents either the earthing and chanelling of some kind of vision and idealism or the dissolution and undermining of power and authority. In our present world it is all too often the latter. Here at Dallas we see that this configuration is exactly rising -0- ME square a culminating MO-180-SA on the IC. This is surely about as difficult and problematic a combination as can be imagined. To make matters more problematic still, the Moon is exactly -45- MC/AS at 3LI58 right on one of the most difficult configurations in the US chart (see p.439). Note how this in turn later becomes the DS of the actual assassination chart (Fig. 6.6). At the same time note that Kennedy's MA-90-UR is here with the DS-IC angles. It is notable that the SA-90-NE on 18 February 1963, 21.59 GMT, occurred at 15AQ/SC40 which is exactly the AS of this chart here at Dallas. (In the chart for this SA-90-NE phase set for Dallas, 2LE08 rises exactly with Kennedy's natal Neptune and the Moon is at 24SG10 on Kennedy's MA/SA 22GE48 and MA/NE 25GE33!) In the light of so much Neptune converging on this point it is hardly surprising that Kennedy's assassination is still surrounded by uncertainties and continuing innuendoes of conspiracy and cover-up!

This example illustrates the power of these cyclical charts, taken collectively, to delineate an 'event' with an unnerving precision which must inevitably raise the question of fate and freewill. (See Addey [1] for a clear and concise summary of the astrologer's position on this vital issue.) But fascinating as this particular example is, we may reasonably ask whether such cycle charts can help us to examine the larger sweep of history retrospectively and prospectively. The great Charles Carter [12] devotes a considerable section of his 'Introduction' to specific examples of the power of charts for the Great Conjunctions for pinpointing different areas and nations. He shows, for example, the crucial indications given by the JU-0-UR of 4 March 1914 and other conjunctions for World War One and the importance of interrelating these charts with national charts. However, because his approach is not cyclical in the full sense, he restricts himself to looking at effects precipitated close to the actual time of conjunctions. Thus he dismisses as 'probably a coincidence, though a curious one, that both these loci (16TA30 and 4LE46, the positions of the last two SA-0-NE) fall in significant points in the maps of Hitler and Mussolini, who did so much to spread ruin and chaos throughout Europe.' In the light of our findings we would in fact argue that it would be impossible for anyone or any nation to have a major impact upon the world if they were not intimately 'tuned in' to such cycles.

   To illustrate the value of these charts in filling out the broad brush

Figure 6.10   The Wright brothers make man's first powered flight, 10.35 EST, 17 December 1903, Kitty Hawk, 36N02, 75W42.

strokes of one area of recent history let us consider the Jupiter-Uranus 'horizon-shattering' cycle in relation to mankind's movement out into space and the dawning of the space age. Obviously, as we have shown elsewhere [23] the potentiality for such a momentous step for mankind is not exclusively described by this one cycle but will have been heralded and reflected in numerous different ways.

The Jupiter-Uranus cycle charts and the space age
We do not have space here to examine the whole of this process in detail but we may note in passing that from the very beginnings of the space age, i.e., from the moment the Wright brothers got the Kitty Hawk airborne (see Fig. 6.10, above) that the 'revolutionary ideas' (Jupiter-Uranus) is involved. In this first chart we find Jupiter was 80° 02′, exactly 2/9th, ahead of Uranus, that powerful phase which often seems indicative of the first fruits of the pursuit of a particular idea or ideal. The JU-O-UR chart prior to this lift-off, and which in part must symbolize this, occurred at 8.17am 20 October 1900 (Fig. 9.7, p.266). This shows MC 17GE56 exactly with Pluto at 17GE30, the AS 19VI08 is -O-MO(!) 21VI33 whilst the JU-UR at 10SG06 falls -O-I.C. in the 3rd and exactly on the USA's AS

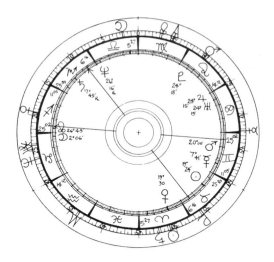

Figure 6.11   The JU-0-UR prior to the launching of Sputnik, 20.34 GMT, 10 May 1955, set for Moscow, 55N45, 37E35.

-180-UR. The Moon of this chart is right on the USA NE 22VI25-90-MA 21GE23. (At the launch of the Apollo XI Pluto had arrived at 22VI56-180-NN 22PI30!) The fact that SA 0CP13-180-NE 29GE10 is with the solar apex (q.v.) at 1CP03, and -90- the super galactic centre (q.v.) 00LI23 and the galactic centre 25SG28 is probably not entirely without significance. However for the period of the actual space programme itself we must turn to the Jupiter-Uranus cycle of 1955-69.

The 1955 JU-0-UR itself is shown in Fig. 6.11. It is set for Moscow as the decision-making capital of the USSR, who were the initial pioneers of space. In this chart we see the Jupiter-Uranus cycle exactly in a closing -30-PL. This is indicative that this cycle is to sow the seeds of some kind of large-scale revolutionary developments. The MC for Moscow is almost exactly at its 2/7 phase to the JU-UR indicating that the consciousness of this place is likely to be inspired in some way by the ideas enfolded within this cycle. The -0- also receives the powerful outgoing -150- from the AS showing that the motivation and effort can be made at this place to actualize the inherent potential.

As will be seen on pp.337 and 338, the fact that the NN at this time is closely rising at Moscow, exactly on the galactic centre (q.v.)

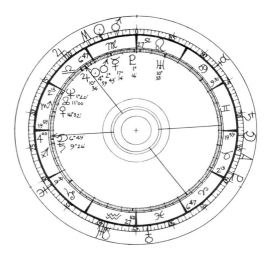

Figure 6.12 The JU-60-UR prior to the launching of Sputnik, 09.27 GMT, 28 September 1957, set for Moscow, 55N45, 37E35.

and that the appropriately rising Moon is on the solar apex (q.v.) at this moment is highly indicative of the 'cosmic' orientation of this cycle (cf., the 1900 Kitty Hawk JU-O-UR above and p.266).

Moving on to the outgoing JU-60-UR 'putting the idea to work' phase, this came exact on 28 September 1957. Set for Moscow, Fig 6.12 shows Jupiter culminating with the Sun and Mars, and -60- the rising Moon and Saturn in Sagittarius, dramatic testimony that the potential of this cycle can become activated effectively at this place. (The launch-site itself was of course at an entirely different latitude and longitude!) The actual successful launch of Sputnik followed on 4 October, just eleven days after this aspect, exactly as the Sun, the timer of the day of an event, came exactly conjunct Jupiter and sextile Uranus and sextile Saturn! The NN/SN axis, which so often seems to indicate what ideas are being focused and channelled at a particular time, is within minutes of the exact -90-UR- and -135 the GC 26SG15 — an 'awakening' for mankind indeed!

The first -180-phase of this cycle occurred on 14 March 1962 at 27LE/AQ28 exactly across the USA's Moon at 27LE10! In this chart the Moon is at 8CN39 — just twenty-two days before John Glenn had become the first American to orbit the earth. On 17 July 1969,

at 4.16pm GMT with the SO 24CN54 (the JU-0-UR occurred at
24CN15 remember!), and as the MC got to 8CN05 (the very position
of the Moon at the JU-180-UR) the Apollo XI blasted off for the
Moon. At 7.59am GMT on 20 July 1969 this JU-UR cycle ended
and a new JU-UR cycle began on 0LI40 -0-SGC 1LI21. At 8.18pm
GMT, with the new cycle less than twelve hours old, Armstrong took
his 'step for all mankind'!

Such retrospective examples serve to illustrate how intimately events
and the cycles they express are interlocked, indeed so intertwined
that they are vivid evidence for the thesis of Bohm[11] and others that
matter and consciousness are one unbroken whole. Astrology in this
sense can be seen as the linguistic/algebraic interface which expresses
both. This said it is of course another matter to turn round and use
these cycles prospectively for constructive forecasting.

To apply these ideas effectively is going to require further patient
analysis of many more cases to establish the hierarchies of the different
cycles and to isolate the principles by which different cycles interrelate and are 'triggered'. This is a job for which computer graphic
techniques will need to be developed. A series of Astrocartographs
superimposed one upon another on the map of the globe is one
obvious approach. Without such analysis and tools effective
forecasting must remain a relatively hit-and-miss affair, because of
the many dozens if not hundreds of cycles and charts from which
to work.

World astrology watch
But just as meteorologists are now able to keep all areas of the globe
under a twenty-four-hour 'world weather watch' so as responsible
astrologers we should be developing an equivalent 'world astrology
watch'. By the systematic plotting of the numerous cycles for every
capital and major population centre in the world it should be possible
to identify the major build-up of potential at any particular time,
and develop ways of assisting society to express these in the most
ideal, beneficial and constructive manner. At one time this idea might
have seemed a Neptunian pipe-dream. Now, thanks to readily
available computer programs — notably the remarkable M65 research
program, produced and made available by the noble dedication and
generosity of Michael Erlewine, we can store all the necessary data
on permanent file. With this we can relocate and print out an
appropriate sequence of maps for any place in the world in a matter

of hours. The advantage we have over the meteorologists is that we can plot out our maps for any distance ahead *now*.

By such a systematic and orderly exploration of the cycles of times past, present, and to come astrologers can slowly but surely assist mankind to fulfil its individual and collective potential.

Non-astrological cycle studies
Astrologers cannot live healthily in a vacuum separated from the rest of the intellectual life of the planet. Astrology cannot grow in the way that it needs to until it begins actively to link up with others working in related fields. And we know 'related' covers almost every conceivable area of human knowledge. This is the potential power of astrology. As a system of universal symbolic logic it is a bridge which can link and cross-fertilize apparently divorced and unconnected areas from cosmology to philosophy, from agriculture to mass psychology. But to develop astrology's full potential as a language for the new consciosness we need to attract to it the best minds, the largest experience and the greatest wisdom that is available in the world today. In the realm of mundane astrology this means that we must start to actively interact with economists, historians, sociologists, social psychologists, biologists, ecologists, meteorologists, chemists, and so on.

The point of contact with such disciplines is of course the rapidly increasing emphasis on cyclic studies in all these areas. As it becomes increasingly apparent that many of the cycles observed have some exogenous, i.e., external, origin it is becoming more and more important for researchers in these fields to discover these external causes and develop a comprehensive theory of cycles.

As this is done, as John Addey[1a] says 'It will be realized that the cosmic bodies are the primary unities of the manifested cosmos and that their motions and inter-relationships are the primary determinants of the patterns in time — those ''rhythmic processes'' which characterize all natural processes of growth and unfoldment.'

This realization is probably still some way off but by becoming familiar with work in other areas astrologers can undoubtedly do work and make suggestions which will accelerate this shift in scientific thinking. As Addey gives an excellent summary of the growing body of cycles in Chapter 21 of his *Harmonics in Astrology* there is no virtue in repeating this here, except to underline the importance of the Foundation for the Study of Cycles[53] as a coordinating body

for this area, and a first port of call for such studies. However since
Addey's work was published in 1976 there have been various works
which have begun to fill out the picture and build the bridges.

From the astrological perspective Geoffrey Dean's *Recent Advances*
gives an invaluable summary of the evidence for some of the possible
connections between astrological cycles and such things as solar
activity, economic cycles, the stock market and so on. From a non-
astrological perspective we have works like *The Rhythms of Life* by
Ayensu and Whitfield[3] , and other respected academics who have
put together a valuable coverage of this area. It is a sign of the times
that such a work includes not only material on the Gauquelins' studies
but also presents material on traditional astrological concepts such
as the Jupiter-Saturn cycle and the use of the charts of nations as
well as individuals. Linking both sides of the picture is *The Cycles
of Heaven* by Playfair and Hill[38] which does a commendable job
of assembling the evidence for 'cosmic forces and what they are doing
to you'. From within astrology there is now a growing desire to link
up with other areas, the most striking recent example is that of Barry
Lynes'[31a] work on astro-economics in which he delineates the crucial
role that astrology must play in developing the New Age economics.

As the tide begins to turn we can expect to see cyclical approaches
being taken in every area of civilization and culture — not just the
sciences. Thus the very change of intellectual climate that is going
on at the present time is no doubt part of a definite alternating cycle
of cultures of the kind suggested by the late Professor Thomas F.
Mayo[33]. He suggests that succeeding cultures swing between
romanticism and rationalism, between emotion and reason, and that
in more recent times these swings are speeding up. This is suggestive
of a swing between right and left hemisphere dominance in the
brain[36]. It is interesting to speculate what astrological factors might
be associated with this kind of shift of emphasis in man's collective
consciousness.

Continuing to keep abreast with what is going on in this all-
embracing area is not easy. However *Cycles*, the monthly journal
of the Foundation for the Study of Cycles, and *The Journal of
Interdisciplinary Cycle Research*, its European off-shoot, will certainly
keep us up to date with the non-astrological picture, with occasional
bridging articles of directly astrological interest. In the field of
astrology The Astrological Association's periodicals — the quarterly
The Astrological Journal, the quarterly magazine *Transit* and the

only fully academic journal the bi-annual research publication *Correlation*[15] — provide between them an improving coverage of the field. Details of other astrological periodicals which occasionally publish relevant material will be found under the list of Abbreviations given in Appendix I.

References
For abbreviations of journals, etc. see pp.471-473.

1   Addey, J. *Harmonics in Astrology* L. N. Fowler & Co., 1976. This is the classic work on the subject and essential reading for anyone wanting to get to grips with the underlying principles.

1a Addey, J. *Astrology Reborn* Astrological Association, 1972. A brilliant presentation of the philosophy of astrology and its relation to Neo-Platonism. It touches upon the significance of Professor David Bohm's ideas for astrology's rebirth.

2   Antoni, H. 'Window on the world' *EC,* vol. 5, no. 2, summer 1980, pp.24-30, and vol. 5, no. 3, Fall 1980, pp.17-21.

3   Ayensu, E. S. and Whitfield, P. *The Rhythms of Life* Marshall Editions, 1981; Book Club Associates, 1982.

4   Barbault, A. *La Crise Mondiale de 1965* Albin Michel, 1965.

5   Barbault, A. *Les Astres et l'Histoire* J. J. Pauvert, 1967.

6   Barbault, A. *Le Pronostic Experimental en Astrologie* Payot, Paris, 1973.

7   Barbault, A. *L'Astrologie Mondiale* Fayard, Paris, 1979.

7a. If mundane astrology is to clarify its principles and techniques it is absolutely essential that adequate methods for evaluating astrological forecasts are developed. But this is in fact much more difficult than might at first appear. What may appear to be a remarkable forecasting 'hit' can be seen on closer examination to be little more than an intelligent extrapolation from the circumstances of the time of the forecast. On the other hand an apparently completely erroneous forecast can on closer examination be seen to be right in principles and in timing but wrong in its particulars. Thus the astrologer who predicted 'major air crashes' for the period around 23 February 1982 when the New Moon fell -90- stationary Uranus at 4SG38 on the degree associated with flight was not only unwise to sow fears in peoples minds but in retrospect wrong. However on closer inspection we find that this time did exactly mark the time of the collapse of Freddie Laker's airline and a major crisis and upheaval in the world's airline industry. Thus the forecast was right in principle: a Uranian impact on matters to do with flight/aircraft. But in attempting to be more specific and translate abstract principles into 'events' the astrologer drifted way off course. As Ptolemy, or a follower, put it in the first aphorism nearly 2,000 years ago:

> . . . it is not possible that particular forms of events should be declared by any person, however scientific; since the understanding conceives only a certain general idea of some sensible event, and not its particular form. It is, therefore, necessary for him who practices herein to adopt inference. They only who are inspired by the deity can predict particulars.

One of the few attempts to make a systematic evaluation of mundane astrological forecasts is a salutary monograph by the French astrologer Jacques Reverchon. In his valuable, privately published, *Valeur des Jugements et Pronostics Astrologiques* (with text in English and French, Residence Gambetta J.6, 91 Yerres, France) he makes a systematic analysis of Andre Barbault's forecasts in connection with the course of the Algerian War and of his '1964; La Crise Mondial de 1965'. The latter was Barbault's attempt to assessess the impact of the major UR-0-PL -180- SA configuration and attendant phenomena on world affairs. Reverchon's approach is two-fold:

1. He lists and dates all the historically important turning points in the Algerian crisis, and all the major events during 1964/1965 and compares them against Barbault's predictions.
2. He lists all the key dates and forecasts made by Barbault and compares these with what actually occured at these times.

Reverchon shows that by both approaches, judged on the particulars he forecast, and did not forecast, Barbault performed no better than chance or the non-astrological informed observer might have done. Indeed he points out that many of Barbault's specific forecasts, such as that Kennedy and Khruschev would remain in power and that Harold Wilson's future was in doubt, were the exact reverse of the facts. Whilst the study can be faulted for not attempting to show in what sense the forecasts were symbolically correct, this study once again illustrates the dangers of attempting to move from general principles to specific interpretations. It also points up the common failing of astrologers: that of developing a single theory and scenario of the future to which all the factors are made to fit. It is extremely tempting to try to paint a global picture but the over simplification involved can only lead to sensationalism and fatalism and clouds the underlying principles in the understanding of which lies man's potential freedom.

Only a complete historical examination of the period can show how sound Barbault's underlying arguments were in this particular case. But despite Reverchon's well-founded criticisms Barbault was certainly vindicated in perceiving this period as the inception of a critical period for the USA, one in which would lead to its decline as a dominant world power (PL-UR-180-SA), and an increase in Communist power. It marked the inception of the Vietnam War and the confrontation between industralized (UR) West and traditional (SA) East. Likewise the 'revolutionary potential' of UR-0-PL in Virgo instead of working out at a physical level of international conflict, can happily be seen, retrospectively, as marking a key period in technological revolution of the micro-chip.

8   Barbault, A. 'The Jupiter-Uranus Conjunction of 1983' *AJ* XXV, nos. 2 and 3, spring and summer, 1983.

9   Benjamin, Elbert = C. C. Zain *Mundane Astrology* Church of Light, 1939.

10 Boeke, K. *Cosmic View — The Universe in 40 Jumps* John Day Co., New York, 1957. Though not philosophical as such this book uses a set of forty illustrations to give an excellent perspective on the scale of the universe from the nucleus of the sodium atom to beyond the level of super galaxies.

11 Bohm, D. *Wholeness and the Implicate Order* Routledge & Kegan Paul, 1981. Bohm is Professor of Theoretical Physics at Birbeck College, London University. He treats matter and consciousness as an unbroken whole and presents a model of the universe in which astrology can readily be accommodated.

12 Carter, C. E. O. *IPA*, pp.29-40. Carter gives a valuable coverage of Great Conjunction charts with numerous compelling examples of their importance.

13 Collin, R. *The Theory of Celestial Influences — Man, the*

Universe and Cosmic Mystery Robinson & Watkin, London, 1954. Collin elaborates his basic thesis in very considerable detail with especial emphasis on the shape, organic development of civilizations, and their sequential unfoldment. He emphasizes the importance of the relative time scales of individuals and collectives and the position of individual man as a specialized cell within the collective organism. He considers the various major phases of western civilization as a series of organic unities with their own major cycles of unfoldment, and he traces the crucial role of the mystery schools and esoteric movements as special 'cells of consciousness' in the regeneration of civilizations.

14 Collin, R. op.cit. Collin presents valuable tables of suggestive evidence for these ideas in the Appendix to *The Theory of Celestial Influence*.

15 *Correlation,* the bi-annual research publication of the UK Astrological Association is the only academic level periodical in astrology. It is very much serving as a bridgehead for the entry of well-tested astrological findings into the world of orthodox science.

16 Devore, N. *Encyclopedia of Astrology* Philosophical Library, New York, 1947. Contains a valuable entry on planetary cycles, pp.74-84 by Charles A. Jayne.

17 Ebertin, R. *The Combination of Stellar Influences* (normally abbreviated COSI) AFA, P.O. Box 22040, Tempe, Arizona 85282. Despite its jaded view of Neptune and its seemingly fatalistic tone this is one of the finest books on the observed effects of planetary combinations, and the standard work on mid-point interpretation. Although written mainly for natal astrology a 'sociological correspondence' is given for each combination and interpretations can be readily adapted for mundane work.

18 Ganeau, C. *See L'AST* no. 35 and 37. A summary appears in ref. 7, above, pp.284-291, and 297-98.

19 Green, H. S. *Mundane or National Astrology* L. N. Fowler. Although originally published at the turn of the century this little book is still one of the finest of its kind, with very practical down-to-earth observations on the likely manifestations of the planetary aspects, and remains a good 'first resort' when considering aspects.

20 Halbronn, J. *Clefs pour L'astrologie* Seghers 1976, pp.143-169.

21 Hamblin, D. *Harmonic Charts — A New Dimension in*

Astrology Aquarian Press, 1983.

22 Harvey, C. *Astrology, Number, and the Transcendant — The Interpretation of Harmonic Charts* Sofia Foundation, 1984.

23 Harvey, C. 'The galactic centre and beyond' *AJ,* XXV, no. 2, spring 1983, pp.74-84.

24 Hoyle, F. *The Black Cloud* Heinemann, 1960. This sci-fi novel by the eminent astronomer explores the interactions of the different levels of consciousness of man and vast cosmic bodies.

25 ISCWA *Cycles in Mundane Astrology* ISCWA, due autumn 1984. A survey of the different cycles, both transit and national, used in mundane astrology today, together with appropriate tables.

26 ISCWA *The Astrology of the Middle East* ISCWA, due autumn 1984. A study of the national charts and major cycles relating to this critical area of the world, including a detailed analysis of the astrology of Israel.

27 Janis, C. 'Vertebrate evolution and the great, great, great, great year' *AQ,* vol. 53-3; vol. 54-1, pp.15-20.

28 Jayne, C. A. See article in ref. 16. Also in the now out-of-print international astrological research journal *In Search* (1958-61), which was one of the finest periodicals of its kind ever produced.

29 Julien P. *L'AST* no. 41, and also summarized in ref. 7 above, pp.291-95.

30 Kenton, W. *As Above So Below — A Study in Cosmic Progression* Stuart & Watkin, 1969. This book uses astronomical and aerial photographs and words to take us through the various levels of the creation from supergalaxies down to man.

31 Lynes, B. *The Next 20 Years* Lynes, P.O. Box 15247, Springfield, Mass. 01115, USA. Despite its rather paranoid and hectoring style this is essential reading. His analysis of the cyclical dynamics of the USA and Russian charts and their implications for the world are extremely fine. Integrated with a broader cyclical perspective this is an essential part of the makings of the new mundane astrology.

31a Lynes, B. *Secret Astrology: Russia's Past and Future and Astroeconomics* are both available from the above address.

32 Martin, C. Although yet unpublished her work on historical cycles is considered by Leyla Rael Rudhyar to be of the highest importance, and far superior to anything yet available. ISCWA will give immediate notice of her work when available.

33 Mayo, Thomas F. *The Great Pendulum,* an unpublished essay and ms. outline for a book by the late Professor of English at the Agricultural and Mechanical College of Texas, in the possession of the writer (CH).

34 Naylor, J. 'The British Elections' *AQ,* vol. 54-2, pp.38-42.

35 van Norstrand *Precepts in Mundane Astrology* Macoy, New York, 1962.

36 Ornstein, R. *The Mind Field* Viking Press, New York, 1976. The fact that it is now clear that we each have two almost autonomous halves to our brain: the left-hand side 'masculine', logical, verbal, intellectual; the right-hand side 'feminine', emotional, musical, intuitive must have important implications for how we apply our astrology. It also leads us to speculate whether there necessarily has to be a parallel mind / emotion split within nations and societies. That there certainly is at the present time is self-evident. We might see parliamentary democracy with its built-in 'opposition' as an instinctive safeguard against this potential social schizophrenia. It is significant that totalitarian regimes find it that much easier to institute a social divorce between thinking and feeling, and are the most adept at double-think, and at repressing unwanted elements.

37 Ouspensky, P. D. *A New Model of the Universe* Routledge & Kegan Paul, 1st ed. 1931, 3rd p/b 1974. In particular see the chapter which gives the book its title, in which he discusses the importance of asking what *form* our world and universe take.

38 Playfair, G. L. and Hill, S. *The Cycles of Heaven* Souvenir, 1978; Pan, 1979.

39 Plato in *Phaedo.* This translation from *The Human Soul in the Myths of Plato*, p. 41, by The Shrine of Wisdom, Fintry, Brook, Godalming, Surrey.

40 Quanier, J. H. editor of *The New Humanity Journal*, describing itself as the world's first politico-spiritual journal, coined the word pneumatocracy to mean 'the rule of the spirit and soul', whereby the inner, higher self within each person guides his / her actions through creativity and intuition. Published 51A York Mansions, Prince of Wales Drive, London SW11.

41 Richfield, K. 'The presidential death cycle: myth and reality' *CAOT,* vol. 4, no. 2, 1980, pp.6-9.

42 Rudhyar, D. *Astrological Timing — The Transition to the New Age* Harper Colophon Books, 1972. (1st ed. entitled *Birth*

Patterns for a New Humanity, Servire, 1969.) One of the few comprehensive attempts to elaborate a coherent theory of planetary cycles and human evolution. His wife, Leyla Rudhyar Rael has recently (1981/82) been doing pioneering work putting flesh on this somewhat abstract skeleton.

43   Rudhyar, D. *The Lunation Cycle* Shambhala, 1971. Though focused on natal astrology the principles outlined hold good in mundane cycles.

44   Rael Rudhyar, L. Shambala Astrological Calendars for 1982 and 1983. (Shambala, 1920 13th Street, Boulder, Colorado 80302.) These contain invaluable essays relating planetary cycles to historic, social, cultural, and political events. The latter essay was reprinted in *AS* 83, spring 1983, pp.13-28.

45   Sepharial *The World Horoscope, Hebrew Astrology — The Key to the Study of Prophecy* W. Foulsham.

46   De Socca, M. *Les Grandes Conjunctions* Editions Traditionelles 1976, 9-11 Quai Saint-Michel, Paris, France. One of the few works as yet available on this vitally important area. Gives approximate dates and positions for the conjunctions of PL-NE, PL-UR, PL-SA, NE-UR, NE-SA, UR-SA, and JU-SA, from 68 BC to AD 2000, together with a selected choice of events from mainly European/French history. Care should be taken with the earlier dates and positions as many errors of one or two years and as much as a whole sign have been noted.

47   Stringer E. T. *The Secret of the Gods — An outline of Tellurianism* Neville Spearman, London, 1974. Dr Stringer is a professional scientist and geographer at Birmingham University. Tellurianism is the belief that the earth and its inhabitants are one. Stringer as a professional geographer beautifully illustrates the organic wholeness of plant Earth with numerous aerial, space, and time-lapse photos. He expands his thesis to the discussion of the levels of consciousness of star systems and galaxies illustrating the different conceptions of time that arise with alterations in magnitude.

48   I have used the word 'enfolded' throughout this discussion of cycles because this is the word the Professor David Bohm (see ref. 11 above) uses to describe the 'implicate' order within the cosmos. Bohm's model of the universe cannot only accommodate astrology but the possibility of astrology is actually implicit within it. Anyone interested in the development of a theoretical

astrology should read this work.

49 An invaluable discussion on levels of consciousness is contained in E. F. Schumacher's profound and delightful little book *A Guide for the Perplexed* Jonathan Cape, 1977. He distinguishes the four classic categories of consciousness: mineral, plant, animal, and human self-consciousness, and goes on to indicate the evident existence of a transpersonal level of consciousness, as reported with great consistency by mystics of all times and from all traditions.

50 There are of course many other points which can be made about Kennedy's assassination. Particularly notable is that Uranus at this time at 9VI49 has just passed the -90- to the USA's natal Uranus at 8GE55, which is almost exactly -45- Kennedy's MC, and also -90- Kennedy's MA/PL at 10GE51. Uranus was also closing to -90- to the USA AS/UR from the Equal House tenth house. Interestingly Uranus was close to this same area, at 10GE22 when Roosevelt suddenly died on 12 April 1945.

51 Details of *L'Astrologue* and other journals will be found under the Abbreviations given at the end of Chapter 14, p.471.

52 Crawford, Arch, *Crawford Perspectives,* Dec. 1981, says that from his anaylsis the New York Stock Market drops about 6% to 7% prior to a conjunction of Jupiter and Pluto. It then reverses direction by at least as much — Crawford is one of the most brilliant and careful workers in this area of research. His newsletter is available from: 250 East 77th Street, New York, N.Y. 10021.

53 The Foundation of the Study of Cycles, 124 South Highland Avenue, Pittsburgh, Pa 15206. Tel: (412)-441-1666.

7.

THE PLANETS

Nicholas Campion, Michael Baigent, Charles Harvey

Whether in natal, mundane, or any other branch of astrology the planets can be seen as symbolic of those archetypal ideas and principles in the light of which the universe is produced and sustained. The closer we can approach and understand these principles in their pure essence the more we will be able to interpret our charts with real insight and establish a 'pure' astrology based on an understanding of causes rather than on a knowledge of particular effects. Such an astrology can be one which is increasingly freed from those natural prejudices and particular sympathies which so often mar and upset our judgement. Most importantly such an approach enables us to see the pure potentiality of a period and situation thus liberating us from the tyranny of fatalism.

The following notes assume a familiarity with the basic planetary archetypes and are only intended to add in something of the mundane dimension to their interpretation. Those seeking further interpretative work on the planets in mundane will find that H. S. Green's little book *Mundane Astrology* though written more than 80 years ago still has a great deal to teach at a practical level. At a deeper level Liz Greene's lectures *The Outer Planets & Their Cycles*[1] deals specifically with the astrology of the collective.

The planets in mundane astrology have exactly the same archetypal meanings as in natal astrology. We are, after all, still working with the same essential symbols and Jupiter still embodies the principle of 'growth' in mundane astrology, and Saturn the principle of 'restriction', just as in natal astrology. It is necessary, however, to make a slight shift in perception away from natal astrology, for we are now dealing with group, rather than individual, behaviour. The concerns are essentially those of politics and may have both a different theoretical basis and practical context to those which arise from a natal horoscope. Nevertheless, the interpretation of the planets in a mundane chart may be approached in a very similar manner to their interpretation in a natal chart.

The Sun (SU)

The Sun is obviously the principal planet in any horoscope, and the Sun sign of a mundane chart will convey much of the essential character of the state or nation, or other organization. It may indicate the supreme authority in the nation — the sovereign body and the leader, the king, queen, president or prime minister. Thus the Sun can represent both the effective political leader and the symbolic head of state. It can also show the way in which a nation expresses itself, the myths and images which it projects and the way in which foreigners view the nation. We have the examples of the UK and the Soviet Union, both with Sun in Capricorn and both very conservative countries. The United States, with its Sun in Cancer first rebelled against Capricorn England, and then selected Capricorn Russia as its principal world enemy.

Thus we can see how global conflicts can be founded on the inability of a Cancer nation to accept its Capricorn opposite, and vice versa. The United States, with its Sun conjunct Jupiter, is obsessed with an ideology of 'freedom' and has a constitution based on clearly defined rights, whereas the chart for Communist Russia (as distinct from the Soviet Union) has its Sun in Scorpio, a position indicating adherence to a rigid State religion and semi-deified national leaders.

The Moon (MO)

The Moon is that on which the Sun, the authority in the State, depends. It is the masses, the common people, and the population as a whole. In particular it rules women in the nation, both in terms of individuals and in terms of the collective's attitude to its female nature and to its women members. In general it represents popular opinion, popular and mass ideologies. The chart for the Polish trade union, Solidarity, shows the Moon as a singleton, the only planet below the horizon, at 23°26′ Taurus, opposing Uranus at 21°57′ Scorpio and Poland's natal Sun at 21°13′ Scorpio. This dramatically emphasized Moon represents the popular, mass appeal of Solidarity. In the Israeli chart the Moon is in Leo, indicating the dominant national philosophy of Zionism, and in the UK the Moon is in the tenth house, representing the institution of parliamentary democracy. In Cancer in the UK chart the Moon also represents the power of English nationalism.

Mercury (ME)

Individuals in a State must communicate with each other, and Mercury represents the means by which they do so. All communication by rail, air, sea, road, post, speech and writing are ruled by Mercury. It represents society's nervous and intellectual systems and all their manifestations through education, literature, postal communications, intellectual movements and trends, schools, and trade. The State authorities have to disseminate their messages to the people, and political speeches and announcements, as well as media events, correlate with Mercury transits. In the chart for Tudor England, Mercury was in Leo, bringing the great age of English literature and William Shakespeare. For the French Third Republic, Mercury was in Libra, bringing the wave of culture and café society pioneered by the Impressionists, the Existentialists and others. In Communist China Mercury is also in Libra, and Chinese art, dance and acrobatics are noted for their delicate grace and beauty.

Venus (VE)

Each planet may be seen as representing a function which helps bind the nation into a State (see Chapter 4). The Sun represents allegiance to a common authority and heritage, the Moon represents the unity of mass opinion, Mercury the necessity of communication, and Venus all those things which make it pleasant for people to stay together. Venusian things enable the State to function without repression. Venus represents the arts, harmony, entertainment and social pleasures. It brings peace, although through its passionate nature it also has associations with war. It rules fashion, glamour, artists, 'bon viveurs' and the 'feminine' archetype. As such it also has particular associations with the women of a country. Through the association of Venus with Taurus there are links with a nation's resources, its financial institutions, bankers, farming and farmers.

In this connection we may also link Venus to its natural metal, copper, in a country's economy.

Nazi Germany had Venus in Capricorn, an interesting reflection of the ideology of 'joy through work' which the government attempted to use to inspire the people without the use of fear. One of the first countries occupied by the Nazi government was Czechoslovakia, and the occupation was accomplished while Venus at 11°6′ Aquarius was transiting the Nazi Sun at 10°15′ Aquarius, an instance of the correlation of Venus with an aggressive act. Charles Carter[2] noted that when used in war, Venus represents victory.

Mars (MA)

Mars represents those forces which hold a State together or drive it apart in terms of aggression. Many countries these days have Martian military governments, while even those which have democratic governments use the threat or fear of war as a means to control their populations. This fact is a commonly recognized part of all international relations theory. At an archetypal level Mars also represents the collective need of a nation or society to have enemies, to express itself aggressively. It can also show what helps a society to grow and to assert itself. It can act divisively and show internal violence from criminal and anti-social acts, or from riots and rebellions. In the UK Mars is in the eighth house and in Taurus, indicating expansion through a global economic empire. The NATO alliance has Mars in Aries, appropriate for a military alliance, while Communist Russia has its Mars in Virgo, indicating the ideology of aggression through international workers revolution.

Jupiter (JU)

A society or nation also needs common values and belief systems if it is to hold together, and these are ruled by Jupiter. We may see these as both a direct expression of the collective unconscious, or as an aspect of political control as in a State religion. Sometimes religion can be a liberating experience, but there is another side to it: Cicero believed that religion saved spending money on police by keeping people well behaved. Thus Jupiter represents the law, both as a means to ensure justice and a means to control the population; and it represents religion, both as a deep experience and as a function of state control. It also represents the monarchy, and its meaning overlaps with the Sun in its rulership of the highest authority in the land. In a more institutional sense it actually represents the courts, Churches, charities. It represents the higher mind — universities, publishing, philosophy, philanthropy — and a nation's sense of well-being. It has links with national wealth and hence with prosperity, wealth, the rich, banks and the financial life of a society. It also represents larger than life images, and in the USA, Jupiter in Cancer represents 'Uncle Sam', while in the UK Jupiter in Leo has brought the emotions of 'Rule Britannia'.

Saturn (SA)

Liz Greene[3] has called Saturn the membrane which separates the personal unconscious from the collective unconscious. In a State it represents the institutions which distinguish order from chaos. Saturn, more than any other planet, represents the State and its institutions and, collectively, the amount of freedom a society permits or denies itself. Institutionally Saturn represents the legal system, the permanent civil service, and all conservative and restraining bodies.

It may also represent the repressive and controlling forces in a State, for example, the police. Saturn shows a nation's attitude to law and order, hierarchies, taboos and old practices. It shows reactionary forces and the fear which resists change. It governs authority and tradition. The American Saturn in Libra indicates the precise and somewhat rigid checks and balances of the American constitution, while the UK Saturn opposed to Venus speaks of the emotional inhibition which is so important to English national discipline.

Uranus (UR)

Uranus, more than any other planet, has characteristics derived from its association with mundane affairs. Its discovery occurred within the same period of time covered by the agrarian and industrial revolutions in England, and the American and French revolutions. Uranus is therefore linked to all revolutions and innovations in society, the need of a collective to permit or deny itself change, and upheaval at all levels in a nation. It rules political revolutions, economic change, strikes, political dissidents, wars (where these represent a breakdown of order), reforms, heavy industry, new technology, and all those who promote such ideas and events. China and Russia both have Uranus squared the Sun and both those societies have undergone tumultuous change. The UK has Uranus conjunct the ascendant, representing the industrial and constitutional innovation of the nineteenth century. The Second World War started as Uranus in Taurus passed over the ascendant of Nazi Germany, bringing a collapse of the old order and stability. Uranus is also associated with uranium, and hence with nuclear energy, and the first atom bomb was dropped on Hiroshima with Uranus exactly conjunct the MC.

Neptune (NE)

Neptune is associated more than any other planet with subversion, perhaps because of its rulership of ideals and links with the 'ideal society'. Hence it rules socialism, and all new visions and dreams of the perfect society, and the people who promote such dreams. It represents the need of a collective to be perfect, but it can also rule delusions and therefore disillusion, glamour, the arts, fashion, a nation's self-image and the image presented to others. It rules oil, and occurs by transit in the charts of those countries which have discovered oil, or is released by the transit of another planet over natal Neptune. Because of its associations with confusion and delusion Neptune can also rule war, and in this respect shows very strongly in the chart of Fascist Italy, where the main motive for war was national glory, and where the main result was confusion. Neptune also rules scandals, the results of confusion and deception.

Pluto (PL)

Pluto represents all things which are hidden and secretive in a society. Perhaps we could say that it rules the shadow of the collective. From the trivial level of sewerage workers, pot holers and archeologists, we can move to the more sinister level of the secret police, organized crime, and all self-destructive impulses. It rules what Jung called psychotic outbreaks in the collective unconscious. Nazi Germany had Pluto conjunct the IC, while the horrific events in Uganda in the 1970s under Idi Amin occurred while Pluto was transiting the Sun. Pluto in general represents the principle of rebirth as well as death, so we may speculate as to whether in the long run it is beneficial for societies to experience traumas such as these. Perhaps, if we return to the analogy of the body politic (see Chapter 4), Pluto represents that healing principle which forces the collective, as an organic whole, to experience violent phases of self-healing, in order to become well again.

References
1   Greene, L., *The Outer Planets and their Cycles* (CRCS 1983).
2   Carter, C., *An Introduction to Political Astrology*.
3   Greene, L., *Saturn*.

Bibliography
GREEN, H. S. *Mundane Astrology*.
RAPHAEL, *Mundane Astrology*.
Both these texts have been published in one volume by Symbols and Signs, P.O. Box 4536, North Hollywood, California 91607, USA.

8.

⁕THE HOUSES AND SIGNS

Nicholas Campion, Michael Baigent, Charles Harvey

The houses in mundane astrology may be interpreted on a number of levels. They may be taken as representing the spiritual development of a society, they may be interpreted as the manifestation of the collective unconscious or they may be seen as direct indicators of precise and day-to-day political events. They may also be seen dynamically as representing the evolution of the collective unconscious or political processes and relationships within the State.

Whilst the following interpretations will have permanent significance in the interpretation of a national and other group charts, the same basic meanings are also traditionally attached to the houses in any ingress, lunation, or cycle chart and can be valuable in locating the area of life which will be most affected by that cycle. If activity in a particular house in a cycle chart is supported by parallel activity in the nation or group's natal chart greater weight can be placed on the such indications.

As in natal astrology the angles, the MC and AS, of a national or group chart are always particularly sensitive to transits. Thus the 1982 Falklands War was almost perfectly timed by the repeat transits of Mars to the UK Ascendant and Saturn to the 1066 seventh house. Intermediate cusps can however also be strikingly sensitive (though, as in natal astrology, which system is most appropriate for which kinds of approach is still an open question!). For example Uranus was almost exactly on the UK's Placidus/Topocentric third house cusp when the government announced 1982 as 'Information Technology Year', and against all the odds the UK rapidly became the largest per capita owner of microprocessors in the world, ahead of even the USA and Japan.

In erecting a national or cyclical chart the MC/AS midpoint should also always be inserted, in addition to the house cusps, since this point is always highly sensitive to transits and directions and, if occupied, will often say something important about the way in which the country puts its ideals and aspirations (MC) to work in the world (AS). The UK has SA in LE exactly -0- this m.p. which speaks reams about 'Imperial Power', British 'stiff upper lip', class consciousness, and deeply monarchist convictions. It is notable that Uranus stationed -90- this MC/AS with an orb of 1°17′ on 28 August 1939, and was exactly -90- to this point at the time of Dunkirk, Britain's 'glory (LE) in defeat (SA)'.

The following notes on the houses are specifically focused towards national charts but the same basic principles will hold good if one is interpreting the chart of a company or even a group of nations, such as the British Commonwealth, the EEC, NATO, the Warsaw Pact, etc. The important thing is to get to the root idea behind each major phase in this mundane cycle. Thus the third house for a company has particular reference to internal communications, and traditionally 'difficult' aspects involving this house can indicate poor employer-employee relationships. The eighth house in a company chart is particularly indicative of outside investment and the stock and share holders. For a group of nations the MC will represent their common interests and shared ideals and the IC their ability to find 'common ground'. For example the EEC came into force with an MC of 29GE so that it can come as no surprise that with Neptune -180- this point during late 1983 and much soul searching and re-focussing as its apparently solid foundations are found to be based upon miscalculations and self-deception. From this we can also forecast with some degree of confidence that the whole idea of the EEC will face further radical changes and restructuring of its foundations its common goals and group interests during January/February 1988 as both Saturn and Uranus pass over the IC of this chart. Such transits to major group charts naturally have their repercussions within the nations that comprise the group.

The first house
The first house is obviously of crucial importance and is said to represent the nation as a whole. The sign on the first-house cusp

may represent the myths of a nation, its image and self-image, national characteristics and, to an extent, the nature of the State. In terms of the evolution of the State we could perhaps take this house as representing the original society which existed before the State was formed.

Nazi Germany had Taurus rising, and the myth which emerged was one which denigrated the intellect and glorified physical action. The image of the Nazi state was of the 'monolithic' solid organization. Taking its cue from the conservatism of Taurus, much of the Nazi myth was based on an image of the past. Communist Russia has Virgo rising — the myth of the 'workers' state'; the United States, in the 'Sibley' chart (see Chapter 15), has Sagittarius rising — the myth of freedom and the wide open spaces; while the UK has Libra rising — the myth of 'fair play'.

Any planet in the first house will, of course, be important. Poland has Mars rising in Capricorn. During its sixty-year history this country has known two periods of internal military rule and has continually had to struggle against foreign domination. Saudi Arabia has Saturn rising, with the Sun and Jupiter in Capricorn, and both the image and the reality of this country is one of great conservatism and fabulous wealth. The Saudi's southerly neighbour, South Yemen, has Pluto and Uranus rising in Virgo, and is the only Arab state to wholeheartedly adopt a revolutionary Marxist philosophy. The chart for the Republic of Egypt has Venus rising, and one of the great aims of President Nasser, the Republic's major leader, was to make his country the diplomatic leader of the Arab world. Thus the first house may manifest through different levels, in some cases indicating the image of a country, and in others showing actual physical conditions.

The second house
Every society has to survive, and so must start producing food and other materials. The second house represents the manner in which this is done. It shows banks, financial resources, material resources, wealth, the economy, the national product. It may also show security and insecurity in the collective and hence attitudes to material and financial resources. At a deeper level this house will show something of a society's values, what they 'hold dear', and possibly the kind of people the nation holds in high esteem and the attitude to the national heritage.

The third house
If an economy is to grow, and different parts of a society to work together, then they must communicate and trade. This house rules roads, railways, telephones, schools, postal services, newspapers, computer terminals, television, literature, freedom of speech and all official announcements. If a society is to hold together then it needs a common language and a unified education system. The third house reflects this need and how far it is expressed by a society.

The third house also represents neighbouring countries, and hence has an influence over foreign affairs.

The fourth house
As people originally settled, they did so in families, clans and kin groups. The fourth house represents the transition from the nomadic tradition, perhaps represented by the third house, to the first settled communities. Communities settled around land and agricultural needs and were ruled by their royal, military and religious leaders. This house represents the foundation or base of society and its deep rooted traditions. It represents the 'common people', the opposition to the government, the ideologies of the mass of the people and of the opposition. This house may be particularly appropriate to nationalism — the ideology which represents love of the land — and socialism — the common ideology of opposition in western countries.

The fourth house also rules the land, agriculture and all produce of the land. The latter are seen as the products of Cancer in its 'mother' archetype. It is interesting therefore that recent research has emphasized the historical role of women in the early development of agriculture.

The fifth house
Once a society is soundly organized and can ensure survival, it can create. The fifth house therefore represents all pleasures, enjoyment, entertainments, theatres, cinemas, sports and social functions. This may have a large influence on certain national characteristics, perhaps, for example, the 'coldness' of the Anglo-Saxons and the 'warmth' of the Latins. The house also rules children and the birth rate, and is said to be particularly linked to 'high society'. Speculation in all forms comes under this house, and there is thus a link with the national economy through financial speculation.

The sixth house

The sixth house rules service, and therefore rules workers, the employed classes and their political institutions such as socialist parties and trades unions, soldiers, armies and national defence. The 'public servant', i.e., the civil service, is particularly ruled by this house. Through its connection with health the sixth house also rules public health, health workers and the health of a society on whatever level we wish to consider it.

The seventh house

The seventh house rules relations with other societies and countries. These relationships often stem from sixth-house concerns, i.e., the fruits of productive labour which need to be sold to foreign countries. This house therefore rules all foreign relations, treaties, alliances, wars, and all related aspects of national affairs.

In psychological terms this house is often very revealing about what we project on to our enemies, and find difficult to see in ourselves. Thus China (see Chapter 15) who has constantly heckled the 'paper tigers' of the West for its 'war-mongering' has both Mars and Pluto in the seventh, positions which Tibet, Korea, India, and Vietnam might interpret rather differently!

The eighth house

The eighth house represents the financial relations which are often so important to seventh-house affairs. All international finance, multinational and transnational corporations are ruled by this house. Issues involving foreign investment in the nation come under this house. The result of seventh-house activity is often death, and the eighth house rules death, public mortality, death duties and all the other arrangements which surround death. We may also see it as the house of national death, rebirth and renewal on a more psychological or spiritual level.

The ninth house

Eighth-house financial relations require long-distance travel and a network of laws. This house is therefore connected to foreign relations and all long-distance communication, especially shipping. The ninth-house rulership of religion, and all belief systems, follows in a natural sequence from the eighth-house rulership of death. It rules philosophy and may show what type of philosophy or religion a society chooses for itself, or whether there are likely to be conflicts in this area. In order to function as a state a society needs belief systems, taboos and commonly-accepted values and morals to guarantee public order. This house also shares with the third the rulership of publishing and education (though it refers especially to higher education). The law and legal system also have a particular affinity with this house.

The tenth house
Standing at the top of the whole structure of society is the government. This house rules that government and the particular 'ruling class' who constitute the government, whether royal family, aristocracy, landed oligarchy, traditional chieftains or party managers. The tenth house also rules national prestige and is an indication of how a society will be seen by its neighbours. As in the individual, the MC indicates the ideals which a society seeks to attain and consciously cultivates.

The eleventh house
The government needs institutions in order to govern, and the eleventh house rules these institutions. It rules the legislature, especially in the UK the elected House of Commons (the House of Lords is non-elective) the civil service (in the same administration) and local government. It has relevance to foreign affairs where it rules countries with more distant connections, and is said to relate to friendly nations. As the eleventh house we may also consider that it relates to a society's collective long-term hopes, wishes, ambitions and ideals.

The twelfth house
The twelfth house rules all that remains wholly or partly hidden. In terms of institutions this represents hospitals, monasteries, boarding schools, prisons and all places where people go, voluntarily or otherwise, to be alone. In terms of ideology this house rules anything which is subversive of the established order, and the sponsers of subversion — secret and underground societies and parties. The occult and mystical aspects of philosophy and religion are also ruled by the twelfth house.

The signs of the zodiac
At this time of radical reassessment in astrology when such eminent researchers as Addey and Gauquelin have cast doubts on the value

of the signs of the topical zodiac in natal interpretation, it might seem surprising to turn to mundane astrology in order to demonstrate their undoubted efficacy. Yet it has to be said, though it is difficult to provide formal proof, that in our experience strong planetary emphasis on a particular sign of the zodiac always leaves its mark in the world, both in the charts of nations and in the 'flavour' of a period, as well as in whole generations of people. Indeed we would go so far as to say that in terms of forecasting the prevailing mood and likely preoccupations of a particular period in the future, the signs of the tropical zodiac emphasized by the outer planets and strong planetary groupings can be depended upon to provide important clues as to the background 'colour', psycho-physiological orientation, and general preoccupations of the collective consciousness of mankind as a whole at the time. Such emphasized signs will normally find their most vivid, and often literal, expression through such manifestations as the current fashions, cultural trends, popular arts, writing, music, theatre, cinema, fashions, the economic and political mood, scientific discoveries, and so on.

Some evidence of the kind of a major shifts in psychology brought about by sign changes is given in Chapter 13 under the *Astro-Economics* section. Thus for example Barry Lynes has observed that in the past, in the world economy, periods when Neptune has moved from a Fire sign into an Earth sign have seen a previous period of unrealistic optimism (Fire) followed by one of drastic deflation and slump and a literal 'coming down to Earth'. On a parallel point, Rieder[1], amongst others, has remarked on the consistent and precise way in which Saturn's entry into the 'money' signs Taurus and Leo (= gold) has coincided historically with dramatic downturns in the market. Likewise astrologically minded commodity traders have long indicated the effect of sign changes, even of Mercury and Venus, on the mood of the market.[2]

Culturally the sign changes of all three outer planets would seem to be important. Thus Reinhold Ebertin[3] has suggested that Pluto's change of sign marks out major shifts in the focus of power within society and that it will indicate the area of life which is likely to be subjected to major transformation. Virginia Elenbaas[4] likewise indicates the importance of Neptune's sign position in colouring the dominating dreams, fantasies, ideals and visions of an epoch. Such sign effects seem to make themselves felt both at the time of the actual transit and through the generation of individuals born with that position. In this way the 'idea of the time', which was first expressed with the transit, resurfaces again with increasing intensity some 20-30 years after the transit itself as that generation reaches its creative peak and begins to express that sign position in living practice through its interests and ideals.

Thus Pluto in Gemini by transit (1882-1914) and generation, saw the beginning of the transformation of world communications, transport and trade and the scientific foundations of the technological era; Pluto in Cancer (1914-39) saw World World One which broke up the traditional family base of world society, saw the rise of the masses and of trades unionism and the transformation of family businesses and family life generally; Pluto in Leo 1939-1957 saw World War Two, the break-up of the old Colonial Empires and the emergence of a new authoritarianism, especially in the Eastern block with the spread of 'dictatorships of the proletariat' (shades of the Pluto in Cancer generation), and the emergence of multi-national companies. At the same time, in the West at least, new previously undreamt of possibilities for individual self-expression and personal growth began to emerge to be consolidated as this generation moves to adulthood; Pluto in Virgo (1957-71) saw the independence and rise to power of former 'servant' colonies especially in Africa, whilst the West saw an enormous growth of power of the civil servants and government officials generally. Advances in genetic engineering and micro-electronics begin the transformation of agriculture and industrial production; Pluto in Libra (1971-1983) saw a shift in the balance of power with the emergence of the Arab world, traditionally ruled by Venus, on the one hand and the rapid growth of feminism, and 'rights' movements of all kinds; Pluto in Scorpio is now with us (1983-1995). Almost to the day of its entry England's Lord Chief Justice Lane launched a national campaign against the corruption of youth through heroin, porn, and violence, whilst within a few days both sides of the House of Commons had voted unanimously for a Bill censoring 'video nasties', and Westminster City Council had refused to renew licenses of most of Soho's notorious sex shops. Meanwhile in the USA exactly on time, as though to propitiate Pluto's advent into the traditional sign of death, near-record audiences watched a nationwide screening of 'The Day After' a 'factional' documentary revealing the full horrors of death and destruction that would be occasioned by a nuclear war. [5]

The signs of the times

For the sceptical student perhaps the most telling evidence of the signs at work comes not so much from these large scale issues as from the details of the daily news. We can appreciate retrospectively, even if it was not apparent at the time, the profound significance of the developments in micro-electronics that were brewing at the time of the 1965/66 UR-0-PL in VI -180- SA in PI, and can smile when, astrologically ignorant, microprocessor buffs declare 1965 to be the watershed year for the birth of 'the computer generation' of children. But this was bubbling beneath the surface. However, what might have caught the contemporary astrologer's eye in 1966 would have been announcements such as that in the *Times* of 26 January, that food technologists had recently discovered a means of turning fish (PI) into flour (VI), and that it was to be used for fighting famine in the Third World. Likewise the astrologer must smile when the British and other governments decide upon 1989/90 as the 'deadline for the withdrawal of lead (SA) from petrol (NE)'. Looking ahead in the ephemeris we find then a triple -0- of SA-UR-NE in CP!

This again raises the issues of the nature of time. For the 'ideas of the time' are normally in preparation during an earlier period. The film director or writer who has a 'hit' by capturing and encapsulating something of 'the mood of the moment' was in fact shooting or writing often several years ahead. Thus Laura Ashley, the designer, working with JU, UR, and NE in SG, chose to focus the 1984 catalogue around extremely Scorpionic looking, sultry, hostile, young pubescent models, a very considerable break from the previous house image of elegant, 'nice', stability. Presumably Ashley was, as any successful designer must be, 'tuned to the future' and somehow sensing the astrologically dramatic change of mood in the year ahead with the shift of planets into Scorpio and Capricorn.

Anyone doubting the importance of signs has only to look back on 1983 which was dominated by the thrice repeated conjunction of Jupiter and Uranus, on 18 February, 14 May, and 25 September. This strengthened and brought out the slow background Neptune in Sagittarius. After a period of world recession 1983 was accompanied, as might be expected, by a marked expansion of the world economy. International airlines (*Note:* JU-0-UR on degree to do with 'flight') which had been going into bankruptcy in 1982 saw a major 'unpredicted' upturn in business, whilst in Detroit and elsewhere the motor industry began to boom again. Most characteristic perhaps was the period of almost unprecedented moral fervour on all sides. The previously long dormant Campaign for Nuclear Disarmament suddenly took on new life. Conclaves of bishops around the world, who had not hit a headline in years, began debating and pronouncing on this and other issues, such as capital punishment, with a new found enthusiasm and authority.

But it was in specific details that this main JU-UR-SG emphasis often expressed itself most vividly. The 'fortune hunting' (COSI) kidnapping of the champion race-horse Shergar (JU in SG) by Irish terrorists/'freedom fighters' (UR in SG) at the time of the first JU-0-UR, or the bizarre theft of the tails of 13 regimental horses two days prior to the third JU-0-UR are typical of the often literal expression of zodiacal archetypes. The lone trans-Atlantic rower (JU-SG with a touch of SA-0-PL) who was miraculously saved (JU-UR) when his boat was dashed against the rocks of a remote island off the coast of Ireland seems to have been living out the time single handedly. Exclaiming 'Thank the Lord' (one of Ebertin's key phrases in COSI for this combination) at his miraculous salvation, he revealed that he had undertaken the marathon row 'in order to discover the existence of God'! More literally still at this same time, an East Berliner made his flight to freedom (JU-UR SG) by shooting an arrow with rope attached into a West Berlin house and swinging across. The 'dramatic freedom bid' aspect was perhaps most vividly expressed when, 'shortly after 2.45pm BST' on 25 September (the JU-0-UR occurred at 2.56pm), there was a mass break-out of Irish terrorist prisoners from the Maze prison in Belfast. As though to vindicate Placidus/Topocentric house cusps, we find that the chart set for 2.56pm at Belfast places the JU-0-UR exactly on the 12th house cusp (= prisons) within 10' (minutes) of arc[6].

Undoubtedly Neptune through the signs is indicative of the underlying focus of collective fantasies, aspirations, and ideals. When the Pope, born with Neptune in Leo, speaks of the Christian ideal that 'each one of us should become a King in our own Kingdom' we know that he speaks from the heart. Elenbaas's pioneering work in this area includes a study of the movement of Neptune through the signs and its relationship to the guiding images of the age, especially as expressed through film, theatre and popular music. Alexis Edwards[7] has likewise made a specialized study of Neptune through the signs and the changing face of Hollywood, as one of the key channels of expression of the predominating unconscious archetypes of the Western World. Recently Neptune in Sagittarius has clearly been related to the immense popularity of horizon-widening science fiction films and novels, with such classics as 'Close Encounters of the Third Kind', and the 'Star Wars' (1977), both winning major awards and huge box-office success in 1977 (at which time additionally JU was -180- NE from GE). More recently in 1982/83 with Uranus also in Sagittarius we have had the moral revolutionary 'Ghandi' with its appeal to higher moral principles (the alchemical quality of the 1982 SA-0-PL is also apparent); 'E.T.' (Extra-Terrestrial), a classic mind-expanding film with a message; and particularly appropriate 'Chariots of Fire', a film superficially about running but essentially dedicated to the true Olympic ideal of man as hero soul. Its title is taken from SO-0-JU in SG poet William Blake's 'Jerusalem', the preceding lines of which are 'Bring me my bow of burning gold, bring me my arrows of desire . . .'!

But such generational effects of the signs may in fact be shaping the patterns of our society in a more immediate and dramatically physical way. There is growing evidence that it is not so much diseases that run in cycles but our inate predisposition to disease. Although it has not yet been proven, there are solid statistical grounds for suspecting that there are strong links between generational sign positions and aspect patterns and the changing pattern of suscept-ibility to disease within different generations.

Thus in John Addey's brilliant astro-medical study of poliomyelitis, *The Discrimination of Birth Types*[8], he draws attention to the shamefully neglected findings of the Scottish surgeon pathologist Dr T. W. Lees. From a systematic study of the UK Registrar General's statistics for causes of death over the last hundred years Lees shows beyond any question that different generations tend to be prone to different diseases. Thus prior to lung cancer the scourge used to be cancer of the tongue, subsequently stomach cancer, and most recently leukaemia, cancer of the blood. With these shifts of disease site the 'new' illness first makes itself known in cases of infant mortality and amongst very young children. Then as that generation gets older and older the disease will begin to appear with greater and greater frequency as the death rate amongst that generation rises by reason of their age. Lees points out that it is usually when this generation is approaching its natural alloted span, around 60 plus, and the number of deaths begins to escalate dramatically that the authorities suddenly take note and campaign against it. By then of course it is too late and, he argues, the subsequent decline in the mortality rate from that particular disease will in fact be related to the decreasing numbers of that generation left to die rather than to the preventative measures taken.

Whilst John Addey expounded T. W. Lees 'Wave theory of disease' he did so in support of his own general harmonic model of astrology and not in connection with the signs which, at least in public, he tended to dismiss. On the other hand Barbault (1979), who retains his characteristic healthy scepticism on the issue of the importance of signs in mundane, feels obliged to point out his brother's observation that Pluto's entry into Gemini (1882-1914) saw a dramatic increase in cases of tuberculosis amongst those born with this position. This sensitivity faded with Pluto's movement into Cancer (1913-1939) when social awareness of the actual disease cancer came suddenly more and more to the fore. Whilst cancer has remained with us and did not fade with Pluto's movement from that sign, Pluto into Leo (1939-1957) can be associated with the upsurge of concern over heart disease and leukaemia. Likewise Pluto in Virgo (1957-1971) may be seen to be associated with the growth of concern over pollution and the trend towards natural food, free from artificial colouring, flavouring and preservatives. Pluto in Libra (1971-1983), is not so obvious in physical terms though we might see in it the development of, and upsurge of interest in, kidney transplants and kidney dialysis machines. Already the advent of Pluto in Scorpio (5 November 1983) is being paralleled by a terrible growth in venereal disease, most notably herpes and AIDS.

But disease would not only seem to be a Plutonian factor but also one in which Neptune is strongly implicated. Thus Barbault[9] notes that Neptune was in Scorpio from 1956-1971 with similar consequences. In 1968 the World Health Organisation reported a four-fold increase in venereal disease since 1954, whilst by 1971 there were over two million sufferers from VD in the USA alone, accounting for more cases than all other infectious diseases put together. Unfortunately what is likely to intensify this problem in the near future is that as Pluto moves through Scorpio it will begin to trigger off the charts of the Neptune in Scorpio generation. Here we must suspect that the long-term effects of the contraceptive pill, the use of growth hormones in animal rearing, artificial fertilizers, and associated matters will need to become the focus of attention of our healers and regenerators. However, happily for the Art of Healing,

Pluto in Scorpio, together with Neptune in Capricorn, are equally likely to bring a new Paracelsus and a major shift of creative energy in the area of natural healing and the subtle transformation and re-visioning of the orthodox, career-structured, medical establishment.

All this is not to say that the signs of the zodiac need no further demonstration: an unequivocal proof of their power is still urgently required. But in our view to ignore the signs in mundane astrology would be to exile us from the kingdoms of the twelve mundane gods, severing us from the very rhythm and sequential pulse of creation, a move not to be lightly undertaken, and certainly not on the basis of the present evidence.

References

1	Rieder, Thomas, *Astrological Warnings and the Stock Market*, Pagurian Press, Toronto, 1972, Chapter 8, 'Saturn And The Money Signs', pp. 45-48.

2	See Daniel Pallant's 'Astrology and the metal markets', in the *Astrological Journal*, Spring 1983, vol. XXV, No. 2, pp. 91-97.

3	Ebertin, Reinhold, *Pluto-Entsprechungen zum Weltgeschehen und zum Menschenleben*, Band I: Aspekte, Ebertin Verlag, Aalen 1965.

4	Elenbaas, Virginia, *Focus on Neptune*, AFA, 1977.

5	This was *Time* magazine's front cover story for the 5 December 1983, on sale 24 November.

6	I am indebted to Michael Harding, Editor of the AA'a *Transit* magazine, for this example. It appeared in issue No. 43, for November 1983.

7	Alexis Edwards spoke eloquently on this theme at the AA on several occasions during 1975/76. His monograph on the subject has yet to be published.

8	Addey, John, *The Discrimination of Birth Types*, 1974, Astrological Association Publications Dept., Temple Field, Anvil Green, Waltham, Canterbury, Kent, CT4 7EU.

9	Barbault, Andre, *L'Astrologie Mondiale*, Fayard 1979, pp. 160-61.

Bibliography

GREEN, H. S. *Mundane Astrology*
RAPHAEL, *Mundane Astrology*

PART THREE:
THE TECHNIQUES

9.

INGRESSES, LUNATIONS, ECLIPSES

Charles Harvey

'The beginning of the cycle of the year is placed at different times by different peoples. Some place it at the Spring equinox, others at the height of summer, and many in the late autumn; but they each and all sing the praises of the most visible gifts of Helios . . . our forefathers . . . ordered the observance of the New Year . . . when King Helios returns to us again, and leaving the region furthest south and rounding Capricorn as though it were a goal-post, advances from the south to the north to give us our share of the blessings of the year.'

The Emperor Julian, AD 331-363[28]

The daily and seasonal movements of Helios, the Invincible Sun, and the monthly motions of Selene, the moon, are the most obvious and dramatic cycles of the heavens. It is not surprising therefore that since at least Ptolemy[47] the ingresses of the Sun into the cardinal signs, marking the start of the four seasons, and the lunations and eclipses, marking out the months, should have become the dominant cycles considered by astrologers. However this emphasis has meant that astrologers have tended to become myopically focussed upon these relatively short cycles, believing, against the evidence, that they can somehow reveal more than they could reasonably be expected to do unaided.

To be used effectively these cycles must be seen within the broad view of the hierarchy of cycles discussed in Chapter 6. By relating the ideas expressed in any cycle to its appropriate timescale of manifestation we will be on the right path. Those few who, even in part, manage to do this, like Andre Barbault and Barry Lynes[33,34] are beginning to unravel the real ground base of time, and come up with forecasts that are based on an increasingly larger perspective and which can therefore have an increasingly constructive and healing value for society.

It can be argued that the narrow traditional approach which has tended to focus upon ingresses and lunations, unrelated to a larger picture of things which includes both other cyclical charts and the charts of nations, groups, institutions and leading figures, has tended to block more fruitful avenues of research. Indeed astrology's poor track record as regards mundane forecasts in modern times is almost entirely due to a false expectations of these charts. Not surprisingly this has produced some fierce reactions to these charts, and some attempts to evaluate them systematically.

The case against ingresses, lunations, and eclipses
Whilst as we shall see, ingresses, lunations and eclipses, do undoubtedly have their own particular place in the hierarchy of things, a survey of the literature is hardly encouraging. Thus despite their popularity and widespread use, they can hardly be said to have produced a crop of outstanding forecasts. Indeed as we shall see in Chapter 14 their rather facile use was a major cause for the embarassing 'no war' prediction made by most European astrologers, including Charles Carter, in 1939.

The reaction against the wholesale unthinking acceptance of these charts is not a new one. Thus Kepler[9] had no use for ingresses at all. He wrote scathingly against the 'nonsensical' use of these charts. This is not surprising for, as Kepler knew, the astronomical tables astrologers were using in the early seventeenth century were consistantly half a degree out for the Sun's position, thus rendering the resultant charts almost totally erroneous! But even when using accurate tables various modern writers have come out almost equally strongly against the use of these maps. Thus, for example, Carter, one of the major students of mundane astrology in this century, concludes in his post-war book[11]:

The experience of examining many of these ingress maps for

the 1939-45 period has convinced me that, unless an angle is nearly involved, they are of little importance except in the most general sense. They form a background; that is all. One cannot safely predict from them save in language so general as to be of little value . . . this writer regards the natal map of the country and of its ruler, if these can be ascertained with accuracy, as being *by far* the truer and more scientific basis for mundane prediction.

Likewise Barbault[3], who is one of the few people who has done a systematic analysis of many hundreds of such charts, also condemns the reliance of his colleagues on these maps. Unlike his significant findings in other areas, his studies of the angularity of planets at the time of ingresses and lunations give results at an absolutely chance level.

Thus Barbault and Le Corre[5] took the 93 major outbreaks of war between 1850 and 1969. On the basis that angular planets have always been considered to be of the greatest importance in interpreting these charts, they noted those planets within 10 degrees of each of the four angles in the 404 appropriate ingresses and lunations attendant on the opening of hostilities. Using these orbs this gives a total of 80 (i.e., ten either side of each angle) out of the 360, or 1:4.5 which can be considered to be 'angular'. Taking the 404 positions of each of the nine bodies Moon, Mercury, Venus, Mars, Jupiter, Saturn, Uranus, Neptune, Pluto, we would, statistically, expect each of these bodies to be angular, by chance in about 91 times out of the 404 cases. The actual observed number of times each body was found within 10 degrees of an angle was as follows: Moon 94, Mercury 92, Venus 90, Mars 80, Jupiter 100, Saturn 88, Uranus 92, Neptune 87, Pluto 87. There is evidently no significant deviation from expectancy here. The largest deviations, MA with eleven cases less than expectation, and JU with nine cases more than chance, though not significant, are deviations which are in fact in the opposite direction to that predicted by traditional astrology! Most astrologers would have certainly expected to see MA above average and JU below average at the time of the outbreaks of hostilities between nations, rather than the reverse.

Although Barbault has published all the related raw data, we have not yet been able to examine and evaluate the charts to see whether perhaps certain categories, e.g. ingresses, or eclipses, may not give better results than all categories taken together in this way, or whether much narrower orbs than those used would improve the picture. But at present the results are certainly not encouraging. Thus even when we examine the overall pattern of the distribution of MA in the diurnal circle for these charts, as John Addey would have advocated, we find nothing of great significance. Thus whilst MA has a slight preference for the area soon after setting, the middle degrees of the sixth house, it is certainly not strong enough to be of any practical value, and certainly does not confirm tradition. Of course these results do not show that MA angular in such charts does not coincide with outbreaks of martial activities of other kinds. But they do indicate fairly decisively that Mars is, if anything, less likely to be within 10 degrees of an angle in such charts at the time of war!

From his studies Barbault himself concludes 'I cannot help thinking that these results block the possibility of localizing events through the use of ingresses and lunations . . . I tremble for my colleagues who make forecasts based on these charts alone.' This conclusion is of course very much in agreement with Carter's empirical experience. When two such giants agree we cannot take their judgement lightly. Clearly these charts are not all they have been cracked up to be. Their possible use has been stretched beyond their limits. Like a musician attempting to play Handel's Hallelujah Chorus on a tin whistle, we must not be surprised if our interpretations are not immediately recognizable. But can we perhaps nonetheless gain some clues as to the 'main theme' if we listen carefully to this instrument?

The case for ingresses, lunations and eclipses

We believe that we can. And in the face of such authoritative adverse criticism we would like to persist in advocating the study of these charts. Both our own personal experience and observation, and all the evidence as to the nature of astrology would seem to indicate that these cycles *must* have *some* value, and that their value must naturally relate to the annual and monthly ebb and flow of ideas and emotions within the collective. It is our view that, whilst these charts are certainly not the panacea they were once alleged to be, to ignore these cycles would be to throw away some extremely valuable parts of the jigsaw puzzle.

As we hope to show, a careful examination of this category of charts would seem to indicate that these annual and monthly cycles, and their phases, do indeed have their part to play in bringing the larger collective ideas and impulses 'down to earth', and focusing them at particular times and places. Thus, as we have already noted in the latter part of Chapter 6, the Earth's annual cycle about the Sun enables us to 'tune in' to the meaning of the outer planet cycles, and the major aspect patterns of the period. So too these charts do seem to focus the manifestation of other cycles within the pattern of unfolding time.

Thus in spite of the weighty evidence to the contrary we must insist that these charts, when used with discretion and placed in relation to other charts, and when compared with the charts of nations and individuals, do have very considerable value in pinpointing events. However we would have to agree that this value may be difficult to demonstrate statistically, and can only be demonstrated by a case-study approach at present.

The work of E. H. Troinski
Probably no one has done more comprehensive work on ingresses and lunations, than the Berlin astrologer E. H. Troinski (b. 18/19 December 1910-82). Probably most famous for his discovery of tertiary directions in 1951, Troinski has dedicated the large part of his astrological career to the area of mundane astrology. In his remarkable work *1001 World Political Horoscopes*[58], published in 1954 and as yet untranslated, he presents a study of the solar ingresses, lunations, and eclipses which accompanied some of the major events of world history. This work illustrates a range of charts, from the Aries ingress for the Founding of Rome in 753 BC, and the Libra ingress for the Fall of Jerusalem in 586 BC, the solar eclipse for Hannibal and his elephants crossing the Alps in 218 BC, through to the major eclipses and ingresses of World War Two, and speculation on the significance of similar charts in the future through to AD 2077. The book gives drawn charts for a large number of these 1001 'most important mundane charts' from his vast collection. He lists all the positions for all 1001 charts including the intermediate houses cusps by Placidus. For the most part Troinski concentrates on the Sun's ingress into the four cardinal signs and the important lunations and eclipses. He does however also consider the entry of the Sun into the other eight signs, as symbolizing further important phases in the annual cycle, and also the cardinal ingresses of the Moon. He develops a case for considering the lunar cardinal ingresses as further

triggers for the solar ingress charts.

It is easy to criticize Troinski's work on several grounds, and Barbault[5] does so fairly strongly. In particular Barbault points out that if you include so many charts during a year as being of significance, you are bound to find something. This 'something' may indeed be real. But such a multiplication of charts, whilst interesting for retrospective analysis, makes them almost impossible to use in forecasting. This criticism is supported by the general failure of any of Troinski's various, often dire and sensationalist, predictions for the past thirty years to materialize in any obvious way. Equally we can point out that to limit oneself to annual and monthly cycles, and not to relate them to larger cycles or to the charts of nations and individuals, is like trying to isolate the part that one colour plays in a wide variety of paintings, without regard to the larger perspectives of each individual canvas or their specific subject matter.

On the other hand it has to be said that, though Troinski can be accused of selectivity, his approach is in fact relatively rigorous and systematic. He presents a great deal of analysis and comparison between these charts throughout the 2,500-year period covered and has discovered some interesting parallels. He comes to many interesting conclusions. Like the French Revolutionaries, he considers that the autumn ingress is in fact the most powerful one of the year, and tends to give it precedence over the others. Of particular interest and worthy of further investigation are his empirically-observed thirteen major groups of planetary patterns, each of which he considers to have its own particular significance. We have been unable to evaluate these as yet but for the record, and to encourage further study these can be summarized as follows.

Group 1
(a) Saturn or Uranus in the tenth or fourth house, with the Sun in one of the four angular houses. Signifies fall or overthrow of governments, revolutions; changes of government; beginnings of new historical periods; death of leaders.

(b) Saturn in tenth, Mars in twelfth, and Sun in first. This appears to be a particularly dangerous and violent combination. For example it occured at the New Moon immediately following the murder of Caesar in 44 BC; at the eclipse accompanying the defeat of the Spanish Armada in 1588, set for Madrid; and at the Cancer ingress for 1934 in Berlin which saw the death of Hindenberg and the rise of Hitler. Troinski also points out the Franz Ferdinand, whose assassination precipitated World War One, had this same configuration in his *natal* chart! That this combination is of some value for forecasting is testified to by Troinski's 1954 indication of a critical time for Europe in 1958 based on the fact that this combination would occur again at the 1958 Spring ingress for Moscow and at the 19 April eclipse of that year for Berlin. In fact Krushchev took power in Moscow on 27 March, and on 8 May the US felt obliged to warn the USSR that an attack on Berlin would be an attack on the Allies.

(c) Saturn in tenth and Sun in eighth or twelfth houses, or Saturn in fourth and Sun in third. Signifies periods of military and political reversals; assassination attempts; earthquakes; violent conditions.

(d) Saturn in tenth -180- or -90- Mars: danger to head of state; fall from power, destructive overthrow of regimes often by the military.

(e) Saturn in tenth with Mars in twelfth or eighth: danger of war; attacks on head of state.

Group 2

The Sun and a heavy concentration of planets in the eighth house. Troinski considers this to be an indication of war, and most particularly the combination of Sun, Mars, Jupiter all in the eighth. Troinski dubs this combination 'the pure war-combination'. It also seems to indicate revolution and rebellion. He gives twenty-four illustrations of such eighth-house concentrations including: New Moon -0-PL and Saturn five days before the assassination of Franz Ferdinand at Sarajevo; New Moon -0- SA and Mercury and Venus in eighth immediately following the D-Day landings in 1944; the Solar Eclipse with Mars, Jupiter, Mercury, Venus in July 1776, set for London, marking the landing of English troops in North America and the beginning of American War of Independence; New Moon -0-UR, Jupiter, and Venus for the Storming of the Bastille; Cancer ingress of 1812 with Mars and Jupiter, and -180-SA, which accompanied Napoleon's invasion of Russia; Cancer ingress 1870 set for Paris with Mars and Jupiter in eighth, SO-180-SA, preceding the Franco-Prussian War.

Group 3

Strong emphasis on first, and twelfth/sixth house axis. Emphasis on the twelfth/sixth indicates political and economic problems and reversals; emphasis on the first, political change, often the start of a better period.

Group 4
Solar eclipses occuring in fourth, sixth, twelfth houses: the sixth/twelfth as for Group 3; fourth usually dangerous.

Group 5
Sun and Moon with Saturn or Jupiter: very clear-cut events for good or ill, depending on the house position.

Group 6
Mars with both Sun and Moon: a fierce combination often leading to explosions of various kinds.

Group 7
(a) Saturn in first with Sun in twelfth. particularly destructive.
(b) Mars in first with Sun in twelfth: aggressive use of force but not always destructive.

Group 8
Sun or Jupiter on the MC or in tenth: essentially highly positive when accompanied by supportive aspects.

Group 9
Sun in ninth with strong grouping of planets. With Jupiter or Venus in tenth peace treaties; with Saturn in tenth destructive.

Group 10
Sun in eighth with Saturn in first: an unfortunate combination.

Group 11
Sun in fourth with Saturn in twelfth or eighth: a combination indicative of great struggles — Sun was -90-SA in twelfth at the autumn ingress for 1914.

Group 12
Sun in twelfth and Saturn in sixth and the reverse: a particularly difficult combination, especially when joined by Mars, as in the winter ingress for 1914/15.

Group 13
(a) MA-180-SA other than fourth/tenth (for which see Group 1c):
helpful or hindering dependent on house position — creates a *tabla rasa* situation and a new beginning. The January 1945 eclipse for Moscow shows this opposition exactly across the horizon with Mars rising, appropriately marking Russia's drive into western Europe.
(b) MA-SA with New Moon in twelfth: 'catastrophic'. Such a New Moon accompanied the outbreak of the Thirty Year War in 1618.
(c) MA-SA-UR in twelfth: very difficult, bringing reversals.
(d) Sun in first -120-JU. Economic and political successes and the beginning of important new periods of development (*cf* Barbault's findings for the period around SO-0-JU each year noted in Chapter 6).
(e) Sun and Moon in ninth and Venus, Jupiter in tenth. An extremely positive combination for peace treaties and long-lasting agreements and settlements (again paralleled by Barbault's findings).

Although it will be impossible to evaluate a work of this magnitude without a large-scale systematic examination (which we hope in due course to be able to undertake) it must be of considerable interest that Troinski writing in 1953/4 was drawing attention to the great importance of the twelfth-house area in these charts. This of course parallels Gauquelin's work on the importance of this area for personality, a fact which first emerged at about the same time. Gauquelin's epochal *L'Influence des Astres* appeared in 1955.

Ingresses: where does the year begin?
With the planetary cycles the seed moment is the conjunction phase. But where does the solar cycle begin? As we see from the Emperor Julian at the outset of this chapter there has always been a diversity of opinion on this. Two hundred years prior to Julian, Ptolemy summed up the problem succinctly: 'in the regular simple motion of a circle no part of it has any apparent precedence'.[47] As we saw with Plato and his predecessors' idea of the Great Year, originally the paramount importance tended to be given to the summer and winter solstices. Then at some point the vernal equinox began to be noted as the point of the 'creation of the world', the point at which the Sun crosses the equator from south to north. The pre-eminence of this point was well established by Ptolemy's time, though the Emperor Julian 200 years later was to argue otherwise. Ptolemy[47] explains its importance from simple material causes as 'because, from that time, the duration of the day begins to exceed

that of the night, and because the season then produced partakes highly of moisture, which is always a predominant quality in all incipient generation and growth'. It is not without interest that this point of the resurrection of the Sun King became coincidental with the Festival of Easter in the Christian Church, which is measured by the first New Moon following the spring equinox. But whatever the reasoning we employ there can be no doubt that a chart set for this moment of 'birth' of the cycle, for any point on earth was, and still is, considered to reveal some of the main archetypal emphasis for that place for the coming year.

However in modern times the great pioneer of astrology in Germany, the highly innovative Alfred Witte[63], and Britain's leading astrologer Charles Carter, both independently suggested that in fact the more fundamental 'birth' of the year might be considered to be at the winter solstice, when, on entering 0° Capricorn, the Sun actually begins its journey northwards. This agrees with Julian's reasoning in the fourth century. This is after all the time of the year when we do in fact symbolically celebrate the 'birth' of the year with Christmas, and the 'New Year' festivities. Yet as we have seen above, so thorough a student as Troinski considers that the Libra ingress should be given pride of place as the most powerful of these four cardinal ingresses. Clearly the matter is still an open one, and indeed perhaps a misleading question.

Whichever we choose as the beginning, the principle involved is the same. The chart reveals the way in which other planetary principles relate to the fundamental Earth-Sun cycle of unfoldment. The only argument is as to how long such charts remain sensitive. Both are claimed to describe the whole year, but with the other cardinal ingresses, Cancer and Libra, marking further important stages of development. The evidence for the duration of these charts throughout the year is ambiguous, and like so much in astrology, awaits further real clarification. One traditional rule, from at least Ptolemy's time, is that their duration will depend on whether cardinal, fixed or mutable signs are rising at the start of the cycle. My own inclination is to consider that each describes the whole year but viewing the solar process from a different perspective. For the dealer in bulbs the life cycle begins and ends with the bulb. For the dealer in flowers the priority must be quite different, and so on.

The timing of ingresses

There is a general consensus amongst those who have experience of
these charts, which is certainly corroborated by our findings, that
they begin to come into operation some two or three weeks *prior*
to the actual astronomical events. Thus the Aries ingress in any year
will start to be felt early in March or even at the end of February,
and likewise the Capricorn ingress will start to become active from
the end of November or early December. This principle seems to
hold good for this whole class of cyclical maps, a clear case of 'events
casting their shadow before them'. Thus lunations tend to become
operative about three days prior to the actual celestial event. This
is another point where the phenomena of astrology as empirically
observed do not sit at all comfortably within our received 'model
of the universe'. Such anomalies must offer vital clues as to the
interrelationship of time and eternity and the real nature of
space-time.

Constructing ingress and other charts

For some practical considerations on the calculation and transposition
of ingress and other cyclical charts see Appendix V, pp.483-6.

Interpreting ingress and other cyclical charts

Any such cyclical chart needs to be thought about first in terms of
what the cycle represents, and refers to, i.e., its referend. All such
ingress charts are revealing something about the interaction between
Earth-Sun and the rest of the solar system, the galaxy, etc. They will
reveal how the interplay of planetary principles and processes are
being focused and 'earthed' during the cycle, and the kind of ideas
around which mankind's consciousness (Sun) is likely to revolve.
So first we need to assess what the larger and broader patterns of
the moment indicate. Then the orientation of the chart itself will
reveal just what aspect of these ideas will be emphasized. Pride of
place should always be given to the angles, to angular planets and
to close aspects to angles, for these show us what can actually be
released into the world at this point. As a Sun cycle the position and
aspects to the Sun will also obviously be of importance. In addition
to normal aspects the mid-point structures, particularly those
involving angles, should be considered.

    In interpreting these and any cyclical charts we should not forget
that the more we understand the prevailing conditions and

circumstances of the place for which the chart is set, the more likely we are to be able to evaluate effectively the kinds of eventualities that are indicated. Thus a strong emphasis on Uranus on the angles of an ingress over an area where there is great civil tension is much more likely to indicate a possible dramatic breakthrough of collective pressures, than the same configuration in a very stable area, where it might simply manifest as attempts to introduce controversial and innovative ideas or a much less dramatic kind of desire for reform and an awakening to a larger view. Often rebellion and reform will go hand in hand. However Uranus can also indicate the imposition of strong autocratic measures to limit outbursts of disruptive energies.

Whilst it is always important to attempt to see and understand the highest possible meaning of any particular pattern it is nonetheless only practical and realistic to keep in mind the fact, that planetary principles, and their aspects, will tend to work out in a balder and less subtle way at a collective level unless they can be deflected and appropriately channelled by imaginative and idealistic leadership. A strong awkwardly-placed Mars is much less likely to be sublimated when occuring in connection with a cyclical chart than in the map of an individual who is relatively aware and awake. It will tend to indicate an increased excitability in the nation, with conflicts and clashes of will erupting in every form from militant protests and stikes, to sporting conflict and even war, if other longer-term factors and national charts show an appropriate build-up of tension. Thus, for example, as we shall see the spring ingress in 1982 showed Mars with Saturn rising at the Falklands.

Some key factors in the interpretation of cycle charts
Apart from Troinski's observations enumerated above, which it is difficult to quantify more precisely, the following summarizes some of the main points which in our experience are of more importance in evaluating any such charts.
1.   The interrelation of the chart to other cyclical charts and to the charts of nations, and leading individuals within the nation, is always of the utmost importance if the significance is to be brought out and localized with any confidence.
2.   Because the interplanetary aspects of any mundane charts are common to every place in the world, the all-important factor becomes the angles and house positions, but particularly the angles. Any planet which is within a few degrees of the angle, especially 1°-2°, is likely

to play a marked role in the period immediately ahead.

3.   Equally, any body configuring the AS/MC mid-point by -0-, 45, 90,135, or 180 within an orb of 2° should be carefully noted. This often-neglected point is of the very greatest importance in all charts since it links together both angles and therefore gives a double intensity to the bodies involved. Edith Wangemann also indicates that the mid-point in time, between MC/AS and AS/DS are extremely sensitive, i.e. the mid-points of the Koch eleventh/fifth and second/eighth houses. She relates the second/eighth house mid-point to actual material creation of the time, and the eleventh/fifth mid-point to the significance of the time.

4.   Close aspects to angles, and particularly where this contact brings some major chart pattern to the fore. The so-called 'minor aspects' can be highly instructive here.

5.   Close mid-point contacts to the angles, within 2° orb.

6.   With regard to cardinal ingresses, Witte[63] draws attention to the fact that the Aries point, as the intersection between ecliptic and equator, represents the relationship of the individual to the group, to the masses, and to the environment, the nation, and the world in general. In this sense this point can be considered to represent 'the world as a whole', and will have reference to such things as natural events, earthquakes, floods, storms, etc., as well as political and economic events. SO-AR (i.e. 0° Aries) contacts and mid-points can be seen as relating particularly to public figures and leaders; MO-AR to people and nations in general; ME-AR to general communications, 'news', and so on. Thus we noted that Armstrong set foot on the moon at the exact time of the JU-0-UR, at 0LI40. We could interpret this configuration as 'an excited world' or a 'global expansion of awareness and consciousness'.

Some examples of ingresses and lunations

Ingress and lunation charts are, then, not a separate technique but part of a hierarchy of charts that we can consider when preparing a forecast for a particular area on earth. To see the kind of information they can supply let us look at our example of Kennedy's assassination that we studied in Chapter 6.

The Libra ingress which preceded the shooting occured on 23 September 1963, 18.23 GMT. The chart set for Dallas is given in Fig. 9.1, p.254. We will want to examine this chart in its own right, and then in relation to Kennedy's chart and the USA chart. (We

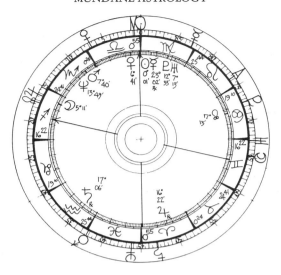

Figure 9.1 The 1963 Libra ingress prior to the assassination of J. F. Kennedy, 18.23 GMT, 23 September 1963 for Dallas, Texas, 32N45, 96W48, MC/AS 8SC38.

may note here that Carter[11] points out that transits that occur at an ingress are in some way 'fixed' and given a continued intensity for the whole of the period. Thus relatively swift transits gain considerable power in this way.) Obviously if we were Dallas astrologers preparing a forecast for the coming quarter we would also want to relate this to the chart of Dallas and her leading figures. The most striking fact about this Libra ingress chart is that we find that the Sun was almost exactly culminating at the longitude of Dallas. This immediately indicates that this is potentially a place where the central meaning of this cycle can be manifested and expressed through leading figures (SO-0-MC), so we must ask 'what kind of Sun is this?'. The Sun makes two aspects. It is -45-NE and -135-SA. In so doing it is highlighting the SA-90-NE of this period. Closer inspection reveals that the Sun and MC are in fact almost exactly -90-SA/NE mid-point at 00CP27. Indeed the SO/MC is 00LI27 which is exact to the minute. The only other close solar aspect is a 1/16th, 22°30′, to Uranus which those familiar with this strongly manifesting aspect will recognize as significant.

SO = MC = SA/NE ideally might be read as the potential to take decisions to earth some kind of vision and put it into practice. However at the present level of collective consciousness such a configuration is more likely to be indicative of 'undermining circumstances', 'sacrifice', 'emotional suffering and upsets' as COSI[14a] puts it. Retrospectively we can see this is a challenge to a particular ideal, a period when some kind of sacrifice, emotional upsets, and difficulties will be likely to occur in connection with leading figures at this place (MC-SO).

Turning to the AS we have at first sight a very different kind of picture. Indeed with Jupiter exactly -120-AS and SA-60-AS we might expect this period to be a solidly expansive and constructive one for the Dallas region, and indeed perhaps at other levels it was. With hindsight, in view of the connection between the Jupiter/Saturn cycle and the death of presidents, it is interesting to note that JU/SA is at 16PI44 only 22' from -90-AS. The other very close aspect involving the AS is from the NN which is on the eighth house forming a close Yod with Saturn and the AS. In other words part of the message of this quarter for the world was SA-150-NN, which could be read as the necessity to take a serious attitude about relationships. COSI gives for the sociological correspondence on the negative side: 'community expressing feelings of grief or depression, e.g. mourners attending a funeral'. Here at Dallas this aspect was made totally local by this double quincunx involving the AS. Linking in the AS we find in COSI amongst other things: 'suffering difficulties with others', 'separation'. So an 8th house, i.e., -150-, aspect is seen here to link a potential 'death' aspect, SA-NN, from the cusp of the eighth. Of course without the benefit of hindsight it is unlikely that we would have focused on this in quite this way.

Taking the MC/AS at 8SC38 to see what will be going on during the time at this place we find it -0-MA and -45-ME. The Mars in Scorpio is of course highly appropriate but joined by Mercury we might have thought more of intense verbal debate, of verbal attacks, abuse and argument rather than of gun shots.

All these factors are ones we would have been bound to consider if judging this chart in prospect. Putting them all together we have, retrospectively at any rate, an interesting and appropriate pattern. We now, with hindsight, need to look at this chart in relation to the chart of the USA and John Kennedy. In relation to the USA chart the most striking factor about this period is the UR-0-PL which is -90- to the USA AS-UR axis. This is loosely localized here at Dallas by the simultaneous -90- to MO and AS (MO/AS = 10SG47 and UR/PL 9VI53). Also striking is the fact that the MA = ME = MC/AS falls closely -90- to the USA's highly dangerous MA-90-NE-45-NN (NN = 6LE36 = MA/NE6LE54). This same axis we remember was sensitized by the MC/AS of the JU-0-UR cycle chart, so that this chart is tending to activate that. In relation to Kennedy's chart we must be first struck by Uranus which is just 21' past the -0- of his MC/AS and within 28' of -90- his SO. At the same time the MA is -150- his SO with an orb of 11'. In relation to the MO/AS = UR/PL above it is perhaps significant that Kennedy's MA/PL is at 10GE51, also very close to the United States' AS/UR. On the same theme we may note that the United States' MA/UR is at 15GE05, widely with this ingress AS axis.

The AS seems to be telling a different story in relation to Kennedy. Here we see it is exactly -180- Kennedy's Venus which seems happy enough. However in fact Kennedy's Venus is -90-MO and -45-NE. This is certainly not a dangerous combination as such but one that can negatively lead to errors of judgement and to being undermined. Again it is interesting to note that the JU/SA is involved very closely with Kennedy's chart in view of the JU-SA linkage with presidential deaths.

Looking now at the New Moon of 16 November 1963, 06.50 GMT, Fig. 9.2, p.257 which occurred just six days before the shooting, we are first struck by the fact that this New Moon falls closely -180-Kennedy's eighth house JU-ME-MA and -90-UR. This would be certainly a warning light of potential sudden upsets, etc. Looking at the chart itself we see that UR-0-PL are just about to rise. In fact the UR/AS is close to Kennedy's MC/AS whilst in the sky we have the picture PL/AS = UR almost exact, for which COSI gives 'extraordinary incidents and upsets, accidents'. Mars interestingly is just about to arrive at the Libra ingress AS and is on the USA's MA/UR at 15GE05. It is also interesting to note that the AS of this lunation chart is not far off the SO-0-UR at 5VI41 of 29 August 1963, 17.53 GMT, a highly relevant cycle which we have not touched upon previously. (The angles of that chart are MC 26LE26, AS 19SC22, MC/AS 7LI54, closely picking out Kennedy's UR-MA-JU. The AS is in exact, 0', -90- the actual assassination AS.) Comparing this lunation chart with the actual assassination chart it is intriguing to note that the ME and IC of the lunation have become almost the exact SO and MC of the event. (It may also be relevant that the

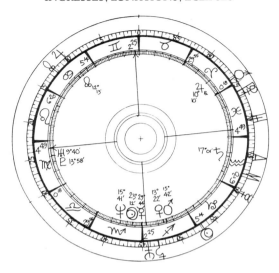

Figure 9.2 The New Moon prior to the assassination of J. F. Kennedy, 06.50 GMT, 16 November 1963, for Dallas, Texas.

SO-0-ME contact also picks up the SO position in the SA-0-NE chart.) But even more exact we find that the MC/AS of the lunation is 18CN37 which is almost precisely -45- the shooting MC. We may recall that this event MC at 3SG44 is -0-MA/NE ('hidden marksman') at 3SG14 and exactly -90- the preceding JU-180-UR position at 3VI/PI33. And so the threads interweave layer upon layer, the picture emerging from the shadows with ever-increasing clarity the closer we look. It is extremely doubtful if using the ingress and lunation alone could have served as a warning. But considered as part of a total picture their implications are evident.

The implications of this kind of interweaving of celestial and terrestrial events may be difficult for some to accept. Some may feel more comfortable with a different kind of example, that of a 'spontaneous' explosion of unknown cause. It is the kind of occurrence which we might hope that an astrology based on sound principles ought to be able to help to minimize.

If we are to be in a position to take action to re-channel, use and positively express these Providential energies we will need to develop an understanding of the way in which pictures of planetary potential build up and develop in the heavens, and exactly how the 'wards of the combination lock' drop into place. Let us then make a step-by-step analysis of this particular case, starting with the event itself and then seeing how the appropriate cycle charts 'signalled' it.

The Betelgeuse Disaster

At 00.55a.m. GMT on Monday 8 January 1979 John Connally, Gulf Oil duty despatcher, was on duty at the Whiddy Island, Bantry Bay, oil terminal in Southern Ireland. At this moment he heard a 'crack or creaking sound' coming from the tanker 'Betelgeuse' which was part way through off-loading her crude oil. Minutes later a 'flash fire' was racing across the water and surrounding jetty. In this horrific fire and explosion 50 men lost their lives, and many others were severely injured. The cause of this sudden explosion, like that of other similar explosions, is not known with any certainty, but appears to result from a spontaneous combustion of a natural build up of explosive gases. A total of 291 people were killed in such explosions between 1968 and 1977, and no less than three such explosions occurred in December 1969 alone. What clues has astrology to offer as to why this 'spontaneous combustion' took place at this particular time and place? If we can understand the principles involved we will be on our way to being able to identify areas of the world 'at risk' at any time. With such knowledge a world-wide 'Astrology Watch' can then be of practical help in encouraging appropriate consciousness-raising measures in such areas.

The chart for the moment of the explosion is shown in Fig. 9.3. We are immediately struck by the SO-0-MA exactly -0- I.C., -90-PL in the first house. We can see this particularly vividly in the 90°-circle round the outside of the chart where we can see that the MC of the moment of the explosion has come exactly to the MA/PL m.p. As COSI puts it: MA/PL 'superhuman power, force, brutality' and MC = MA/PL '. . . the misfortune to face overwhelming force without power, danger through the intervention of Higher Power.' It goes without saying that intense (PL) burning heat (MA) is a very obvious correlate of this combination.

Let us now look more closely at the planetary picture in terms of our principles, and see exactly how it is built up. What we have here is MA at its outgoing 'manifesting' -90- phase with PL, with an orb of 59'. The unfolding idea of 'superhuman power' has arrived at that part of its cycle where it seeks direct, 'challenging', actualized, physical, expression in the world. (i.e., the -90- aspect.) It has been

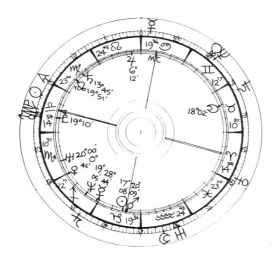

Figure 9.3   The explosion of the oil tanker 'Betelgeuse', 00.55 GMT, 8 January 1979, Whiddy Island, Bantry Bay, Southern Ireland, 51N37, 09W38.

within orb of 1°00′ of this phase since about Noon GMT on 5th. At this point in time on the 8th the SO is closing its conjunction with MA, always a potentially explosive time, and thus 'focusing' the MA-90-PL energies to 'this day', which is in line with both Witte and Barbault's findings on the role of the solar cycle. Indeed if we look again at the 90°-circle we also see that the SO is closing up on the MA-PL in such a way as to form the picture SO/MA = PL, with its potential for an intense, and possibly violent release of energy. What else is happening at this point? Are there any other m.p. configurations involved?

Running our eye around the 90°-circle we see UR with the MO and NE with tNN (the mNN is at 20VI52) all equidistant from PL. Calculating their m.p.s. we find: UR/NE 4SG32, UR/NNt 19LI55 (UR/NNm 20LI25), MO/NE 3VI33, MO/NNt 18CN56, (MO/NNm 19CN26). This means that PL is stimulating all of these m.p.s. by either 0°, 45°, 90°, 135° or 180° aspect. These m.p.s. divide naturally into two groups. The slow moving combinations of UR, NE and NN and the fast ones involving the MO. The slow one will define a whole period. The MO ones will help to define 'the hour', to use Witte's rules.

The broad background planetary picture is dominated by the slow, long-term PL = UR/NE. This is a combination which is indicative of deep changes, purgations and transformations at the deepest collective level of society. (As we shall see below and in Chapter 10, a variation on this combination, UR = NE/PL, was angular through Iran at the 1978/79 Capricorn Ingress which accompanied the beginning of the Iranian revolution.) At a physical level we can see that this UR/NE = PL is highly indicative of 'deep transformative explosions, and explosions involving oil'. (In Iran of course the fall of the Shah was accompanied by earthquakes and disruption of the Middle East oil supplies.) Also classifiable as part of the broad background planetary picture is PL = UR/NN which speaks of deep shake-ups, changes and dramatic upheavals within groups and communities. Again this is obviously appropriate to what was going on in Iran at this time.

Back at the Betelgeuse and focusing in upon this *day* we have seen that the SO is also completing the picture SO/MA = PL. Thus for this day right around the world there is a potentially explosive grouping PL = SO/MA = UR/NE = UR/NN. Then at around this *hour* we find the Mo approaching -180-UR and forming the m.p.s. MO/NE and MO/NN with the PL axis. COSI says of MO/NE = PL 'an emotional shock or upheaval', whilst MO/NN = PL is given as 'separation through higher power or providence'. Finally within these hours at this *minute* we find the MC is triggering off the whole picture by forming the incoming 'manifestation' -90-phase with PL. Finally focusing this day (SO) 'at this time and place' (MC/AS) we see SO in the 90°-circle is in fact exactly between MC and AS, i.e., SO = MC/AS. The actual m.p. is 2VI15 so that the SO is within 7' of the exact -135- to this crucial point.

In sum we see that the potentially violent, explosive, and dramatic configuration (MA-PL) which is seeking to manifest itself (-90) is localized and released at this particular place on the earth's surface at this particular time. This is a satisfactory planetary picture as far as it goes but we must now needs ask ourselves whether there are not larger cyclical factors which identify this particular spot? After all this combination and variations on it will have been angular over quite a range of areas even on this day.

Turning to our hierarchy of cycles we note that the Capricorn Ingress occurred just 18 days prior to this event. Setting this Ingress for Bantry Bay, Fig. 9.4, we find that as the SO entered 00CP00

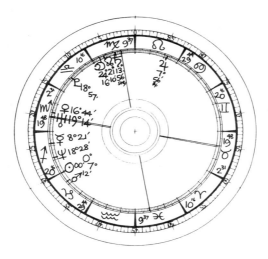

Figure 9.4 The Capricorn ingress prior to the 'Betelgeuse' explosion, 05.21 am, 22 December 1978, set for Bantry Bay.

to begin its annual cycle UR was exactly on the AS. (This can also be seen on the AstroCartoGraphy of this Ingress which is shown in Chapter 10, Fig. 10.2, where UR's rising line can be seen passing right through S.W. Ireland.) This in itself is indication enough that this place will be likely to see 'sudden incidents, awakenings, upsets, accidents' during the coming cycle. But what kind of UR is this? First of all it is at the NE/PL m.p. at 18SC42, which is a variation of the PL = UR/NE already noted. This is again suggestive, on the material plane, of amongst other things 'sudden oil explosions'. Examining this UR-AS axis we also find that this falls closely-180- the SO/MA in the 90°-circle, at 3CP36. Thus we have UR = SO/MA = NE/PL, which might be translated as 'sudeen fires, explosions, possibly involving deep maritime matters, oil', being focused exactly here at Bantry Bay. It is noticeable that UR was here on the AS right up through Ireland (see Fig. 10.2 p.283) and that later in August of the year Ireland was also to witness the assassination of the Royal Warrior (SO/MA) Lord Louis Mountbatten through a bomb placed in his *boat*, as well as the murder on the same day of 22 soldiers at Warren Point by a remotely detonated explosion.

Noting the explosive potential of both the Ingress and the event, we may ask what were the specific 'timers' which linked the event with the potential of the annual cycle for this place. Taking the SO as marking 'the day' we note that the SO will within the next 48 hours complete the -90- to Ingress PL but that additionally it has just passed -90- Ingress SA/UR = 16LI35. SA and UR are of course *both* closely angular at the Ingress so that this day in particular might be expected to focus on both the 'sudden, explosive' and the 'sense of loss' qualities of the year. The MO as the 'hour marker' is just about to complete the -180- to the Ingress AS-UR and -135-SO/MA. Such periods each month when the Moon transits the angle of an Ingress chart will inevitably tend to 'trigger' its potential. (Likewise other transits seem to be able to trigger such charts.) Looking at the 'time and place' MC/AS of the event we see that this, like the SO, has just configured Ingress SA/UR. Relating the actual 'place', AS, of the event to the Ingress we find that this is conjunct Ingress MC/AS at 14LI41 within 15′! The event AS is also with MO/SA (15CN53) = VE. COSI say of AS = MO/SA 'Meeting with sick or depressed people, mourning or breavement'. Thus at this place, AS 14LI54, we see the 'time and place' (MC/AS) potential of the Ingress, 14LI41 is released into the world at a MO/SA = VE 'separations from loved ones' hour.

So far we have seen that the event occurred at a particular point within the annual cycle. But since we have argued that this explosion occurred at the time of the outgoing, 'manifesting' -90- phase of the MA-PL cycle we now also need to examine the relationship between the 'manifested event' and the 'seed potential' signalled by the chart for the MA-0-PL at this place. Turning to our ephemeris we find that the MA-0-PL occurred on 28 August 1978 at 02.41 GMT, and that it fell at precisely 15LI01! The chart for this moment, Fig. 9.5, shows that whilst the MA-0-PL was not exactly angular that 'at this time and place' the MC/AS was 4GE18 exactly -90- to SO 4VI27 -0- SA 4VI02. This could be read as 'During the course of this intense-release-of-energy-cycle (MA-PL) this time/place will focus upon the lesson of Saturn, of shortcomings, inadequacies, and potential losses'. This MC/AS = SO = SA was of course exactly triggered by -45-/-135- by the MC = PL = SO/MA of the event! We may also note that MA at the event has coming exactly (orb 2′) to the -90- 'manifesting' aspect of the seed-moment MC!

Thus to summarize the key features we can see that the seed potential of the MA-PL cycle was focused at that 'time and place'

Figure 9.5   The MA-0-PL prior to the 'Betelgeuse' explosion, 28 August 1978, 02.41 am, set for Bantry Bay as Figure 9.3.

by MC/AS = SO = SA. It was exactly pin-pointed by the MC/AS of the Capricorn Ingress, and was subsequently released by the transiting AS. This occurred at the very point when that MA-PL had reached the days of its -90- 'actualization and materialization' phase in its expression. The final timing of the day was triggered by the SO joining the MA-PL, by the MO configuring SO/MA, and the MC of the moment 'actualizing' the whole process by its incoming -90-to PL and -180 SO/MA which were in turn with the original seed moment MC/AS = SO = SA.

We would suggest that this example is archetypal of the kind of build-up, layer upon layer, of points of emphasis, which culminate in the release of a particular 'picture' in a particular place. In other words, what 'happens' in the world is not the result of isolated configurations but of an accumulation of threads that have been inexorably weaving themselves into this *predetermined* tapestry of planetary conditions and circumstances.

If we are to make progress in this area it is important to recognize that these patterns *are* predetermined. To pretend otherwise is to side step the central issue. The planetary patterns of all time were there in potential from the beginning of time. They were enfolded within the very structures and geometries of the Cosmos at the outset.

If this is so then the most important role of the astrologer is to suggest ways in which individuals and collectives may become increasingly conscious of the potential of each cycle and work for its highest unfoldment. For, as Jung put it, what we will not accept into our consciousness will simply return to us in an external guise as 'Fate'. In other words we can only receive those manifestations of any cycle or moment of a cycle that we are open to receive. Increased consciousness is the only key.

Let us now take a happier example where human consciousness seems to have been atuned to the higher vistas.

Man takes wing
Life is not all shootings and explosions, even if these are the kinds of energy release which astrology might hope to be able to draw attention to so that we can consciously tranmute and channel them. So let us now return briefly to our theme of mankind's evolutionary movement out into space. Fig. 6.10, p.205 shows the historic moment itself, when Orville Wright, having won the toss against Wilbur, flew the plane they had built for twelve seconds and 120 feet. This

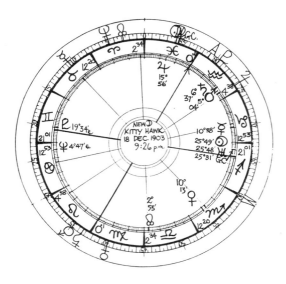

Figure 9.6   The New Moon following the Wright Brothers' first flight, 21.26 GMT, 18 December 1903, set for Kitty Hawk, 36N02, 75W42.

chart is a valuable one and is undoubtedly still valid for following the course of flight. It is almost always strongly activated at the time of major developments, strikes, crashes, etc. and those connected with air transport often show close contacts to it. It is interesting to note that Freddie Laker's sudden bankruptcy and the subsequent shake-out throughout the world's airline industry occurred in February/March 1982 just as Uranus stationed at 4SG38 on the MC of this chart, (and on Laker's IC at 2SG. In fact the Uranus station was exactly configured with his MC/AS).

Looking at this chart we note that this crucial moment occurred right on the eve of a New Moon -0-UR, a classic example of how in fact celestial events 'cast their shadow before them' by a few days. The New Moon is shown in Fig. 9.6, p.264. As we can see it falls just 1′ from Uranus in SG, a highly appropriate piece of symbolism for mankind leaping out over old horizons to new vistas. What makes it doubly appropriate is that Uranus is at this point only 17′ from the galactic centre. The whole of this configuration is here localized at Kitty Hawk by falling across the AS/DS -180-PL, and by the harnessed energy of SA-0-MA forming the powerful productive and manifesting -135- aspect with the AS from the cusp of the ninth. It would obviously be absurd to claim that this lunation was the main significator of this major step for mankind, but it certainly does hold within it the magnitude of the moment, even if it is doubtful if its full significance could have been in anyway perceived at the time.

What does help to reveal the significance of the moment is to consider this lunation in relation to 20 October 1900, 08.17 GMT JU-0-UR, Fig. 9.7, p.266. We note that Pluto, 'the Idea whose time has come', is exactly on the MC for the JU-0-UR. In the lunation it is closely rising almost exactly -90- the JU-0-UR AS, whilst the Moon position at the JU-0-UR is almost exactly -90- the New Moon AS. The importance of Pluto is brought home by the fact that 'take off' occurred exactly as the AS made its incoming, 'fruit bearing' trine to Pluto. We find that the New Moon MC/AS is at 25AR31 almost exactly with the Sun position in the JU-0-UR chart whilst the MC/AS of the JU-0-UR chart, at 3LE32, has just been activated by the -180- from Mars and Saturn by the time of the lunation. Looking at the moment of flight in relation to each of these we find that most symbolically the Moon at this moment is just 6′ past the -0- of the JU-0-UR, or in other words that the first-ever take-off occurred just twelve minutes in time after the Moon had crossed

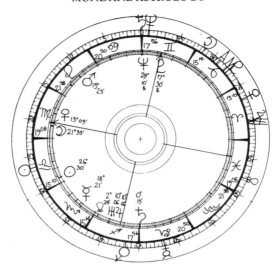

Figure 9.7   The JU-0-UR prior to the Wright Brothers' first flight, 08.17 GMT, 20 October 1900, set for Kitty Hawk, 36N02, 75W42.

the actual position of this key conjunction. Furthermore the all-important SO/MO mid-point at take-off was 17SG22, almost exactly -0- the JU-0-UR IC and -180-PL.

In seeing these interconnections we are seeing 'the wards' of John Addey's 'combination lock' slipping into place, with a kind of precision that must make us question very seriously the choice we can have over the *external* course of events. Orville and Wilbur Wright could no doubt have given very clear reasons as to why they were there on that particular day and exactly ready at that particular moment, yet somehow their reasons and intentions exactly reflected the ideas of the time and the intentions of the Heavens.

These examples do not in any way vindicate the practice of attempting to use ingresses and lunations alone to make forecasts, but they do make clear that, contrary to Barbault's statistical findings, that each case in fact *retrospectively* makes remarkably precise sense. As we clarify the principles at work which interlink cycle with cycle so we will be able to apply these with increasing confidence *prospectively*.

Eclipses

But before we leave this area we must deal with one very special kind of lunation cycle, the solar and lunar eclipses.[42] From the earliest times in all civilizations these phenomena have understandably been greeted with awe and trepidation and have been considered immensely powerful for good or ill. The sight of darkness at noon and the sound of birds twittering into silence before the approaching shadow of an eclipse was for early man evidence enough of the powers of heaven to affect life on earth. In effect what is happening at a solar eclipse is that the Moon is beginning both a lunation cycle and a latitude cycle almost simultaneously. Such eclipses occur when the Moon is crossing the plane of the ecliptic at the time of the New Moon. At this point the body of the Moon comes between ourselves and the Sun, effectively blotting out all or some of it. Indeed when the Moon is at perigee, i.e., nearest the Earth and therefore appearing bigger, the eclipse will be total in certain regions.

There is much debate as to just how much more powerful than a lunation an eclipse is and since Ptolemy's day there have been rules of thumb indicating that eclipses will last as many months or indeed years as they last in hours. It has also been asserted that eclipses are only, or most powerfully, felt where they are visible.

André Barbault[4a] has played devil's advocate in doubting, if not denying, the especial place of eclipses amongst the astrological forecaster's tool kit. Certainly the case needs clarifying but of their basic power there can be little real doubt. What we do not know is whether eclipses can in fact have an effect for the full nineteen years of their cycle, i.e., until the next eclipse in that particular area of the zodiac, as some allege. Certainly there seems good reason to suppose that their impact is often not felt for several months after their occurrence.

What makes eclipses particularly noticeable is that they often presage the 'eclipse' of those in power. This is particularly the case with solar eclipses where we are, as it were, seeing the solar, authority, principle being cut off by the Moon, the regulator of earthly activities.

Some examples

Taking the case of Kennedy's assassination, is it simply coincidence that on 20 July 1963 at 20.43 GMT there was a total solar eclipse at 27CN24 exactly conjunct Kennedy's natal SA 27CN09 in his tenth house? This is the classic picture of a 'fall from power'. What of course greatly intensifies this is the fact that this eclipse also fell exactly -180- the USA Pluto at 27CP37. That this followed on a partial lunar eclipse of 6 July 1963, 21.55 GMT, at 14CP06 closely -180- the USA SO must also be compelling evidence for this case. Clearly if such lunations were considered to last but one month we would have to discount this picture as mere coincidence. But how long they do last is obviously a matter of practical interest. Only when we know this can we place them appropriately on the hierarchy of cycles, and use them effectively. Thus, for example, nineteen years later in July 1982 these eclipses repeated themselves at 13CP55 and 27CN43. For how long has this sensitized these critical degrees of the USA Sun and Pluto which must have so much to do with the power and authority of the nation? Although the Secretary of State Alexander Haig did resign shortly after this there has not been to date (May 83) the kind of deep administrative crisis and transformation that might have been expected.

The course of World War Two saw various striking testimonies to the apparent power of eclipses. Most notable perhaps is the case of the eclipse of 1 August 1943 which occurred just six days *after* the resignation of Mussolini on 25 July. This eclipse was exactly rising at Rome conjunct Pluto and Jupiter. This not only fell on the dictator's own Sun and square his NN, but was also closely square to the Sun in the chart for Fascist Italy. At the same time Uranus was on Mussolini's MO-0-SA.

There was also a solar eclipse the very day of the 20 July 1944 bomb attempt on Hitler. This fell on the Third Reich MC and closely square Hitler's AS on his Equal House tenth. Pluto was closely square the Berlin MC. The MC/AS mid-point is -0-SA and -90-NE, probably signifying the terrible purges that were to follow. However for the Führer himself Venus was almost exactly on his MC and Jupiter was rising in 28LE50 -0- the fixed star Regulus, both traditionally significators of protection and good fortune for those in power. However it is notable that General Tojo, who masterminded Pearl Harbour, resigned in Tokyo on 18 July, just two days prior to the eclipse.

Equally striking in another way was the eclipse of 9 July 1945 at 13.35 GMT in 16CN58. At London this places Pluto in 9LE11 right on the MC 8LE20. 28LI39 rises. This coincided with the General Election which was held from 5-12 July. The upshot of this election was that Churchill, who had taken Britain through the war, was totally defeated in a landslide Labour victory, at the very moment when he might have been expected to be bathed in glory. The MC and Pluto of this chart are exactly -180-1066 MA 8AQ28 and Churchill's Saturn at 9AQ36. The eclipse itself fell with Saturn and NN right on UK MC and Moon but exactly -90- Churchill's Mars at 16LI34. Mars was -0- his Pluto, whilst the AS is exactly -180- his Neptune — an astonishing catalogue of contacts. This eclipse -0-SA also saw the sudden death of the Australian Prime Minister, John Curtin, on 12 July. For Canberra the angles are MC9CP12, exactly -0- true NN 9CP12. This falls exactly on the Australian SO 9CP30 and SO 7CP39f, whilst Uranus at 15GE14 was exactly -90- the Australian Uranus 14SG17 and PL 16SG16, i.e. -90- their mid-point 15VI16 by only 2′. Pluto is also exactly -150- the MC with a 1′ orb.

Cases like this demonstrate the importance of multiple factors, and the interaction of eclipse with national and leaders' charts — it is not just the eclipse but the eclipse as a catalyst for a web of interactions.

However the work of Charles Emerson[16], Al Morrison[37, 38] and others has shown that eclipses have a far more intriguing impact upon world affairs and world leaders in particular. Using von Oppolzer's remarkable compilation the *Canon of Eclipses*[42] Emerson has shown that the actual eclipse-path prior to birth of a future leader seems to indicate in a very remarkable way the region of the earth where their influence will be most felt. Thus for example Karl Marx was born at the time of an eclipse (in Taurus in the second house as befits a committed materialist!) which occurred not far from the longitude of his birthplace, Trier. The path of the eclipse sweeps from Central Africa in the south, up through Libya across Turkey and then right across the Russian Empire from the eastern shores of the Black Sea, across the Ural Mountains and Siberia all the way to the Kamchatka Peninsula. The case of Alexander the Great is if anything more dramatic. Its noon position was at the longitude of Pella, Alexander's birth place. The eclipse swept over Egypt, Mesopotamia, and Persia ending at India, exactly demarcating the lands he was subsequently to conquer with such dramatic consequences for the future. The path of the eclipse prior to Muhammad's birth is shown in Fig. 9.8, p.270. Here it will be seen, as Emerson says:

Every nation, every people anywhere near the line of this eclipse path are either Muslim today or had to throw off the yoke of

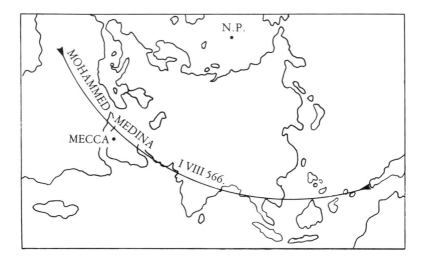

Figure 9.8 The path of the eclipse of 1 August 566 AD which preceded the birth of Muhammed in 567. The path neatly demarcates much of Muhammed's main sphere of influence in the world. As Charles Emerson comments, 'Muhammed's chart responded mightly to the thought behind the phenomenon.'

Muslim conquerors in the past. Reaching in its physical path of totality from western North Africa to the western tip of New Guinea this eclipse crosses directly over the city of Muhammad's refuge after his flight from Mecca during the famous Hegira of AD 622, an event which traditionally marks the founding of Islam. Something in Muhammad's chart responded mightily to the thought behind the phenomenon.

And in that final sentence Emerson sums up the picture that is emerging in the astrology that is being reborn. It is of a universe that is more like a great mind than a great machine, a universe in which as Bohm expresses it 'consciousness and matter are an unbroken whole'. As we become increasingly familiar with the cycles of heaven, from Great Years to the harmonics of the daily cycle, instead of feeling trapped we can know, as Dean Inge puts it[23]:

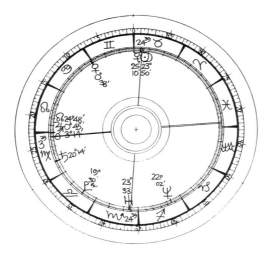

Figure 9.9   What happened at this New Moon? The potentially violent
New Moon of 12.00 GMT, 14 May 1980, set for London, 51N30, 00W07.5.

We are not merely cogs in a machine, we are the machine itself
and the mind that directs it. But this is only fully true of the
personality which has realized its own inner nature. The
imperfect man is pulled and pushed by forces external to
himself, just because he is still external to his true Being.

A cautionary note on interpretation: when forecasts fail
One of the main problems about interpreting shorter cycles is that
we may forget that we are looking at a very small section of time
and will be misled into generalizing. Thus whilst a lunation can trigger
other, deeper, longer-term cycles it will not do so if these are not
'primed'. A classic example of such a 'damp squib' is the New Moon
of 14 May 1980, which is shown set for London in Fig. 9.9, (above).
It would be difficult to imagine a more dramatic, volatile and
potentially dangerous configuration. The *exact* -180-UR is not the
kind of thing that one expects to go unnoticed. Furthermore this
chart 'hits' the chart for Queen Elizabeth II in no uncertain way,
the lunation falling right across her MC-0-SA and triggering off her
very problematic T-square. In addition the angles of this chart are
exactly with those of the chart for the opening of the new debating

chamber of the House of Commons, (26 May 1948, 11.10 GMT).

We would be justified in imagining that something fairly dramatic and far-reaching might occur at this time. In fact this actual day in London was marked very appropriately by a widely-heralded Day of Action against the Government by the trades unions. But despite the omens and the careful organization the event had little support and in fact rather fizzled out as a non-event. Protest there was, but not the kind of explosive violence one might have expected from such close angularities of Uranus and Mars. Perhaps the mass rallies acted as a 'lightning conductor'; if so then there is a valuable lesson here for working with the heavens. The only act of explosive violence on that day was a bomb in a south London police station which severely injured the duty officer. Nor was there anything particularly violent or volatile about the surrounding period in Britain generally. It could be argued astrologically that the -120- of Saturn to the lunation controlled it. This may be true to some extent, but the more important message is that lunations *of themselves* cannot 'make things happen', and that we should not draw too many large-scale conclusions from such relatively parochial maps. However this is not to say that this lunation does not indicate the potential for an enormous release of Uranian energy. Obviously it does. Thus it can come as no surprise that immediately following this Mount St Helens, in Washington State, USA, blew its top in the largest single recorded explosion since Krakatoa. Presumably at that point on the globe, where the lunation fell across the horizon, the lunation triggered other cumulative patterns.

Other ingresses

An ingress is an 'entering into', and the term can be applied to any body entering any defined point in a cycle. Charts set for such moments represent either the beginning of a cycle or of a phase of a cycle. It is of course important to understand the referend of the circle in question. The planets passing through the phases of the tropical zodiac will be telling us something different from the planets passing through the sidereal zodiac since they refer to different levels of order in the cosmos. It is possible to draw up charts for the moment that any of the planets enters 0° Aries, or crosses other nodal points in its cycle, and consider this as the beginning of a new cycle of that planet. Jacques Halbronn[70] considers such cycles, especially of the outer planets, as being potentially important for tracing historical phases and developments. In such an approach it is of course possible to demarcate the different stages of the cycle. Halbronn particularly emphasizes the main eight-fold division of each cycle. Thus the content of the cycle tends to manifest particularly strongly when a body reaches these points in the cycle. Thus in the zodiacal cycle: 15° TA is the -45- phase, 0°CN the outgoing -90-, at 15°LE the -135- and so on.

Tracing the unfoldment of the zodiacal cycle in this way can obviously be very instructive and there can be no question that when a planet enters a particular area of the zodiac it stirs up and activates the appropriate archetypal ideas in the collective (see 'Zodiacal cycles' in Chapter 8 for further discussion on this point).

Sidereal ingresses

These lie outside the immediate scope of this book but do represent another potentially important cycle. This measures the movement of the Sun and planets in relation to the 0° Aries point of the constellations. This zodiacal cycle would appear to be a higher 'galactic level' of organization within the cosmos. The 0° Aries point for this cycle is fixed amongst the constellations. Relative to tropical Aries this 0° Aries point is considered by Western sidereal astrologers to be at 24°27′31′′ of tropical Aries at 0 hrs 1 January 1980, and due to the precession of the equinox it is advancing in the tropical zodiac by one degree every 71½ years, so that for 1 January 1985 it is at 24°31′27′′. This value, known as the Ayanamsa, is based on the historical and statistical studies of Cyril Fagan and Donald Bradley. It indicates a coincidence of the two 0° Aries points in AD 221. Various other Ayanamsa are used in the Hindu tradition. These range from about 19°30 through to 29°00, though the main ones use a value fairly close to the Fagan-Bradley one. Those who hold that the Aquarian Age began at the entry of the Sun into Aquarius in 1881 imply that the difference is now over 31°00. Obviously the precise value for this point is critical if one is attempting to set up charts for solar and other ingresses. Even a small margin of error must render the angles in such charts worthless. See Appendix III, p.477.

The authors have as yet relatively limited experience of these charts but preliminary observations are encouraging. Thus in studies on the major Israeli wars the solar ingresses into the cardinal signs of sidereal zodiac are often very revealing. Fig. 9.10, p.274 shows the sidereal Libra ingress for 17 October 1956 set for Tel Aviv. This

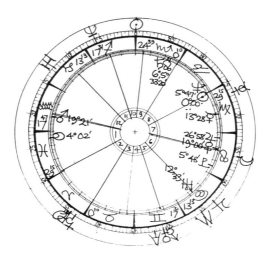

Figure 9.10 The sidereal Libra ingress prior to the Suez crisis and Israel's invasion of Egypt, 17 October 1956, set for Tel Aviv, 32N07, 34E45. The Anyanamsa is 24°08′27″, i.e., add this on to above positions to obtain positions in the Tropical zodiac.

immediately preceeded the Israeli decision to invade Egypt on 29 October and the Suez Crisis. It is an entirely appropriate figure. Not only is there an exact MA-180-VE right across the horizon but the MC/AS is closely -90-NE. A fuller discussion of these charts is given in ISCWA's *The Astrology of the Middle East*. Many examples are illustrated and discussed by Firebrace[19] and others in the pages of *Spica*, and Lewis[30] includes the four sidereal cardinal ingresses for observation in his annual book of mundane maps.

References
For references see pp.361-8.

10.
WHERE ON EARTH:
1 Astrocartography

Charles Harvey

Background

Having established that heavenly events are in some mysterious way
reflected on Earth, then the most pressing practical question that
confronts us is to identify *where* a particular conjunction, major
configuration, etc. is most likely to manifest itself and find expression.
If we could answer this question with any certainty the evaluation
of mundane trends would be transformed. Without such a knowledge
our attempts at forecasting must, all too often, be vague and
unfocused, and lacking any real conviction. As we have seen in the
last chapter, in connection with ingresses, this is unfortunately once
again an area in which astrology presents us with a plethora of
mutually contradictory traditions, theories, ambiguities, and very
little attempt at systematic observation and evaluation.

But as we shall see, what appears at first sight to be a simple question
capable of a simple answer in fact turns out to be a very complex
one. It is a question which raises many subtle yet fundamental points
about the nature of astrology, and astrological effects, and how we
think of such things as countries, nations, and peoples.

There are three main approaches we can take to this question of
where a particular celestial event may manifest. Ultimately we would
expect each to have its part to play in finding the answer.

1.   Astrogeography: This is a spatial, static, approach, by which we
assume, on the basis of the doctrine of correspondences, that the
macrocosmic zodiac must be inherent in some way, or ways, in the
microcosmic Earth, imbuing precise 30° divisions of the very land

and ocean of the earth with the zodiacal ideas. In this scheme we can expect, for example, that a conjunction in a particular degree of the zodiac will resonate particularly strongly with a very specific degree of longitude on the earth's surface.

2.   Planetary angularity: A temporal, dynamic approach, by which different areas of the earth are temporarily sensitized and brought into prominence because of the angularity, or exact aspects to angles, of planets at major conjunctions, stations, ingresses and lunations at that locality. Some would consider that these sensitivities may not be noted immediately but will remain latent for the full duration of the particular cycle which brought them about.

3.   The individual charts of towns, cities, nations and groups: This approach sees each grouping of people as a unity, an organism in its own right, with its own horoscope and inner life, and sensitivity to the cosmic cycles. This approach is complicated by the fact that the collective unconscious of any one group and the area of the earth on which they live, will, in fact, be imprinted with many layers of planetary and zodiacal ideas, deriving from significant moments in its history. Thus it is impossible to allocate an absolutely definitive rulership to any particular area, though certain degree areas may be of singular importance. Again we may ask whether each particular cultural group of people, e.g the Greeks, the Irish, the Italians, the Jews, the Poles, take their own particular sensitive degree areas with them as the emigrate. Thus does Chicago resonate particularly to the root patterns of Poland, or New York especially to an ancient Jewish pattern? Or do immigrant peoples become immediately subsumed under the local chart?

An additional and more general approach can also be involved: the principle of symbolic resonance and sympathy. Thus, as we saw in Chapter 6, a society, like an individual, with a strong Jupiter-Neptune, will tend to respond to the cycle of Jupiter-Neptune regardless of whether Jupiter-Neptune are making precise transits to sensitive degrees in the chart. Equally we might expect any areas in the world involved in coal mining and the iron and steel industry would reflect, to some extent, the cycles of Mars-Saturn. Likewise, for example, the cycle of Jupiter-Uranus is likely to strike a responsive cord in entrepreneurs and 'fortune hunters' in every society regardless of their geographic location. Naturally an area where Jupiter-Uranus was already an important factor might be expected to resonate with these ideas the more strongly.

This chapter and the next two will look at each of the three main approaches separately, so that the main principles invloved in each can if possible be clarified. But whilst we can study each approach in isolation, it will be apparent that ideally, and in practice, a living mundane astrology needs to combine all that is most certain and well supported from each approach. It should be reiterated that most of the work presented here is urgently in need of clear, systematic investigation, of a kind that the authors have not yet had time to undertake. Pending such research these methods should be taken as hypotheses for testing rather than as entirely reliable and demonstrated systems!

Planetary Angularity and the Location of Planetary Effects: Astrocartography

It has been suggested that, to some extent, we are all responding all the time, at some level, to the cycles of heaven, though each organism has its own particular familiarity, or 'tuning', with some cycles rather than others. As we noted in Chapter 6 the effects of these cycles tends to become very much more noticeable as they reach points of exact phase, and particularly 0, 90 and 180. Likewise in Chapter 9 it was suggested that the intensity of action of a particular cycle will be yet further accentuated in those areas of the earth where the planets involved or other planets are on the horizon or meridian at the moment of an exact phase, and especially if this area is close to the capital city of a nation.

As will be explained, the advent of the computer, and the ingenuity of Jim Lewis's Astro Cartography [30] has now made it a relatively simple matter to plot out on a map of the world exactly where each planet is on an angle for any moment. This now enables us to pinpoint immediately some of the main regions where, in theory, the maximum activity of a particular cycle ought to be manifesting. However we should keep in mind that, as yet, these maps do not allow us to identify where planets are on the all-important and catalytic MC/AS mid-point, though developments are in hand to add this facility in the near future. Likewise the scale of these world maps does not, at present, allow room to plot in where planets are making exact aspects to the angles and MC/AS, though Michelsen does show aspects to angles on his large-scale astro-locality chart for North America and for Europe.

A lack of unambiguous evidence

Whilst the examples to be presented shortly do certainly tend to support the value of these maps we do need to keep the picture balanced. Thus it is only appropriate that we should at this point recall the negative results of Barbault and Le Corre's study of Mars within 10° of the angles for the ingresses and luncations associated with the outbreak of 93 major wars (see Chapter 9). This certainly demands explanation! It is possible that these results might have been improved if latitude had been considered, or if the cumulative picture over each significant area were given. However a further study of Barbault and Le Corre on the angularity of planets at the time of 147 cases of SO-0-JU and 101 conjunctions of SO-0-VE at the time of major periods of detente, proved only a little more significant, though not at a level which has a great deal of practical use in itself. Thus considering the SO-JU together with Mercury and Venus as a group and allowing a 10° orb to each of the four angles for 112 places where 'peace had broken out' compared to 35 places where there had been not such events, they obtained the following figures:

Détente (112 cases)	*Control* (35 cases)	*Control* X 3.2
49 angular	12 angular	38 angular
28 within orbs	9 within orbs	29 within orb
35 beyond orbs	14 beyond orbs	45 beyond orb

It will be seen that when the two samples are equalized, that there are 77 cases either angular or within orbs in the cases for détente and 67 in the equivalent control. Though in the right direction this is certainly not a result which can be considered to have great practical significance!

A further analysis using the Moon and Mars as a control shows that whilst Mars was underrepresented and Venus was most frequently angular, the deviations from expectancy were not large enough to be useful. Thus Barbault gives the following figures for the planets within 10° of each of the four angles:

	☉	♀	☽	☿	♂	♃
112 cases of detente	26	35	31	29	20	26
35 control cases	3	14	4	11	4	8

Since none of the figures deviates outstandingly from expectancy, except Venus and Mars which are above and below average for both sets, there is little that can be concluded from these figures. However distributions of Mercury and Venus around the diurnal circle were found to be much more promising. These show that Venus does concentrate quite strongly around seventh cusp, towards the sixth house side (15 cases in 10°) and in the last part of the ninth and early tenth houses (15 cases within 20°) and twelfth and early first houses (14 cases in 20°) and to a lesser extent around the IC (8 cases in 10°). This gives a total of 52 cases in these areas, which closely parallel Gauquelin's 'key sectors', as opposed to the 19 cases which we might have expected by chance. Mercury also shows a strong, though more dispersed concentration around the seventh and fourth houses.

If these results are disappointing, it can be said that a subjective examination of mappings of angular planets made in this way for the ingresses, lunations, and eclipses over the four years 1979-82, whilst far from conclusive, leaves no doubt that planetary angularity can indeed be a vitally important factor in locating the areas of maximum impact, of these ingress and lunation cycles. Whilst we have not yet been able to study any large number of charts for other cycles, we can say that there is sufficient evidence for supposing that this principle will be found to hold good for the whole range of conjunctions, and planetary phases, though in a much more subtle way than simplified tradition implies.

This said, it is clear that an isolated angularity does not necessarily, of itself, indicate very much. Indeed, as the Barbault-Le Corre work indicates, from a statistical viewpoint we are still a very long way from being able to quantify such effects, or apply any single factor with any high degree of confidence. Once again the message is that single factors on their own can tell us very little. However such planetary phase charts ought, when considered over their total time span, to be able to offer us vital clues about the way in which specific ideas are likely to be unfolding within the collective. The total symbolic picture can only be expected to emerge from an examination of the cumulative build-up and interrelationship with other cycles and in relationship with the charts of the individuals, groups, and organizations in the geographical region indicated.

Indeed cumulative build-ups of angularity in the same geographical region seem to be a vital clue, directing us to examine charts for countries in the area. The effects of such a repeated emphasis are graphically expressed by the Anthroposophist astrologer Willi Sucher. [56] He speaks of major planetary configurations as leaving 'wounds' or scars in the 'aura' or etheric body of the earth, at the point where they become exact. He sees these scars remaining sensitive to future planetary activity in the same area, which may 'reopen the old wounds'. Taking this image we can see that whilst one single angularity of a planet at a particular place may not have much impact, the repetition of important celestial events over a particular region may build up an acute sensitivity in that locality, of a kind represented by the planets involved. When additionally such sensitive points coincide zodiacally with important areas in the charts of nations and groups in that region of the world we can be fairly certain that the ideas represented by the cumulative planetary configurations will be resonating strongly within the organism and will therefore need to be 'played out' in some way.

The question of latitude

Before we go further there is one technical matter which needs consideration. Whilst all students seem to be agreed that it is the places where planets are closely angular that will see the maximum manifestation of a particular configuration, there is some disagreement over the question of whether such angularity should be measured purely in terms of zodiacal longitude, or whether it is in fact the body of a planet on an angle which is important. If the latter is the case then this necessitates taking the planets latitude into account, something which is rarely considered by most astrologers.

Latitude is the measurement of a body's angular distance north or south of the plane of the ecliptic, which is defined as being the point of 0° latitude. Whilst the plane on which most of the bodies of the solar system circle the Sun are approximately the same planes as the Earth's, i.e. the ecliptic, they are in fact inclined to this plane by up to 4° of latitude for most planets, and by up to 5°18′ for Moon, 7°00′ for Mercury, 8°30′ for Venus and 17°19′ for Pluto. The effect of this is that when a body's latitude is much greater than 0°, the actual body of the planet will not rise with the degree of the zodiac in which it is placed.

The reason for this latitude effect is illustrated in Fig. 10.1, opposite. Here we can see that, measured on the plane of the ecliptic, Venus is in exactly the same degree as the Sun and AS, i.e. it would be placed in the chart as exactly -0-AS. Yet in fact we can see that the body of Venus has in fact been 'up' for quite some time, and

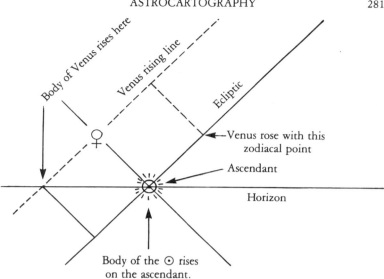

Figure 10.1   The effect of latitude on the rising position of a planet. Here
Venus is in conjunction with the Sun when measured on the plane of the
Ecliptic. However, because Venus has several degrees of N. latitude its actual
body has already risen some time.

is well into the twelfth house. In extreme cases the actual body of
Pluto may cross over the horizon with a degree of the zodiac that
is several signs removed from its zodiacal position. Even for the Moon
and Mars there can be as much as 20° difference between their point
of bodily rising and their ascendant degree in some parts of the earth,
up to 10° for Saturn and up to 5° for Jupiter.[12a] If actual bodily
position is considered of key importance this will of course often
substantially alter the physical house-position of a planet.

In mundane work such differences can obviously move the point
of maximum impact of a plant from one country to another. By a
comparison of results it ought to be possible to assess whether
longitudinal positions, or actual bodily positions give the best results.
No thorough study has yet been done on these lines but informal
observation and theoretical considerations would seem to indicate
that both positions may have their own symbolic significance. Thus
Pluto's angularity by longitude in cyclic maps appears to be an
important factor in marking out where the seed 'ideas of the time'

will manifest and where key issues are likely to come to some kind of head. For example, it was precisely conjunct the MC in longitude at the moment of the explosion of the first hydrogen bomb (8.15pm GMT 6.11.1952, 162E10, 11N30), and closely rising by longitude at the lunation immediately following the Wright brothers first flight (see Chapter 6). On the other hand Pluto's bodily position in Astrocartography maps (see following section) where latitude is allowed for, often seem to mark areas of extreme crisis as we can see in the example on p.403, with Pluto on the I.C. for Japan.

Mapping moments on the world: astrocartography (ACG)

Given that the maximum impact of any particular ingresses, luncations, conjunctions, etc. will be likely to be at those places where planets fall angular, then it is obviously of great importance for anyone wanting to assess world trends to be able to identify the areas of angularity with the minimum of fuss. Until recently to identify such areas of angularity on a systematic basis was almost impossible. It meant calculating numerous separate charts for each capital city and area that might be considered important. Whilst such individual charts are still extremely valuable and, in many sense, essential for a full assessment of the impact of any particular moment, we can now simply have a computer draw lines across a map of the world exactly through those places where the body of each of the planets is exactly on the MC, IC, AS and DS. An example of such a chart is shown in Fig. 10.2, opposite.

These computer-drawn charts, known as Astrocartography (ACGs) or astro-locality charts are the brainchild of Jim Lewis[30] of San Francisco who developed them for plotting out the relocation charts for individuals, a field in which they are also a powerful and indispensable tool. Although Lewis invented his ACG charts himself he was in fact rediscovering a tool that has been used on an off by individual astrologers since at least 1960 when Brigadier Firebrace reproduced coloured versions of these, laboriously plotted by hand, in the sidereal journal *Spica*[19] for mundane purposes. When I (CH) saw these charts, in 1978, remembering Firebrace's work, I suggested that they would make invaluable tools for mundane work if a set of these could be published for the year ahead. Almost at once Lewis had put together his first edition of the *Sourcebook of Mundane Maps for 1979*[30] from which Fig. 10.2 is taken. This now totally indispensable publication is printed each year, for the year ahead,

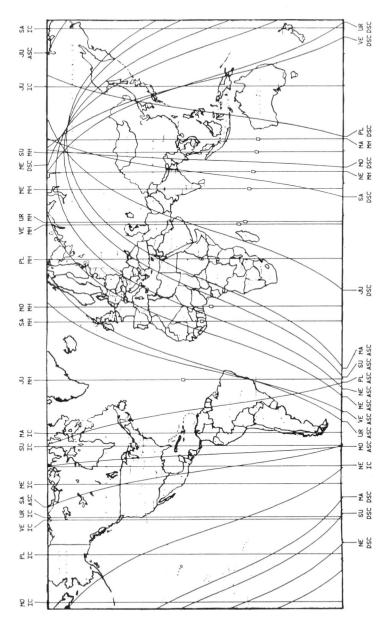

Figure 10.2 Astrocartography for the Capricorn ingress. 22 December 1978 17.21 GMT.

and includes charts for the year's four ingresses, both tropical and sidereal, and for all the New and Full Moons and solar and lunar eclipses. In addition it gives the personal ACG maps for the US president, and for the 1775 US Declaration of War chart, and for the 1801 UK chart. More about the application of ACGs for nations and leaders is given below.

The example chart

Our example ACG, Fig. 10.2, p.283, is for the Capricorn ingress in 1978, which, according to some authorities, is said to depict the basic pattern for the whole of the year 1979 and certainly the first quarter. At the bottom of the figure are the planetary positions for the moment that the Sun entered Capricorn. Above on the map of the world, we can see a criss-cross of lines. These are labelled by the initials of their planet and angle along the top and bottom. (NB For technical reasons the map of the world has had the polar regions slightly truncated at top and bottom.) On examination we find four lines marked in for each planet. The two absolutely vertical lines mark those localities where the planet is on the MC and IC and the moment of the ingress. The two curving lines mark where the body of the planet is on the AS and DS at the moment of ingress. Note that these AS-DS lines are for the *body* of the planet rising and setting as Lewis's program takes account of latitude (see section on latitude above). If these lines were marked on a 3-D globe it would in fact be seen that the MC-IC planetary lines are in fact one continuous line, a great circle passing up and over the pole. Likewise the AS-DS line is in fact a continuous circle passing right about the earth.

Thus at a glance the ACG gives us immediate information as to exactly where on earth at this particular moment each planet can be theoretically considered to have its maximum effect and, by implication, which countries' and cities' charts we might do well to examine further.

Parantellonta

It has been suggested by Lewis that an additional set of sensitive areas on these ACGs may perhaps also be important in mundane work. These are the parentellonta, those parellels of latitude where two planets are simultaneously on an angle. Lewis[31] has amassed considerable anecdotal evidence that these are certainly significant areas in the charts of individuals, and he gives a persuasive case for their consideration in mundane work in his introduction to his *Sourcebook of Mundane Maps*. The latitudes at which such parantellonta occur can be readily identified on the ACG map. They are those parallels of latitude which pass through any intersection of an MC-IC line with an AS-DS line. For example on the ACG illustrated we see that the Jupiter on the MC line intersects with the Venus and Uranus on the ascendant lines just north of Rio de Janeiro on the east coast of Brazil, at approximately 21°S. At the moment of the Capricorn ingress these bodies were simultaneously angular at this point on the earth's surface. What has been suggested is that as the earth rotates under them so this pair of angularities, this parantellonta, will sweep along this latitude bringing these planetary ideas into the consciousness of those areas. Such is the theory. However, compared to the actual line of angularity itself, it would seem unlikely that these parantellonta latitudes should be given much weight, unless supported by other factors.

Interpreting the ACG
If in 1978 we had wanted to look ahead at 1979 as a whole, this is certainly one of the maps we would have wanted to examine. But before we examine any ACG we should always first consider the basic planetary pattern of the ingress and the kind of ideas and energy patterns that it potentially contains. This we did in part in Chapter 9 when we looked at the Betelgeuse explosion (see p.261). To continue from that point, and because the action of Uranus is usually fairly clear cut, we might now first consider how the same UR = NE/PL = SO/MA, and VE = SA/PL, manifested on other parts of the world.

We first see that on the ACG the lines of Uranus and Venus are close together, reflecting their conjunction (orb 2°30′). But we may also note the way in which the Venus and Uranus rising lines merge and cross over one another through Rio de Janeiro, and likewise with the setting line just south of Japan. This is because in these areas the bodies of the two planets were rising and setting exactly together, even though they were of course still 2°30′ apart in longitude. This effect is, as we have seen above due to the planets having latitude. In this case it is mainly due to Venus's latitude which is 3°21′N at this time. Uranus's latitude of 0°21′N will also have had a small effect.

Going systematically over the map, and seeing which areas are touched by this conjunction, we note that: (1) the VE-0-UR was exactly on the MC down through the Urals, past the eastern shore of the Caspian, right through the geographical centre of Iran and southward across Oman and the Arabian Sea. (2) At the Same time this conjunction was on the IC down the west coast of California. (3) As noted already, it was on the ascendant on a line through Rio and the east coast of Brazil and up through both S. and N. Ireland and Scotland. (4) It was setting on a line down through Japan and the Queensland coast. Here then at a glance we can see those areas in the world where the meaning of this VE-0-UR 'theme' for the year, or at least the first quarter of 1979, may be sounded and expressed particularly clearly. These then are the areas where we can expect to find dramatic awakenings, impulsive eruptions (SO/MA) and 'bubbling through' of very deep level collective, transformative ideas (NE/PL), sudden changes, disturbances of equilibrium, upheavals, reforms awakening of revolutionary ideas of all kinds, calls for 'freedom', and change, and also of forceful autocratic rulership. At the physical level, as we saw in Chapter 9, this signals the danger of 'unusual catastrophes' (= NE/PL) and sudden accidents, explosions, and releases of intense energy (= SO/MA).

We do not have time to consider all these areas in detail but we can look at one more closely and hope that students will care to explore other areas and other themes in the chart more fully by themselves. For it is only by such systematic work and background research that we can hope to really get to know the scope and limitation of our tools. Those students, and we hope they will be the majority, who do want to explore this further will find that in addition to contemporary newspapers and periodicals there are various publications which give chronological listings of major events for past years. A summary of some of these is given in the main Bibliography.

1a. Starting with the MC, where the Uranus principle was, theoretically, most likely to be most consciously expressed, we see that this line, running as it does through the geographical centre of Iran, in fact pinpoints[65,68] the most dramatic, and in many respects 'unexpected' event of the year, the Iranian crisis and revolution, and the overthrow of the 'oldest Empire in the world'. What makes this particularly striking is that the CIA and the western intelligence services had considered such an event impossible right up until the moment that it happened. Indeed so unforseen was it that the Queen of England was due to pay a state visit to Iran at the very time when the unfortunate Shah was travelling into exile. Whilst it would be foolish to pretend that astrology, from this map alone, could have forseen these events, this Uranus line would most certainly have presented a major storm signal which would have had any astrologer worth their salt reaching for the chart of Iran (see Ref. 71, p.368). On examining the chart of that country, and its 45 ephemeris for the year, we immediately note that this culminating Uranus was in fact configuring both the AS and MC by 45/135 and was 90 to the all important MC/AS point which falls at 19LE36! At the same time we would have seen that the Iran's ruler Venus at 18PI27 was receiving both an almost partile square (orb 1′) from Neptune and a stressful quincunx (orb 30′) from Pluto, thus bringing in the full force of the major UR = NE/PL configuration. Besides these transits, the fact that Mars was just past Iran's IC, and -90- to the natal MO-180-ME and approaching the -180- to the natal 10th house Pluto, which might normally have aroused our suspicion of unsettled times ahead, seem but firecrackers.

We can see from a timetable of events how the nation's long-building tensions were released within weeks of this ingress. Thus more and more violence began building up from early in December 1978, with widespread demonstrations and clashes between pro and anti-Shah demonstrators, and the police. On 21 December, with twenty-four hours of the ingress, Parliament adjourned for three weeks in an attempt to form a new government; 23rd, deputy head US Oil Services Corporation (NE/PL) was shot dead (SO/MA); 26th-30th, oil production (NE/PL) dramatically cut to less than even national needs — widespread stikes, troop-student clashes, repeated failures to form government; 3 January 1979, Queen of England cancels her three-day visit; 16th: as transisting Sun-0-MA passes over the ingress ascendant which is conjoined Iran's SA/UR at 25CP52, the Shah flies into exile and an earthquake shakes the country — nature echoing and foreshadowing the traumatic events of the nation.
1b.   Oman, where Jupiter was also exactly on the DS (it passed to the south of Iran): 28 February: Queen Elizabeth II state visit, but no record of Uranus type manifestations.
2.   Uranus on IC on west coast of California produced no dramatic earthquake, please note! But it did, 180 from Iran[66] on 3 January, produce a firebomb and mob attack on the home of the Shah's sister in Beverley Hills.

3a.   UR-VE on AS, and Jupiter on MC for Brazil. As from 1 January fundamental reform measures took effect to 'set Brazil on a normal democractic course', allowing for the creation of new political parties, and depriving the president of exceptional powers over the executive. After many years of dictatorship the year, as a whole, saw widespread reform and liberalization in Brazilian politics.

3b.   Uranus on the AS through Ireland. The *Betelgeuse* explosion had already been discussed in Chapter 9. On 15 December S. Ireland broke its ties with sterling an joined the European Monetary System (VE-UR = financial reforms). A good example for those who consider the Capricorn ingress chart to be valid for the whole year is available here in the fact that his UR = NE/PL = SO/MA line passes exactly through Mullaghmore, where Lord Mountbatten was assassinated on 27 August. On 21 December three soliders were murdered by IRA machine-gunners, and on 1 January there was a new wave of nineteen bomb explosions.

4.   VE-UR on the DS and Jupiter on the MC for Japan. On 18 December an assassination attempt was made on the Prime Minister by a right-wing extremist. 25 January, record trade surplus and 20 per cent increase in exports reported (JU-MC). 30 January saw an increase in tension between Japan and USSR because of the latter's build-up of military installations on the occupied southern end of the Kurile chain. As well as the general VE-UR on DS indication here for 'disturbances with neighbours' we may also note that ME = SO/UR passes exactly through the island under debate!

   Such a listing of events is inevitably selective. It is possible to argue that since so much is going on in the world at any time, events could have been found to fit any such pattern. Certainly the element of chance does need to be controlled for. Thus if we use another chart (e.g. the one for the 1945 Aries ingress on p.403) as a control, for the above we can see that it is possible to argue that Pluto on the MC through Brazil and through IC for Japan could be equated to the Uranus on the AS and DS in the 1979 map. Likewise, though Uranus is no longer on the MC for Iran it is on the IC for India in the 1945 chart. This period 19-26 December saw Mrs Ghandi temporarily imrpisoned and a spate of rioting and hijacking on her behalf, which certainly seems most appropriate. The 1979 map shows only inocuous Mercury angular for Delhi. (Though with ME = SO/UR not as innocuous as it might at first appear!) Yet if we take the symbolism of the two maps and full symbolism, and relative magnitude, of the events into consideration it has to be conceded that it would be difficult to interchange them on any really consistent basis.

ACG for nations and world leaders
Another extremely valuable approach to the 'where' question which has been made possible by the advent of ACGs is to examine the ACG for the moment of a nation's birth or the birth of her leader, and see where on the earth each of the planetary principles is likely to find its maximum outworking. Jim Lewis who has pioneered this technique has come up with some very compelling results. Lewis points out the remarkable case of the US 'Declaration of War' chart (see Ref. 7, p.464). This many regard as a highly significant moment in the formation of the US, one which can be considered to mark the beginning of the USA's self-assertion in the world as a warring nation. In this ACG we find for example that Pluto is exactly on the MC at Hiroshima, that the MA-0-SA of the chart fall on the DS through South-east Asia, and on the AS through Cuba, site of the 1962 missle crisis, and that Neptune and Mars are on the MC through Germany. Neptune, Mars and Saturn fall on the IC through the Bering straights and west Alaska, the line of the US's main early warning radar stations and the point where the two super-powers confront each other. Equally remarkable is the fact that Uranus falls exactly on the MC through Alamogordo, where the first atom bomb was exploded, using of course uranium!

This would be an interesting catalogue of coincidence if it were one map but Lewis has gone on to show that, for example, both the US presidents involved in the decision to develop and use the atom bomb, Roosevelt and Truman, each also had their Pluto on an angle through Hiroshima! Likewise he points out that President Carter had his on the AS through eastern Iran, whilst his ME-180-UR falls across the AS through eastern Iran, exactly where his task force sent to rescue the US hostages met its abortive end. The 1801 chart for the UK, it has to be said, is nothing like so impressive, but it was not of course specifically a 'war' oriented chart. It does however show some interesting points. For example Uranus is on the AS through Ireland. Not a good omen at the time for lasting stability in that area of the UK. It shows Jupiter on the MC down through the boundary between Egypt and Libya not far from El Alamein — an appropriate significator perhaps for the crucial victories of the North

Africa campaign which marked the turning of the tide in World War Two. Most topically it shows Mars on the MC and Sun on the DS close to the Falkland Islands. This is given added interest by the fact that Margaret's Thatcher's own Sun and Mars fall exactly on the Ascendant through the Falklands! Used in conjunction with other techniques ACGs obviously have as important a role to play in the future development of our collective awareness through mundane astrology, as they do in the area of individual astro-therapeutics, and self-awareness. [32]

References
For references see pp.361-8.

11.

WHERE ON EARTH:
2 The Search for the Earth Zodiac

Charles Harvey

'The Earth looked at from Heaven, is like a ball with twelve leathern stripes, each of a different colour . . .'

Plato

Astrogeography

Following the ancient doctrine of correspondences, many astrologers have, quite logically, considered that there ought to be some kind of natural, exact, macrocosmic-microcosmic interrelationship between the zodiac, as a whole, above, and the earth, as a whole, below. If this is really the case, it is argued, then it implies the very tantalizing thought that there must be a precise, geographically plotable, 'astrological anatomy' of the earth, an 'earth zodiac', which is waiting to be discovered. Indeed, as we shall see below, many have set out in pursuit of this Rosetta stone, and some even claim to be convinced that they have discovered it. Certainly this area, despite the chaotic abandon of its growth, has thrown up some provocative results which deserve closer scrutiny.

This 'earth zodiac' model suggests that in some sense the very earth and rocks, or indeed sea, of a particular area will be in tune with, and respond to, one part of the sky rather than another. Simply put, using such a scheme, we might expect a major configuration in for example, 10° Aries to have its maximum impact in that area of the earth which corresponds with this degree. Obviously the key challenge of this approach is to determine the geographical 0° Aries point of this terrestrial zodiac. But in addition we also need to discover on what plane the ecliptic is projected on to the earth, and in which direction around the earth the zodiac is moving.

If there is indeed such an earthly zodiac we might expect it to have been definitively located by this time. However despite the observations of many different astrologers since at least Ptolemy, the situation unfortunately still remains, like so much in astrology, confused, ambiguous, and in need of solid research. As we have seen, in Chapter 1, Ptolemy's own solution, which has dominated our thinking in this matter for nearly two thousand years was, curiously, not in terms of a circular zodiac at all. But since his time such projections have usually been made either on the plane of the ecliptic or on the plane of the equator, though additional divisions have been suggested on other planes and even from pole to pole. The zodiac has usually been considered to run in an easterly direction though, as we shall see, at least three systems, including the earliest yet discoverd, have proposed the opposite, whilst Davison[12] has suggested that the zodiac can be measured in both directions.

Regarding the crucial question of locating the starting-point of this earthly zodiac, there is here, as we shall see, as much uncertainty and debate as in so many other areas of astrology. To date, despite isolated attempts, none of the many variations proposed can be said to have been adequately evaluated using past events. Nor do we know of the advocate of any system who has yet demonstrated that its use in fact improves an astrolger's capacity to make accurate forecasts. This is surely the acid test, since astrology is already overburdened with a vast accumulation of factors invoked for making *ex post facto* judgements!

Comparing the different methods proposed

In order to compare the different methods we have prepared the table on p.305 which shows the mid-heaven degrees that some of the main methods produce for some of the world's capitals. The proponents of most of these systems also advocate the use of the ascendant for each place as another significant sensitive point. This is derived by using the MC for the location and then taking out the ascendant for the appropriate latitude. Presumably local house cusps by the preferred method could also be added in the same way.

Faced with this vast array of different possible angles for any one location many readers may at this point simply wish to hurry on to the somewhat more secure ground of the next section! For those who feel tempted by the promised El Dorado that the answer to this riddle offers, the following notes will supply a basic groundwork to some of the main systems proposed. Whilst none of them may be of more than ludic value, there is also the possibility that there may be more than fools gold in one, or even several, of these systems, or in some such method that has yet to be discovered. Certainly this is not an approach that should be abandoned too lightly.

Let us then look at some of the main systems that have been put forward. These are presented in approximately chronological order of publication.

1.   The Ptolemaic Allocations
The most famous of these methods and the most ancient is, as we have see that of Ptolemy. [47] He was quite happy to divide the then known ancient world into four quadrants (Fig. 1.3, p.43) allocating each to one of the four elements, and alloting the planets as co-rulers of specified regions, within these areas. Whilst he does give some particular rulerships for individual places which may still have some value, it is difficult to see how we can now class his main scheme of allocations as anything but entirely arbitrary and worthless. Indeed it can never have made more than the vagues symbolic sense, even in ancient terms. Nonetheless his rulerships are so deeply entrenched that many prefer to cling to these rather than have none at all. What has probably made these rulerships stick is that certain of the allocations that arise from this method seem to be at least in part appropriate, such as Britain being under Aries. The lists of rulerships [67] of different countries and regions given in early textbooks and repeated down to the present day can in very large measure be traced back to this one source.

2.   de Boulainviller's World Zodiac
Perhaps the first astrologer to attempt to project the zodiac on to the globe in a systematic manner was the enthusiastic French nobleman Count Henri de Boulainviller. [9a] Having solved to his satisfaction the question of the Chart of Creation, which we discuss later, de Boulainviller, sometime prior to 1711, turned his attention to the way in which the Creator had placed the zodiac about the earth. He concluded from his observations and the incomplete

geographical knowledge of the period that 0° Aries began in the
Middle East and that the zodiac then ran westward giving a value
for London's MC for example of 27GE45, for Edinburgh of 0° Cancer,
and for Buenos Aires of 22LE00. Assuming his measurements to have
been in Right Ascension we can see that his sources were about two
degrees in error for the longitude of Buenos Aires. Curiously enough
he gives the ascendant of Buenos Aires, from this MC as 12SG30,
which is identical to the ascendant normally attributed to the first
Argentine Republic!

3. Sepharial's Geodetic Equivalents and the work of Parsons
This scheme, usually attributed to Sepharial (Dr Walter Gorn-Old,
1864-1929), begins an earthly reflection of the microcosmic zodiac
exactly at 0°E as 0° Aries, and follows the ecliptic around the Earth
in an easterly direction so that 1° terrestrial longitude = 1° zodiacal
longitude. Thus Paris at 2E20 is given an MC of 2AR20, and is
corresponding AS for the latitude of 26CN06. The scheme would
seem to imply that God is either an Englishmen or that He took
a very precise hand in the placing of Greenwich Observatory. Yet
curiously the scheme appears to have been discovered independently
by different observers, and still has, as we shall see, many keen
advocates.

Sepharial writing in about 1923[52] claims, by implication and
certainly according to his publisher's note, to have discovered this
system. If he did it is a point in its favour, for it is in fact identical
to a theory which appears to date back at least thirty years earlier
to an American astrologer Parsons (b.1847-?). Parson's work[46] was
given enthusiastic coverage in Alan Leo's high quality, and widely
circulated *Modern Astrology* for May 1913 by an experienced astrology
teacher Gertrude de Bielski[8] who had been using his theory in her
classes and lectures for 'a period of about fifteen years'. In the event
it would seem very curious if Sepharial, one of the most eclectic of
astrologers of the period, had not come across her work, or Parson's
original book. Whatever the truth of the matter it was certainly
Sepharial who did much to promote this system, and who seems
to have coined the term 'geodetic equivalent'. Its original promotion
by de Bielski arose from a dissatisfaction with the Ptolemic rulerships,
a dissatisfaction which was already widespread amongst astrologers
by the end of the nineteenth century! Parson's scheme in fact
theoretically places 0° Taurus through the Great Pyramid of Gizeh

whilst at the same time mapping Greenwich as 0° Aries rather than as 28°50' Pisces where it would need to be to be consistent, since the two locations are 31°10' apart in geographical longitude. This discrepency of 1°10' is not noted or explained by de Bielski. After ten years of her own studies of the question and after experimenting with this scheme for fifteen, de Bielski states that her observations of 'the effects of transits, especially of the superior planets through the signs over the countries which correspond to them . . . give some very convincing proofs of the feasibility and reliability of this system'.[8]

Though at first sight it seems implausible that the Greenwich Meridian should be placed so conveniently at exactly 0° Aries, it is of course possible that such a scheme does have some validity (see Johndro[25,26] for further thoughts on the significance of Greenwich). de Bielski's evidence, as she presents it, is highly generalized and intermingled with Theosophical speculations though she does give some specific examples of how the then current Chinese Revolution corresponds to Neptune through Cancer, which covers most of China under this scheme, and how the *Titanic* sank close to the area governed by 1° Aquarius where Uranus was posited at the time. Sepharial presents his case for this same idea with more specific examples of this kind. Unfortunately Sepharial's own very first example[53] does little to inspire confidence in the method. He illustrates it with a discussion of the outbreak of the Spanish-American War of April 1878, showing how the MA-90-NE, which occurred in 16 April, places Mars exactly on the geodetic MC of *Lisbon*! Madrid, presumably the appropriate capital, is in fact 5°27' further east, much too far out or orbs to be useful for these purposes. Although Sepharial himself warns[53a] against unquestioningly accepting traditional rulerships, sensibly advocating that only 'very close study of transists and eclipses in connection with the history of a country can determine with any degree of certainty what sign of the zodiac has predominance in either its political or social life', his own work lacks any such 'close study'. In fact his original book launched the theory upon the world with but a dozen or so suggestive examples and various dramatic and, as it transpired, erroneous predictions based on these methods, such as that 'we may confidently look to the year 1927 as inaugurating the greatest change in the constitution that has been made since the famous code of Alfred over one thousand years ago'.[52] None of this would matter if it were not for the recurrent, and relatively uncritical recycling of this scheme without any kind of systematic analysis and evaluation. To be taken seriously any such evaluation needs to take into consideration the many similar methods which have been advocated.

One writer who has at least attempted to present a larger background to the problem is Davison. [12] After a survey of the whole question of the earthly zodiacs, as known to him, he concludes that 'an examination of the merits of the various systems . . . has led me to the conclusion that the most effetive is the one proposed by Sepharial'. He then elaborates on Sepharial, suggesting that the zodiac can be measured in *both* an easterly and a westerly direction, so that each place has two corresponding MC degrees. The case he cites in support of the geodetic equivalents are for the most part cases of individuals for whom certain geographical regions have been important, though he also enumerates some cases of transits to the degrees. A particularly striking example that he gives is that of Cape Canaveral which is located at 80W33 W. This places 9CP27 on the MC by the easterly count-method. John Glenn, the first US astronaut to go into orbit, was born at almost the same longitude, 81W35 and has his Pluto in 8CN52. Mercury was at 11CN09 at this first space launch. Neil Armstrong, first man on the Moon, had Jupiter in 8CN42 and Saturn at 6CP14. His companion Aldrin had Uranus in 7AR58, and Collins Saturn in 7CP00.

Hiroshima produces another striking example. Its eastern place degree is 12LE28. When the atom bomb fell Pluto was at 9LE58 and the Sun at 13LE09. However the problem is that positive examples can always be found to support any thesis. If we simply ignore the cases that do not appear to work we can soon convince ourselves. Some devil's advocacy and 'control' examples are essential when attempting to evaluate these methods. Thus we could argue that if these degrees are really so important we might expect them to show up in outstanding events for any locality. But taking as example the case of Pearl Harbour with Geodetic MCs of 7VI59 and 22LI01, which Davison cites in this study (he points out that Hirohito's ME is 22AR20 = MA/PL at 21CN22 and the USA's UR 8GE53), the only transit to these points either on the day of Pearl Harbour, or at the preceding New Moon for that matter is from ME 7SG25, not perhaps the weightiest of transits! Since the Japanese massive pre-emptive strike was by far the biggest event in this locality's history this hardly encourages much faith in these MC degrees, at least for the purpose of forecasting. Their great attraction must obviously be their ease of calculation. We trust that, of itself, this temptation will not seduce too many students into assuming that this is therefore the correct method! At the same time it would be invaluable if someone would undertake a systematic and impartial study of this scheme and the methods which follow.

4.   The Hamburg School — The Friedrich/Grimm Method

This method, which gives results close to Sepharial's has a considerable following amongst the Hamburg School in Germany at the present time. It also takes Greenwich as its starting-point, but measures the geographical longitude of a place in terms of Right Ascension, i.e. as it is, measured along the equator, and projects this on to the ecliptic, and then notes the appropriate MC and AS. This method was apparently developed entirely independently of Sepharial, or of Johndro (see below), by Theodor Friedrich of Leipzig, in about 1937, following the ideas of the German astrologer A. M. Grimm, put forward in about 1933. The results give angles that are usually within 2° of Sepharial's. If anyone is interested in testing out and comparing these methods this difference ought certainly to be sufficient to show whether one, both, or neither is significant. Adherents of Friedrich's method may count it as a significant improvement on Sepharial's method, just described, in that using the examples given, this method gives the MC for Cape Canaveral as 8CP41, in much closer -180- Armstrong's Jupiter, and for Hiroshima an MC of 10LE01, within 3' of transit Pluto! For those who wish to experiment and compare, a set of cross-indexed tables of MC and AS for the main cities of the world by this method has been produced by Brummund[9a] of the Hamburg School. This includes a short discussion of the pros and cons of the issues involved and cites various suggestive examples and case studies.

5.   Johndro's Locality Angles

In 1929 Johndro[26] writes of the need 'of coordinating the heavens and the earth' and of how 'the solution of this astrologically important problem has engaged the author's attention for twenty years'. He goes on 'after testing and discarding scores of equinoctial-geographic coordinates during this period of research it is now believed a solution has been attained that will stand the severe test of time . . .' He then goes on to elaborate a scheme which is tied to both the Great Pyramid of Egypt and to Greenwich.[26] Like Friedrich, above, Johndro uses Right Ascention. His starting point gives Greenwich a RAMC of 29°10′ = 1°19 Taurus in 1930. Johndro however considers that this point is advancing at the rate of 46′10″ per year in line with equatorial precession. Using this base line Johndro gives tables of MC, and the AS derived from these, for the major cities of the world. This is supplemented by a chapter of 'Verification by world events' in which he demonstrates the efficacy of these angles in much the same selective way that Sepharial proves his version.

As the product of twenty years research these results certainly deserve some consideration, especially as Johndro[25] had in 1914 put forward an entirely different scheme which gave 9GE19 on the MC at London, which he felt obliged to abandon. However Dean[12a] points out that Johndro himself also later rejected at least part of his own 1929 findings for a period, as the result of a series of negative tests on the locality ascendants. Johndro went on to say that the same lack of accuracy 'was found to hold true of (locality) ascendants based on any single Greenwich base'. Following this categorical statement he however then changed to Sepharial's base-line of Greenwich = 0° Aries, which he had earlier rejected. Then to confuse the matter yet further it appears[12a] that he reverted to his 1929 base-line in an unpublished article written a few months before his death. Thus there is serious ambiguity even on the author's own evaluation of this method. Since Johndro's books are kept in print, (there have been two reprints and a paperback edition in the past twelve years) and since he still has many devoted admirers it is to be hoped that someone will undertake a clear assessment of his work.

This said, however, there are features of Johndro's scheme which are provocative. For example it is notable that the MC his method (published in 1929) produces for London is 1TA12. Is it simply coincidence that at the outbreak of World War Two we find SA 00TA54 -0- MO 29AR44, -90- PL 2LE08? It may be, and one would like to see a systematic study of major transits to this point. Again another highly suggestive allocation is that for Warsaw, Poland. Under this scheme Warsaw turns out to have an MC of 22TA41. As will be seen under *Poland* in Chapter 14, this falls very close to an area which turns repeatedly at key moments in Polish history. It seems extremely unlikely that Johndro could have known this or considered it in his work. Also intriguing is the allocation of an MC of 15TA02 to Berlin. This is again close to one of the degree areas that appears to be important for Germany as a whole. Thus we find that Pluto in the chart of the German Empire falls at 17TA00, Hitler's MA-0-VE falls at 16TA23 and 16TA42, -90-SA 13LE27; that at the creation of Greater Berlin (00 hrs 1 October 1920) we find MO 13TA55-90-NE-13LE11, whilst for the 1925 refounding of the Nazi part there is MA 13TA10-180-SA 14SC18, -90-NN 13LE32. Equally it is interesting that two separate German astrologers, Ritter and Andersen (see below), neither of whom shows any knowledge of Johndro's work, both independently arrived at the conclusions that the area between 5E00 and 35E00 which covers Germany is under Taurus. Andersen's starting-point for the zodiac places — 24°55 Aries on the MC for London — makes Berlin MC 8TA23, a difference of 6°39′, which though wide of the mark is perhaps sufficiently close to Johndro to encourage the thought that there may be something here that deserves further attention.

6. *The Great Pyramid Base Line of Williams*
David Williams[61] in his studies of the problem arrives at a division of the globe based on the Great Pyramid of Gizeh at 31°07′57″E as marking 15°00′ of sidereal Taurus (cf Parsons value of 0° Taurus for the Great Pyarmid). This is based on the precessional studies of David Davidson's *The Great Pyramid* and the assertion that the pyramid is located at the exact centre of the land area of the world, Given that the pyramid is situated at 31°08′E this gives a value of 13°52′ sidereal Aries for Greenwich, which is close to the value of 15° tropical Aries proposed by Wise. Approximate sidereal allocations for this system can be obtained by subtracting 1°08′ from the values given by Wise in the final column of the table below. As Williams makes his allocations in terms of RA, adjustment for this would be required. According to Williams the first point of Aries precessed into Aquarius in 1844. Conversion of values into the tropical zodiac will need to be made accordingly.

7. *The Pyramid-Based Sidereal System of Spencer*
Another advocate of the Great Pyramid as the primary starting-point is Spencer[56] who takes the pyramid as having originally marked the dividing line between the constellations of Aries and Taurus. In this she is in accord with Parsons (see 3 above). But whilst he proposed equal divisions of the Earth, Spencer uses a sidereal zodiac of unequal length constellations, with an ayanamsa (i.e. difference between 0° sidereal and 0° tropical) of 24°00′ for 1930. She, again like Parsons,

marks out the zodiac about the earth in an easterly direction. She considers the boundaries of these constellations for the 1930 epoch to have been as follows: 0° Aries stretches from 11W49-18E1; Taurus = 18E11-44E4; Gemini = 44E40-77E05; Cancer = 77E05-110E36; Leo = 110E36-140E43; Virgo = 140E43-168E20; Libra = 168E20-162W00; Scorpio = 162W00-134W20; Sagittarius = 134W20-101W51; Capricorn = 101W51-69W24; Aquarius = 69W24-40W22; Pisces = 40W22-11W49. These are of course sidereal values and 24°00′ needs to be added to these to obtain their tropical equivalent for 1930 and precession allowed for other years.

8. Astrogeography: The Work of Hans Andersen

By far the most comprehensive of these 'global zodiac' schemes is that of the contemporary German astrologer, Hans Andersen.[2] His extensive work in this area is not, as yet, available in English. It merits consideration as one of the most elaborate attempts to develop these ideas on at least a quasi-empirical bsis. Andersen has made wide-ranging studies of the positions of eclipses and major conjunctions in relation to different areas of the earth and most specifically with Germany. As a result he has come up with an extraordinarily complex series of interlocking world zodiac, each with its own equator. Andersen's work is not for the faint-hearted dabbler. Not content with one main 'earth zodiac' on the plane of the equator, he has also postulated at least a dozen further global zodiacs. Only a rigorous analysis and evaluation will tell us what is in fact of value amongst this plethora of possibilities, and this has yet to be made. Without such an approach we must suspect that much of it may be like the works of the author's namesake, strong on symbolic content but weak in realism when it comes to making actual forecasts.

Andersen considers that the basic global-zodiac has about 25°00′ Aries on the MC at Greenwich. He notes that this places the area from about 5E00-35E00 under Taurus. This is curiously enough exactly in agreement with the findings of another German astrologer Dr G. Ritter (see below). Ritter however suggested that the zodiac ran from east to west with 0° Aries being placed at about 65E. Thus though their schemes agree exactly on a Taurus allocation for this precise area of Germany and Central Europe, the actual degrees of Taurus are reversed. Interestingly, as noted above, Johndro also comes up with a Taurus MC for most of this same area. Like Sepharial, Andersen equates degrees of zodiacal longitude with degrees of

Figure 11.1 H. J. Andersen's 'Solar Zodiac' with its pole at 52N30, 08E30. The zodiacal positions of some of the major cities of the world are noted in around the circumference. Andersen has hypothesized the existence of equivalent 'zodiacs' for each planet.

geographic longitude, rather than working in Right Ascension like Johndro.

However the global zodiac is only the first step in Andersen's scheme. Over this basic framework he then superimposes a whole range of supplementary global zodiacs which divide the Earth along quite separate planes of their own. Each of these empiracally derived subsidiary zodiacs is considered to have a special afinity with one of the planets, and the way in which that planetary principle is experienced upon the Earth. Thus his Sun-system has its North Pole at 52N30 and 8E24 from which point all the signs radiate out as shown in Fig. 11.1, above. The resulting allocations of degrees for some

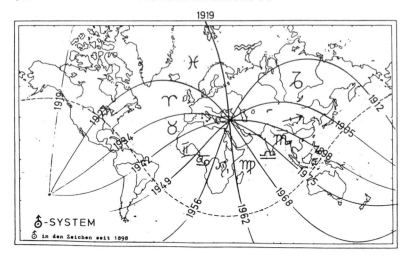

Figure 11.2   H. J. Andersen's 'Uranus Zodiac' with its north pole at
c.37N00, 37E00. (NB the vertical 'Mars') symbol with a dot is the one
commonly used in Germany for Uranus.) The dotted line shows the path
of Uranus through the signs this century. Andersen suggests that this zodiac
will reveal where Uranus will be particularly active during its occupancy
of a sign.

of the major cities of the nothern hemisphere are shown in the
comparative table below. Is it simply coincidence that Andersen's
empirical studies led him to suggest that the pole of this important
system is in his native Germany? Perhaps. Alternatively he could
be giving indirect confirmation to the idea of Hitschler that each
national centre can be treated in turn as the centre of its own zodiac.
Andersen's other systems have their poles in entirely other parts of
the globe. Thus, for example, the North Pole of his Moon-system
is at 92.25E and 33.51N; of his Venus-system at 54.59N and 177.09E;
of his Jupiter-sytem at 46N and 20E; of his Uranus-system at 37N
and 37E.

Figs. 11.2 and 11.3 show the projection of the Uranus-system on
the globe. This, Andersen suggests, represents the sequence in which
different geographical areas will undergo change, revolution, and
'awakenings' of various kinds. Fig. 11.2 shows the periods when
Uranus was passing through each of the signs. Presumably the
orientation of the system was adjusted to obtain the best fit for past

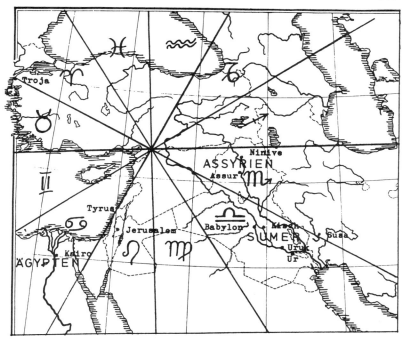

Figure 11.3 A close up of the polar area of Andersen's 'Uranus Zodiac'. This shows the concentrated area covered by each sign near to the pole of such a zodiac. The actual pole then becomes the focus of energy of that planet.

transits of Uranus. Thus the predictive value of this hypothetical system can only really be tested on Uranus' movement since its promulgation in about 1970. The turn of events in Iran, if not India, during Uranus' transit through Scorpio are intriguing. The entrance into Sagittarius is indeed coinciding with major shifts within China. Does the pole of this system falling in the Middle East imply that this region will continue to be an epicentre of change? The terrestrial projections for this other planetary zodiac are illustrated in numerous issues of *Sein und Werden* and in various of the Ebertin Yearbooks.[15] Andersen has published a systematic listing of precise degree allocation for different cities in these other systems in *Astrogeographie und Geschichte.* An article giving the trigometric formula for their calculation is available in *Sein und Werden*[2a].

9. Ritter's Cosmogeography

As noted, unlike most other researchers the German astrologer and expert in astro-meteorology Dr Gerhard Ritter[50] considers that the zodiac should circle the earth from east to west, with its origin point at 65° east. This places 5°00 Gemini on the MC at Greenwich . He also suggests that the Earth can be divided into twelve 15° bands of latitude starting with Aries at the North Pole to Pisces for the final 15° around the South Pole. Ritter employes a complex system of sub-rulership within each sign, rather than actual degrees, in order to obtain fine grain distinctions of location.

10. The Time Zone System of Wise

Wise[62] suggests that the Earth be divided up starting with Greenwich as 15° Aries. He does this on the basis of the 1894 international agreement on time zones, which he sees in some sense symbolizing an orderly and conscious sectioning of the globe. He argues that Greenwich is the centre of a 30° zone rather than the boundary. Like the authors of each of the other systems he claims that such a division produces highly appropriate results symbolically. He offers no additional empirical observations, but points out that this system produces almost identical results to that of Williams (see above), based on the Great Pyramid. The unusual feature of this model is that Wise proposes that oppoiste signs rule the southern hemisphere. Thus the area 15° either side of the meridian is given to Aries in the nothern hemisphere and to libra in the southern.

11. Hitschler's Method

The Swiss astrologer Hitschler, best known for his astro-medical work which interlinks the 360° of the zodiac and the periodic table of the elements, has made some interesting observations on the problem of the earth zodiac.[22] He, like Ritter, also advocates that it runs in a westerly direction. His value for Greenwich is 26AR00, thus placing most of central Europe under various degrees of Aries, and putting the east coast of America under Cancer. Interestingly this puts Washington DC's MC at 12CN53, almost exactly conjunct the US. Independence Sun, exactly oppoiste 13CP00 the MC degree by Sepharial's method. Curiously, as can be seen from the table, this method also gives an almost identical MC to Sepharial for Berlin. He suggests that the MC degree obtained by these means is the ruling degree for that country and can, paradoxically, be considered as its rising degree. (Hitschler's further elaboration on this method are outlined elsewhere in Chapter 12, p.316-317.)

Comparative table of midheaven degrees for some major cities according to different systems

	Sepharial[1] Geodetic	Hamburg School	Johndro (1930)	Andersen Earth	Andersen Sun	Ritter	Wise[2]	Hitschler
Madrid	26PI19	25PI58	29AR27	21AR19	25CP00	8GE41	11AR19	29AR34
London	29PI55	29PI54	1TA12	24AR55	9PI00	5GE07	14AR55	26AR07
Paris	2AR20	2AR32	3TA45	27AR20	4AQ00	2GE40	17AR20	23AR33
Berlin	13AR23	14AR30	15TA02	8TA23	10-14VI*	21TA37	28AR23	12AR30
Cape Town	18AR30	19AR54	20TA17	13TA30	10SG00	16TA30	3TA30	7AR23
Warsaw	21AR00	22AR40	22TA41	16TA00	12VI00	14TA00	6TA00	4AR53
Cairo	1TA17	3TA28	2GE30	26TA17	00SC00	3TA43	16TA17	24PI36
Jerusalem	5TA13	7TA34	6GE15	00GE13	22LI00	29AR47	20TA13	20PI40
Moscow	7TA38	9TA52	8GE29	2GE38	23LE00	27AR22	22TA38	18PI15
Tehran	21TA29	23TA29	21GE21	16GE29	27VI00	13AR31	6GE29	4PI24
Delhi	17GE13	18GE03	15CN06	12CN13	12VI00	27AQ47	2CN13	18CP40
Peking	26CN25	24CN10	23LE19	21LE25	7LE00	8AQ35	11LE25	29SG28
Tokyo	19LE48	16LE55	17VI56	14VI48	23CN30	15CP12	4VI48	6SG05
Canberra	26LE51	26LE29	28VI08	21VI51	***	7CP09	11VI51	28SC02
San Fransisco	27SC52	00SG05	27SG02	22SG52	6TA00	7LI08	12SG52	28LE01
Washington	13CP00	12CP06	9AQ43	8AQ00	8AR30	22LE00	28CP00	12CN53
New York	16CP10	14CP57	12AQ41	11AQ10	10AR00*	18LE50	1AQ10	9CN43
Buenos Aires	1AQ32	29CP32	28AQ39	26AQ32	***	3LE28	16AQ32	24GE21

[1]   Sepherial Davison also considers that these can be counted westward giving a series of complimentary values, e.g. by the west count Madrid = 3AR41, and Paris = 27PI40
[2]   Williams (see 5 above) Sidereal values based on the great Pyramid of Gizeh can be obtained by subtracting 1°10′ from the values of Wise.
*   It is difficult to give precise values for areas close to the pole of zodiac.
**   Estimated value from map.
***   Not available.

NB   This table does not include all the methods that have been advocated. de Boulainviller's values can be obtained by adding 22°38′ to those of Ritter. Spencer's constellational values can be calculated from the positions given in the text (see 7 above).

Local Zodiacs Within Nations, Cities, and Communities

Hitschler,[22] amongst others, has pointed out that astrological symbolism must allow us to treat any nation, or indeed city, town, or community, as a microcosm in itself. It follows from this that we should expect to find some kind of zodiacal effect within any organism, and hence the possibility of localizing planetary effects within countries. Thus if we take the capital city of a nation Hitschler has proposed that its MC degree, calculated according to his system, will become its natural ascendant, and that the zodiac will circle out from this point around the capital and the country. Although he gives some brief examples neither he nor any other astrologer that we know of has tried to follow this idea through on a consistent basis.

Taken to its logical conclusion this implies that each one of us not only lives within our own microcosmic zodiac, which, it is alleged, dictates that we will be more prone to damage to our heads if we have stressful aspects from Aries, the throat from Taurus, etc. but also that we live amidst hierarchy of such zodiacs, perhaps starting with our own home, and then up through our community, the local administrative capital, the country, the nation, the grouping of nations, such as the EEC, and finally the world zodiac.

However since there is still so much uncertainty about even this final-level zodiac the utmost caution is required before we pursue this idea too far without really substantial evidence. Whilst undoubtedly certain areas of countries do have very distinct characteristics, the question is whether these areas link together zodiacal patterns, whether they depend mainly on their own foundation, or whether both factors intermingle. For example is Poole in Dorset, which Carter, who grew up there, places under Pisces, bordered by areas with Aquarian and Arian flavour? If so where is their focal point? Or do such qualities stem not from the area but from some original foundation of the town itself at a strongly Piscean moment? Or do both factors have a bearing? Likewise within London, Addey[1] and others have pointed out the very strongly Virgo-Pisces qualities of the area around Queen Square, where the Astrological Lodge meets at the Art Workers Guild, a centre of fine craftsmanship, where John Addey, with his SA in VI-180-UR in PI first conceived the AA. It is an area strongly connected with health and hygiene, which includes many hospitals, including the Royal Homoeopathic where John Addey died. Is this an area unto itself or is it part of an underlying zodiacal order of the natural zodiac of London itself? John Addey gave considerable thought to the question of the subjective experience of zodiacs and spoke in the last months of his life of his own 'discovery' in the street where he lived.

The Cheam Road zodiac

Every morning until the severe winter of 1981/82 and his final illness, John Addey used to set off with his sticks to circumambulate the block where he lived, for his morning constitutional. A naturally observant and enquiring man he soon began to notice a very curious thing.[1a] Counting his own home as Cancer, naturally, he noticed that proceeding clockwise the next house was occupied by a family with identical twins and indeed that there were a further two sets of twins in the next houses, clearly a Gemini area. Following this there was an area of extremely solid housing with well-tended gardens, and the local ear, nose and throat specialist in residence, the very names of the inhabitants proclaimed this to be a Taurus area. The ex-Army character had obviously settled under Aries, the prominently displayed fish-pond obviously demarcated the Pisces zone. As he continued his walks he soon discovered that it neatly divided into the twelve signs, with the hypochondriac specialist in health diets living under Virgo, the retired insurance broker located securely under Capricorn, and so on. Indeed once he had established the pattern every new piece of information rapidly confirmed this most remarkable discovery on his very own doorstep — no less than the 'Cheam Road zodiac'!

However being of an experimental turn of mind before proclaiming his discovery to the astrological community he decided to do a control experiment. What would happen he wondered if he demarcated his own house as Aries, instead of Cancer? During the following days he kept his eyes peeled for signs, and behold were there not keen brewers of wine next door, and how had he overlooked their fish tank? And was not the former Taurean in fact rather eccentric and given to helping good causes? And the throat specialist, was he not in fact a leading scientist in his area? The Aries ex-military man had in fact confessed his great love of mountain climbing, and was now involved in local politics, clearly a Capricorn of the officer class. And so on around the block. The former zodiac had evaporated and an even better fit had taken its place!

It is with this experience in mind that we should perhaps approach any consideration of other alleged zodiacs of this type. The capacity of the human mind to project order and system onto random patterns is well known. Who can resist seeing pictures in the fire, faces in the wallpaper, castles and fabulous creatures in the clouds?

The Glastonbury and other local zodiacs

The most famous of all such suggested local zodiacs is the one at Glastonbury in Somerset, England. Its persuasive protagonists[10] suggest that there is a zodiac circle some thirty miles in diameter in the area around Glastonbury, Somerton, and Castle Cary, which contains the signs of the zodiac and various other figures outlined by ancient tracks, field boundaries, and water courses. No certain suggestion of its existence is known prior to its discovery and exploration by a mythologically inclined sculptress Katherine Maltwood in the twenty years prior to 1935, when her major work *Glastonbury's Temple of the Stars* was published. Since then it has attracted growing attention, modification and improvement from its devotees, and has become part of the myth of the whole area. However the emphasis in the approach of modern students, is away from 'psuedo-archaeology' and objective evidence to a subjective approach to the zodiac as a ground for deep meditation in this admittedly mysterious area. As Geoffrey Ashe writes in his introduction to Mary Caine's comprehensive and stimulating book[10] on the subject:

> If the . . . aerial photographs were shown to a group who had not been told what to look for, I doubt very much if they would pick out the fiures. . . . I would say, though, that if you discuss the figures in a purely objective way . . . you are discussing them wrongly . . . . What matters is the experience of those who do see them — the wide-ranging meditations which they can set in motion, the complex imagery they can conjure up.

In this approach we cease to be concerned with whether there is or is not an actual zodiac, rather we are using and allowing the rich symbolism of the concept of a zodiac to order our experience. Whether all of the protagonists of the Glastonbury zodiac, and the other zodiacs that have been alleged since in London, at Kingston-on-Thames and in Wales, would agree with this approach seems unlikely. Map readings and physical measurements still seem to play a key role for most of those committed to these ideas.

References
For references see pp.361-8.

12.

WHERE ON EARTH:
3 The Astrology of Towns and Cities

Charles Harvey

Once we start dealing with such complex notions as 'nations', 'states', 'peoples', cultures', which are living, changing, evolving entities, and not static geographical regions, we can see that the 'celestial conditioning' of a particular area will tend to build up in layers as it were, over the natural and basic rulership, the underlying *genius loci* determined theoretically on the basis of the earth zodiac. But in addition geological factors can be expected to play their part. Thus any region that actively develops its iron ore deposits will begin to activate and emphasize the Mars archetype within itself, whilst coal-mining areas and areas of heavy industry might expect to intensify an affinity with Mars-Saturn configurations, and so on. Later 'overlay' charts might be expected to reflect these developments in the area's focus of consciousness if they are of long-term consequence.

The most important overlays here will be the inceptional charts marking the foundation of nations, states, and cities, and other charts for moments of collective significance for the people of a region. Such moments as the signing of Magna Carta, or the opening of a Parliament building can continue to echo through the unconscious. The pattern of planetary ideas, and the ecliptic degrees occupied, at such moments of collective decision seem to become etched into the collective memory as constellated energies, as myths. These archetypal patterns seem able to live on in the collective unconscious, in a timeless state of vitality, ready to be reactivated by appropriate celestial circumstances or by the embodiment of particular transits within an individual who may become a future leader. As can be seen this approach greatly complicates things for it allows, at least in theory, the possibility of an almost infinte number of possibly significant charts, each with their sensitive degree areas. Here, as as in all other areas of astrology, we will see that it is essential to define carefully the exact reference of each of our charts. Equally it will be important to establish some sense of the priorities amongst our charts, some kind of hierarchy of importance in the manner suggested in Appendix IV on p.481. .

After the chart of the individual, there is presumably a chart of the family, of the local community, the town, the administrative area, the state, the country, the grouping of countries and finally, presumably, of humanity as a whole. All these interconnect like a series of Chinese boxes, together with other charts for sub-groups and organizations to which the individual belongs through work and other involvements. In this way any one individual is probably interrelated with many dozens of different wholenesses, each with its own chart. And this is not only of philosophical and theoretical interest. In practice cross-referencing between such different charts can give a 'fix' on possible eventualities. Thus Charles Carter points out how death is often to be seen more clearly through the charts of the deceaseds' nearest and dearest than in their own chart. This was certainly the basis on which he predicted his own likely departure.

Chapter 15 gives the charts of some of the main countries of the world. Here we will specifically consider the question of the charts of town and cities. Few of us are likely ever to become intimately involved with national affairs; many of us are likely to be involved fairly closely with our own communities. Such studies can open up the possibility of increasing collective awareness at a local level. If we can learn to channel potentially dangerous build-ups of energy into positive collective consciousness at the national and international levels. This perhaps suggests the importance of active 'town meetings' with real power, of the kind that exist in Switzerland and parts of the US such as New England. Only conscious action at this level is likely to enable communities to use the archetypal energies in their locality really positively. Thus of recent years it has been reported that Yorkshire, in England, has a particularly bad record for crimes of violence and perversion, the most famous of which have been the Moors murders and the Ripper killings. Could it be that past areas of exploitive heavy industry, emphasizing the negative application of the Mars-Saturn-Uranus principles, may have had their part to play in this? Astrology ought to be able to shed some light on such developments and be able to offer clues as to ways in which the community can begin to redirect these same energies constructively. One can imagine the advertisement: 'Wanted: Regional Psychotherapist — experience with negative Jupiter-Neptune an advantage'.

The charts of towns, cities and states

If, as in natal astrology, we can detect the operation of the planetary cycles through the charts of individuals, so too we can expect to find these principles reflected at each level, in each nation and its smaller sub-divisions, in its separate states, counties, cities, towns, and even villages, and families within communities. Of course, as always, we have to recognize that there will be a hierarchy here. The smaller unity will normally tend to be subsumed under the unities of which it is a part. But we should never lose sight of the fact that because of its unity, any single cell within a larger organism has the potential to constellate particular 'ideas of the time' and activate the parent organism appropriately. This is what democracies intuitively enshrine when emphasizing the importance of individual liberty. Within a healthy society presumably each 'cell', each level of organisation, will have sufficient autonomy to allow it to respond positively to the times, so as to be able to contribute the maximum awareness to the greater whole. By the same token the chart for any such collective enterprise must inevitably reflect the kinds of experience that the community will be likely to constellate at a given time. Thus, as Carter[11] points out, the charts of Hiroshima or Nagasaki would, if known, surely have indicated in some fairly clear way the catastrophe that was to befall them, just as the true charts of London, Paris, Madrid, New York etc. ought to show their subsequent rise to power. Unfortunately, today, reliable charts of this class are no less wrapped in ambiguities and uncertainties than are the charts of their parent nation.

In Ptolemy's day this would seem to have been a less common problem for he states:[47] 'In certain cases . . . where the date of foundation of a metropolis cannot be ascertained, the Mid-Heaven in the nativity of the reigning king or other actual chief magistrate, is to be substituted, and considered as that part of the zodiac with which it chiefly sympathizes'. This would seem to imply that knowledge of the foundation charts of cities was relatively common at this period. Ptolemy continues: 'those points or degrees of the zodiac, over which the Sun and Moon were in transit, at the time when the construction of any such city was first undertaken and commenced, are to be considered as sympathizing with that city in an especial manner; and that among the angles, the ascendant is principally in accordance with it'.

With the major new cities of the Roman Empire the election of charts for foundations was considered commonsense, as it still is today throughout the Indian sub-continent. Thus when the Emperor Constantine decided to found his city Constantinople, the present Istanbul, he consulted the astrologers who elected for him to lay the foundation stone of the future city's walls 'at the hour of the Crab' on 26 November 330 AD. Knappich[27] notes that the actual rising degree of many other major cities are given by the Arabic and classical astrologers. Lists of these are given in the works of Cardan, Gauricus, Rantzau, Junctinus and other Renaissance astrologers. It would be a noble work indeed if somebody could collate this material, for at present we are for the most part still in the position of the great Al-Biruni. In AD 1029 he advised:

. . . to find an association between a particular place and a sign of planet is a matter for investigation and research, but how are we to draw a horoscope or ascertain the Lord of the hour for a place unless we know accurately the time of its construction? And what city is there of which such a recollection is preserved? Even if a religious ceremony be associated with the foundation of a city, the history of its early condition has passed into oblivion.

A start on this enormous work of systematically listing and indexing all known foundation data has been made in certain areas. Thus in Britain Wigglesworth[60] was awarded the Astrological Association's Astrology Prize for his exemplary work on researching the Incorporated Boroughs of England. This is an important start on the problem for Britain. The USA has been well served by Dodson,[13] who has compiled an invaluable collection of the foundation charts for each of the States of the Union and of many of the major cities of the nation. In Germany von Beckerath,[7] and Baumgartner[99] have listed the sensitive degrees for many leading cities. We do not know of other such compilations, but ISCWA are planning a monograph to survey this important area.

Empirical studies
Whilst a chart for the formal incorporation of a town must of course be important, this date normally occurred many centuries after the community first became established. Where no founding date is known the only way to overcome this problem is to take an empirical approach and see if, by a methodical listing of major events in a town or city's history and examining the transits for such times, it is possible to reconstruct by inference the main features of the town. To our knowledge work of this kind has been done on Richmond in Surrey, England, Frankfurt, Bristol and York, the last as yet unpublished.

Richmond
Perhaps the most immediately dramatic example of the potential value of this kind of study occurs in the case of John Addey's work on the horoscope of Richmond, Surrey, in England in 1952. In this case as a result of his researches, he detected an extremely sensitive area around 18° Cancer. He mentioned to a newspaper reporter that in the following year (1953) there would be a particularly violent eclipse with Mars and Uranus on this degree, and that this suggested some violent and unpleasant event connected with the river (Cancer). A few weeks before the eclipse the 'Towpath Murders' occurred. Two young girls were stabbed to death with exceptional violence on the banks of the Thames. Scotland Yard mounted the largest-scale murder hunt ever, and at the time of the eclipse in Cancer the Thames was actually drained in the area in a search for the weapon. From the afflictions in 17-21 of the cardinals on the night of the murder Addey deduced that the murderer was likely to have been born with heavy afflictions in this area and identified 12/13 July 1931 as a possible birth date. When the murderer, Charles Whiteway, was finally arrested it was discovered that his birth date was in fact 21 June 1931 with the T-square between SA-UR-PL in 19-20 of the cardinals being activated by his progressed Sun coming -0-PL in 20° Cancer at the time of the murder. The progressed date was in fact 13 July 1931 thus linking Whiteway in both time and place with this outworking of Fate.

Frankfurt
This is another less dramatic case of the retrospective value of empirically-determined degree areas. In 1935/6 Erich von Beckerath in the spirit of Al-Biruni's call for 'investigation and research',

published[7] a study on the reconstruction of the chart of Frankfurt-am-Main. Taking a wealth of historical events, including the foundation of churches, major royal visits, fires, floods, wars, and the charts of famous scions of the city, together with considerations of the symbolism of the city's armorial bearings, he discovered, that there is a concentration on 4°VI/PI and 21°LE/AQ. For its re-publication in 1969 Bekerath gives the chart for the first night of the Allies devastating bombing raids on the city, 21/22 March 1944, though of course the city had been bombed less intensely for a long time prior to this date. The beginning of the raid shows Uranus at 5GE28 in -90-to one axis and Neptune 2LI57 -135- JU 17LE48/MO 25AQ configuring the other axis. The Moon went on to transit the 4PI during the next day's raid. Uranus had stationed at 4GE49 on 12 February. Anyone noting this sensitive degree area ahead would in the circumstances of the war been altered to the fact that this was a period of increased danger.

Bristol
A very similar kind of study to von Beckerath's was undertaken by R. Marshall-Harmer[34] in the 1950s based on a careful study of some of the major events in the history of Bristol. His conclusions are that the MC is probably in the region of 15 TA and the AS at 26 LE around a highly sensitive area of 23-26 LE. Other important areas appear to be 20-23 GE/SG, 17-27 VI, and 26 AR. He considers that 'perhaps the surest way to place the ascending degree of a town . . is to observe the place of Mars or Uranus, or the degree of the MC at the time of matters of serious importance to the town'. Interestingly Marshall-Harmer's detection of the sensitive area in Leo in fact bears out the traditional rulership of Leo for Bristol. The value of this AS degree and the area in the mutables was terribly confirmed when, with Uranus at 26 SC and MA-180-NE in 23 SG, the severe and unprecedented race riots broke out in the city in July 1981, part of a wave of riots that went on to sweep various other major city centres. These followed the New Moon on 1 July when Mars and Mercury opposed an exactly-rising Neptune at Bristol, a configuration which the ACG for the time shows arching right across Britain from the South-west and up over Liverpool, another severely hit area. Pluto, which so often purges and brings issues to the surface, was on the MC through London at the same time. Happily the riots did much to speed up appropriately 'eliminative and regenerative' Plutonian

action in these depressed inner-city areas. Happy will be the day when we can be prepared to use these energies constructively ahead of time. Undoubtedly detective work of the kind cited above will be of immense value in such work.

The advent of computers, with long-term historical ephemerides on board and appropriate research software — such as Matrix's M-65 program,[17a] opens up the possibility of much deeper and more elaborate studies of this kind. One would expect that transisting midpoints would be an important additional factor that should be considered in such studies. The authors would be interested to hear of other studies of this kind, both in connection with the charts of communities and nations.

Vienna
An important empirical study of this city by the great astronomer-historian Wilhelm Knappich has come to our notice. Published in January 1938 issue of the *Ersten Astrologischen Gesellschaft,* Vienna's journal. In it Knappich sets out the steps for reconstructing a city's charts by the examination of events. He concludes that the MC is between 13° and 14° Cancer and the AS 10°-11° Libra. Interestingly enough, he notes that this places 18°-19° Leo/Aquarius on the III/XI Placidus Cusp, a degree area noted by Von Beckerath as important for Austria as a whole (see p.332).

Traditional allocations and fixed stars
Various cities have long had specific degrees associated with them (see 'Sensitive degrees' in Chapter 13 for further examples). These are usually considered to be the city's ascendant degree. Whalley[47] in his commentary on Ptolemy notes that the gradual progress of fixed stars 'from one sign to another, is in an especial manner to be regarded in considering the mutations, manners, customs, laws, government, and fortune of a kingdom'. The most famous application of this approach is the case of Lilly's prophecy of the plague and the Great Fire of London which he is said to have made on the basis of the arrival of fixed star El Nath, the Bull's north horn, at 17GE54 the ascendant for the City of London (see Robson[51]). Taking the same approach Morrison (Zadkiel I) studied the chart of Liverpool. He concludes: '. . . we have been able to decide that the exact ascendant of Liverpool is 18 degrees 12 minutes of Scorpio. And we find that the North Scale, a very benevolent fixed star, first

came within orbs of influence (5 degrees) of Liverpool's ascendant in the year 1558 when cottons of Manchester were first bartered for wine with Liverpool merchants . . .' He continues by showing that the equivalent MC will be 8VI55 and that at the time of writing (1834) a malefic Venus-Saturn star had just arrived at this degree bringing discredit and dishonour upon the town, which had just had its freemen disenfranchised by a Bill in Parliament. He interestingly goes on to predict that when the North Scale arrives at the ascendant in 1916 this will produce wonderful improvements in Liverpool and that the city will flourish greatly about the early part of the twentieth century. He goes on to suggest that London's fate will decline around 2077 when Rigel comes to the ascendant, and that Liverpool will become the seat of government in the year 2291.

Names of towns
A further consideration in identifying the sensitive areas of a city is its actual name. The name of a thing can be thought of as its vibration. Many astrologers, including such outstanding students as Carter[11], Addey[1] and Elwell have pointed out how names have a definite resonance with astrological principles, with the signs of the zodiac and the planets. It has been suggested that this may have some bearing on the question of allocating town rulerships. Thus a name like Blackpool would suggest perhaps a combination of Saturn and the fixed water-sign Scorpio. Interestingly enough its date of incorporation, which occurred of course long after it received its name, shows MO-0-JU in Scorpio -90-SA-0-VE in Aquarius. However things are not always so clear cut, thus Leominster disappointingly shows no sign of Leo at its incorporation in 1554. Another problem is raised by the fact that the same town will have different names in different languages. Thus the romantic and 'perfumed' name Cologne becomes the somewhat harsh (to English ears) Köln in its original German. Similarly actual name changes as from Petrograd/St Petersburg, to Leningrad, or Constantinople (named after the Empeor Constantine) to Istanbul, must surely have changed the affinity of that city. Interestingly in the case of St Petersburg the protection of the heavenly rock (St Peter) is here replaced by the earthy materialist 'St Lenin' with his rigid, rocklike qualifications of both Sun, Mercury, Jupiter and Pluto all in Taurus.

The Swiss astrologer Hitschler,[22] suggests that there will indeed be a strong affinity between the names of towns and their namesakes chart. Thus we might expect events in Washington DC, and indeed in Washington State and other towns and communities named after the president, to respond to transits in George Washington's birth chart. John Addey noted how Churchill's Mercury degree was being activated on the day that Paris dedicated the Avenue Churchill to his memory. We might expect something of the events in all such avenues and streets to be reflected in the charts of their namesakes. A new slant on accident prevention suggests itself! Systematic work on this kind of resonance would make an interesting and valuable study.

With towns Hitschler notes in particular an intriguing relationship between the Sun's degree on a saint's day and towns named after that saint. For example a miraculous healing took place at San Severo in Italy in mid-March 1950. Jupiter at this time was in 23° Aquarius, exactly conjunct the position of the Sun on Saint Severin's Day, 1 February. An outbreak of polio in the town of Saint Quentin, France, during the week of 20 September 1954, coincided with Saturn passing over 7° Scorpio, conjunct the position of the Sun on Saint Quentin's Day. Similarly a severe epidemic of measles broke out on 24 July 1960 at Saint Georges in Switzerland, as Mars crossed 3° Taurus which corresponds to St George's Day, 23 April. Which saint's day, one wonders, does Petersburg/Leningrad now respond to — Peter or Lenin? Such cases as Hitschler quotes may be happenstance or they may be pointing to deeper layers of connection within the collective. They are certainly worth keeping in mind in the coming years as more and more work is done on this important area of research into the charts of communities.

References
For references see pp.361-8

13.
OTHER TECHNIQUES

Charles Harvey

Whilst mundane astrology has tended to cling to ingresses and lunations for forecasting, the *ex post facto* explanation of world events probably employs more different techniques than any other area of astrology. Retrospective analyses of earthquakes, sudden national upheavals, and the latest eye-catching headline call out methods which are rarely heard of when forecasts are being made. These same techniques can be, and are, however often useful to employ in connection with known future events. The perennial question of 'who will win' a forthcoming election or contest has in particular, produced a range of techniques for application to individual, party, team, and national charts. This specialized area of group and political forecasting techniques cannot be covered here but is the subject of a separate monograph.

When we use specific techniques for attempting to forecast the future trends in national and international affairs, the important thing is not to lose sight of the broader picture which is being spelled out by the major march of the planetary cycles, and the particular unfoldments of national charts. Keeping a sense of perspective is the key to all successful astrological prediction. We need to constantly steer a course between the large view and the daily detail, and not be too swayed by isolated particulars. We should constantly remind ourselves of the scope of the particular technique we are employing, and not attempt to draw from it information which it cannot reasonably expected to show. A single lunation of a major conjunction, or cycle phase, is unlikely to be localized to the specific day of its occurrent, though some symbolic even may indeed occur on that day, as witness the moon landing on the exact JU-0-UR and SA-135-PL in 1969, or the outbreak of the Falklands war on the day of the SA-45-UR.

The charts of national leaders
This is a major study in itself. Since at least as early as Ptolemy the national leader's chart has always been considered to be of great importance in mundane astrology. As we noted in Chapter 12, Ptolemy suggests their MC as the ruling degree for a city when this is not known. Charles Carter[11] considered that the chart of national leaders, together with the chart of the nation itself, where the times of these are accurately known, constitute by far the most reliable basis for mundane forecasting. They certainly represent the whole 'inner' aspect of forecasting and must therefore constitute one half of the process of preparing a forecast. This is not surprising since in practice a nation's ideals, aspirations, and efforts, or lack of them, at any one time, tend to be personified and expressed through the nation's leadership. This is perhaps more obviously so in the case of dictatorship such as are found in the Communist and Facist systems of government, where the State becomes to a great extent an extension of the leader's own personality. For better or worse absolute leaders like Brezhnev, Franco, Hitler, Mussolini, Stalin, and Tito directly express and constellate in their own person the unconscious development of their people at a particular time. In so doing their own personal birth chart takes on national dimensions.

As we saw in Chapter 6 when considering the outworkings of cycles in J. F. Kennedy's chart, this is also very much the case with US presidents who, since they are elected by popular franchise every four years, can be particularly expected to express and act out the underlying mood of the nation during their period in office (observations on Kennedy and the US chart are given below). On the other hand in modern hereditary monarchies such as, for example, the UK, Belgium, Denmark, Holland, Japan, Norway, Spain, or Sweden, the chart of the reigning monarch, in as far as they are truly identified with the nation's highest interests, can be seen to symbolize the 'ground base' of the nation's attitudes and development during a particular period, whilst it is the chart of the prime ministers, who come and go with changes in popular sentiment, that tend to constellate and express particularly phases in the developing themes of the national consciousness.

Needless to say there are usually strong contacts between the charts of leaders and the nations they rule. The nature of the contacts will be a astrong indication of the chief characteristics of their period in power, and the aspect spontaneous and almost instantaneous. Thus as was noted when discussing Jimmy Carter's Astrocartography (p. 289) the fortunes of a nation often change dramatically with new leadership.

A classic example of the effect of one person on a nation's collective psyche is that of Hitler and Germany, as personified by the 1871 chart of the German Empire (see Chapter 14, part 1). His partile MA-0-VE was exactly -0- 1871 PL, his Uranus fell exactly -180- 1871 Neptune, and his AS-180-ME completed a Grand Cross with the 1871 SO-0-ME-180-UR. Thus his chart activated all three of the 1871 'collective planets', stirring up and awakening the folk memory. In addition his MO-0-JU fell on the 1871 SA-NN-MA T-square constellating this potentially destructive area. The way these dangerously powerful collective energies were then 'fixed' in the chart of the Third Reich is discussed more fully in Chapter 14.

Violent aspects of the collective unconscious were activated in a different kind of way by the interaction of John F. Kennedy's chart (Fig. 6.4, p.195) with the US chart. Here we see his MC falls exactly on the US Mercury, his Sun = MC/AS is on Uranus, his SN is with the SO, and perhaps most significant of all, his potentially violent Pluto at 3CN16 -45-MA at 18TA26 (on Placidus cusp 8), is exactly with the US's Venus. This seemingly innocent contact in fact stimulates by hard angle aspects one of the most highly sensitive and critical strings of mid-points in the US chart: SO/MA 2CN21 = SO/NE 17LE52 = MA/SA 18LE06 = VE 3CN07 = UR/PL 3LI16 = SA/NE 3LI37. It is perhaps significant that at the moment of the assassination Saturn was 17AQ19 and the AS 19AQ22 and thus the SA/AS 18AQ21, exactly triggering this mutually dangerous axis.

These contacts, and notably of the Sun with Uranus and Pluto etc. clearly indicated that Kennedy's relationship with the USA could be a potentially disturbing and perilous one, but we should not deduce from this that he would best not have been selected as president. Addey uses this very case to discuss the profound issue of the purpose and purposes of the human soul. He concludes:

The Late President Kennedy had a nativity fraught with danger.

When he was elected, astrologers of insight were disquieted because they knew that dangerous nativities are required to fulfil dangerous purposes and must be confronted by dangerous situations. In his short term of office he was called upon to face many explosive situations and one moment of quite appalling danger (the Cuba crisis). The world held its breath; no one wanted to be in his shoes then, but after it was over everyone praised his courage and resolution.

From this we learn that no nativity is good or bad in itself, only in relation to a purpose, and that even nativities which are fraught with danger and difficult have their due place in the scheme of things and can be devoted to the service of good ends . . .

Addey here points to a central issue which will become increasingly more important as astrology becomes increasingly used by government and decision-makers. If astrologers become involved in choosing our leaders, what criteria should they use? It is perhaps salutary to recall that an English college of art which began choosing its students by astrology soon gained the reputation amongst the Inspectors of Education of being particularly uncreative! By emphasizing what he believed to be 'artistic' qualities and avoiding 'difficult' combinations the headmaster had unwittingly filtered out the creative frictions and tensions. Extending this to government we can see that badly-applied astrology could help to create a bland, 'play safe', unadventurous, uncreative leadership unwilling to take the kind of radical measures that a country may drastically need.

Certainly astrologers familiar with the UK chart (Fig 15.4, p.433) might have hesitated before endorsing the choice of Margaret Thatcher as Prime Minister. Her chart with its SA-0-AS, 120 PL, -60-JU, and JU = PL = SO/MA shows a remarkably powerful potential for deliberate and sustained reforms and transformation. But with this JU-PL = SO/MA falling right across the 1801 SO-180-MO-MC, -90- NN, and her rising Saturn falling on the UK second house Neptune ('squeezing out inflation') and -180- MA the timid astrologer might have blenched somewhat at the thought that here was someone who would forcus uncomfortably directly on the radical issues of the relationship between government and people. The sight of her MC exactly -180- the UK Pluto would further confirm the very deep level of 'elimination, purgation, and regeneration' that she would evoke. Likewise on seeing her MA = MC/AS — 'the iron lady', right on the 1801 AS, 'conservative' astrologer would be obliged to see that here was the possibility of dangerous tension and frictions within the country and even the danger of actual war. The Falklands was was thus totally appropriate, and the more so since it was, exactly at the Falklands that Margaret Thatcher's Sun and Mars were on the AS at birth. Equally an astrologer concerned with Thatcher's public 'image' would be bound to see her Saturn -180 1801 MA, and -90- 1801 VE, as creating a sense of harshness ('Mrs Thatcher — milk snatcher') though the sight of her exact NN -120-VE, falling in 1801 Jupiter and -60- Uranus would indicate that in her dealings with the world she would be extremely 'lucky' for the nation and be likely to greatly increse the nation's standing in the world and her fortunes at the bargaining table.

Declination cycles

Most of our astrological tradition deals with cycles measured along the plane of the ecliptic. But there is obviously no reason why we should not study cycles that are measured in relation to other planes. Elbert Benjamin (= C. C. Zain) of California's Church of Light in his *Hermetic System of Mundane Astrology* has elaborated a system based on the cycle of each planet in relation to the plane of the Earth's equator. He considers that a new planetary cycle begins at the moment a body crosses the equator from south to north, i.e. when it enters north declination. A second, 'Full Moon' type chart may be drawn for the moment that the planet crosses the equator moving south.

A chart for the capital cities of the world set for the moment when the body of the planet arrives in the Earth's equator, can be used in the same way as any other cyclical chart, in order to throw light on subsequent events in that area which reflect the nature of the planet. As with planetary ingresses in longitude, the positions of all the planets at this moment can in theory mark sensitive points which endure throughout the life of the cycle which brought them into being. In the case of the outer planets this will be for their full cycle of the Sun. Thus for example Pluto's cycle (Fig. 13.1) is calculated by Zain[72] to have begun at about 13.29h GMT on 20 February 1864. It will form part of the ground basis of events well into the twenty-second century. In view of Pluto's very slow motion the precise angles and the Moon's position of this chart should be ignored. For most planets the 0°N declination cycle will of course

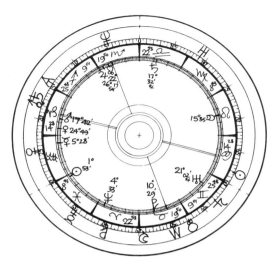

Figure 13.1 Pluto declination cycle 21 February 1864, 05.08 GMT. Set for Greenwich, 00E00, 51N30. RAMC 15.09.32.

normally occur when the planet is within a few degrees of the planet's entry into 0° Aries. But, in the case of Pluto, its great latitude can make a very considerable difference; and as can be seen in Fig. 13.1, Pluto was in fact well into Taurus at the start of its last declination cycle.

If we accept the idea that the chart at the moment of a planet's ingresses into 0° Aries is sensitive then there can be no question but that these charts ought also to have symbolic value. Practice seems to bear this out. Being related to the plane of the equator we might expect them to be particularly related to the Earth in a physical sense, and to mankind taken as a whole. Benjamin advocates that these charts be calculated on the plane of the ecliptic. A good case could be made for setting them up in Right Ascension since this is the normal measure used along the equator. The authors have had inadequate experience of the technique to speak from first-hand experience, though the initial evidence, as will be seen below, is encouraging. Russell,[73] who has worked with them over many years, speaks favourably in their support. The times that each of the planets crosses the equator does not appear in most ephemerides, but is now given in Michelsen's ephemeris for the twentieth century.[36] In the case of the outer planets his figures can vary by up to nearly three-quarters of an hour from those given by Zain.

We have taken the Pluto cycle as an illustration (Fig. 13.1) since it is the slowest and therefore theoretically the most powerful of these cycles. It is generally agreed that Pluto seems to be particularly connected with the mass destiny of mankind and we might therefore expect this chart to partially reflect some of the main ideas and events which have shaped man's history since its inception.

The Pluto cycle chart (Fig. 13.1) is given for London. Its Greenwich RA is 150°21′ (ST 10.01) and, as with any other chart of this kind, it can be relocated anywhere in the world simply by adding or subtracting the longitude of the place we wish to examine (see Appendix V). First we have to ask: Does the chart make interpretational sense? The most outstanding features of the chart are perhaps:

1.   The MO-PL-ME T-square, with NE -60-ME, and UR -135-ME. This would seem to speak of a transformative cycle which will be focused on the masses (Moon) involving both strongly idealistic (Neptune) motives and compulsive pressure (Pluto). This might be seen to reflect the transformation in thinking (Mercury) about the masses generally, and woman's place in society (Moon), and also the powerful movement to mass (Moon) literacy and the attendant growth in the press, publishing, propaganda (ME-PL, ME-UR), to mass transport and communications systems generally. It is interesting to note that this cycle began in the midst of the American Civil War, which was fought over the issue of slavery.

2.   The SO-45/135 the exact MA-90-SA. This can be seen to reflect the tendency to the ever increasing focus (Sun) of authority on actualizing (90) the energy (Mars) and material resources (Saturn) of the planets, and for the forces of labour (MA-SA) to take increasing power (Sun). Equally it can be seen to reflect the danger that war, death, and destruction (MA-90-SA) will become a central preoccupation of those in authority (Sun).

3.   The JU-0-NN, -60-VE. This emphasizes the formation of alliances, and common-interest groups, and the growth of mutual cooperation and trade. It is interesting to note the consolidation that came about in Europe shortly after this, with the formation of the German Empire, and the final unification of Italy, both occurring in 1871 with UR-120- this JU-0-PL, and 180-VE. France's third Republic was formed in 1870 with the same contact.

These features could certainly be related to some of the quite extraordinary transformation that has taken place in the world over the past 120 years. But the crucial question is: Do the main 'transformative' events of this period show any kind of concepts with this chart which ideally ought to reflect them? It is difficult to provide a control for this kind of evaluation, but certainly, on the face of it, the main chart factors would appear to be highly sensitive. An exploration of this and similar charts would require a whole book. All we can do here is present the reader with some admittedly selective evidence.

There have been many fundamental changes and transformations in the collective (un)consciousness of man since 1864. At a social level most nations of the world have gone through radical changes and reforms. A general shift of consciousness as regards the value of the individual has been taking place. Depth and height psychology has begun to probe our inner world and its relation to the creative principles of the universe. Intellectually through a concentration on science and technology, man has begun to harness the forces of nature. Pathologically man has engaged in two world wars of unprecedented scale and destruction. In the limited space available we can only examine briefly a few of the landmarks: (1) The development of atomic energy; (2) Man's movement out into space; (3) The two world wars.

1.   The first release of atomic energy[74] (see p.368 for chart) occurred as the AS was -180- MA right across the 1864 JU-0-NN, with JU-120 the 1864 JU-0-NN. (Not surprisingly the interactions between the atomic power chart (AP) and the 1928 Uranus cycle chart also make interesting reading. Note in particular the way the AP UR-120-NE-0-MO-MC Grand Trine so closely configures the close 1928 SO-30-UR). Looking at the destructive and purgative side of the Pluto cycle, we find at the time of the first atomic explosion that Saturn was exactly rising -90-MO applying to the 1864 SA-90-MA, whilst Mars was -180- the 1864 NN-0-JU (exactly on the AP AS!). At Hiroshima itself Pluto was 9LE58 approaching the exact -90- of the 1864 Pluto, NE 4LI22 was -180-NE 1864 4AR32, whilst the lunar occulation of Saturn less than an hour afterwards fell at 18CN13 triggering off the potential 1864 'death and destruction' MA-90-SA. Whilst by no means conclusive these contacts seem appropriate and close to time.

2.   In terms of mankind's evolution the move out beyond the forces of gravity into space must be as significant as that point at which the first amphibeans moved tentatively up the shore of the primeval sea, from water on to land. The first step in this 'conquest of space' occurred on 4 October 1957 with the Soviet Union's launching of Sputnik. On this day Pluto was at 1VI26 -180- 1864 SO, Neptune was at 1SC33 -120- the 1864 SO, and Uranus 10LE48-90-NN 10SC55 was 90/180 to 1864 Pluto. Such precise and appropriate contacts by the three outer planets are impressive by any standards. By comparison Armstrong's actual moon landing is less obvious. The main feature is a Grand Trine of Neptune 26SC01-120-NN-22PI29-120-ME 25CN51-0-SO 27CN55, which ties in very closely with the 1864 NN-JU-VE pattern. PL 23VI01 -180-NN is -90- 1864 Uranus, although wide in terms of the other contacts. The strong nodal connections in and between these charts are interesting.

3.   As might be expected there appear to be strong contacts between this Pluto cycle chart and the two world wars. As will be seen in Chapter 16 under 'Degree areas' in World War Two, Germany responds to a highly sensitive area around 7-10 LE/AQ exactly with the 1864 ME-PL, and with England's 1066 MA 8AQ36. This may of course be entirely independent of this Pluto cycle chart.

Clearly the next key transit to this chart will be in 1985-87 as Pluto in Scorpio triggers off Mercury, Uranus, Pluto and Moon. As Neptune will be -90- 1864 Neptune for much of this time also, and Saturn will be with the NN-JU in 1985 we can expect some fairly fundamental changes and transformations to be occurring within the collective at this period. At least this chart points us to this time as one to examine in greater detail.

Uranus and other cycles

Space does not permit a further discussion of the other cycle charts. The important thing to remember is that each chart only relates to matters connected with the planet for which it was erected. However with the outer planets there can be some blurring, and we ought not to be surprised if certain facets of conflict and war, and equally of scientific and technological advance, are shown up in the Uranus cycle chart as well as the Pluto. In this connection it is interesting to note that the Pluto and the 1928 Uranus cycle charts have their Suns in almost exactly conjunction, whilst the place of Venus in the Pluto cycle is the place of Mars in the Uranus cycle, 24CP55.

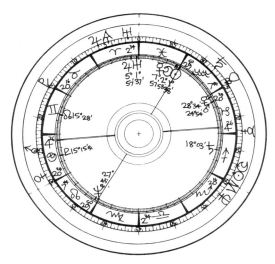

Figure 13.2 Uranus declination cycle 21 February 1928, 12.07 GMT. Set for Greenwich, 00E00, 51N30. RAMC 22.07.22.

Is it coincidence that the invasion of Poland in 1939 we find Mars at 24CP22?

The last Uranus cycle began on 21 February 1928 at 12.39pm GMT according to Benjamin, whilst Michelsen's ephemeris gives the time as 12.07pm. The Neptune cycle began, according to Benjamin, on 7 March 1944 at 4.05pm G,T, Micheslen gives the time as 3.22pm. The Neptune declination chart is an extremely interesting figure with a tight pattern of aspects. A tight MA-0-SA is -90- SO. This harsh configuration perhaps relates to the immense upsurge of terrorist violence for obtaining Neptune 'idealistic' ends. This pattern is to some extent offset by the much softer, but possibly confused idealism, expressed by Neptune at 3LI19 -135- VE 18AQ23, with VE-180-JU-MO. This can be seen to relate on a mental plane to the growth of idealistic internationalism, as with the formation of UNO. On the emotional plane it can perhaps be related to the rapid growth in the 'glamour' aspect of life, the growth of pop music, TV, and the media as purveyors of dreams. On a material plane we can see this as a dependence of the world on oil. It is certainly appropriate that at the time of the 1973 Middle East war and the sudden escalation of oil prices which brought about the slide into recession for nearly ten years, that Pluto was exactly on this Neptune position -90- SA, and both bodies -135- VE and -45- JU, bringing the unrealistic position 'down to earth'.

Degree areas

In contrast to the degree symbols these are empirically observed areas of the zodiac which seem to occur repeatedly in connection with certain countries or ideas. In contrast with the fixed stars, these degree areas would appear to move with the tropical zodiac, though we know of no formal study that has been undertaken to distinguish between the two zodiacs in this respect. The most comprehensive empirical studies of such degree areas are those done by Carter[11a] and Wemyss.[69] Whilst Carter concentrated on the psychological and medical interpretations and their application in individual maps, Wemyss extended his work into the wider world. An example of this was given in Chapter 9 where we saw that the area around 4-5 Sagittarius is attributed by Wemyss to flight. He has many other such attributions. For example he associates 9LE/AQ and 6-7 TA/SC with oil, and fifteen of the fixed signs with the refining of oil. He places coal under 11 CN/CP and 6AR/LI, iron under 15 AR/LI and 9TA/SC, cotton under 5 AR/LI, wool under 8 VI/PI, 3-6 TA-SC and 18 AR/LI, and so on. A great deal more research needs to be done to assess whether these an many other attributions have any real practical value. With commodities, an analysis of price movements in relation to the appropriate areas would be the obvious approach.

Degree areas associated with countries and institutions are particularly valuable for making forecasts. Thus in British history and the British Royal Family, Carter and others have noted the importance of the area around the last degrees of the mutable signs, which appears with remarkable constancy. This area is triggered off repeatedly in connection with British affairs. It appears at least as early as the 1066 map for England, where the Moon at 29PI08 is -90- Uranus at 28SG13, and as recently as the birth of Prince William, who has Neptune 25SG34 with the Ascendant at 27SG32 (interestingly enough this is closely with the galactic centre, whilst his Sun and Moon oppose the solar apex). The important, though often neglected, Union with Scotland chart for 1 May 1707, shows the Moon 28VI10. Queen Victoria energized this area strongly with her Saturn 28PI45-0-PL 27PI18, closely -90- NE 27SG59 and Uranus 23SG59. It of course appears again in the charts of Elizabeth II, Uranus

27PI23, and Prince Charles, JU-180-UR 29SG/GE. That the galactic centre is now approaching close to this area gives it an added interest for Britain and the Royal Family. We may wonder what will happen when the galactic centre arrives at about 27SG30 around 2050.

Another area which occurs with great frequency in connection with Britain, the old Empire, and present Commonwealth, is that around 7-10 CP/CN.. Thus the 1066 chart has Sun 9CP55 and the 1801 chart has the Sun 10CP11 and MC 9CN15. Of course many countries have been granted their independence as from 1 January when the Sun is in this degree. But quite apart from this we find for example that the Statute of Westminster, which was the legislation which brought the Commonwealth into existence (9.30am, 12 December 1931) shows Mercury 6CP22 R, Venus 13CP18, bracketing the ascendant at 9CP12. The House of Commons new debating chamber was opened on 26 May 1948 at 12.10pm BST with Venus 10CN04-90-NE 10LI23. Mercury 27GE54 was on the first mentioned degree area in conjunction Uranus 25GE01. Australia was created a separate Commonwealth Dominion on 1 January 1901, 00.00hrs with Sun 9CP28, MC8CN47, Saturn 7CP39. Again we find the late mutables degree strongly tenanted with Jupiter 25SG52-0-ME 27SG03 -180- NE27GE32. This latter is perhaps not surprising since this first symbolic loosening of links of Empire occurred only three weeks before the death of Queen Victoria on 22 January. The Canadian Dominion came into being on 1 July 1867 with Sun 8CN51 -0- UR 8CN39, and the Moon 28GE51. Pluto was at 10CN31 when Northern Ireland voted itself back into the UK on 7 December 1922. Pluto was at 9AR40, -90-SO 13CP00, when the Union Jack was raised over the Falklands on 3 January 1833, 9am, Saturn was at 28VI05 -90- ME 24SG45, thus 'freezing' stressful configurations for the future.

Looking ahead, we might well be preparing now to think of ways of putting the Neptune transits over these areas, at the end of the decade, to constructive use. If Britain works with its idealistic and elevative aspect the Neptune station of April 1987 at 8CP00 -90-JU 9AR12 could offer an opportunity for great altruitistic cooperation and leadership within the British Commonwealth and the world. Neptune will continue within orbs of this area through to the end of 1988, being joined at that time by Saturn. This must obviously mark a very tough time for those in power, but also an opportunity for a fundamental consolidation of constitutional matters. That

Uranus and Saturn will also be going over the late degrees of Sagittarius at this time must add to the emphasis on radical reforms, change, and innovations around December 1987 and January/February 1988. The SA-0-UR on 13 February occurs at 29SG55 with Neptune at 9CP17. This cannot but mark a very important transition for Britain and her rulership at this time. This shift and reorganisation in the structure of power is likely to continue throughout the Commonwealth countries for some time, for Uranus moves on over the 7-10 Capricorn area through 1990 and 1991.

Naylor[39] assembles telling evidence for Sepharial's empirical allocation[53a] of MC9GE and AS 14VI for London and the importance of these degrees at the times of British general elections. In an analysis of all the general elections from 1900, presented on 19 February 1979, he considered that it would have been possible to judge the likelihood of a general election in fifteen out of the twenty-two elections. He showed that in ten out of twenty-two cases either Saturn or Uranus was on one of these degrees close to the time of the election, that in two others the Moon's NN occupied 9 VI/PI and in another that Jupiter along with Mercury, Venus, Mars was on these points. He indicated that Saturn at 9 GE/SG always seemed to indicate a critical time politically for Britain. He went on to indicate that mid-March, June or September seemed the most likely times for the 1979 election. He added that he saw that the next Parliament seemed the most likely times for the 1979 election. He added that he saw that the next parliament, which was in fact elected by polls of 3 May following the Labour Government's defeat on 28 March, would probably last until the spring of 1983 when an adverse MA-JU (see Chapter 6) and the JU-0-UR close to 9 SG would be likely to signal the next general election (by the time that you read this, the accuracy of this prediction will be known). The next emphasis on these areas will be of Uranus at 14 SG in March and December 1984, and the long station of Uranus at 9 SG in mid-August '84. The strong double emphasis of October/November 1986 when Jupiter is at 14 PI and Saturn is at 9 SG, may well mark the end of the Parliament elected in 1983, and fresh elections. By Naylor's criteria this would certainly be likely to mark a time of great political uncertainty and problems. In connection with the area around 9° of mutable signs it is interesting to note that the British Labour Party has its Sun 8PI28 -90-JU 9SG38, that the Liberals have their Sun at 10GE19 and MC at 7VI32, the SDP has Moon 8SG31 -90- 10PI06, and the 1867 Conservative Party chart has NN 10VI42 -90-ME 7SG44 St R.

Other degrees that Sepharial gives are those for Calcutta: 7 VI and 2SG, and for Tokyo of 29 LI and 14VI. Naylor[39] points out that the Independence of Bangladesh occurred when SA-180-NE fell across the 2 SG ascendant degree, whilst he had himself been able to predict the change of government in Japan when Uranus passed over 29LI, despite his complete ignorance of Japanese affairs at the time.

Extremely powerful empirically-observed degree areas have been noted for various countries. The case of the area around 21 TA/SC for Poland was noted in Chapter 11, as was the emphasis around 15 TA for Berlin, (see under Section 5: Johndro). Other degree areas for Germany around 7-10 AQ/LE, 22-25 mutables, and 4-5 cardinals are discussed in Chapter 14. von Beckerath[7] published an historical study for Austria identifying an area around 19-27 AQ/LE and to a lesser extent similar degrees of TA/SC as extremely powerful in the nation's history. From this von Beckerath was able to predict that the time around 13 February 1934 would be important for the nation because of a major concentration of planets in this area. On 11-15 February Austria entered a period of major crisis as Dollfuss dissolved all political parties. At the Anschluss (11-13 March 1938) Jupiter was at 19AQ. At the declaration of the Second Austrian Republic (15 May 1955, 10.27am GMT) Pluto 24LE19 conjoins the AS 27LE30, -180-MO 28AQ09, -90-SO 23TA48. All interesting corroborations that von Beckerath's original observations are soundly based.

In the case of the US there is considerable controversy over the correct chart. However, in a study of a speculative chart for Columbus, Al H. Morrison[7] indicates that the area round 10 SG appears to be very important for the nation. He points out that: 'The ascendant was 10° Sagittarius at the time the Declaration of Independence was signed in 1776, according to the best records, the minutes of the Congress itself. When Paul Revere looked at the church to see whether there would be one lantern or two, the ascendant was 10° Sagittarius. When General Cornwallis sent forward a white flag of truce — the effective end of military conflict — the ascendant was 10° Sagittarius'. It is interesting to note that the sudden death of F. D. Roosevelt (12 April 1945) occurred with Uranus 10GE23, and the assassination of J. F. Kennedy (see Chapter 9) with Uranus at 9VI49. The movement of Uranus and Jupiter over this area during 1983, and in particular the station of Uranus at 9SG32 on 18 August 1984, which will colour the whole period from July-September, will be a further opportunity to observe this area in relation to the US.

Degree symbols
The idea that each degree of the zodiac is in fact as distinct as each sign has an ancient history. In Hindu astrology even the degrees are broken down again into ten distinct segments of 6′ each. Over the centuries there have been many attempts to capture the essence of each degree in sets of symbols and interpretations. Freddie Gladitz, who was compiling a definitive work on the subject at the time of his death, had already listed over thirty different sets, the earliest going back to the early Middle Ages and from thence back to the Greeks at least. If a clear-cut meaning could be attributed to each degree this would obviously be of immense help in clarifying the meaning of major conjunctions, lunations, eclipses etc. The great problem is however which of the many sets to use, as there is often no apparent connection between interpretations in different sets. Various writers, notably Hitschler and Davison, have proposed using these individual degrees for locating and describing specific events. However, Hitschler uses the degree meanings of two different French writers: Janduz and Andre Costeseque. Unfortunately his use is totally undisciplined. He employs so many factors, their anti-scion and contra-antiscion points (i.e., their reflection points over 0° Cancer/Capricorn and 0° Aries/Libra), not to mention their heliocentric positions, and 90 and 180 aspects to these points that the whole exercise soon becomes diluted beyond any possible practical use!

That said Hitschler does in fact cite cases where he was able to use methods to good effect in published mundane forecasts, though the details of the particular charts and degrees he used are not given. An example he gives of this approach is that Saturn was exactly rising in the 16th degree of Cancer as the first atomic bomb exploded at Alamogordo. Janduz's symbol for this degree is: 'A new Samson threatens to totter the pillars of the temple. At his feet on the staircase is a dead lion, further down a hedgehog rests its little foot on a dead serpent'. We cannot deny that there is something curiously evocative about the image, especially in the context in which the atom bomb was being developed. But why would we particularly single out Saturn's degree at this time in advance? Degree symbols may be a seductive area for retrospective work but perhaps not a promising one at present as far as practical mundane forecasting is concerned.

Fixed stars

Specific stars have been used in mundane work from the earliest times, though of recent years they have been rather neglected, with the move to simplify the tradition for mass marketing. Their very numbers do pose problems and it is difficult to justify the inclusion of one fixed star and then not go on to include all of the millions available. Yet it would seem that certain stars do appear to have a very definite character and considerable value in forecasting when they are brought into sharp focus. Originally they were associated particularly with weather phenomena. For example the rising of Sirius in July was supposed to give rise to the feverish heat of the 'dog days'. Ptolemy seems to have been the first to describe the characteristics of the stars in terms of the planets. Thus he says: 'The stars in the head of the Ram show a blend of the nature of Mars and Saturn. However those in the mouth of the Ram have a nature similar to Mercury and a little of Saturn'. Such distinctions were elaborated with further interpretations by the Arabs.

Of the fixed stars whose nature seems beyond question (though the great Barbault remains to be convinced) perhaps the most famous is Regulus, currently at 29LE15. It was known as a royal star in Persia at least as early as 3,000 BC when it marked the summer solstice. Regulus does very often quite literally seem to be associated with monarchy, and particularly the British Royal Family. Thus the solar eclipse conjunct Regulus on 22 August 1979 with UR-0-MC five days before Mountbatten's assassination, was the classic hallmark of the impending death of royalty. Likewise the Full Moon on 18 February 1981, conjunct Regulus, attended the announcement of Prince Charles' engagement and marriage. That Lady Diana had her NN conjunct Regulus was the clinching factor that led Suzi Harvey to forecast that Diana was 'the one' in the written report she made for the Press Association the previous December. Likewise Charles Carter predicted the marriage of Princess Margaret, who has her conjunct Regulus, from an occultation of Regulus by Venus.

Barbault reports on the studies of the German astrologer Hans Schwarz[4a] who made a systematic study of eclipses and conjunctions of Mars and Saturn with Regulus. Schwarz points out how there was an eclipse conjunct Regulus on 21 August 1914 visible over Europe

immediately after the start of World War One. This was a classic
presage of the downfall of royalty and leaders. The actual day of
reckoning came in full in November 1918 when Saturn transited
the point of this eclipse and Regulus. Again Schwarz points out that
Mars conjunct Regulus accompanied the assassinations of Ferdinand
at Sarajevo in June 1914, Alexander of Yugoslavia in October 1934,
Trotsky in August 1940, and the attempt on Hitler in July 1944.
Ebertin points out that Bismarck was forced to relinquish office the
very day that Saturn came exactly conjunct Regulus on 20 March 1890.

By contrasting the double-star Algol — 'Al Ghoul' the demon
or evil spirit — which was placed at 25TA28 in 1950 has a reputation
for violence and destruction. As a binary star it is occulted for about
nine hours in every 69 creating changes in its brightness. Arab
commanders would not begin an important battle when Algol was
being occulted. Algol was exactly rising at the moment that the first
atomic energy was released (p.368) and Mars was only 6′ from its
conjunction at the moment the first atom bomb was exploded at
Alamogordo. It was with UR-0-SA on the MC/AS at the moment
that Pearl Harbour was attacked, as was of course being conjoined
by Saturn and Uranus on an off for much of the early years of World
War Two.

To be of real value in mundane work the fixed stars will need to
continue to be evaluated systematically, for cycle after cycle, on the
lines of Schwarz so as to discover what conditions make their presence
crucial. In this connection it should be mentioned that the great
French astrologer Volguine claimed that charts set for the moment
that the Sun comes in the conjunction with Sirius each year, and
that the Moon comes conjunct Sirius each month, are of significance,
in the same way that a ingress or lunation chart is. If such a technique
has value, and we can certainly see its logic, it would obviously offer
a means for assembling a large amount of observations for analysis
over a relatively short space of time.

Another approach is that of Elbertin and Hoffman[14] who mention
two effects of the transit of outer planets in conjunction with fixed
stars. Ebertin[15] had made a special study of transits to the fixed star
Benetnash, the 'hired mourners' over several centuries. He concludes
that ancient tradition is essentially correct and that this fixed star,
which was at 26VI08 in 1950, is of great importance in mundane
astrology. He says: 'Benetnash will claim human lives in calamities
such as mine accidents, collapse of houses and bridges, mountain

slides, earth tremors and catastrophes caused by weather'. He goes on to illustrate the period of major instability that occurred as Uranus came conjunct Benetnash at the end of July 1968. This marked the culmination of tensions in Czechoslovakia, followed by the Russian invasion; a period of massive build-up in the Vietnam war; rioting, rebellion and racial strife broke out in various parts of the world simultaneously, and a major volcanic eruption occurred in Costa Rica. Another star Ebertin indicates as being highly suspect for mundane conditions is Akrab, at 1SG51 in 1950, which he relates to mass catastrophes when conjoined by Mars, Saturn or Uranus.

The Fixed Stars and other Factors in Ancient Chinese Astrology

The rich Chinese tradition in mundane astrology has not, as far as we know, been investigated by Western astrologers, though various academics such as the great Dr Joseph Needham have opened up the area and encouraged others to explore further. Ancient Chinese astrology in fact appears to have beem almost exclusively concerned with mundane and political matters, and other than the Emperor, the stars and astronomical events were considered to effect 'mainly the bureaucracy, seldom the masses and never the individual'. The main text on the subject are the three astronomical chapters in the *Chin Shu*[65] — the Official History of the Chin Dynasty (AD 265-420), which was finished in AD 635. The three chapters include an historical survey and discussion on astronomical/astrological writings, the main schools of cosmological thought, the relationship between the stars and different regions on earth, and the astrological implications of the planets, conjunctions, occultations, and so on. The approach is very empirical, listing observations, their 'standard prognostications' and then following them by an account of what actually occurred. Thus we find for example: 'On the i-wei day in the fifth month (11 June AD 351) Mars trespassed against the large star Hsien Yuan (Regulus) — an ill-omen for the Empress according to the standard prognostication. Venus . . . trespassed against the left 'arm' (Aldebaran): its prediction pertained to General and Ministers'. It goes on to enumerate other phenomena of Mars and the Moon occulting other fixed stars which occurred during the period, each with their standard prognostications, all of which are indicating the same basic predictions of a period of great unrest. It concludes: During the seventh year (AD 351) Liu Hsien put to death Shih Ti and a number of Generals, chaos reigned throughout Chantung, and many died during an epidemic'. As was the case in western astrology, the main concerns are with military movements, epidemics, famine, abdications, executions, and death generally. An analysis of the standard prognostications shows that of 215 omens 122 were essentially negative, 65 positive and 28 neutral.

At this period there was a definite allocation of different degrees of the zodiac to different areas — administrative prefectures — of China, and the station of Jupiter in that particular area was considered of especial importance. Some interesting parallels are that, for example, Venus with Jupiter was considered in certain circumstances to 'forecast a very rich harvest during the year', whilst 'the conjunction of Mars and Saturn is an omen of great anxiety, for it governs evil ministers'. This is clearly an area for future comparative study.

The galactic centre

Whilst the realm of the Fixed Stars may seem too diverse to ever be approachable, in fact the seemingly random mass of stars out there are in reality all proceeding along completely orderly orbits around their own centres of attraction. In the case of our nearest star, our own Sun, it is part of the Milky Way galaxy. Just as we move about the Sun once each year, so the Sun moves at 1,000 kilometres every second around the galaxy, completing one complete solar year in about 220-240 million earth years. The centre around which it moves, our galactic centre (GC) is currently situated at 26SG30. Landscheidt, Erlewine, and others have suggested that the GC represents a higher level solar principle, which is the source of instructions and information for the solar 'cells', such as our own sun, in its attendant galactic system. So, just as the Sun at this level relates to our sense of purpose in life, the GC relates to the higher purpose for mankind, and will be the directing source for new levels of inspiration and insight for man. These new ideas will be modulated and flow into our solar system level as planets, and particularly the outer ones, line up or form hard aspects or mid-points to the GC, which we might visualize as a sort of higher level 'mission control'.

This is more than a nice theory, for Landscheidt has shown that for example if we plot out the Jupiter/Pluto mid-point in its orbit around the Sun, as it lines up with the axis of the GC, there is a significant increase in solar activity. From such studies he was able to predict a good fifteen years ahead that the period centred around 1982, with NE -0- GC, would be likely to be one of great economic uncertainty and recession. Likewise the Foundation for the Study of Cycles has reported that when planets line up with the GC, the stock market tends to show much more intense activity. In a study of the charts of all the US presidents Landscheidt[29] found that a significant number, at the .008 level, tended to have their MC/IC axis within + / − 30° of the GC.

If we look at individual cases it is interesting to note how the GC seems to play an important part at key moments in history, and in the charts of key people. Thus for example we find that the Wright brother's first flight, the first time man had left the earth's surface using mechanical power, took place on the eve of a New Moon exactly conjunct Uranus conjunct the GC. Likewise we find that the man whose compelling obsession almost single-handedly landed man on the Moon, Wernher von Braun, was born with PL-0-MA-0-AS-180-GC. And the man who set foot on the Moon for him, as it were, Neil Armstrong, was born with the Moon(!) setting *within 1'* of the GC.

It seems significant that the USA declared its Independence when the GC was at 23SG44 opposed by Mars 21GE23, and squared by Neptune 22VI25. This fact may well explain the very acute sensitivity of this area in the US chart so brilliantly traced out by Barry Lynes in his remarkable *tour de force The next 20 Years.*[33] It is equally interesting to note that Lynes assigns Russia an MC of 25GE14 and As 26VI50. In 1917 the GC was at 25SG42 right on this suggested IC, -90-AS. This again may acount in part for the sensitivity that Lynes so expertly demonstrates in his analysis of Soviet history in terms of transits to these angles.

On a less epochal level, but certainly of profound significance in terms of the change of consciousness that it has brought about, we find that at 3pm GMT on 2 November 1936, when the world's first regular TV service was started by the BBC, the MC was 26SG48-0-GC 25SG58-0-NN 25SG06-0-JU 23SG45, all -180-MO 27GE01. (MA-NE are setting, 'the drug addict in the hands of others'?) Likewise it has been noted that there has been a strong move towards Christian and inter-religious unification during 1981/82 as Neptune has been approaching the GC. With Neptune stationary -0- the GC through August-October 1983 and Jupiter conjunct this point in January 1984 we can expect further vital developments in this direction, and the likelihood of a rapid recovery in economic confidence. The New Moon of 20 December 1987 is, like that of December 1903, conjunct Uranus and the GC, and it could well mark important innovations, inventions and insights of an equivalent kind.

The super galactic centre (SGC)

Erlewine in his remarkable survey of the whole area of cosmic structures has drawn attention to the fact that we now already know that our galaxy, around which our Sun travels in 220- 40 million years, is in turn part of a whole spiraling collection of galaxies comprising a 'super-galaxy'. The centre of the super galaxy, as at 1983, is placed at 1LI33, and is subject to precession like the GC (see above). Its 1950 value is given by Erlewine as 1LI05′29′′. This point might be considered to be a yet higher level of focus and purpose than the GC, the centre of our own galaxy. It might be seen as the 'long-term' pull of our collective consciousness upwards to yet higher heights, and deeper insights into the nature of things. In this connection it is remarkable that just as the GC shows up in the charts of the first space pioneers so too we find that this point, the SGC, also turns up in space exploration. Thus the launching of Sputnik 1, which can be said to have begun the space age, occurred just eleven days after a New Moon at 0LI29, immediately following the Libra ingress. Armstrong's actual landing on the Moon occurred on the very day of the JU = 0 = UR at 0LI40! (see also under Jupiter-Uranus in Chapter 6). Another suggestive case is that for the first-ever atomic chain reaction (Chart on p.361). We find the moon at 1LI15-0-NE1LI46, in a Grand trine with Uranus 2GE15 and MC 2AQ24. As with the GC a great deal more work needs to be done on evaluating this point if it is to be made a practical tool for forecasting. However where it is featured strongly in a mundane map we may certainly to give that chart some added weight.

The solar apex (AP)

It can be argued that the location of the SGC so close to a cardinal point over the past 100 years (it was at 00LI00 about 1873) is perhaps one of the factors that may have accelerated mankind's consciousness of the natural world. In a similar vein we could argue that this process has also been accelerated by the fact that the solar apex (AP), the direction in which our Sun is moving in the Milky Way, has been close to the Capricorn point for a similar length of time. Its value in 1983 is 2CP13. In 1900 it was 1CP03, and in 1800 29SG39, and at 00CP00 about 1825. Landscheidt considers the AP to have a somewhat similar meaning to the GC. Since the AP is the 'target or objective of the Sun as it hurtles us through space at 1000 kilometres every second. Landscheidt suggests that this point may in some sense represent the 'target' towards which an individual, or collective, is heading at a given moment. With the SGC and AP close square to one another it will obviously require some very fine grain research to disentangle one from the other. A possible approach would be to study charts set for the moment of conjunctions to these points, as with sidereal ingresses.

Heliocentric astrology

There has of recent years been an increasing interest in heliocentric astrology. In fact astrologers were interested in the possibilities of heliocentric astrology as soon as it was realized that the Earth went round the Sun. In connection with mundane astrology the work of Nelson, which is however now considered suspect, was a classic study which appeared to support the value of heliocentric aspects. A different kind of work has been done by the Anthroposohist W. O. Sucher. [56] He pays particular attention to the question of the planetary nodes. Sucher considers that heliocentric configurations build up areas of stress and emphasis and specific meaning with the solar system and that future contacts in these areas will release these stored ideas through both events and people. Those who are predisposed to a material-causal chain explanation of astrology are attracted by the possible relationship between solar activity, the sun-spot cycle and the cycles of the heliocentric movement of the planets. That such interactions do exist seems beyond any doubt but the precise interrelationship has still to be uncovered. In the meantime heliocentric astrology, because it produces absolutely clear regular cycles, undistorted by retrogradation, ought to offer invaluable ground for all types of correlation research on harmonic lines, as applied to everything from economic cycles to weather, church attendance and international aggression (see pp.209-11).

Planetary nodes

Various writers have considered the planetary nodes to be of importance in mundane astrology, most notably Nelson in connection with storms in the ionosphere (though as noted his work is now very seriously questioned) and Sucher whose work using heliocentric positions is outlined above, and Landscheidt who has developed a computer program for their interpretation in general. The planetary nodes are the points where the plane of a planet's orbit intersects the plane of the Earth's orbit about the Sun. Viewed heliocentrically these move very slowly, a matter of a minute or so per year, and the north and south nodes are always exactly opposite each other. Viewed geocentrically the planetary nodes are not necessarily 180° apart, indeed the node of the inner planets, Mercury and Venus, move through the full 360° in the course of a year and can be found in any relationship to one another including conjunction. With the geocentric nodes of the other planet the movement is less extreme and oscillates around their heliocentric position. This oscillation decreasd from almost + / − 45 in the case of Mars to less than + / − 2 in the case of Pluto. (Positions are available in Dobyns.) *The Node Book* TIA Pub, P.O. Box 45558, Los Angeles, Calif. 90045.

The asteroids

To date very little consistent study of the asteroids has been made in mundane astrology. The one serious attempt is that of Donath who has made a systematic study of the position of the four asteroids in the last forty-two US presidents, and in important events in American history. The authors have not had sufficient experience of these factors to comment on their practical utility for forecasting. Lynes in his brilliant, if erratic, study of the US and Russian charts and their cycles, *The Next 20 Years,* points out that Ceres, goddess of grain, cereals, of both nourishment and famine, and of the common working-man, was conjunct the Sun on the day of the Russian Revolution. He points out that its symbol is appropriately enough the sickle. The fact that, with the Sun, it is exactly -90-SA, and also -90-UR, can be seen to related to the inability of modern Russia to grown sufficient grain. Lynes also relates the Saturn-Ceres square to the virtual enslavement of the working population, and its centralized bureaucratic control. This may be rather too much to read into one asteroid, but it does at least suggest that they may be worth investigating further in mundane work.

Chiron

This small planetoid which was discovered on 1 November 1977 moving between Saturn and Uranus is still too new to have accumulated any definitive litrature on its possible mundane significance. The newsletter of the Association for the Study of Chiron

(ASC), under the enthusiastic direction of Zane Stein, is studying its position in every conceivable kind of chart. It is agreed that his principle is probably a blend of Saturn and Uranus, a mixture of wise healer and maverick. Lynes points out that it was discoverd the same month that Sadat made his historic visit to Israel, and suggests that this is possibly highly symbolic of the nature of the planetoid.

New Year charts

These are charts set for 0 hours local time for the capital city of any country, and can often be highly symbolic of 'the year ahead' for the nation. In this case there can be no arguments as to what period the chart covers. It covers the complete 365 / 366 days until the stroke of midnight of the next New Year. It can be objected that the New Year is an artificial, civil concept, and does not relate to any astronomical reality. However there can be no doubt that man gives profound significance to the 'stroke of midnight' of 31 December each year. It is felt by millions to mark the beginning of a clean slate, the possibility of starting afresh. Countless resolutions and affirmations are made at this moment. As such this moment must be of profound psychological significance for a nation as a whole, and thus also it must be of astrological significance. In these days of mass communication it is a moment whose significance is likely to be drunk by the united collective, and not only in champagne or Scotch!

These charts are of course subtly different for each country, as January 1 begins over the whole period of 24 hours in different parts of the earth. It should also not be overlooked that, although the western calendar dominates most of the world's secular activities, and tends to mark a new beginning for most peoples of the world, there are several other important New Years. In particular it would be foolish to overlook the Chinese New Year which for one billion Chinese is the true start to their new cycle of possibilities. The date of this three-day festival varies from year to year but occurs in January or February. The Hindu New Year or 'Diwali' can occur in either mid-March or October. Al Hijra, the Muslim lunar calendar which produces slightly shorter annual cycle in that the date slips back each year. In 1983 it occurs on 8 October. Rosh Hashanah, the moment of annual renewal for the world's Jewish community, occurs on September 8 1983 according to our calendar. One would expect that charts set for the significant moment on any of these dates ought to be symbolic of that communitie's perception of the year ahead. We do not know of anyone who has studied such charts.

Any such chart can be taken as a straight horary question applying to a whole group of people both collectively and individually. In effect at this moment most of us are all likely to be asking: 'What will the New Year bring?' Such a mass-horary obviously raises some interesting problems of interpretation. Is such a chart invalidated if the first or last degrees of the sign are rising? This would seem unlikely. Is a Moon void-of-course of significance? and so on.

An example of a New Year's chart is given in Fig. 13.3. It is for 1982 for Britain, the year that found her engaged in open warfare again for the first time since the Suez crisis of 1956. Here we see Mars exacty rising at Westminister, exactly on the UK ascendant, and square the Sun. (Except in those years when Britain has been on Summer Time throughout the year the angles for New Year charts will always be very close to those for the UK 1801 chart since this came into force on 1 January.) It would be difficult to think of better symbolism. That Saturn is also -90- the UK Moon, and -0-1066 DS can only add to the problematic nature of the year ahead. That Venus is 120-AS might be seen as a classical signifactor for victory. The UR-120- 1801 JU, -60-1801 UR, and JU-120-1801 MC and Pluto are obviously more encouraging. The former can be seen to relate perhaps to the fact that 1982 was declared 'Information Technology Year' for Britain, with a major campaign to boost the use of microprocessors in business and industry. These transits to the 1801 chart occur in any case but, as with the Capricorn ingress, can be considered to be brought into sharp focus by occurring at this time. Looked at from the point of view of Argentine, because of Summer Time the New Year chart angles were MC 27GE12 and AS 25VI15, placing NE-0-IC, -90-AS. For the Falklands the MC was 11CP29, AS 29LI00, showing the SA-0-PL just risen as well as the SO-90-MA from the 4th.

Carter discusses these charts with further examples, and testing them on World War One and World War Two shows that they do in general provide charts which give important clues as to the state of the collective at these times.

Horoscopes of centuries
This is a further extension of the principle at work in charts for the year. At the turn of a new century there has always been an enormous

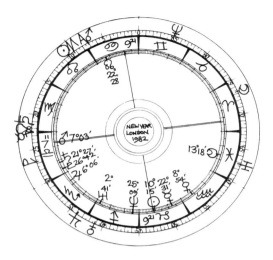

Figure 13.3   New Year 1982, London — i.e., 00.00 GMT, 1 January 1982.

sense of anticipation and millenarian anxiety followed by a new influx
of energy as the idea of the new century takes hold. These turning-
points repeatedly seem to mark times of death and re-birth as the
dread of the 'end of the world' gives way to the new opportunities.
It is remarkable how different we feel about each century. Something
that occurred in the nineteenth century, albeit by a few days, seems
of a quite different era to the twentieth, and likewise with each
century. Various astrologers have considered the chart for the
twentieth century. Most consider that it began in 1 January 1900,
but there are those who claim that 'officially' 1900 was the final year
of the nineteenth century and that 1 January 1901 began the
twentieth. We frankly very much doubt that anyone at the time
postponed their twentieth century sense for a year though it is true
that Queen Victoria waited until 22 January 1901 to die. A chart
for that moment might be seen as 'the end of an era' which marked
out a period of history in western Europe almost more than any other.
Having decided on 1 January 1900 we then have to decide whether
to set the chart for the world as a whole by taking the very first moment
of 1900, which occurred at the International Date Line 180 E, or
whether to set separate charts for the leading nations of the world
so that each views the twentieth century from their own perspective.

Both have their advantages. A study by Maria Dolores de Pablos[44] of the chart set for 180 E seems to indicate that this chart can be progressed. An interesting feature of this chart for the literal start of the century is its most outstanding feature: Moon 25SG18-0-SA 27SG40 in exact -180- NE 25SG14. This falls exactly on the galactic centre which, we have noted, appears to be very much related to mankind's movement out into space. This in itself is interesting. The 180E chart, set for 23N07 has an MC of 9CN, AS 8LI50, and the third / ninth house is 8 GE / SG. Thus this opposition across the GC also falls across the third / ninth house, an altogether remarkable placement!

Astro-economics
'Millionaires despise astrologers but billionaires thrive on them' goes the quip, and certainly various US multi-millionaires have employed astrologers, most notably J. P. Morgan, whilst it is well known that Saudi Arabia's Oil Minister Sheik Yamani is a dedicated astrologer. But at an official level western economists remain untouched by astrology. Yet as we saw in Chapter 6, economists and cycle experts have detected numerous important and persistent cycles in the world economy, such as the now increasingly accepted Kondratieff 54-year cycle, and in the production and price of a large number of basic commodities, and products. Various astrologers have made specialist studies of such moevements both for particular commodities and for the world economy in general, in relation to the main astrological cycles. Some of their results have been extremely striking. A useful summary and evaluation of much of this work is given in *Recent Advances* pp.516-27. The work of Williams,[61a] Reider,[49] Crawford, *et al,* tends to show that the main movements in the world's economy, as reflected in stock-market confidence, tend to be accompanied by important planetary configurations of the outer planets, notably Jupiter, Saturn and Uranus. Traditionally 'good' aspects, the trine and sextile, are essentially related to periods of increasing prosperity and upswings in the market, and the 'bad' aspects, the square and opposition, to decline in confidence and economic depression'.

That this is not the whole story is evident from the fact that different nations' economies and the world's different stock markets, do not necessarily rise and fall together. Clearly there are other factors, and it would be a foolish astrologer who ignored the national charts in these matters. As Lynes says as a result of his brilliant and intensive work on the US chart and the American and world economies: 'the astrology-economic link is irrefutable'. But all national charts if accurate should give reasonably clear-cut indications of changes of economic fortune, as well as more day-to-day financial matters. Likewise experienced astrologers working with the charts of the main stock exchanges, the charts of currencies (e.g. the German Mark, 'born' 6pm 18 June 1948 in Frankfurt) find that these too reflect the important shifts of market feeling, as it would seem do the charts of major companies. The study of individual businesses and multi-national companies is of course an important sub-division of astrology in itself, even if as yet still poorly documented.

At the level of macro-economics Jensen and others have related the 20-year cycle of Jupiter and Saturn in Earth signs, from 1840 onwards, to the marked increase in material prosperity of the last century and more. On the other hand Barry Lynes[33a] relates Neptune's entry into Earth signs as signalling the beginning of major economic recessions. He forecasts a major recession for 1984 and beyond as Neptune enters Capricorn. He cites the movement of Neptune from Leo into Virgo in July 1929, which was followed by the Great Crash in October, as an example. By contrast Naylor[39a] associates Neptune's entry into a nation's dominant sign as being indicative of a time of new growth and prosperity. Whatever truth there may be in such theories, and one cannot deny the appropriateness of the symbolism, it is contrary to all astrological theory and experience to believe that any one factor alone will be entirely responsible for such changes. As always we need to be considering a complex interaction of cycles. Thus Dr Theodor Landscheidt[29] for example successfully predicted the economic slump of the early 1980s many years ahead from the line-up of Neptune with the galactic centre. This is a point which he belives to be important in modulating the 'controlling information' which comes to our solar system from the galactic level of organization.

At the level of micro-economics there are a growing number of metal and commodity brokers who use astrology for forecasting daily as well as long-term price movements. A director of one of London's largest merchant banks speaks of a Belgian client who, using astrological methods, enters the commodity markets about once every few years, makes an enormous 'killing' and then disappears again. Robert Hand, the outstanding US astrologer, tells us that his father used to play the markets using heliocentric astrology. He would be very perplexed if the market did not move in the way anticipated within a few minutes of the time calculated. This picture is corroborated by the careful work of the commodity-broker Daniel Pallant.[45a] Using a combination of harmonic techniques based on John Addey's work, a close study of all kinds of ingress charts, and a study of aspect patterns, notably the simulataneous interaction of 'hard' and 'soft' aspects, Pallant reckons to be able to forecast when the market will make a major move with 90 per cent accuracy, and to be able to read the direction of the move with some 75 per cent accuracy. Likewise in the USA the great commodity analyst W. D. Gann used astrological methods to make his fortune, although the astrological component is less evident in the work of his contemporary followers.

Whilst there is clearly a great deal of money to be made, and being made, by private individuals using such methods, the really important impact of astro-economics for mankind as a whole can only come when these matters are studied and incorporated into western economic planning at an official level. The tragic consequences of man imagining he understands, and is in command of, his economic destiny are all too evident. A formalized astro-economics could hardly do worse than the hundreds of thousands of alleged 'economists' who have been increasingly guiding the fortunes of the world with their conflicting theories over the past century. As the world's economy becomes increasingly unified we can expect it to resonate more and more strongly with these larger cycles and rhythms, rather than less. This makes a real understanding of astro-economics a matter of considerable urgency.

By a real understanding we must mean an understanding that is based not only on particular observations but on sound and consistent principles that we understand. The findings of people like Williams, Rieder, Lynes, and others, can obviously be applied to economic and business matters, and will certainly be an improvement on complete 'blind flying'. But the truth is that we do not in all honesty as yet have a sufficient graps and understanding of exactly what is going on to lay down the law and demand an instant hearing. Indeed it could be argued that the immediate adoption of partial results could lead to worse problems in the long run. A little knowlede *is* a dangerous thing. However if the findings of Barbault, of Lynes and of the growing band who are increasingly beginning to work in this field, can be integrated into a larger, more coherent theoretical framework, based on that provided by Addey, we can then expect astro-economics to be taken seriously by our decision-makers. The silence that Lynes reports[33] from officialdom in the face of his persistent efforts to awaken them and obtain a hearing is not really that surprising. We must take it as a challenge to clarify our understanding. But the different threads are coming together, and there can be no doubt that as our picture clarifies that this is one aspect of astrology that can serve greatly, in Lynes' words, 'for the renaissance of a united world'.

Graphic ephemeris
To do an effective job of predicting mundane trends is likely to mean monitoring many dozens of charts and being able to assess all their main transits within measurable time. Such a job demands some form of efficient visual presentation. Graphic ephemeris can give us exactly that. Fig. 13.4 shows a blank 45°-graphic ephemeris for 1982. Fig 13.5 shows the same graph with the positions for the chart for the UK drawn in on it. Once familiar with this technique it does not take more than ten minutes to complete such a graph, and little longer to assess and assimilate the outstanding features of the whole year.

If we look across the top of the graph we will see that time is plotted across the page from 1 January to 31 December, divided up day by day, and labelled every ten days. Down the left-hand side of the graph, zodiacal space is measured in an unorthodox way with positions given for cardinal, fixed and mutable signs in the three left-hand vertical columns. As will be explained below, this graph is set out on a 45°-scale format, with 45 lines of squares down the page each representing 1°00′ of longitude. Although difficult to see in this reduced form, each 1°00′ square is subdivided into five smaller sections of 12′ of arc each.

Graphs using various different formats or 'scales' can be used, and these are now becoming available commerically. The simplest of all such graphs would be a 360°-graph. This would start with 0° Aries at the top of the page and end with 29°59′ Pisces at the bottom of the page. If we then drew in movements of the planets on this graph we would see the picture of the planets' movement across the sky moving down the page with direct motion, and back up the page for retrograde. If we then drew horizontal lines across the page at exactly the positions where our natal planets fall we would be able to see and measure exactly when a transiting body crossed this line, and that would mark the point where it became exactly conjunct. Though very simple, the 360° graph is not very useful because it can only show us transits by conjunction.

However, experience shows us that transits by other aspects are also important. In particular we find that 'events' and happenings in the world tend to be the product of transits by the 'hard' angles, the -180-, -90-, -45- and -135 — those aspects in fact which are multiples of 45. Therefore if instead of measuring our space down the page as from -360 we instead measure it from 0-45, we will find that we construct a graph which will show us whenever a planet is making an aspect to a radical planet by -0-, or by some multiple of 45.

How this is done may be easier to understand if we divide a 360° zodiacal circle into eight equal sections. The first 45° takes us from 0° Aries to 15TA00 Taurus. The next 45° takes us from 15TA00 to 0° Cancer, the next from 0° Cancer to 15LE00 and so on. In this way we have eight 45-degree segments. Four of these start at 0° of a cardinal sign, cover the whole of that and half of the next fixed sign. The other four start at 15°00 of a fixed sign, cover the remaining 15°00′ and then the 30° of the next mutable sign.

If we now superimpose these eight segments on top of one another, we could say that the beginning of a 45° segment is either 0° of a cardinal sign, or 15° of a fixed sign. Likewise halfway through any segment will be either 15° of a cardinal sign of 0° of a mutable sign.

On the right-hand side of the graph we see a scale measured from 1-45. This is using a '45°-scale' to measure how far the position of a planet is through its particular 45° sector. Whilst we can familiarize ourselves with translating planetary positions into this 45°-scale, it is much simpler to use the more familiar zodiacal numeration on the left-hand side of the graph. Here there are three columns marked. The first measures positions in the cardinal signs: AR, CN, LI, CP. The next column measures those in the fixed signs: TA, LE, SC, AQ. The third measures positions in the mutable signs: GE, VI, SG, PI.

If we had to construct this graph we would turn to a normal ephemeris for 1 January 1982. Starting, perhaps, with Pluto we would look up its position, 26LI42. This is in a cardinal sign, so we trace down the left-hand column until we reach 26. The bottom of the square marked 26 is 26°00′ of any of the cardinal signs. Since each square is divided into sub-divisions of 12′ arc each, 42′ will be 3½ of these 12 ′ sub-divisions or almost ¾ of the way through the next square marked 27. Here we see the beginning of the Pluto line marked. To continue the construction of the graph we then follow the same procedure for, say, the 1st of each month, making a dot for Pluto's position. Then with our twelve positions marked (one for each month) we draw in a smooth curve that links these all together. This line is the line we can see marked for Pluto (PL) on this graph. It moves forward in motion in a gentle slope down page through until the end of January. It then stations at 26LI51 ′, as indicated. It then begins to proceed in a gentle slope, retrograde, back up the page, until the end of June. Here it stations and turns direct, at 24LI07, and begins moves across again slowly moving down the page as it goes.

To construct a complete graph of this kind we would do the same for each planet, plotting in their positions for each month and then joining up the dots. Let us take Jupiter as another example. It started the year at 6SC04. This is a fixed sign, so we look in the second column. The column starts at 15 goes to 30 and then stops. But ⅔ of the way down it starts again with square 1. We go down to square 6. The bottom of the square is 6°00′ of a fixed sign. Jupiter's position is just a shade over into the square marked 7. We mark a dot, and do the same exercise for each month. If we join up the dots and we find we have the much faster moving curve that we see sweeping down to 10SC20 in late February, stationing, moving retrograde up the page until the end of June. Here it stations at 00SC26, almost halfway through the square marked 1 in the second column, which marks those positions between 0°00′ and 0°59′ of the fixed signs. Juiter then moves on, its curve getting steeper as it gathers momentum and disappears through the bottom of the graph as it gets to 15SC00 on 17/18 October. It simultaneoulsy reappears at 15°00′ of the fixed signs at the top of the page at 17/18 October, moves on steeply down through the remaining 15°00′ of Scorpio and can be seen entering 00SG00 on 26/27 December.

If we examine this graph in greater detail we see that the different planetary lines sometimes cross over one another. Thus about 7/8 November we see the Saturn line and the Pluto line intersecting at 27°36′. This is their conjunction. However if we look back at the beginning of April we see the Uranus line is intersecting the Saturn line. They then separate slighty and then in early July recross. Where these cross one another they are in an exact 45°00′ relationships to

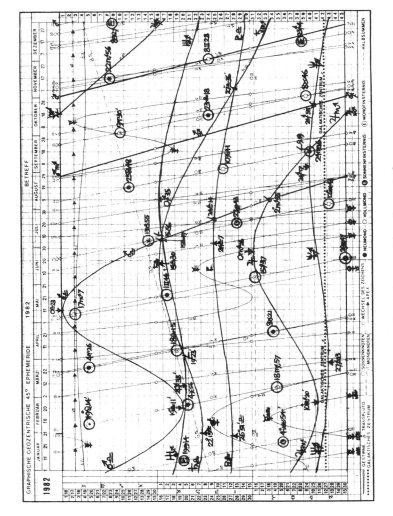

Figure 13.4 A 45° graphic ephemeris for 1982.

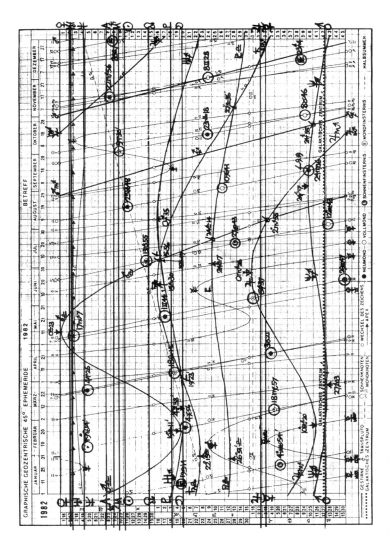

Figure 13.5 The 45° graphic ephemeris with the positions for the United Kingdom's chart drawn in.

one another. In fact wherever we see two lines crossing, those two planets will be either in conjunction or some exact multiple of 45 ° 00 ' apart.

Putting the natal chart on the graph

Even the explanations given above are not completely understood, it is well worth using the graph and learning by experience. Figure 13.5 shows the same graph filled in with the natal positions for the birth of the United Kingdom. If we study this we see that the UK chart positions have been draw in as horizontal lines, using the appropriate one of the three columns on the left of the graph to locate where each line should go.

Until experienced, it is best to use a soft pencil to first mark in the positions down the left-hand side, but do not at this stage draw in any horizontal lines across the graph. If we mark in these positions systematically it will minimize the chance of mistakes and omissions. First, using the far left-hand column, we make a mark for each of the positions in the cardinal signs and label them with their symbols. Then using the scale provided in the second column on the left, we mark in positions that fall in the fixed signs, labelling them as we go. Some of these will probably intermingle with the first half of the cardinal-sign positions and, if there is a right grouping, we may need to juggle the symbols to make them legible. Finally, using the scale in the third column, we mark in all the positions in the mutable signs, labelling them.

When filling in the positions we must always include the SO / MO mid-point and the MC/AS mid-point as these are of the greatest importance in any chart. It is also worthwhile to include the NN. IF we are not sure whether to use the true node or the mean node it is a good idea to note both, and discover which is the more sensitive point. It is also a good idea to count up how many positions have been marked in. If we use the SO, MO, ME, VE, MA, JU, SA, UR, NE, PL, NN, MC, AS and SO/MO and MC/AS we should have a total of fifteen positions marked in ready to draw their lines. If there are less than fifteen we need to discover which we have left out.

Using a suitable coloured pen (the graphs are normally either in light-blue and red [Ebertin] or black [ACS and AGS]) and a ruler we draw an exactly horizontal line through the mark for each chart factor. Having drawn in the lines we then work systematically through the graph starting first with the circles, if marked. These indicate where the New and Full Moons and eclipses fall during the year. if any of these fall over one of the radical chart lines just drawn in, we use another coloured pen to circle this circle bodly so as to draw attention to it. We now work systematically through each of the planet's lines, starting with Pluto, since it moves the least. If it crosses one of the radical chart lines we highlight this with a pen. We do the same with Neptune, Uranus, Saturn, and Jupiter. Finally we can pick out those points where Mars in its speedy motion crosses over any radical lines. But so as to avoid to many blotches it is best to pick out only any conjunctions of Mars, and those places where Mars is crossing a radical line at the same time as a slower-moving body. This will mark a time when the slower-moving transit may be activated or reactivated.

Interpreting the graph

Now we need to sit back from the graph and take a large overall view. Are there any places where several things seem to be happening at once? Such clustering of intersecting lines is bound to indicate a period of increased activity in connection with that area. This area can be reemphasized with a coloured pen. Likewise where the station of one of the outer planets is 'sitting' within close orbs (say 30 ′, i.e., about half of a square of a natal line) then it is a good idea to oval this in and hatch-line it, for this indicates a sustained period of this type of activity. At this stage we may also take note of periods when a long-term transit is being activated by even Sun, Mercury, or Venus, for these can severe as triggers for the longer-term factor.

   In interpreting a graph it is always important to keep in mind its harmonic base. A 45°-graph, as illustrated, is **not** telling us the same thing as a 30-graph, which will pick our all the 30, 60, 90, 120, and 150 and 180 aspects. The eighth-harmonic graph, the 45°, is essentially telling us about what is likely to mainfest in and around the organism, organization, nation, in question and where that organism is going to need to make efforts, and exercise its will to meet challenges and master inadequacies. Hence it is particularly valuable for examining what is likely to 'happen' in terms of actions, events, and will-oriented behaviour. It is closely connected to the idea of cause and effect in its fullest sense. It relates to the profound idea of the absolute Justice of life, that whatever happens to us, or to an organization, or group is the precise result and consequence of the thoughts, ideas, ideals, words and deeds that have been fostered,

10

By contrast the twelfth-harmonic, 30-graph, is better suited to presenting us with information about the opportunities that life is likely to present to the group or society, the kind of motivation the group is likely to experience (120) and the kind of effort (90) and reconciliation (30/150) that may be required to be made and performed in order to actualize this potential. In this sense the 30-graph might be considered to be a better tool for indicating in one picture the main opportunities for national and group progress through conscious aspiration and effort.

Unless one is engaged full-time in making forecasts for specific groups, it will obviously not normally be possible, in terms of time, to use more than one or two graphs for a particular organization. When one does it is important to look at them first separetely and then together, to build up a composite interaction.

Although a graph may seem rather bewildering at first, by using it in conjunction with a normal ephemeris it soon becomes clear exactly where each line is, and what is going on. The really great advantage of this approach, apart from the speed and simplicity, is that once we get used to reading graphs they give us a very much better idea of how different pressures and possibilities are building up over a period of time. We can see the transit approaching and get some measure of just how long it will last. If we use a 1° orb for transits then this will amount to the period when the planet is visually within the width of one square's distance of a particular line. Probably orbs of 30′, i.e., half a square, are more appropriate for this kind of work. Whilst we can allow a wider orb for the -0- and -180-, the -90 and -45-/-135- seem to operate to the same orb.

Other scale graphs
It is now possible to obtain this type of graphic ephemeris in any scale we may wish to use of experiment with. This opens up remarkable possibilities in all areas of astrology, not least mundane where one has, at least in the free world, a constant feedback from the environment and the media as to what ideas are bubbling beneath the surface. Some students find the 30°-graph very valuable. A 36°-graph enables us to study the effects of transits in the fifth/tenth-harmonic, the quintile and decile series, whilst a 51°26′/25°43′ one will allow us to study transits in the seventh/fourteenth-harmonics, a very important and much neglected area. In theory

transits in the fifth / tenth should show us the way in which knowledge and power is being used in the world, and the kind of creative ideas that are likely to be building up at particular times. The seventh / fourteenth-harmonic graph will enable us to look at the more mysterious, inner workings of the time and the kinds of creative inspiration and 'ideas of the time' that will need to be worked through and channelled.

Indeed, when fully understood the seventh / fourteenth-harmonic transit patterns ought to reveal the inner workings of the time — its guiding vision and image. This pattern should enable us to probe into the real inspirational mainsprings behind the outer happenings of the hour, and help us to interpret the wholeness behind the apparent random movements of the moment. Clues for the study of these seventh-harmonic ideas will come from the latest films, books, plays, and the subtitles of thinking and changes of collective attitude that can only be caught by those with their ears tuned to the undercurrents rather than the outward razzmatazz. There can be little doubt that work in this area will do much to transform our understanding and interpretation of mundane events. Similarly a 20°-graph, which reveals the ninth / eighteenth-harmonic transit patterns, will no doubt help to reveal something of the longer-range implications and outworkings that can be expected of patterns set in motion at a particular time. In forecasting work this scale could hold great possibilities for understanding the deeper trends and purposes of the world situations and events. These are of course as yet highly-specialized research tools which have yet to reveal their potential. They will inevitably be followed by the higher primes such as the eleventh, thirteenth, seventeenth, and nineteenth-patternings, which must relate to increasingly specialized and refined ideas and process, and which might not be expected to reveal themselves very clearly in the immediate preoccupations of present-day man!

Horary astrology

Horary astrology is a strictly divinatory application of astrology, analogous to the *I Ching*. It is very much deserving of study on its own merits but it demands especial consideration here because for many hundreds of years horary techniques were the very foundations of mundane astrology. The fact that as a technique it can be extremely effective cannot be ignored in any real consideration of the nature of astrology. Intelligently used, it undoubtedly still has its part to play in unravelling the promise of the future.

Horary involves the interpretation of a horoscope for a particular moment to answer such specific questions as may occur to the astrologer or his client at that particular moment. A good horary practitioner might hope to arrive at not only an answer but even an elucidation of the background factors involved in such questions as 'Will the Government fall?', 'Who will win the election?', 'Will the President be re-elected?'

The rules for reading such charts are somewhat complex and differ considerably from those used in the usual chart interpretation. The more clear cut and deep felt the question the clearer the answer is likely to be. The beginner should therefore experiment at first with clear questions to which he seriously wishes to know the answer. Whilst the 'pure' horary chart is one which is set for the moment that a particular question is voiced, the technique has also been extended to apply to event charts such as, for example, the Close of Poll for an election, or the moment of the swearing of a new government, monarch or President. As was discussed in the section on 'New Year Charts' (q.v.) such moments can be considered to symbolize such unspoken questions as 'Who will win?', 'What will the new government bring?' and so on.

In horary great emphasis is laid upon the precise interpretation of the houses and planets taken as 'significators' of the question. For example in a question concerning the future of the Universities the ninth house would obviously be most important. Additionally attention would be paid to the natural ruler of the ninth, Jupiter, the planet ruling the house on the ninth cusp, and any planets within the ninth house. These planets would be analysed in terms of the aspects they made to other planets, their relationship to other positions, such as the Fixed Stars, and their location in certain degree areas such as the 'terms'. Traditional ideas of 'good' and 'bad' aspects are strictly adhered to.

If the question involves a challenge from one party to another then a 'contest' chart might be drawn, timed for the beginning of the battle, election, or other dispute. Such charts can of course be most usefully interpreted simply in terms of the cycles and transits to the charts of the contestants, but applying an horary approach the first house would be taken to signify the holder, the party in power, and the seventh house would be taken as the attacker or challenger. (A subtlety here is that the first house may also be taken as the ruler of the party or person who initiates the action.) The ruler of the first is compared to the ruler of the seventh house. Whichever is considered to have the most positive contacts would be judged to be the winner.

An Example Judgement

One of the great exponents of horary astrology who brought his skills to political use was William Lilly (1602-1681), the author of *Christian Astrology*, the first major astrological textbook in the English language. He was regarded as the unofficial 'court-astrologer' during the English Republic in the 1650s.

Several examples of Lilly's work are reproduced in Vol. I of *Christian Astrology*, and one of the most notable is a question concerning the future of Presbterianism in England. A consideration of how Lilly handled this case allows us to see the way in which this kind of astrology can be employed by a master practitioner to throw light on a complex issue. Lilly was asked 'Whether Presbytery shall stand?', or in other words whether the Calvinist Presbyterian faction would succeed in taking over the country. The question was asked in 1646 by a member of the House of Commons at a particularly volatile time. The King and the Royalists had been defeated in England and Wales but Scotland and Ireland remained loyal. Amongst the Parliamentarians there was a major split between the Independents, who were Puritans but believed in freedom of worship for all Protestants, and the Presbyterians, who wished to impose a rigid and uncompromising hierarchy. The Independents were based in the army and looked to Cromwell as their figurehead (even though he crushed the more extreme factions), whilst the Presbyterians made their base in the House of Commons. Lilly sympathized with the Independents and firmly opposed the Presbyterians, who were making a bid to crush their rivals, and the astrologer's sympathies show through his very skillful reading.

Lilly's first judgement on the chart (Fig. 13.6), was that it was weak because the angles are in mutable signs, and only one planet, Saturn, was in a fixed sign. Thus he considered the chart as a whole to lack stability. It was clearly essential to establish the significators of the question in the chart and Lilly decided that since the Presbyterians were seeking to establish a religious orthodoxy, the key house was the ninth. This gave him three planets to analyse: Jupiter, the natural ruler of the ninth and 'the general significator of religion'; Saturn which was placed in the ninth, and Venus the

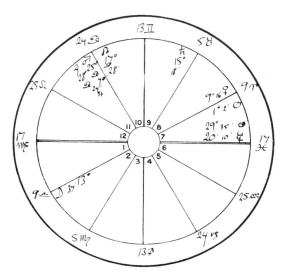

Figure 13.6 'If Presbytery Shall Stand?'

ruler of Taurus, the sign on the ninth cusp.

The judgements Lilly made on these significators were as follows: (a) Jupiter is exalted in Cancer which is good. It is however conjoined by Mars and is moving into Leo where he will be in the terms of Saturn, and will aspect several malefic fixed stars. He will then enter the term of Mercury, which planet is in Pisces (bad), but is angular and in the decanate of Mars (good). His general verdict on Jupiter is that it is poorly placed. (b) Venus is in Aries, which is her detriment and therefore bad. She is in the eighth house which is bad and in the twelfth house from her own (i.e., the twelfth when counting anti-clockwise from the ninth as the first house), which is definitely bad. Additionally before she arrives at the safety of her own sign Taurus Venus must pass through 21° of Aries and the eighth house, when she will make squares to Mars and Jupiter at which time all three planets will be in the terms of Saturn. This is definitely very bad. (c) Saturn in the ninth represents all that Lilly disliked about Presbyterianism, mainly its strict, humourless and authoritarian manner. At this point Lilly's personal prejudice intervenes for he attacks the Presbyterians for their greed and concedes that if they could overcome their bad habits Saturn might possibly work in their favour. However, as Presbyterianism is not a religious order, like the monastic orders ruled by Saturn, he doubts if it will receive any material benefit from Saturn. As it is Saturn is peregrine, occidental, has no essential dignity, and is making no aspect to Fortuna, all of which is bad. There is a reception from Saturn to the Moon (Saturn in Taurus, the Moon in Libra) via their exaltations, but there is no aspect between them. This is an important consideration for the Moon not only rules the People in mundane, but it is also the single most important planet in any horary chart.

Lilly concludes that the chart is weak for religion in general (Jupiter) and also for both the elders of the Presbyterian church (Saturn) who shall lose respect because of their authoritarian ways, and the junior members of the Church (Venus) who shall be reluctant to submit to this authority. Looking at the other planets, only one is Fixed (Saturn) and only Jupiter is dignified but he also is afflicted by Mars. The Moon is entering the Via Combusta, Mars and Mercury are in their Fall and Venus is in her Detriment, all of which may be considered bad.

Lilly concludes from the application of Venus to square Mars and Jupiter that the gentry would oppose the Presbyterians and, noting that Mars ruled the English (1066) Ascendant stated that the Mars-Jupiter conjunction meant that the people as a whole would oppose Presbyterianism. Looking at the Moon, Lilly noted that it separates from the opposition of Venus and is applying to square Mars and Jupiter and 'going to vacua cursus', and concludes that Presbyterians would have to 'struggle hard and wrangle stoutly'. The tenth house rules the authorith in the land which Lilly took to be the gentry. Gemini on the MC is ruled by Mercury which is separating from the sextile of Saturn. From this Lilly concluded that the gentry were moving away from the austerity represented by the Presbyterians.

If the Presbyterians should fail who should oppose them? Lilly took Saturn in ninth as the threat, and identifying him as Oliver Cromwell, the 'Countryman' (who was at that time still in retirement), judged that it would be he, with the support of the army, that would overthrow the Presbyterians. Moreover Lilly judged that with the Moon, natural ruler of the fourth, applying to the square of Jupiter, Lord of the fourth and ninth, that Cromwell would have overwhelming popular backing.

Not only was Lilly remarkably correct but he also added some, astrologically unargued, judgements including the statement that within three years a more amenable government would rule and that 'all shall be even as when there was no king in Israel'. In fact, just under three years later in January 1649 King Charles I was executed and England became a Republic.

Few modern astrologers at present have the skill or technical knowledge to make such a judgement, yet in Medieval and Renaissance Europe this was the substance of mundane astrology. This had to be, for astrologers were continually faced with questions of immediate importance by the politicians who so often turned to them for political advice. Amidst the proliferation of modern techniques such a structured, divinatory approach can add another dimension to our understanding and is deserving of serious exploration and experimentation.

For further reading see William Lilly's *Christian Astrology*, Vol. I, London 1659. A 1981 facsimile edition of this is available from the Lilly Chapter of the Astrological Lodge of London, the Art Worker's Guild, 6 Queen Square, London WC1. The above study is contained in pp. 439-442. Modern works on the subject include M. E. Jones' *Horary Astrology*, London 1975, and Barbara Watters' *Horary Astrology and the Judgement of Events*, Washington 1973.

These references include all those for Chapters 9-13. They are listed in alphabetical order of author. Specific unnamed footnotes continue at the end.

Sources
Most of the reference material cited can be consulted at the Astrological Association Research Library by appointment. In the USA the Library of the AFA also holds run of many of these periodicals, and the NCGR are also building up a comprehensive library.

References

1 Addey, J. Selected Writings, AFA 1976.

1a Addey, J. Lecture at AA Conference , September 1981.

2 AFA, Publishers, "Mundane Data: Lunations and Eclipses". This valuable publication contains drawn charts for each ingress and lunation, together with the charts for the current declination cycles. It also includes geographical maps of the year's eclipse paths and much else from the "Astronomical Ephemeris". Available for years *c*.1969-1985 direct from the AFA, PO Box 22040, Tempe, Arizona 85282, USA.

3 Andersen, H. *Astro-Geographic und Geschichte* Ebertin-Verlag, 1976. See also *Cosmobiology International*, no.22, January 1976, for a very brief summary in English of some of Andersen's work. Many issues of the German periodical *Sein und Werden* from 1967 onwards, contain detailed analysis of Andersen's different 'planet-systems' applied to different geographical areas in the news, and current events. A special supplement on *Astrogeographie* was issued in December 1969.

3a *SuW*, 4/1975.

4 Barbault, A. *Le Pronostic experimental en Astrologie,* Payot, Paris 1973.

4a Barbault, A. *L'Astrologie Mondiale,* Fayard, Paris 1979.

5 Barbault, A. *L'Astrologue* no.11, 1970, third quarter, pp.183-6. This includes a diagram showing the distribution of Mars in the diurnal circle for the 404 charts in question. The list of wars and the data for the charts studied are given in issue no.12, pp.252-8.

6 Barets, J. *L'Astrologie Recontre la Science,* Dervy Livres, Paris, 1977.

7 von Bekerath, E. *Staedte Horoskope,* Ebertin Verlag, Aalen, 1969.

8 de Bielski, G. 'The signs of the zodiac and countries they rule over' *MA,* New Series vol. x, no.5, May 1913, pp.184-93. The issue includes a photographic frontispiece showing Parson's scheme (see ref. 46 below) which allocates the zodiac and the twelve tribes of Israel to the globe starting with Greenwich as 0° Aries. The author gives an enthusiastic outline of her work and experience with Parson's theory.

8a de Boulainviller, original work in possession of R. C. Davison.

9 Brackenridge, J. B. (Ed.) 'On the more certain fundamentals

of astrology' by Johannes Kepler, American Philosophical Society, vol. 123, no.2, April, 1979. As a separate offprint from the society and through the AA of Great Britain. The important feature of this translation is the very important essay on Kepler and the history of astrology by Brackenridge which it contains.

9a Brummund, R., *World Tables,* L. Rudolf (Hamburg).

10 Caine, M. *The Glastonbury Zodiac,* Grael Associates, Torquay, Devon, 1978. This contains a comprehensive bibliography. A useful introductory article appeared in *AJ,* IX-1, pp.5-13, winter 1966/67, 'Notes on the Somerset zodiac' by Kara M. Pollitt.

11 Carter, C. E. O. *An Introduction to Political Astrology,* p.44.

11a Carter, C. E. O. *An Encyclopaedia of Psychological Astrology.* Contains findings on degree areas.

12 Davison, R. C. 'The place degrees' *CAOT,* vo. I-1, spring 1975, pp.5-13; also *AQ,* vol. 50-1; spring 1976, pp.25-42.

12a Dean, Geoffrey, *Recent Advances in Natal Astrology,* Analogic, 1976.

13 Dodson, C. R. *Horoscopes of the US State and Cities* AstroComputing Services, 1980.

14 Ebertin and Hoffman *Fixed Stars and Their interpretation* Ebertin, 1971. This contains a valuable listing and description of the main fixed stars. Though mainly devoted to personal charts it mentions the alleged effects of some transits of planets over fixed stars.

14a Ebertin, R. *Combination of Stellar Influences* abbreviated COSI.

15 Ebertin, R. *Jahruch füer Kosmobiologische Forshung.* The 40th Yearbook for Cosmobiological Research 1969, pp.154-61. He considered not only Benetnash, but also Deneb Kaitos, 1AR51 in 1950. Vindemiatrix, and others, though he comes to no conclusions on these others.

16 Emerson, Charles A. 'Historical Nativities and Eclipse Paths', *AJ,* XIV-1, pp.23-29, Winter 1971/72.

17 Erlewine, M. *Astro-Physical Directions,* 1977.

17a Erlewine, M. Matrix Software and notably the M65 research package are transforming this kind of research.

18 Erlewine, M. and M. 'Some preliminary comments on the interpretation of higher order structuring', *CEB* nos.8 and 9, 1979.

19 Firebrace, R. C. Editor of *Spica* (see abbreviations).

19a Firebrace, R. C. *Wars in the Sidereal,* available through AA,

13pp. text, 6pp. of drawn charts. Many examples of solar and sidereal ingresses into the cardinal signs are given in the pages of the now defunct *Spica*.

20 Firebrace, R. C. *John F. Kennedy 1917-63* Moray Series no.7, 1964, 58pp, 26 drawn charts. Evaluates Kennedy's chart, the 1775 USA chart, and the Kennedy Inauguration Chart, in terms of various sidereal solar and lunar returns. An evaluation indicates the power of the angular houses in these charts.

21 Harvey, C. 'The galactic centre and beyond: signposts to evolution' *AJ*, vol. 25. no.2. spring, 1983, pp.74-84. Gives a survey and discussion of the symbology of the GC, SGC, and AP and some suggestive evidence for their value in interpretation.

22 Hitschler, K. *Les Correspondences entre Planetes, Sons, Couleurs, et Corps Chimique* Geneve, 1956.

23 Inge, D. *Philosophy of Plotuius.*

24 Janis, C. *'Vertebrate evolution and the Great, Great, Great, Great Year' AQ,* vol. 53-3; vol. 54-1, pp.15-20.

25 Johndro, L. E. *The Earth in the Heavens — Ruling Degrees of Cities* 1st ed. 1929; reprinted, Weiser, New York, 1970, 1973, p/b 1979.

26 Johndro, op.cit., p.4-12. Johndro shows ingeniously the startlingly fact that, taking the value of the precession of the equinoxes on the ecliptic as 50′.25″ per year, and the same on the equator at an average of 46″ per year, that the complete precessional cycle from Greenwich to Greenwich on the plane of the Equator is 28,184 years which is virtually the same as that of the complete precessional cycle on the ecliptic of the Great Pyramid to the Great Pyramid plus the distance to Greenwich, of 28,174 years! From this he concludes that '. . . it was not by chance that the Greenwich meridian was chosen for astronomical reference thousands of years after the Great Pyramid had been built for that purpose in earlier times'.

27a Knappich,

27 Jones, M. E. 'Mundane perspectives in astrology', *AFA,* 1975. Illustrates the influence of the transits and progressions in the charts of US presidents on national events during their terms of office.

28 Julian *The Works of the Emperor Julian,* Loeb Classical Library, (trans, Wilmer Cave Wright) 1913, vol. 1, Hymn to King Helios, p.427. This whole section which discusses the reasons for starting

the year at the Capricorn solstice is included in the ISCWA publication *Key Texts in the History and Philosophy of Astrology,* due December 1984.

29 Landscheidt, T., private communication.

30 Lewis, J. *Sourcebook of Mundane Maps,* published annually since 1979. Available direct from ACG, Box 22293, San Francisco, or from ISCWA, 48 Castle Street, Frome, Somerset BA11 3BW. England. Personal ACGs are available only from the US address.

31 Lewis, J., Lectures and personal communications as yet unpublished.

32 Anyone who has experienced the power and appropriateness of relocation charts will immediately appreciate that ACGs have enormous potential as a medical and therapeutic tool, highlighting those areas which will help bring out specific aspects of the psychosomatic potential for exploration.

33 Lynes, B. *The Next 20 Years*

33a Lynes, B. *Astroeconomics,* pub. Lynes 1983, PO Box 15247, Springfield. Mass. 01115. A pioneering attempt to bring together astrology and economics, and to encourage the conscious use of these by decision-makers.

33b Lynes, B. *Capitalism and Astrology,* AS, spring, 1983, pp.43-50.

34 Harmer, M. 'The Horoscope of Bristol' *AJ,* IV-4, Sept. 1962, pp.18-27.

35 McCraig, H. *The Ephemeris of the Moon, 1800-2000* Macoy, 1951. The times of lunations and sign ingresses are accurate down to 1950 but increasing error's occur towards the end of the century. The listing of actual positions for all lunations and eclipses in the nineteenth century makes this a valuable research tool.

36 Michelsen, N. Produces a superb range of ephemerides of all kinds including heliocentric and sidereal. Astro Computing Services will also produce, to order, monthly ephemerides *for any period in history* with complete aspectarian.

37 Morrison, A. H. A study in *The Horoscope,* May 1834, quoted in Robson below.

38 Morrison, A. *Canon of Solar Eclipses 1895-1974,* AFA. A useful section from von Oppolzer, see below.

39 Naylor, J. 'Sensitive points in mundane astrology' *AQ* vol. 54-1, pp.28-30; vol. 54-2, pp.38-42.

40 Niggeman, H. (trans.) *Rules for Planetary Pictures,* unauthorized

translation of Alfred Witte's major work. Published by the translator New York, 1932, with an introductory essay by E. Richard Wagner.

41 Niggeman, H. *The Principles of the Uranian System,* self-published, 1961.

42 von Oppolzer, T. R. *Canon of Eclipses 1200 BC-2131 AD.* This remarkable work gives the rising, culminating and setting points of all solar eclipses with diagrams showing the actual eclipse paths for the most important ones.

43 Osten, G. *The Astrological Chart of the USA 1776-2141,* Stein and Day, N.Y. 1976. Using a 20GE AS chart Osten presents evidence for the theory that presidents born in years when there were no major progressed aspects in this USA chart tend to be relatively insignificant presidents compared to those born in years of strongly marked progressions. Contains a useful potted history of the US.

44 de Pablos, M. D. 'Sigol XX', 'Sigol XXI', *Anuario Alfonso X* El Sabio, 1982. Discusses the destiny of the twentieth and twenty-first centuries in terms of charts set for 00.00hrs, 1 January 1900 at 1800.00 E, i.e. the International Date Line.

45 Pallent, D. 'Astrology and the metal markets' *AJ,* vol. XXV, no.2. Spring, 1983, pp.91-7. Pallent trades successfully exclusively on astrological signals. He says of his empirical researches, which have been directly tested on a professional basis for many years: '. . my researches confirm some of the most ancient concepts on the subject, including aspects, signs of the zodiac and diurnal effects. I believe that definite confirmation of the existence of zodiac harmonics can be obtained by observation of planetary ingresses and their effect on prices'.

46 Parsons, A. *New Light from the Great Pyramid,* pub. The Metaphysical Pub. Co., New York, 1883, sub-titled 'The astronomico-geographical system of the ancients recovered and applied to the elucidation of history, ceremony, symbolism and religion'.

47 Ptolemy, *Tetrabiblos.* There are various editions and translations available. The authoritative Loeb Classical Library edition, which includes both the original Greek and the translation, is available through ISCWA.

48 Raphael's Ephemeris, W. Foulsham, published annually in summer for following year, with details of ingresses and other phenomena since 1906 edition.

49 Reider, T. *Astrological Warnings and the Stock Market,* Pagurian Press, Toronto, 1972.

50 Ritter, G. 'Kosmogeographie-Astrogeograpie', SuW, 6-69, pp.7-11.

51 Robson, V. E. *The Fixed Stars and Constellations in Astrology,* Though mainly related to personal astrology, Chapter VI is concerned with the mundane applications.

52 Sepharial (= Dr Walter Gorn-Old), *The Theory of Geodetic Equivalents,* W. Foulsham, c.1924.

53 Sepharial, op.cit., p.12.

53a Sepharial, *The Law of Values,* W. Foulsham.

54 Sepharial, *The World Horoscope, Hebrew Astrology — The Key to the Study of Prophecy.* W. Foulsham, 1900.

55 Spencer, K. Q. *The Zodiac Looks Westward* David MacKay CO., Philadelphia, 1943.

56 Sucher, W. O. *The Drama of the Universe — A New Interpretation,* Landvidi Research Centre, 1958.

57 Thompson, C. J. S. *The Mystery and Romance of Astrology,* Brentano, 1929. A popular, dismissive, compilation of astrological information. Chapter X contains material on famous comets of history.

58 Troinski E. H. *1001 Weltpolitische Horoskope,* Baumgartner-Verlag, Hannover, 1955.

59 Tyl, N. *The Principles and Practice of Astrology. Vol. XI; Astrology Mundane, Astral, Occult,* Llewellyn, 1975.

60 Wigglesworth, H. "The Incorporated".

61 Williams, D. *AFA Research Bulletin* No. 4, 1969. This includes, on p.13, a comparative table of the geographical allocations for 0 and 15 of each of the signs according to five authorities. This includes one by L. J. Jensen, which is not listed in our comparative table. Apparently from 'Astro-Economic Interpretation' it places 0° Aries at 1.07.5E. He measures his zodiac westward so that his values can be obtained by adding 1.07.5 ′ to those given for Sepharial.

61a Williams, D. *Astro Economics,* AFA, 1982.

62 Wise, A. *AFA Bulletin,* vol. 30, no.9, 22 September 1968.

63 Witte-Lefeldt, *Rules for Planetary Pictures,* (trans. Curtt Knupfer) Ludwig Rudolph / Witte Verlag, Hamburg. This is the authorized English translation of this classic work. See also the Niggemann translation and writing listed above.

65 Yoke, Ho Peng. *The Astronomical Chapters of the Chin Shu*
    Mouton & Co, Paris, 1966. Includes a very valuable bibliography
    of works on Chinese astronomy/astrology.

65 Most students in this area agree that it is the very close angularity
    of a planet over a national capital or the geographical centre
    of a country, say within 1°-2° maximum, that really brings that
    idea into high focus during the period. This is not in agreement
    with the Gauquelins' well-known findings with natal astrology
    where Addey's analysis shows the maximum amplitude of effect
    to occur about 5°-8° after the angle for the pure traditional idea
    of a planet. Those who wish to experiment with adapting the
    Gauquelins' findings will need to allow visually for this by
    considering a position a few degrees to the east of each line to
    perhaps mark the position of greatest intensity.

66 Various writers, as in Hitschler (22 above), have pointed out
    that each point on the Earth's surface can be taken as a zero
    point and that it will thus automatically have aspectual
    relationships with specific other points on the globe. The most
    classic example of this is the exact 180° relationship between
    Washington DC. and Hanoi, Pnom Penh, Saigon in Vietnam,
    part of the US's projected 'shadow' as it were. M. Jordan explores
    some further examples in an article 'The astrology of geo-political
    relationships', reprinted in *CAOT* 2-2, p.18.

67 Lists of rulerships: traditional lists can be found in Carter's *IPA*
    and also in the Appendix of von Beckerath's *Stadte-Horoskope*
    cited above, which gives actual ascendant degrees for a large
    number of, mainly German, cities, though the origin of these
    is not stated.

68 The actual angles for the capital were in fact MC: 14SC38, AS
    23CP59, placing the MA/AS at 19SG18 exactly conjunct
    NE = 18SG29 = UR/PL = 19SG05. Although Uranus was exactly
    angular about 4°30′ further east, over central Iran, the Tehran
    angles in fact in themselves pick out other highly significant
    points. Thus the Tehran MC almost exactly bisects the exact
    MO-MA bi-septile, MO/MA is at 15SC44, adding a quality of
    'fated' and collective possession and 'inspiration' to the
    MC = MO/MA. This mid-point could in any case be expressd
    as 'at this time the will of the people' (or negatively 'the anger
    and fury of the mob') 'is made known'. Likewise the
    AS = ME = SO/UR which is highly descriptive of what COSI

describes as 'the young reformer', the voice of revolution amongst the youth and students and the whole climate of nervous tension and uncertainty.

69 Wemyss, Maurice, *The Wheel of Life*, L. N. Fowler. Contains great detail on degree areas in relation to specific aspects of life.

70 Halbronn, Jacques, *Clefs pour l'astrologie,* Seghers, Paris 1976, pp.142-169. Gives a succinct exposition of the eight-fold zodiacal cycle in relation to history with graphed curves for the cycles of Mars, Jupiter, Saturn, and Uranus. He emphasizes the Platonic concept of considering each cycle as a movement from unity at conjunction into multiplicity and back to unity again. He is critical of the simple Gouchon-Barbault Cyclic Index because it lumps together outgoing and incoming phases and is thus not truly cyclical unlike the later variations. He also advocates that such an index should include Mars but exclude Neptune and Pluto.

71 **Iran:** The key chart would appear to be that for the Coronation of Reza Khan, 25 April 1926, 4.10 p.m. L.T. = 12.44.16″ p.m. GMT., Tehran, 35N44, 51E26. MC 4CN51; AS 4LI21 M/A 19LE37; SO 4TA33; MO 5LI35; ME 7AR48; VE 18PI27; MA 24AQ05; JU 23AQ10; SA 24SC08; UR 27PI35; NE 22LE00 R ; PL 12CN45; NNt 19CN39; NNm 20CN14. Source: Press, researched M. Baigent, AJ XXIII-4, Autumn 1981.

72 The Pluto Declination chart given by Zain is almost 16 hours too early by modern calculations. This chart angles should still be treated with caution as Pluto moves so slowly.

73 Russell, James, *Cycle Charts,* AJ XXI-3, Summer 1979, pp.135-8.

74 Atomic Energy: First controlled chain reaction began 15-20 C.S.T. ended 15.55 C.S.T., 2 Dec 1942, Chicago, 4IN50, 87W40. Source: Official records. MC 2AQ24; AS 25TA00; SO 10SG05; MO 1LI15; ME 11SG04, VE 14SG07; MA 21SC06, JU 24CN34 R , SA 8GE57; UR 2GE15 R , NE 1LI46; PL 7LE07; NNt 28LE37; NNm 29LE04.

PART FOUR:
THE APPLICATION

14.
THE ASTROLOGY OF WAR AND PEACE: A STUDY OF THE SECOND WORLD WAR
Part 1: Collective Pressure

Michael Baigent

Our news broadcasts, our newspapers, our popular books feed us constantly on a diet of conflict after conflict. World Wars One and Two, Korea, Vietnam, Israel, Lebanon — all examples of humanity;s inability to live with itself. The tragedy of such disasters is all too obvious — the lives ruined, the soldiers and civilians killed, the children psychologically crippled, perhaps forever. To end such wars is the hope of many people but one so idealistic as to defy the practical limitations of mankind's frequently selfish and violent temperament. A lesser hope — to understand and possibly to predict wars — is perhaps the place to begin. Here we have a chance of success and here astrology can offer a useful contribution. This section of the chapter will explore the possibility of using the outer planet transits to crucial areas of a state's natal chart as indicators of the increasing tension between states — tension which all too often leads to conflict.

War is not merely the existence of mutual hostility between nations. It is also characterized by the outbreak of fighting, the breakdown of those delicate balances which maintain order. This outbreak of violence can be seen in psychological terms as the eruption of a mass psychosis in the body politic. The nation is in the throes of a mass psychological breakdown. And once the nation breaks down, once rational action disintegrates and becomes replaced by emotional slogans and nationalistic dreams, then the result is a variety of mass hysteria rushing headlong into a mass psychosis. When this happens, when a society becomes collectively abnormal, the latent psychotics — who feel at home in this social environment — emerge to take control. [1] Jung explains National Socialism which erupted in Germany in the 1930s as such a mass phenomenon, an outbreak of the collective unconscious. [2] The forces then driving the society are archetypal and as each archetype contains, both good and evil, such mass movements then can lead equally to creation or destruction, to life or to death. Once a mass becomes activated, history shows that it always produces a leader, a charismatic individual who becomes the focus point for the mass fantasies. Cried Jung: 'Can we at last get it into our heads that any government of impassioned patriots which signs the order for mobilization should immediately be executed *en bloc?*'[3]

Wars are eruptions following a period of strain. Such strain can lead to an implosion — civil war, as happened in Spain in 1936 — or, if the tension is paralleled by that within a bordering state, an explosion, an international conflict. En masse, man becomes much more negative, much more 'fated', much more liable to succumb to the collective pressures and hence more liable to break under the strain of continued tension. All that is needed is the spark to ignite the increasingly explosive situation.

Astrological symbolism can aid in tracing this building tension. By watching the transits of the outer 'collective' planets, particularly Uranus and Pluto (whose symbolism connects them with revolution and destruction) a pattern of changing tension can generally be traced. However even though, as will be demonstrated, this pattern of tension can be shown, the breakdown of rationality, the root cause of the flashpoint, cannot. This point does not find any astrological correspondence: none which has been proposed over the years is at all convincing. This flashpoint is the mass equivalent of the individual's act of either self-determination or irrationality. These points do not show up in the symbolism of the natal chart.

Despite the apparent inevitability of tension, the flashpoint is not inevitable. Wars do not have to be fought, it is just that they erupt more commonly than does a desire for peace. This is the area of mass 'free-will', which is much smaller than that of an individual, but nevertheless does exist. It is simply a tragic fact of history that in periods of tension, flashpoints often erupt. One of the dramatic examples in recent history is the origins of the Second World War. The background to German, indeed to all European pre-war difficulties has been exhaustively explored, but never from the point of view of the astrological symbolism and the cycles that it can reveal. This particular study will deal with the mutual tension between Germany and Poland as shown by the transits of Uranus and Pluto primarily to the Sun (leadership), the Moon (people) and the ascendant (the nation) of the astrological charts drawn for the regimes of Poland and Nazi Germany.

Poland and the astrological cycles

In any country the transits of Uranus should provide insight into sudden changes in the *status quo,* the challenges made to tradition. Uranus symbolizes those social elements which do not desire the *status quo* to be perpetuated and so initiate reforms or revolutions. Because of this opposition to tradition any cycle of such change will often evoke tension and pressure. In mundane astrology the maximum orb allowed for an aspect from a transit of Uranus is 2 degrees, which is approximately one month in time — unless of course Uranus is stationary.

The Pluto transits reflect a pattern which lies behind that of Uranus. Pluto symbolizes the social energies which seek change, but over a much longer timescale. Pluto energies support an erosion, rather than the open rebellion of the Uranus elements. This causes the social structure to decay so as to allow the new forms to be born. Pluto symbolizes that which seeks to destroy and that which seeks to take control. Such a transit often reflects a period of power struggles, especially within the leadership of a country. The orb used for Pluto in practical work is about 1 degree, which again assuming the planet is not stationary, represents approximately one month in time.

In Poland the slow build-up to World War Two was preceded by a long period of internal problems. If a flashpoint had erupted at this early stage perhaps civil war could have ensued. As it was, in 1926 a military coup erupted but the increased centralization forestalled revolution if not street riots.

The republic of Poland, as Fig. 14.1, p. 374 shows, was not born with a central leadership imposing dictatorial rule upon its people. In fact, the leadership (Sun-Venus in the tenth house) appears benign and well-meaning — these qualities are symbolized by the trine both to Jupiter and to the Moon. Their popularity, or rather the popularity of the republic, is reflected by the second of these trines, to the Moon (the people). Naturally though a benign government will find it hard to please every interest in the country. Storms on the horizon are symbolized by Mars opposition Pluto across the ascendant, representing a fiery passion in the people which could so easily turn from the creative to the destructive, or even suicidal. Mars in Capricorn, a combination of aggression and tradition, is expressed by the militarism shown by subsequent governments.

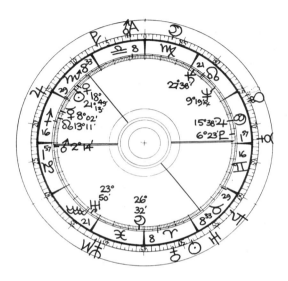

Figure 14.1   The chart of Poland set for 09.30 GMT, 14 November 1918, Warsaw, 21E00, 52N15. The mNN is 14SG05.

The second black spot is the T-square running from the Sun to Uranus — placed in the second house ruling finances — and to Saturn in the eighth. This suggests a continual failure of leadership to solve the economic problems consequent upon the lack of resources and lack of heavy industry. Indeed, these problems were to occupy the attentions of the leadership for the entire duration of the republic until the war — unfortunately, with little success. These problems became eventually overshadowed by increasingly ominous foreign developments, in the escalation of which Poland played its part.

The transits
Uranus trine Sun: April 1924 to February 1926
From mid-April to September of 1924 transiting Uranus formed a trine aspect to the natal Sun of Poland at 21 degrees Scorpio in the

tenth house. Uranus transiting the second house suggests that financial concerns would receive some innovative attention, or if not, some body blows. And so it developed. At this time Poland saw a major currency reform and the formation of the Bank of Poland. On the negative side the transit suggests an instability of the leadership — this too developed. This aspect repeated from February 1925 until February 1926. With this repetition of aspects, common enough and due to a period of retrograde motion, it is usually the final transit which coincides with the most important result of the cycle involved. In this case, a Saturn transit was adding to the Uranus transit. In November Saturn passed the Midheaven and Venus, and in December, the Sun. This symbolizes a time when any weaknesses in the leadership would become apparent. And as expected, late 1925 saw the economic situation in Poland deteriorating rapidly. There was some 30 per cent unemployment, general strikes, financial scandals and near the end of the year, a critical leadership crisis. In November 1925 General Pilsudski, who had been instrumental in gaining Polish independence and was regarded as a great patriot, emerged from his retirement to air his views in public on the chaotic political situation. It is now known that this period saw the beginning of the planning for his later *coup d'état*.

December 1925 saw a very positive aspect of the cycle emerging. The Polish parliament ratified a major land reform bill. As a nation where 60 per cent of the population were agricultural workers, of whom few owned sufficient land to work economically, land reform had been one of the major priorities of the republic's leaders.

Uranus conjunct Moon: March 1926 to May 1926

This aspect would be expected to coincide with some eruption from the people, an eruption with popular support. And so events proved. On the evening of 12 May 1926 General Pilsudski entered Warsaw with a large body of troops with whom he proposed to take over the government. Power was effectively his by 8.30 pm when he had gained control of all the major centres of the city. As would be expected, the chart for this moment (see Fig. 14.2) connects with the chart for the republic. The two Sun's oppose one another — 5 minutes of a degree. Saturn at the time was transiting the Sun of the republic's chart. The government forces fought for two days when the government resigned between 7 and 7.15 pm on 14 May. The chart for this movement too, fits (Fig. 14.3, p.376) both the republic

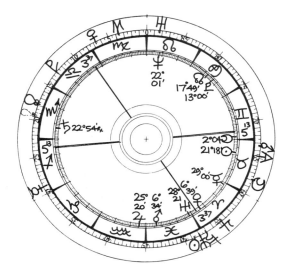

Figure 14.2   Pilsudski takes power in Poland, 12 May 1926, 19.30 GMT
Warsaw. The mNN is 19CN23.

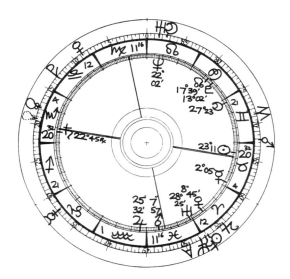

Figure 14.3   The Polish Government resigns, 14 May 1926, 18.00 GMT,
Warsaw. The mNN is 19CN17.

chart and that of Pilsudski's taking of power two days earlier. This is another demonstration of the astrological adage shown to advantage in Part 3 — that the end of a cycle is contained in its beginning.

Following the coup, Pilsudski's increasingly authoritarian manner reduced the opportunities for internal change. External affairs gradually became dominant. Unfortunately for Poland, the enthusiastic revolutionary of the First World War had changed into a very tired old man, frequently sick and mistrustful of his subordinates — all well symbolized by Saturn crossing the Sun in the Polish chart.

Pluto trine Sun: August 1931 to June 1933

The stage upon which the Second World War was to be fought was, for Poland and Germany, set in the early 1930s. In Poland this stage was symbolized by the slow transits of Pluto. Here was the foundation of Poland's destruction as later, Pluto reflected Germany's destruction. In four separate periods between August 1931 and June 1933, Pluto formed a trine with the Polish Sun, moving through the seventh house — the house of treaties, of the diplomatic side of foreign policy. Additionally Pluto touching the Sun by trine is considered the classic aspect of the dictator — an apt symbol, as will be seen. As usual, the final passing of Pluto coincided with the most dramatic effect which occurred from February to June 1933.

At the end of January 1933 Adolf Hitler came to power in Germany. Thus there was suddenly a dictator in a neighbouring state (Pluto in the seventh house). Also, in March 1933, the Polish government passed the 'enabling act'. This allowed Pilsudski to issue decrees which had the full backing of law. It thus conferred dictatorial powers on him. Poland itself then had a dictator also.

The major cause for the later conflict came in the somewhat undiplomatic decision by Pilsudski to annex the free city of Danzig (today known as Gdansk). There was no justification for this move, especially as the city had an overwhelmingly German population. At the same time Pilsudski began plans for a preventative war against Hitler. It was Danzig which was eventually to provide the reason for the German invasion of Poland and the subsequent bloody hostilities. A fitting event then to coincide with a transit of Pluto.

Uranus opposition MC: June 1936 to April 1937

The tension which was to lead to World War Two can be seen,

astrologically, beginning in earnest with the Uranus transit of the MC-IC axis, to enter the fourth house, which rules land and the national heritage. This aspect occurred from June 1936 until April 1937. Apart from the slow build to tension as Uranus slowly comes to the opposition with the Sun (indicating maximum pressure upon the leadership for change), alterations and tensions affecting the very basis of the country (the land) could be expected. Again astrological symbolism proves accurate. Expressing the negative side of this aspect was the final despair of the peasants desperate for land and a decent life. In June 1936 a group of peasants occupied by force a provincial town, deposing the government authorities. Frustration too made the largest opposition party, the Peasant party, much more radical. This event was to lead eventually to a bloody national strike by farm workers.

On the positive side, the government at this time proposed a four-year economic plan in an attempt to reduce unemployment. As part of this plan they organized the creation of a central industrial region which was in part aiming to draw workers off the land. By 1937 the economic strategy was oriented more towards the increasing defence needs. In June 1936 transiting Saturn trined the Sun. This is a symbol of strength available to the government as well as an indication of the inflexible nature the government would adopt. Certainly the government had the strength to withstand the turmoil among the peasants. But rather than become more flexible it became more centralized, more intransigent, more concerned with military and international affairs as the bordering countries expressed their own fears by building up their forces.

Uranus opposition Venus: June 1938 to June 1939
This aspect, due to a period of retrogression, occurs twice. It can though be expected to coincide with a period of tension coupled with a change in alliances. The involvement of the tenth house indicates a large measure of self-interest in these manoeuvres. With Uranus passing through the fourth house, activating the elements of society desiring reform, the government, symbolized by the tenth house, can either relax or tighten up. It chose the latter course of action.

1 June to October 1938
In September 1938 a manipulated election meant that effective one-

party rule was achieved in Poland. In October Poland annexed the border areas of Czechoslovakia near the Carpathian mountains. Also in October, Hitler offered to extend the non-aggression treaty with Poland, if the Poles returned Danzig to German control. Naturally the Poles rejected this out of hand. War moved that small step closer.

2 April to June 1939
Again events which coincided with this final passing of the aspect proved to be the most crucial. April 1939 saw the signing of the Anglo-Polish treaty. Astrology sees a Uranus opposition Venus aspect as symbolizing those relationships which neither last long nor produce much good. As a result of this treaty an annoyed Hitler renounced the German-Polish treaty. So the final alliances were in place for the catastrophe.

Uranus opposition Sun: June 1939 to August 1940
On 1 September 1939, German troops invaded Poland. Uranus was within 44 minutes of a degree from the opposition to the natal Sun of Poland — well within orb. Here we have a symbol of the final crisis which ended in the destruction not only of the leadership but of independent Poland. As Part 3 shows, the chart for the signing of the invasion order has an ascendant which is conjunct the Sun of the Polish chart. It would seem that a successful invasion is one which is started at a time which synchronizes with the charts of both the attacker and the defender, for this chart of the extremely successful invasion links both the Polish and the Nazi German charts.

Germany and the astrological cycles
Nazi Germany was born on 30 January 1933 at 11 am when Adolf Hitler was appointed Chancellor. The chart (see Fig. 14.6) for this time indicates a country under severe tension. There are numerous tension points which, if transited, would be expected to coincide with crises in the State. And so events proved.

Uranus square Mercury-Saturn-Sun: May 1935 to April 1938
This is the period which began with the open declaration of German rearmament and reintroduction of conscription (March 1935) and ended with the invasion of Austria in March 1938. This period saw Hitler preparing for war not only by the rearmament but also by the increase in social strictures and repression, all of which were

designed to lead the German nation towards those aims which the Nazi party held. It saw too the breaking of the power and independence of the army. By the end of this cycle Hitler was indisputably master of all Germany: it was he who made the decisions; it was he who embodied its destiny. During this time Germany had become inextricably linked with this man. Their destinies became the same. The stage was set for their simultaneous destruction.

The astrological symbolism would suggest success as a result of hard national effort (this is the mundane interpretation of the square). With the tenth house Sun-Saturn involved, this national effort would be expected to augment the dominance of the leadership. Indeed, during this time Germany broke free from the limitations consequent upon the treaties which ended the First World War. This whole period can be usefully split into three parts.

1. Uranus square Mercury: May 1935 to April 1936
This period saw Hitler being made supreme chief of the armed forces. It saw the beginning of his plan to break the Locarno treaties. It saw too the Anglo-German naval agreement which allowed Germany to build 'pocket' battleships and submarines. It ended with the breaking of the treaties — the German occupation of the Rhineland.

2. Uranus square Saturn: May 1936 to April 1937
This period saw the increasing centralization of the State coupled with increasingly authoritarian measures: the disappearance of civil liberties, the persecution of the Jews, the measures aimed against the Christian Churches. It saw too German involvement in the Spanish Civil War. And, true to the symbolism of Saturn in the tenth house, it saw the years of Nazi respectability.

3. Uranus square Sun: May 1937 to March 1938
This period saw an acceleration in the pace of events. Hitler became more reckless and more confident. Additionally he became very worried about his health — all to be expected from an *individual* under a transit of Uranus square Sun. The fact that Hitler was showing effects symbolized by a transit to the German chart is an indication of the increasing identification of Hitler with Germany. Transits to Germany symbolized Hitler and, indeed, transits to Hitler's chart symbolized Germany.

In late 1937 Hitler revealed to his high-ranking officers details of his long-term plans. He wanted war: he wanted to conquer first Austria and Czechoslovakia, then Poland and the Ukraine. In February Hitler, after some high level scandals (one top officer married a prostitute and another proved to be homosexual) was able to take over the supreme command of the army. The independance of the army was broken; Hitler no longer feared his generals. The preparation for Hitler's dream of a thousand-year Reich was complete: he was in command.

Uranus conjunct ascendant: May 1938 to May 1940
This covers the outbreak of World War Two. The time when, as would be expected with Uranus crossing the ascendant, Germany struck quickly outwards, breaking free from all restraints. During this time, viewing Hitler as the embodiment of Germany, it would be expected from the symbolism of this aspect that he would attract violence to himself. History indicates that this is correct. In September 1938 an abortive coup was planned by military officers. In November 1939 a bomb went off in a beer hall where he had just finished a speech.

Open violence was erupting within Germany. November 1938 saw the infamous *kristalnacht* when synagogues all over Germany went up in flames; in August 1938 Germany mobilized; September saw the conference at Munich where the allied compromise allowed Hitler to gain more confidence.

In May 1939 Hitler told his military chiefs of his decision to attack Poland, which he did on the 1 September. From November to January 1940 he was poised to attack in the West but instead moved against Scandinavia. Finally in May 1940 the long expected attack on the West came, ending with capitulations and Dunkirk.

The invasion of Poland, 1 September 1939
Works on the occult aspects of World War Two often mention stories to the effect that Hitler was closely guided by astrologers. It should be simple to clarify this matter by looking at the chart for the invasion of Poland. For if an action is precisely planned astrologically then the planetary aspects at the time would reflect that. But as experience shows, even though an aspect will symbolically represent a collective cycle, the events rarely happen exactly on aspect; for the planetary cycles do not *cause* the world effects: rather there is a coincidence of cycles — albeit at times remarkably close.

As has been explained there is, by virtue of the planetary orbs used on transits, a range of at least one month in the coincidence of aspect and event. Because of this we should note any events of the expected type which occur on the exact day of the planetary aspect, for in these cases it is most likely that the date and time have been chosen by astrologers (though, of course, coincidence must always remain possible).

Looking then at the invasion chart, together with the charts of Germany and Poland, it is clear that the aspects are not exact — even though they are close. We must conclude that the war was not planned astrologically. Additional points which support this conclusion are:

1.   On September 1 several planets were retrograde. An astrologer would have advised against beginning an important action at this time.
2.   The chart for the signing of the first order of the war (see Part 3) has a 'void of course' Moon. An astrologer would avoid this at all costs.

Ellic Howe in his study of astrology in the Second World War reaches the same conclusion, though not from the astrological evidence just presented. [8]

The coincidence of the various charts, close but not exact, is an indication rather that Hitler was closely 'in tune' with the collective cycles. He was in a very real sense fulfilling the task the German, indeed the European, collective demanded of him. What he was not to know was that the currents which drove him were also to demand his destruction.

Such currents of destruction are symbolized in astrology by transits of Pluto. Not surprisingly then, the final set of major transits crossing the chart of Nazi Germany are those of that planet. During the 1940s Pluto aspected the same cluster of planets as Uranus had done in the 1930s. Both planets, Uranus transiting by square and Pluto by opposition, aspected the Mercury-Saturn-Sun grouping in Nazi Germany's tenth house. The effect of Uranus was to coincide with the coming of Hitler and his party to power. The second aspect — of Pluto opposing this grouping — began in 1940 and was not to finish until both Hitler and Germany had been destroyed.

Pluto opposition Mercury-Saturn-Sun: October 1940 to August 1946
This aspect began with the first clear defeat for the German forces — their failure to destroy the Royal Air Force and ended, in August

1946, with the dissolution of the German army. As in the earlier transits, this too had three phases.

1. Pluto opposition Mercury: October 1940 to September 1941
Following the successful invasion of western Europe and the withdrawal of British troops from the mainland, the German generals were led to understand that the war was over. In June 1940, 35 divisions of the army were demobilized. If the war had in fact ended at that point the future of Europe may well have been different. However, as is symbolized by the rapidly-forming Pluto transit, a further grasping for power was inevitable. Hitler wanted to invade England. His troops were not prepared and so the battle was begun in the air. The story of the survival of the much smaller British air force (admittedly operating from close to base, unlike the German air force) is well known. The point here is that the German attempt to gain air supremacy failed. They lost the Battle of Britain. This realization that they had lost their first battle came in October 1940 with the cancellation of Operation Sealion — the invasion of England. This coincided with the beginning of Pluto's long period of opposition. If Hitler had truly been advised by astrologers he would never have attempted further expansion at this point. However, the next year he invaded Russia. The end of this period, September 1941, coincided with Hitler's uncertainty on how to proceed with the Russian invasion. As a result his huge army sat uselessly for almost two months before resuming the advance upon Moscow. This delay, caused by Hitler, was to prove fatal. It was as though the collective wanted the invasion to fail.

2. Pluto opposition Saturn: October 1942 to June 1945
This period saw the end of the Third Reich. It started with the two battles which spelled the breaking of German power: El Alamein late in October 1942 and the beginning of the successful Russian counterattack at Stalingrad in late November 1942. The latter ended with the retreat and surrender of immense German forces. The German army was now on the defensive. This fits the symbolism of Pluto opposing Saturn — ever increasing power opposing the armed might of the German government. The end of the period coincided with the end of Germany, for on 7 May 1945, the final surrender of all German forces was made.

3. Pluto opposition Sun: October 1944 to August 1946

This is tangled in with the earlier aspect. However, in October 1944 Hitler and his HQ staff planned the Ardennes offensive which eventually, in terms of losses to the German war effort, became a second Stalingrad. Hitler was still insisting upon bringing Germany to complete destruction. The end of this period, August 1946, was when the German army ceased to exist. This final dismantling of power came on the orders of the occupying allied forces who dissolved the Wehrmacht.

Two countries, side by side, both in the throes of a cycle affecting the leadership — the very focus point of the nation — symbolized by the transits of Uranus and Pluto to the Sun, found a flashpoint and war erupted between them. Both nations were destroyed. Today, one exists under foreign domination; the other is divided in two, physically and idealogically. The end of the war brought peace but not harmony or tranquillity.

In a sense both countries have returned to their natural situation — as far as history can reveal it. Poland has mostly been under foreign domination and Germany was always fragmented.

References
1   Jung, C. G. *Collected Works* vol. 10, p.248.
2   ibid., p.237.
3   ibid., p.243.
4   Carter, C. *Political Astrology* p.62.
5   12 May 1926, 19.30hrs GMT, Warsaw: *The Times,* 17 May 1926, p.4.
6   14 May 1926, 19.00hrs GMT, Warsaw: Rothschild, J. *Pilsudski,* pp.146-8.
7   Goering, H. *Germany Reborn,* p.114.
8   Howe, E. *Astrology and Psychological Warfare during World War Two.* Hitler had all astrologers arrested after Hess' flight to England.

Bibliography
CARTER, C. E. Q. *An Introduction to Political Astrology* 3rd edition, London, 1973.
GOERING, H. *Germany Reborn* London, 1934.
HOWE, E. *Astrology and Psychological Warefare during World War Two* London, 1972.

JUNG, C. G. *Collected Works* (trans. R. F. C. Hull) 19 vols. London, 1953.

ROTHSCHILD, J. *Pilsudski's Coup d'Etat* London, 1966.

Part 2: The Cyclical Background

Charles Harvey

A mundane astrology developed on real first principles can transform mankind's understanding of our individual and collective destiny. By coming to a real understanding of the deeper process of war and peace and of the relationship between peoples we may fashion a tool by which we may be able to say 'Collective mankind know thyself'.

This chapter examines how some of the techniques outlined earlier actually performed in connection with understanding the archetypal processes at work during World War Two. In the limited space available priority has been given to examples which will help to illustrate the main principles involved. Emphasis here has been placed on the German / Polish perspective. For those interested in following this example further an ISCWA study[1] covers the charts of all the main countries.

Hitler and the German charts

'In this column for years, I have constantly laboured these points: Hitler's horoscope is not a war-horoscope . . . . If and when war comes, not he but others will strike the first blow.'

R. H. Naylor *Sunday Express* 1939

Mass psychology and the extraordinary power of the collective are only just beginning to be understood. R. H. Naylor was a gifted astrologer, but in terms of real social psychology he was as naive as most people of the period. His assessment quoted above, based no doubt on the Libra / Taurus emphasis in Hitler's chart, would have been totally changed if he had had the modern techniques of mid-points and harmonics, which reveal with intense clarity the *potential* for 'total destruction' that this man could release.[2] Likewise had Naylor been aware of the importance of comparing the charts of leaders and nations, an examination of Hitler's chart with that of the 1871 Empire and the Third Reich could only have led him to replace his judgement with the gravest warnings as to the 'fire' with which Hitler was playing.

World War Two is now of course often called 'Hitler's War. He was undoubtedly the catalyst, and any study of it must therefore start from a consideration of Hitler's chart and its relationship to the main charts for Germany. A preliminary discussion of his interaction with the chart of the German Empire was given in Chapter 13. Hitler through the Uranus, Neptune and Pluto contacts indicated there, was able to constellate some of the very deepest archetypal processes at work within the German psyche. Such archetypal processes are living ideas with a life of their own. As such when they are contacted they impel the soul to action, and do so in terms of the level of the ideals which the nation holds dear. Like grass breaking though reinforced concrete these archetypal principles, once awakened, will transform and reshape all they touch after the image of the ideals evoked. Tragically Hitler awakened these vital processes more at the level of the self-assertive, self-preservative, and self-expressive *instincts,* in the name of hate, aggression, and superiority rather than love, dignity and service. Thus whilst in the space of a few years he was able to galvanize and regenerate a broken and dispirited nation into becoming a world power, he inevitably also reaped the harvest of those predominantly negative guiding ideals. Figs 14.4 and 14.5 show the charts of Hitler and of the 1871 German Empire whose idea, power, and glory he sought to resurrect. Fig. 14.6 shows the moment he chose to crystalize this aspiration: the chart for the Proclamation of the Third Reich, which 'fixed' the interaction of Hitler and Germany and the traumatic release of collective energies that this permitted. The chart shown in Fig. 14.7 is set for exactly 11.00am, MET, the beginning of the ceremony. Some German astrologers take 11.07am as the key moment in the ceremony. This gives angles of: MC 22CP31, AS22TA23, MC/AS 22VI27. Whichever chart is taken, the outstanding feature is the VE-180-PL across the MC/IC exactly -90- UR and -45-NN. This of

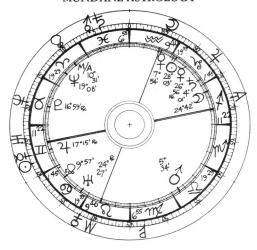

Figure 14.4 The German Empire: This is for the time of the Proclamation of William I as German Emperor at Versailles, France, 2E08, 48N48, at 13.00 LT, 18 January 1871. The mNN is 9CN07. The angles for this precise time are MC 10AQ00, AS 11GE49. Those given are as slightly rectified by Carter (IPA) in the light of experience.

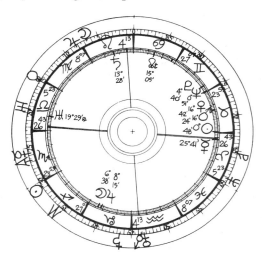

Figure 14.5 Adolf Hitler: This is exactly for the time given in the birth records, 18.30 LT = 5.38 pm GMT, 20 April 1889, Braunau, Austria, 13E03, 48N15. The mNN is 16CN04. The AS/MC is 15VI28 = SO.

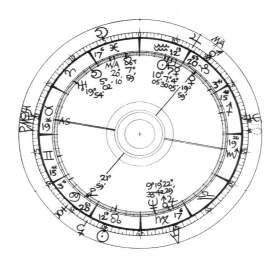

Figure 14.6 The Third Reich: Set for the Inauguration of Hitler as Chancellor at 11.00 MET, 30 January 1933, Berlin, 13E23, 52N30. The mNN is 9PI21. Some German astrologers take a later point in the ceremony at 11.07 am which gives angles of MC 22CP31, AS 22TA23, MC/AS 22PI27, exactly with JU.

course falls exactly with the 1871 Empire's NE-90-UR and Hitler's UR-AS-ME. At the same time the slow moving mid-points NE/PL at 15LE46 and PL/NN at 14TA58 are still in the area of the 1871 Pluto and Hitler's MA-VE.

As though to say that Hitler not only 'awakened' the 1871 Empire but also 'spoke' and put it into practice, we find here 1933 ME-0-SA-0-SO on Hitler's I.C. and exactly with the 1871 MC-0-VE. Note the Sun representing the *day* is exactly with the 1871 MC: 'today we focus upon our Empire's aspirations', whilst the Moon representing the *hour* is exactly -180- 1871 Mars and -90- 1871 Saturn, and with Hitler's PL/MC 4CN26 = MO 6CP38 = SA/NE 7CN09: 'at this hour we respond and evoke the nation's steely will (MA-90-SA) through our leader's striving aspiration to regenerate and give power to the masses (PL/MC = MO) through an appeal to a spirit of self-sacrifice and xenophobia (MO = SA/NE)'. Whilst at the *minute* of the ceremony we find that 'at this time and place: MC/AS = 20PI09, is evoked the 1871 UR/PL 20GE42, ability to build anew upon the ashes of the old, and, 1871 MO/JU 20PI50 expand the aspirations and homeland of the Empire, through the capacity of our leader's power to transform and regenerate the people: Hitler's MO/PL 20PI39!'

There are so many other remarkable interactions between these charts that it would seem as if all three moments are in fact simply different ways of looking at the same idea in different stages of manifestation. Each chart reflects a different stage of the process of the emergent German nation. They each represent as it were critical points, phases, in the unfoldment of a cycle of growth of a body politic. In this process Hitler can be seen as a specific specialized 'cell', as it were, giving precise conscious expression to the collective unconscious at this critical juncture in Germany's development.

This is perhaps most vividly reflected in the precise interaction of degree areas in these charts, as can be seen in the case of the degrees around 5° of the cardinal signs noted above. Another such area is about 9°30′ of the fixed signs/24°.30 of the mutables. Thus Charles Carter, in *IPA* pp.29-30, notes the immense sensitivity of the MC degree, 9AQ40 in the 1871 chart (which is also exactly -45- MO 24SG47), a degree which is stimulated over and over again throughout World War One. The JU-0-UR — that potentially colossally destructive combination — of 4 March 1914 fell at 9AQ33, whilst Uranus had retrograded to this same degree and minute on 4 August 1914. We likewise find Neptune 9LE30 -0- JU 10LE26 at the founding of the Nazi party, being in fact on the MC/AS, 8LE43, at the opening ceremony (19.30 MET, 24 February 1920, Munich, MC 23GE01, AS 24VI25). It can hardly be a surprise then when we find that Hitler has SA/MC 8LE50 = PL/NN 24GE52 = UR/NE 10LE10 = MA/MC 25GE18 = VE/MC 25GE27 = UR/PL 12LE05. This says: 'My conscious ambitions and fears (SA/MC) are interwoven with mass-movements of transformation (PL/NN) and the awakening of unconscious collective elements (UR/NE) which I can put into action by the conscious direction of my will (MA/MC), and ability to gain popularity (VE/MC) so as to rebuild again on the ruins (UR/PL)'. By falling in with the nation's conscious aspirations (MC) the whole process is released in a mutual interaction. As will be seen in Part 3 of this chapter when the UK declared war on Germany the MC, the focus of the moment, was at 9LE12 with the English 1066 MA at 8AQ28, and Winston Churchill's SA 9AQ36! And these are but some of the most obvious interweavings of this tragic, traumatic period of mankind's evolution. Further considerations of these issues are given by Liz Greene in *The Outer Planets*.[3]

The cyclical background to World War Two and the Cyclic Index

The famous 'no war' prediction of some of Britain's leading astrologers at the Harrogate Conference of 1939 led the then Astronomer Royal, Sir Hugh Spencer Jones to retort that if *he* were an astrologer he would be obliged to predict war. His historical understanding of the astrological tradition was that the times of great conjunctions indicated periods of change, crisis and major upheavals. He pointed out that the next few years 1940-41 would see a very rare thrice-repeated conjunction of Jupiter and Saturn, and that Jupiter and Saturn would then go on to form a multiple conjunction with Uranus during 1941.[4] As we astrologers now know to our embarrassment, this simple restatement of tradition by an outsider in fact proved to be of more value than the detailed considerations of all the experts who had somehow lost grip of the larger picture.

It would of course be foolish to pretend that these conjunctions alone would have been sufficient grounds for forecasting the crisis of the world civilization represented by World War Two. However these patterns ought to have been, as we now know from Barbault's studies, very important considerations for any astrologer attempting to assess the qualities of the time that lay ahead. Retrospectively we can now see that taking these major conjunctions together with the long-term Uranus-Neptune trine of 1938-45, and the general interactions of the collective planets Uranus/Neptune/Pluto by sextile aspect and by mid-point combinations during 1943-45, we obtain a picture of a sustained period when major transformative and purgative processes would be likely to be at work within the collective psyche, in a way that they had not been since 1914-18.

The Cyclic Index

We saw in Chapter 6, p.167, how the essence of this broad symbolic picture can be illustrated in quantitative terms by the Gouchon/Barbault 'Cyclical Index'. From Fig. 14.6 on p.389 we can see that the period 1940-44 was a time, like 1914-18, when, with the ending of so many cycles, things were, in Barbault's terms 'reverting to a primary chaos', to a death and dissolution, to a fresh 'seed time', as all the planets move closer and closer to one another at the end of so many of their cycles.

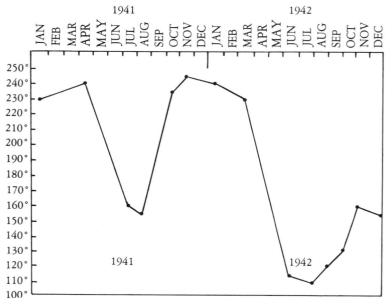

Figure 14.7   A detailed Cyclic Index for 1941/1942. This shows the
fluctuations at the very bottom of the graph shown in *Figure 6.1*.

Viewing this period of 'dissolution' in further detail, (Fig. 14.7),
Barbault suggests that the detailed fluctuations at the very bottom
of this curve, which is based on the elongation of all the planets for
1941-42, can be seen to closely parallel the key shift in the dominance
of action and reaction of the war during these years. Thus the first
months of 1941 marked a period of the consolidation of German
supremacy in Europe, and a relative slowing in the destructive
processes. Then as the planets begin to close up on one another once
again, on 6 April, the 'end of the cycle', disintegrative processes begin
to reassert themselves in full with the German invasion of Greece
and Yugoslavia, followed by the invasion of Russia on 22 June. After
the rapid string of German victories of July and August, the
momentum of world conflict is slowed as the planets begin to spread
out and we see the graph mount to a new point of momentary
maximum stability for the year with the check of German forces
outside Moscow at the end of November. But then almost at once
on 7 December, and for the next eight months, with the falling graph
the disintegrative process begins again. This time it is both in the

east with Pearl Harbour and the Japanese invasion of Dutch East India. Burma, Java, etc, and in the west with renewed German offensives, first in North Africa and then again in Russia. This new wave bottoms out just before the Germans are halted at the gates of Stalingrad at the end of August and it climbs to a new plateau in the next months with the Battle of El Alamein in October in the Russian counter-offensive and final surrender of von Paulus at Stalingrad in the January of 1943.

Such a simplified interpretation of complex events may perhaps seem naive. Yet just as we can learn a great deal from the graph of temperature during an illness, though it be only one measure of many complex interacting bodily functions, so too this Cyclic Index would seem to be giving us an eloquent account of certain aspects of the primary forces of dissolution and reaction within the collective. This is a promising approach and certainly one that deserves a thorough evaluation, in all its possible variations, for a sustained period of history. [5]

With this broad quantitative synthesis of prevailing conditions provided by the Cyclic Index we need now to make a qualitative assessment of the ideas and processes at work in the collective at this time. This we can approach by an examination of the key phases of the major planetary cycles. Let us examine some of these.

The major planetary cycles

To fully understand the place of World War Two in the evolution of European and world consciousness we would need to examine the whole range of charts for the main phases of all the great planetary cycles set for each of the major capitals of the world. Such a presentation would occupy a large book. But some measure of the importance of these charts can be gained from the examples below.

Fig. 14.8 shows the Great Mutation Conjunction, the JU-0-SA of 26 January 1842, 5.29 am GMT, set for Berlin. This is considered by many to lay the foundations of the 220-year Earth phase of the Jupiter-Saturn great 960-year cycle of the elements. As noted in Chapter 6 this cycle has been specifically related by Barbault to the unfoldment of Europe. Since the unification and development of Germany has played such a critical part in European history over the past century we might expect to find some contacts. We are not disappointed. We immediately note that the JU-0-SA was closely rising at Berlin. Turning to Fig. 14.4 we see that the German Empire

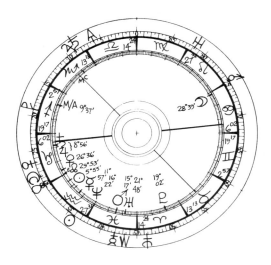

Figure 14.8 The Great Mutation Conjunction of 26 January 1842, at 05.29 am GMT, set for Berlin. This appears to remain an important chart and can transposed to other capitals. The Greenwich ST is 13h.41m.45s.

was founded almost an exact Saturn cycle later as Saturn -90-MA come to mutation AS. At the same time Neptune had come exactly -0-PL, whilst Uranus had come -135- the MC/AS at 9SG37. It was founded on the very *day* that SO-0-ME came -0- mutation VE-0-NN and -180-MO, and close to the *hour* that MO/JU 20PI58 was coming to mutation UR 21PI48, and to the point that was 'later' to be occupied by Hitler's MO/PL 20PI50 = ME/MA 6TA12 = JU/PL 21PI27 = MA/AS 6LE34! At the *minute* the MC-0-VE has just arrived with the SO-ME-NE stellium in Aquarius.

The contacts between this chart and Hitler's are no less impressive. It will be seen that his MO-0-JU is falling right with the AS and the mutation conjunction itself; his SA -90- mutation MC, his AS-ME -90- mut. MO-VE-NN, his IC -0- mut. SO, and perhaps particularly significantly Hitler's MC/AS 15VI27 with mut.MA 15PI17, his MA-0-VE in -90- mut Neptune, and his Uranus with mut.Pluto.

There is unfortunately not space to discuss and show the three NE-0-PL of 1891/92 or the five occurrences of UR-180-NE of 1908/09, but the former fell in 8GE35, 8GE20 and 7GE36 near the Empire AS and -120- Empire MC, as well as on the MC/AS of the

Great Mutation for Berlin. Presumbly such localized interweavings of cycles must be an important part of the hierarchy of such cycles. The UR-180-NE fell in 13CN/CP18, 14CN/CP46, 16CN/CP07, 17CN/CP59, and 18CN/CP55. It is presumably not without significance that these fell closely across Hitler's NN/SN, so that he was a natural 'earth' for these energies. The first UR-180-NE is in fact with the NN/SN at 14CN/CP13 and puts Mars exactly on the AS at Berlin in 00AR50 (AS 00AR25), and Jupiter 10LE52. The fourth and fifth closely trigger the Empire/Third Reich/Hitler NE/UR/UR. The fourth rises at Berlin (MC 24TA49, AS 18CP55). It is also noteworthy that the UR-120-NE of 1940/41, which represents the harvest phase of this process, closely configures both the Empire and the Third Reich charts with UR falling on the IC at Berlin. Not surprisingly, as we shall see below, this Uranus-Neptune and its later configurations with Pluto seem to be vital to an understanding of the underlying process being worked out in World War Two.

Figs. 14.10 and 14.11 show the -0- and the last of the -180 phases of the Saturn-Neptune cycles which lasted from 1 August 1917, 5.15am through until 1952/53. The cycle undoubtedly has to do with earthing visions, with self-sacrifice for a higher cause, and with everything from structuring Eutopias to becoming fixated on nightmare and phobic elements in the collective. In the highest sense it must have to do with 'purifying the collective vision' and squeezing out illusions, so that a purer, clearer, vision may flow. In a lower sense it relates all too closely to 'creating the pure State' through the sacrifice of 'inferior' or 'subversive' elements, as was seen on a horrendous scale during this cycle in Germany under Hitler, and Russia (created at this conjunction) under Stalin. Hitler had SA-72-NE as a key part of his extraordinary fifth-harmonic patterning,[2] in 72/144 AS and Moon-Jupiter. It is therefore not surprising to find him resonating strongly with this cycle. In Fig. 14.9 we see that this SA-0-NE fell with the Sun close to the Empire IC and exactly on Hitler's MC. At the same time here for Berlin the MC/AS 5CN43 is closely with the MA-0-PL which are exactly with Hitler's NE/MC 2CN32 and PL/MC 4CN26. This conjunction is of course also a key one for Russia's development and when transposed to St Petersburg (as then was) and Moscow makes interesting reading.

The three SA-180-NE all make fascinating reading. The first, 21 March 1936, 9.48am, fell at 14VI/PI59 with UR/PL 14GE22, right

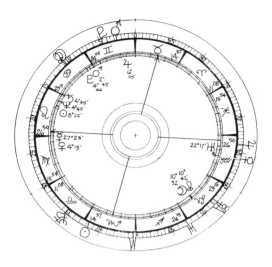

Figure 14.9   The SA-0-NE of 1 August 1917, 05.18 GMT set for Berlin.
The mNN is 9CP07 exactly -0- 1871 German SN. The AS/MC is 5CN43
-0-PL-MA. It is an important background chart for the period down to
1952/3.

across MC/AS. Combined with Uranus/Pluto this combination is
indicative of very profound revolutionary changes within the
collective, changes which Hitler was able to articulate and bring into
'this time and place' (MC/AS). Perhaps significantly Jupiter at this
time was at 23SG47 on the Empire Moon, indicating a cycle focused
on popular expansion amidst the 'revolutionary discipline' of the
SA = NE = UR/PL. The second SA-180-NE, shown in Fig. 14.10 is
exactly -90-JU and again with UR/PL at 18GE37, and exactly on
the MC/AS at 18GE41. This is with the Empire JU 17GE15 (and
UR/PL) 20GE43), and with Hitler's SO/MC 17GE3135, whilst the
AS at Berlin is exactly on his Saturn. The MC is close -90- Empire
Uranus. The Berlin-Rome Axis was formed by Hitler and Mussolini
on 25 October following this opposition. Figure 14.10a shows the
third -180- on 18 January 1937, 02.21am fell at 18VI/PI45 across
the MC/IC in Berlin (MC 14VI31, AS 22SC28, MC/AS 18LI29).
The MC/AS is with JU/PL 19LI09 exactly with that sensitive degree
in the German charts. The SO 27CP36 is with the Empire Sun, whilst
Moon at 4AR57 falls with the Third Reich Moon and Empire

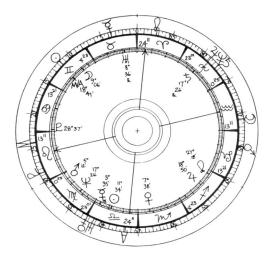

Figure 14.10 The second SA-180-NE of 4 October 1936, 23-42 GMT, Berlin. The mNN is 28SG12. The AS/MC is 18GE41 = JU 18SG50 = UR/PL 18GE36 = SA = NE. See text.

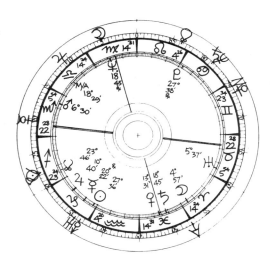

Figure 14.10a The third SA-180-NE of 18 January 1937, 02.21 GMT set for Berlin. The mNN is 22SG38. The MC/AS is 18LI29 = JU/PL 19LI09, a critical polarity in the German charts. See text.

MA-90-SA. With such intimate interconnections Germany might be said to have been destined to become a focal point of these deep transformative and purgative collective processes. These might be seen to have reached their terrible final 'fruition' with the incoming SA-90-NE of 2 July 1944 at 1CN/LI34, of 8 January 1945 at 6CN/LI26, and 6 April 1945 at 4CN/LI46, the latter of course falling exactly with the critical 4-6 of the cardinal signs.

We now need to examine how these longer-terms cycles are focused within the year. This is of course the role of the solar cycle which we can focus by an examination of the cardinal ingresses and finally by the actual Sun-planet cycles.

Ingresses

The pressures for survival mean that the responses of the collective tend to be at their most stark, primitive and immediate during times of war. Thus we might expect the ingress charts covering World War Two to be particularly eloquent in their description of subsequent events and collective responses. By and large this is certainly the case. Whilst these annual cycles, by their very nature, cannot describe the overall course of a war, which unfolded over five and a half years, they do seem to mark out many of the key issues for each of the main theatres of war. It should be said however that such charts could not, in isolation, be expected to indicate that a global war would definitely break out, or that it was in fact going to continue. At any time we can only interpret them, and make inferences from them, in the light of the background of the period.

There is only space here to examine a few such charts and so we will concentrate principally on examining the Aries ingresses related to the outbreak of the war in 1939 and the close of war in 1945. However in general terms it is of interest that Neptune entered 0° Libra in October 1942 and was within 5° of the 0°, 90°, 180°, of the Sun at each of the cardinal ingresses for much of the war, indicating a period when 'the world in general' (0° Aries) 'will be going through a process of refinement, and a dissolving of existing forms'. The importance of the NE-120-UR and -60- PL for this war period is examined further below. It is also notable that on 20 June 1944, shortly after the D-Day landings, Saturn moved into Cancer forming -90-NE on 2 July. Thus the 1944 Cancer ingress, which marked the beginning of the final harrowing sacrifices of the war, was both -0-SA and -90-NE: 'the world in general faces self-abnegation and sacrifice for its ideals'.

It has been pointed out, by Carter[6] and others, that the problem about ingress charts is that they are the same the world over except for the angles, and that they cannot therefore be expected to show a great deal for any particular nation. Yet in a sense we can see that as the world shrinks this feature is a positive advantage. For in fact increasingly the world does appear to respond en masse to cosmic indications, rather than as separate nations. Thus whilst a hundred years ago each nation might to some extent pursue its own internal economic system, we now live in a world which is becoming almost entirely economically interdependent, with the instant transfer of credit by electronic impulses from one part of the globe to another. Likewise we now live in an era when wars can no longer be readily contained but tend to have a dramatic impact on the whole earth, as witness the very possibility of two 'world' wars this century, something which would have been impossible prior to the advent of modern methods of rapid transport and telecommunication (the shadow side of the epoch shaping 1891-92 NE-0-PL in 8°-9° Gemini).

This said, whilst the overall 'message' of the time may be similar for everyone its impact will be different according to the perspective from which it is seen, and we can still expect that the charts set for the different capitals will focus on a different and appropriate part of the same underlying story.

The 1939 Aries ingress

Turning to the Aries ingress for 1939 we must ask ourselves whether, in the light of current methods of interpretation, this chart in fact indicated the danger of war during the year. As we saw in Chapter 9, some of the best astrologers in Britain, having examined this chart, declared for 'peace in our time'. Carter (IPA) in voicing regret over his part in this judgement concludes that it is the technique of ingresses that has 'been weighed in the balance and found wanting'. To conclude otherwise he considers 'would condemn too many able astrologers'.[7]

Yet in the light of the highly unstable world situation at the time, even a cursory examination of this chart set for London (Fig. 14.11) would hardly be reassuring to an astrologer using modern techniques. Considering the positions in the 90° circle it would be impossible to ignore the extremely close SO-MA = UR axis, reflecting the exact SO-90-MA, -45-UR — hardly the most pacific of configurations.

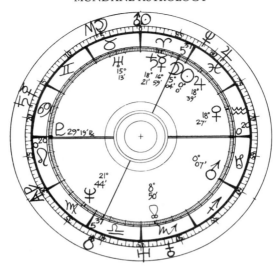

Figure 14.11 The 1939 Aries Ingress, 21 March, 12.28 GMT, set for London. The mNN is 10SC40. The MC/AS 2GE58 = SA = UR/NE = VE/JU ('destroyed hopes') and 7 other mid-points. 'No War!' was the judgement from this chart in 1939 by leading british astrologers. Pluto was still little used and mid-points were almost unknown. PL = SA/NN ('Sacrificing oneself for others . . . mourning and bereavement') SO-90-MA and -135-UR threatens violent self-assertion and confrontation by world leaders, and 'military call up'. Here for Britain the MC is exactly with the MO-90-SA/NE at 5CN03 indicating the forthcoming need for the people (MO) to be prepared for 'readiness for sacrifice, suffering, and renunciation . . .'. The Third Reich Moon was at 5AR02! As can be seen in Fig. 14.14 SA was -90-NE at this same point at the 1945 Aries Ingress bringing this period of 'sacrifice and suffering' to its final culmination. (All quoted interpretations from COSI.)

Pluto rising, whilst -120- SO is also close -180- SA/NN (10' with mean NN and 44' for true NN), an indication of great collective mourning and bereavement in the offing, and of mass suffering and sacrifice. The AS itself is -90-SA/UR at 1TA47, an indication of pressures and tensions and the need for great determination and powers of resistance. Likewise the MC-0-MO exactly -90-SA/NE 5CN03 speaks of the need for self-sacrifice on the part of the people, whilst the extremely difficult and problematic SA = -90-UR/NE 18CN29 — 'depression, instability, pessimism — a painful loss,

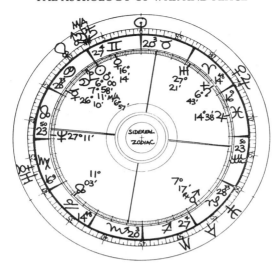

Figure 14.12   The Cancer sidereal ingress of 17 July 1939, 09.13.34 GMT, for London. The AS/MC is 6CN57! The Ayanamsa is 23° 54′ and this should be added to the positions shown to obtain the equivalent tropical zodiac positions.

mourning or bereavement' (COSI) is found to be -45-MC/AS 2GE59, focusing it 'at this time and place'.

The 1939 tropical and sidereal Cancer ingresses
The tropical Cancer ingress, 22 June 1939, 07.39.20 GMT, for London, which immediately preceded the outbreak of war is equally problematic. It shows an exactly culminating SA 28AR59 = JU/UR 28AR24, -90-PL 00LE12, and -90-MA 4AQ42. At London the MC 26AR14, AS13LE57 gives an MC/AS 20GE05 = NE 20VI39 = MA 4AQ42 = MA/NN 20SG50, indicative of an extremely tough period with the likelihood of disappointments, and difficulties.

   The Cancer sidereal ingress, 17 July 1939, 09.13.34 GMT, set for London, is shown in Fig. 14.12. If one chart will convince us of the sidereal zodiac and that the Fagan-Bradley ayanamsa is correct, then this is it! Here we find an almost exact MO-0-PL -180-MA, -90-SA and the whole configuration *exactly* on the MC/AS — a devastating testimony of harsh struggles ahead. The AS is very close to the PL/NN and SA/NN. Intriguingly the sidereal AS is exactly on the position of the UK's tropical SA. Does this represent a kind of sympathetic resonance between the two zodiacs perhaps?

The 1945 Aries ingress
Our final example illustrates the immense value of Jim Lewis' Astrocartography in identifying where planets will fall angular. Fig. 14.13 shows the moment of the 1945 Aries ingress projected on the map of the world, whilst Figs 14.14, 14.15, 14.16, 14.17 show this same map set for London, Berlin, Washington, and Tokyo. It will be seen that the geometry of this ingress is such that important bodies appear angular in all these major capitals simultaneously. (It may perhaps be that such *simultaneous* precise angularities over major foci of collective consciousness and decision-making is an important clue in assessing the global significance of such ingresses.)

Starting with Fig. 14.14, set for London, we see that Jupiter is exactly culminating. At this stage in the war this must be seen as encouraging. When turning to Britain's leaders' charts we see that this exact JU-MC echoes the King's own JU-0-MC, falling exactly on George VI's[8] 'victorious' VE/MC 21VI22 = SO 21SG65 = MC 6LE59 = VE/JU 22VI11 = JU/MC 7LE47 = JU 8LE36, and that this point also exactly coincides with Winston Churchill's[9] 'victorious' VE 22SG02 = JU/PL 7LE29, and exactly -120 Churchill's Pluto at 21TA25. We can be confident that this cycle will see some kind of triumph. The fact that the ingress MC/AS 24LI50 = 9GE35 = MA/JU 9SG11 is also indicative of 'sudden successes' but is also a clear signal that there may be a revolt against 'the powers that be' during this cycle, or as COSI puts it: '. . . the urge for freedom an active resistance to guardianship or to tutelage . . .'. Thus Churchill the 'great war hero' (JU/MA) was to be suddenly and dramatically rejected by the people later in this cycle (see under 'Eclipses' in Chapter 9).

Turning to Berlin (Fig. 14.15) we have a very different picture. As we can see on the map the SO-180-NE falls across the MC/IC through Germany and down through Italy, whilst Uranus is setting. In the actual chart we see how devastatingly the Berlin MC is picking up the full impact of the T-square with MO-SA, which of course cannot be shown on the map as such. This would be problematic enough but as we noted above, this SA-90-NE is also falling exactly on the highly critical 4-6 cardinals area of the German charts, the Empire SA-90-MA, the Third Reich Moon, and of course Hitler's PL/MC = MO = SA/NE. In addition we may note that MC/AS

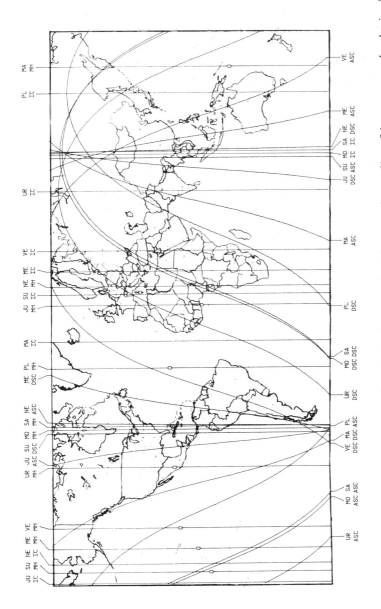

Figure 14.13   Shows the Astrocartography for the Aries ingress 1945. A better understanding of these maps can be obtained by comparing this with the individual relocated charts for this ingress given over.

Figures 14.14 — 14.17   These show the Aries ingress of 20 March 1945, 23.37.11 GMT, set for London, Berlin, Washington, and Tokyo. mNN 14CN38. To relocate this for other areas the Greenwich ST is 11.29.43.

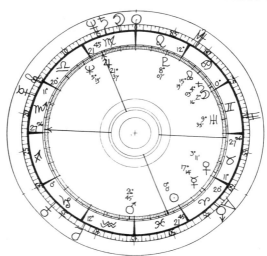

Figure 14.14   The 1945 Aries ingress set for London. AS/MC 24LI50 = 135-UR.

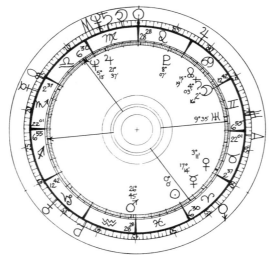

Figure 14.15   The 1945 Aries ingress set for Berlin. AS/MC 6SC42 = -90-PL.

Figure 14.16 The 1945 Aries ingress set for Washington DC. AS/MC
19LE46 = SA/NE.

Figure 14.17 The 1945 Aries ingress set for Tokyo. AS/MC 4AR54 =
NE = SA.

6SC42 is -90-PL, a critical configuration potentially indicating a period of major 'elimination and regeneration', but made the more critical by the fact that this is closely with UR/NE 7LE24 for which COSI says 'the abandonment of resistance, the necessity to give in, great losses, calamities, catastrophes'. (The same configuration was operative at the time of the US withdrawal from Vietnam.) The significance of this picture is made personal for Germany by the fact that it falls close to the IC of the 1871 chart, on the Third Reich Saturn, and of course with Hitler's MC. Interestingly the MC of the AH/1871 composite chart (a valuable technique in this context) is 6TA47. It is also more exactly -45-/-135- Hitler's SO/SA 22GE08 = NE/NN 22GE58. There are many other factors. An interesting detail is the placement of NN close to cusp 8 at 15CN19, thus this is almost exactly Hitler's NN return (cf. JFK assassination).

Transposing the chart to Washington (Fig. 14.16) we may be forgiven for wondering if this does not in one fell stroke demolish the value of these charts. For here is a chart which, although it admittedly does not have the MC/AS = PL, is quite as problematic as that for Berlin. Furthermore we may note that the culminating MO-0-SA falls exactly with the US VE-0-JU, whilst the rising Neptune is close to that hightly problematic area in the US chart. Additionally the ruler Venus is -0-cusp 8, admittedly -60-MO-SA but also -90-PL and -150- rising NE. What could we reasonably predict from this chart? Blows to national prestige, losses, suffering, mourning and bereavement would certainly have to come into the picture. Just 23 days after the start of this cycle on 12 April at 3.35pm War Time in Warm Springs , Oklahoma, President Roosevelt who had been the 'Father of the Nation' since 1933, suddenly died of a cerebral haemorrhage. At 7.09pm Harry Truman took the oath of office. [10] That this was to be a critical period for Roosevelt is shown by his chart[11] which has Moon at 6CN06, whilst Pluto has just crossed his exact VE-90-SA in 6TA/AQ06G and is moving to -180- his Sun. (A comparison of this chart with the German charts makes interesting reading.) Of course this ingress also covers the continuing heavy loss of US lives in the war in the Far East and the traumatic decision to drop the atomic bomb, and its harrowing aftermath for the American people.

Finally, in the chart set for Tokyo, Fig, 14.17, the first thing we note is the PL = UR/NE on the IC exactly -0- VE 8LE07, the AS ruler of the 14 July 1853 Japanese chart. This also falls with the IC 2LE and SA 16LE28, SA/IC 9LE14 of the 11 February 1889, 10.30am, Japanese Constitution chart. This is also exactly -90- to the Emperor Hirochito's MC ruler VE 8TA07 and SO 8TA31, whilst Mars, which is -90-AS, is exactly -180- Hirohito's MA 26LE31. This is highly appropriate but what about the cathartic ingress T-square? If any place on earth 'suffered and sacrificed' and went through the SA-NE 'refiner's fire' it was Japan with Hiroshima and Nagasaki. Not surprisingly then we find here 'at this time and place' the MC/AS is 4AR51 exactly placing this SA-90-NE process at the heart of the Japanese Empire. Turning to the AS we find that it is close to the 1852 Saturn 28TA40, and to the 1889 Neptune at 29TA31, thus bringing out the SA-0-NE between these two charts and 'tuning the charts to the time'. The AS is also exactly -90- ingress JU/PL 29LE52 which in its negative manifestation COSI says is 'loss of social standing . . . the misfortune to lose everything . . .'. Jupiter is about to make its outgoing -45-PL = UR/NE with both factors configuring Hirohito's Moon at 22VI39 indicating the potential of his people (Moon) 'losing everything', and having to 'abandon resistance'. The AS is also -45-SN which is with Hirohito's JU-0-SA indicating that an important restructuring of his life, and all that it represents, is likely to begin during this cycle.

Space does not permit discussion of this chart set for Moscow but readers will note from 14.13 that Venus, planet of Victory, falls exactly on the IC. Comparison of this position with Russia's chart in the next chapter makes interesting reading.

Such a study as the above certainly does not 'prove' that ingresses work in isolation. But we can see that, when considered alongside the charts of the nations and their leaders in an already known general context, that they can give extremely powerful signals as to what will be unfolding at that time and place for that nation. Of course not all ingresses are so starkly dramatic. What appear to be highly critical ingresses can come and go without any very obvious large-scale effect, though their general symbolism is usually seen to work out at some level. To assess the level of manifestation ahead from such charts we will need to see these threads of the tapestry in relation to the major cycles, and develop an understanding of the principles on which these interweavings operate.

From the ground-base of the slow outer-planet cycles and these annual cycles we can now turn to see how the fast synods of Mars and the Sun trigger these larger processes. Mars will tend to precipitate latent processes into action whilst the Sun seems to measure the approximate day on which they will be likely to occur.

The Sun and Mars cycles to outer planets in World War Two
At the opposite end of the scale to the major conjunctions and the cumulative approach of the Cyclic Index, is the consideration of the 'trigger' effect of simple fast-moving cycles of the Sun and Mars as they pass over the collective planets Uranus, Neptune, and Pluto each year (Sun) and two year (Mars). Taking World War Two as a collective crisis and transformative process for mankind as a whole, we might expect appropriately significant events to occur around the times that these outer, collective planets were brought into high focus and activated by conjunctions from the will-centred and decision-making planets Sun and Mars.

A modified and adapted version of a study by Barbault of the Sun and Mars cycles, with Mars-Pluto conjunctions added to complete the picture, is given below. Whilst in theory Barbault allows an orb of up to + / − 12°, in practice the average orb he uses is less than 4° and few examples go beyond 8°. If these orbs seem at first glance rather large, we must remember that we are here concerned with specific events as symbolic foci of collective processes, which seldom occur overnight! Even allowing a conjunction aspect of 15°, as he does on one occasion for the Sun, we are still only looking at 1/12th part of the planets' total cycle, i.e. one month of the year. In fact most events are within a week of the exact aspect.

When making and evaluating this kind of study it is a good idea to consider the complete sequence of events as a whole prior to attempting to assess the appropriateness or otherwise of isolated examples. We should not forget that we are looking at what would normally be considered extremely transitory factors, some of the last 'wards in the lock'! This, and the similar studies of Barbault, point to such solar and inner planet transits as vitally important links in the unfoldment of time. Their very speed of movement must make them invaluable for picking up important clues as to the underlying meaning of slower-moving configurations.

During 1940-45 there were a total of 27 conjunctions of Sun and/or Mars to Uranus, Neptune and Pluto. These are shown and numbered from 1-27 in Fig. 14.18. Some of the main events associated with these periods are given in the appropriately numbered paragraphs below. The figures in brackets after the date indicate the actual orb in degrees and decimals of a degree.

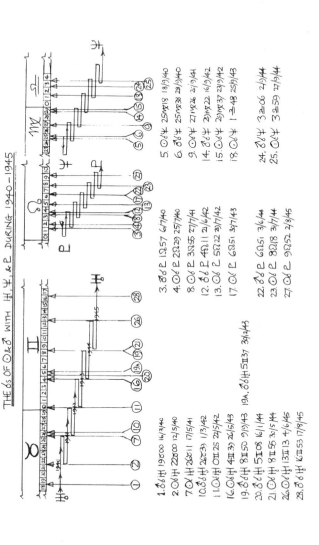

Figure 14.18   The 29 conjunctions of the SO and MA with UR, NE, PL during World War Two. Some of the attendant events are listed in the text. From the upper section of the diagram it can be seen that these conjunctions almost all occur very close to the station points of the planets. This is particularly the case with the conjunctions to Uranus. A comparison of these points with the charts of the various belligerent nations and their leaders makes instructive reading.

1940

1.   MA-0-UR, 16 March: 19th (2) air raids on London resumed. 20th (2.5) Yugoslav pact with Germany. 27th (6) Paul of Yugoslavia deposed in *coup d'état*. 9 April (15: exceptional orb), Germany invades Norway and Denmark.

2.   SO-0-UR, 12 May: 10 May (2.5) Germany invades Holland, Luxembourg, Belgium.

3.   MA-0-PL, 6 July (6), USSR invades Rumania. 3rd (2), Royal Navy sinks French Fleet. 5th (1), Vichy France breaks relations with Britain. 9th (2.5) RAF begin night bombing of Germany.

4.   SO-0-PL, 25 July: 18th (7), formation of Japanese 'war' cabinet. 1 August (6), occupation of Tonkin by Japanese, and annexation of Baltic States and Bessarabia by USSR (to 6th).

5&6.   SO-0-MA-0-NE: 18-28 September: 27th (MA-NE: 1), Germany-Italy-Japan economic and military pact. 19th (SO-NE: 1, SO-MA: 6), USA halts **steel** exports to Japan.

1941

7.   SO-0-UR, 17 May: From end of April Wehrmacht occupies most of Western Europe. 10th (6), London's heaviest air raid. 14th (3), Vichy endorsement of Darlan-Hitler agreement. 19th (1.5), Germans invade Crete.

8.   SO-0-PL, 27 July: 23/25th (4/2), All Japanese funds in US/Britain frozen. 27th (0), Germans enter Ukraine, and Japanese troops enter Indo-China.

9.   SO-0-NE, 20 September: 17th (3.5), Shah of Persia abdicates. 19th (1), Germans take Kiev. 29th (8), US/UK/USSR war supply Conference in Moscow.

1942

10.   MA-0-UR, 1 March: 15 Feb (8.5), Singapore surrenders to Japan. 28 Feb (1), Japan invades Java. 9 March (5.5), Java and Rangoon surrender.

11.   SO-0-UR, 22 May. 20th (2), Germans take Kech peninsula. 26th (3.5), Rommel resumes major tank assault in Libya: Anglo-Soviet treaty/alliance. 30th (7), first 1000-bomber raid on Cologne.

12.   MA-0-PL, 21 June: period of severe British losses in North Africa. 21st (0), Rommel takes Tobruk, and heavy British-Malta convoy losses. 28th (4.5), Eighth Army retreats to El Alamein. German counter-attack in Kharkov.

13.   SO-0-PL, 29 July: 28th (1), Germans take Rostov, overrun nothern Caucasus.

14&15.   SO-0-MA-0-NE, 16-28 Sept: 23rd (SO-NE:0, MA-NE:4), Russian counter-offensive near Stalingrad begins.

1943

16.   SO-0-UR, 26 May: 22nd (4), stepping up of air offensive on Germany. End May (2-4), Roosevelt-Churchill 'Trident' Conference, decision on Allied invasion of Europe.

17.   SO-0-PL, 30 July: 26th (4.5) Fall of Mussolini, dissolution of Facist Party.

18.   SO-0-NE, 25 Sept: mid-month major Russian victories. 24-25th (1), cross Dneiper, take Smolensk. 1 Oct. (5.5), Italy declares war on Germany.

19.   MA-0-UR, 9 Sept-in orb until 7 march 1944: Sustained period of major assault on Axis powers, intense fighting on all fronts. 3 Sept. (3), invasion of Italy, unconditional surrender 8th (5).

1944

20.   MA-0-UR, orb 1 through 1-23 Jan: Major battles of Italian campaign. Massive RAF bombing of Berlin, 20th provokes British protest.

21.   SO-0-UR, 30 May: 4 June (4.5), Rome taken. 6th (6), D-Day landings.

22.   MA-0-PL, 3 June: 4 June (0.5), Rome taken. 6th (1.5), D-Day landings.

23.   SO-0-PL, 31 July: 25th (6), Allies demand unconditional surrender of Germany and Japan, 30th (1), US breakthrough in Normandy. 1 Aug (1), Warsaw rising begins.

24.   MA-0-NE, 2 Sept: 25 Aug. (5), Paris liberated. 31 Aug. (2), Russians take Bucharest. 3 Sept. (0), Brussels liberated. 5th (1.5), USSR declares war on Bulgaria. 12th (4), Roumanian armistice.

25.   SO-0-NE, 27 Sept, Dumbarton Oaks Conference for post-war planning lays groundwork for UNO began 21 Aug-ends 29 Sept. (17-27 (10-0), abortive Battle of Arnhem.)

1945

26.   SO-0-UR, 4 June: 5th (1), Germany divided into four zones of occupation under control of Allied Control Commission.

27.   SO-0-PL, 2 Aug. 27 MA-0-UR, 17 Aug: 6th Hiroshima and

USSR invasion (SO-PL: 3.5, MA-UR: 7.5). 9th, (SO-PL: 6, MA-UR: 4.5), Nagasaki 14th (SP-PL:11, MA-UR: 2.5), Japanese surrender ends World War Two.

USSR invasion (SO-PL: 3.5, MA-UR: 7.5). 9th, (SO-PL: 6, MA-UR: 4.5), Nagasaki 14th (SP-PL:11, MA-UR: 2.5), Japanese surrender ends World War Two.

Space precludes presenting a similarly suggestive study of Barbault for the period 1932-39 showing the correlation of these same Sun, Mars cycles to Uranus, Neptune, and Pluto in relation to the build up to World War Two.

Summary
With hindsight, we can see from the above that each of the hierarchy of cycles and charts discussed contributes something to a cumulative understanding of the tragic picture of World War Two. Much remains to be uncovered but it is clear that such methods when fully understood will enable us to read in prospect as well as in retrospect the way in which Eternal Ideas are interwoven on the loom of Time. This does not mean that World War Two was inevitable or that our future is predestined.

However this study does reveal that we are far more circumscribed than we might like to imagine. For we must remember that, barring cosmic changes, the future interweavings of the planets most certainly *are* totally preordained. All such future patterns are in one very real sense 'already there'. Thus the only way in which mankind can change its future is by making a shift in its level of consciousness. Only in this way can we give expression to these same creative and destructive processes of the Cosmos on higher and deeper planes. We only receive what we are open to receive, so that as long as we persist in conducting our affairs at a mass level of instinct, opinion, and prejudice, and primitive self-interest, then these great archetypal processes of the cosmos will inevitably continue to express themselves on that plane.

If we can as individuals, and as groups of individuals, raise our consciousness so that we are operating on the level of true Reason then the cycles that unfold Eternity in Time will express themselves in like manner. Understood and harnessed at a higher, inner, individual, level these energies offer us all an infinite potential to use and be of service in ever increasing consciousness. With such an awareness mankind can begin to transcend and transmute his instinctive impulses and soar into the Empyrean.

In a full understanding of 'the harmonics of cosmic periods' we will find descriptions of the interfaces between man and man, man and nation, nation and nation, between man and Cosmos and the Creator. However terrible World War Two, through its full analysis, and the analysis of current affairs, we can begin to see these harmonic processes made visible. By perservering in our exploration it is certain that the 'waves and particles' of the different levels of consciousness within the Whole, will begin to become self-evident.

So now if, learning from the past, we would embark upon such celestial interpretations of the future, let us aspire first to become true philosophers, that we may be worthy to join with Plato and, as worthy 'spectators of all time and existence', bring not only prophecy but real understanding, wherein must lie the seed of mankind's transformation.

References

1 ISWCA, *The Astrology of World War Two,* ISCWA, Summer, 1984.

2 For a detailed study of this chart and other in the light of harmonic and mid-point techniques see: Harvey, C. *Astrology and Human Potential,* Sofia, Summer, 1984; Harvey, C. *Midpoints — An Archetypal Approach,* Sofia, Summer, 1984.

3 Greene, Liz, *The Outer Planets and Their Cycles* — The Astrology of the Collective, CRCS Publications, 1983.

4 This conjunction was at its most intense at the Full Moon on 11th May 1941, when SA, SO, UR, VE, ME, JU were all within 8°05′ opposed by the Moon. At this lunation PL fell on the IC for London. The preceding day the British House of Commons was destroyed in a massive bombing raid. This also coincided with Hess's flight to Scotland.

5 See *L'Astrologue,* no.61, 1983, for computer-produced graphs of the Cyclic Index covering every century from 1,000 AD.

6 Carter, C.E.O., IPA, p.44.

7 ibid., p.47.

8 George VI was born at 3.05am GMT, 14th December 1895, Sandringham, according to official records. MC 6LE59, AS 27LI14, SO 21SG55, MO 24SC52, ME 18SG15, VE 5SC46, MA 1SG22, JU 8LE36R, SA 14SC46, UR 22SG09, NE 16GE30, PL 11GE30, mNN 7PI28, tNN 6PI57.

9　Churchill was born 30 November 1874, at 01.30 am, in Blenheim Palace, 51N50, 1W22, according to a letter from his father written on the day. This time is LT = 01.35.28″ am GMT. MC 1CN09, AS 00LI53, SO 7SG43, MO 29LE40, ME 17SC36, VE 22SG02R, MA 16LI34, JU 23LI34, SA 9AQ36, UR 15LE14R, NE 28AR26R, PL 21TA25R, tNN 26AR551, mNN 24AR22.

10　Front page story of the 'Oklahoma Morning Post', 13 April 1945.

11　Roosevelt was born at 8.45pm LT, 30th January 1882, New york, according to his father's diary MC 22Ge11, AS23VI19, MC/AS 7LE45, SO 11AQ08, MO 6CN15, ME 27AQ11, VE 6AQ03, MA 27GE01, JU 16TA56, SA 6TA03, 17VI57, NE 13TA50, PL 27TA22, tNN 7SG10, mNN.

Bibliography

For anyone wishing to make further detailed examination of the period of World War Two there are several detailed, day-by-day accounts available. There is some discrepancy between these sources on specific incidents and none of them can be entirely relied upon for detail.

ARGYLE, CHRISTOPHER, *Chronology of World II*, pp.200, Marshall Cavendish, 1980. A basic sketch outline of 6,300 + main events from 1/9/39-30/9/45 categorized under 8 different heads. Analysis of 10 key turning points. Maps and photos.

GORALSKI, ROBERT, *World War II Almanac 1931-1945*, A Political and Military Record, pp.486, Hamish Hamilton 1981. Covers 18/9/31-2/9/45. Includes maps, photos, statistical tables, and useful bibliography.

SALMAGGI, CESARE, & PALLAVISIN, ALFREDO, *2194 Days of War*, pp.754, Arnoldo Mondadori, Milano 1977, English translation, Windward 1979. 620 illustrations, 84 maps. Covers 29/9/38-2/9/45. This is the most complete chronology we have come across. It often contains precise times of events, though these are not always reliable, and often lack time standard used. (e.g., Hiroshima time is 75 minutes in error.)

YOUNG, BRIGADIER PETER, *The Almanac of World War Two*, pp.624, Hamlyn 1981. pp.346 of chronology, outline 1919-39, detail 12/8/39-12/9/45. pp.159 on the combatants and their weaponry. pp.91 of some 400 brief biographies of key personalities (birth/death years only). pp.16 of colour maps and photos.

Part 3: Astrological Timing

Nicholas Campion

The progress of the Second World War of 1939-45, and of certain events which produced the war, offers astrologers a valuable chance to observe in detail certain aspects of mundane astrology. If we conceive of war as an outbreak of mass psychosis, in which the entire 'body politic' exhibits the symptoms of such an outbreak, then we must assume that, in accordance with long-stated mundane theory, the people involved in such situations are acting as slaves to the stars. The sequence of events in a war situation should therefore be highly 'fated', that is, outside the control of individual free will. It follows that the timing of political and military events in the war should theoretically be reflected very exactly in astrological correlations. Such a proposition may be tested, and the Second World War offers us ample opportunity to do this for over a period of six years it involved a large number of independent countries in a complex interlocking of invasion and counterinvasion. The material can thus supply us both with sufficient evidence on which to test our hypotheses, and sufficient proof for us to make some highly valid conclusions on political events, and the relationship of the microcosm of human society to the macrocosm of the planetary spheres.

Examining some thirty charts concerning the war between Germany and the UK, France USA and USSR, we may make the following conclusions.

1. Mundane horoscopes pertaining to a particular country, or a
    related sequence of events (such as a war) form part of a series

of horoscopes which illustrate successive incarnations on the physical plane of psychic changes in the collective. This fact should be demonstrated by the repetition of important degree areas in the charts.

2. Horoscopes may also be related to each other in a 'horizontal' sense, i.e., horoscopes for different countries may relate to each other through being created at a close date, perhaps deriving from the same event. This shows clearly in the charts for Nazi Germany and Independent Poland where both horoscopes derived from the upheavels of World War One.

3. A national chart contains the potential for all events affecting that nation, so long as it remains the functioning national chart. Within this framework the potential is continually modified for the event charts for major points in the nation's history.

4. Horoscopes for events in which more than one country is involved may combine significant elements from the national charts of the respective countries.

5. There is a hierarchy of manifestation in political events from the ideal plane through to the physical. This is reflected in astrology in that there is a sequence of horoscopes from, for example, an order being given to carry out an invastion (the realm of thought, the ideal plane), to the actual invasion (the physical plane).

6. There is a hierarchy in astrological timing from general conditions of stress set up by outer planets transiting a national chart, down to the precise timing of events which express that tension. Thus a transit of Pluto or Uranus may indicate a year of tension, the progressed Moon a month, transiting Mars the week, transiting Sun the day, transiting Moon, the hour, and finally the degree of the ecliptic rising, the minute, of a particular event. This 'hierarchy of timing' is not a perfect system, but it may frequently be observed in outline.

The origins of the war

A common view of World War Two is that its origins lay in the unsatisfactory terms of the peace settlement following World War One, terms which are said to have been responsible for the deep desire in Germany for a reversal of the settlement. World War Two is in part seen as the culmination of an explosion of German resentment, fuelled by other factors which we will not discuss here. We may test this hypothesis astrologically by taking the dates for the ending of

World War One and the Peace Treaty, and examining whether key degree areas repeated in the horoscopes for Nazi Germany and the beginning of World War Two. The areas which we might expect to see repeated would be those occupied by the Sun (the soul of a country), the Moon (the mass will) and the ascendant and Midheaven (the incarnation of the collective psyche in the State).

The Armistice which ended the fighting between Germany and the western Allies was signed on 11 November 1918, and the Treaty of Versailles, which fixed the peace settlement in the west, came into force on 20 January 1920. We find that on the first date the Sun was at 18° Scorpio, while on the second, the Sun was at 19° Capricorn, and we would expect these degrees to be repeated in the subsequent charts. It is therefore remarkable that at the time of the swearing in of Adolf Hitler as Chancellor (from which point we date Nazi Germany), the ascendant was at 19°26′ Taurus, and the Midheaven (MC) was at 20°53′ Capricorn (Fig. 14.7). From this we see how the settlement of World War One planted a seed in the German collective unconscious, a seed which was embodied in the position of the Sun in the two charts relating to the end of the war. When finally a regime came to power which was sworn to undo the peace, the Sun positions in the earlier charts were 'incarnated' in the angles of the regime's chart. We may make two further observations of technical importance:

1. It is degree *polarities* rather than single degrees which are important, so that we find the Sun at the Armistice of 1918 at 18° Scorpio, but the ascendant in the Nazi chart at 19° Taurus.
2. It is degree *areas* rather than single degrees which are important, so that the Sun at the Treaty of Versailles was 19° Capricorn but the MC in the Nazi chart was almost 21° Capricorn. We will find that such a degree area extends over perhaps four of a particular pair of opposing signs.

This chart for the swearing in of Hitler as Chancellor (which we shall refer to as the 'Nazi chart') is important, for, just as German aggression initiated World War Two, so this horoscope was to be the foundation for the astrology of the entire war in Europe, right up to the final armistice. In particular we should note the extremely powerful conjunction of the Sun, Mercury and Saturn in Aquarius, the Moon at 5° Aries and the Mars-Jupiter conjunction at 19°22′ Virgo representing the society's capacity for aggression. Also of

considerable interest is Neptune, at 9° Virgo, for this planet rules
fantasies and dreams which can be the cause downfall, a key factor
in any war situation, especially those in which (as in Nazi Germany)
the warrior spirit is exalted.

The relationship of the Nazi chart to other national charts
The Nazi regime was historically a result of World War One and
represents astrologically the transition point which enabled World
War Two to begin from the legacy of World War One. The war was
initiated by the German invasion of Poland, an event in which the
status of the Free State of Danzig was the trigger. These latter two
States were created in the settlement after World War One and both
Danzig and a substantial part of Poland consisted of former German
territory. We should therefore expect these two States to have a close
astrological relationship with the Nazi chart, a relationship which
is indeed expressed in the position of the Sun in the Polish horoscope
at 21° Scorpio, exactly opposed to the Sun in the chart of Danzig
at 23° Taurus, repeating the degree area which we have already found
to be so important in the Nazi chart.

Contacts between the charts of Germany and its other opponents
are not so powerful, for the charts of these other countries originated
in other events, although we should note the Sun of the Russian
chart at 16° Scorpio, within 3 degrees of the Nazi asecendant. In
the UK chart the Moon (public opinion) is at 19° Cancer, opposed
to the Nazi MC, and the French Pluto (death) is at 18° Taurus
conjunct the Nazi ascendant.

The build-up of tension — 1939
We may consider that the build-up of tension towards the outbreak
of war is contained in essence within the Nazi chart, for Pluto in
that chart is opposed to both Venus and the MC, indicating a powerful
threat to both the government, and to peace, and opposed to the
Sun in the Treaty of Versailles. The essence of the chart indicates
that its purpose is to provide a dramatic rearrangement of forces,
by violence if necessary. In certain events prior to the actual outbreak
of war we see the sensitive degree of the Nazi chart repeated. In
particular the occupation of Czechoslovakia occurred with the Moon
at 19° Capricorn, and the ascendant at 11° Pisces, emphasizing the
surprisingly powerful symbolism of natal Neptune. If anyone doubts
the strength of this apparently weak planet in a mundane chart, let

it also be noted that the Nazi-Soviet pact — Hitler's last major act of diplomacy before the war — was signed as the MC was about 7° in Pisces. In the first of these two charts we also notice that the MC at 22° Sagittarius, and in the second the Moon at 23° Sagittarius, are squaring Mars-Jupiter in the Nazi chart. Thus we may draw certain conclusions:

1. We may see Neptune, normally considered a 'spiritual' planet, associated with war in its role as a bringer of fantasy and of confusion.
2. The Mars-Jupiter conjunction in the Nazi chart is such a powerful significator of war that the equivalent degree area in all the mutable signs (that is in a tense, square relationship) are repeated in subsequent charts.

The long-term framework for these events was the transit of Uranus through Taurus to reach the critical area of 18°-23° Taurus-Scorpio at the end of 1939. As it did so it released the potential inherent in that degree area, the deep desire to reverse the balance or power in Europe at any cost. Also, Pluto in 1938 moved briefly into Leo, retrograded out again, and finally began its long path through Leo in June 1939. From this position Pluto was to make an opposition to the Sun-Mercury-Saturn conjunction in the Nazi chart which was to last for the duration of the war, fulfilling its role as Lord of Destruction.

The declaration of war — August-September 1939

The circumstances surrounding the beginning of the war are instructive as much as for what did not happen as for what did. The original decision to invade Poland was made on 25 August 1939. the plan being to invade early in the morning on 26 August. The plan, however, came to nothing due to the failure of negotiations between Hitler and Mussolini, and the invasion was cancelled at the last minute. It is significant that the horoscopes for these two events show no major contact with any of the charts which we have designated as our base, or 'founding', horoscopes for the war except, that is, for the Uranus transit through Taurus. There are none of the indications of timing which we would expect and in particular neither the Moon, nor the angles, are in a close relationship to the Nazi chart.

It was at 12.30pm CET on 31 August 1939 that Hitler finally gave

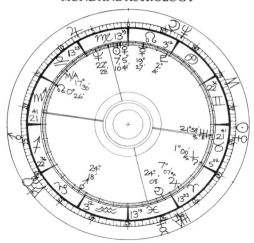

Figure 14.19 Hitler's Order to Invade Poland, 12.30 MET, 31 August 1939, Berlin, 13N23, 52N30. The mNN is 2SC03. N.B. AS is forming the exact -180-UR, and is exactly -45- Hitler's MO = SA/NE. The MC = MA/tNN = MA/PL, which grouping is on Hitler's SO/ME = SO/AS. The MC/AS is applying to Hitler's JU/AS = NE/PL = SO/MO = UR = SU/JU = PL axis.

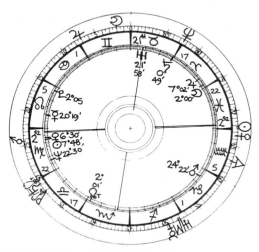

Figure 14.20 The First Shot in World War Two, 04.17 MET, 1 September 1939, Danzig, 18E38, 54N21. The mNN is 0SC22. NB tNN-90-PL exactly with Fig. 14.20 MC.

the order to invade Poland, and the first hostilities broke out at 4.17am CET on the following morning; the charts for these two times may be taken as those for the outbreak of the war. Both these charts have an exact relationship with the Nazi chart, and were to act as the 'intermediary' charts between the Nazi chart and all subsequent charts for the war in Europe. The chart for the 'first order' shows an ascendant of 21°41' Scorpio and an MC of 13°19' Virgo, emphasizing the ascendant and, again, the Neptune of the Nazi chart, When fighting finally broke out some sixteen hours later, in the port of Danzig, (Fig. 14.20 opposite) the Moon had moved into Aries where it was about to make its monthly transit over the Nazi Moon, but the impeccable timing of the event is demonstrated in the MC of 21°41' Taurus opposed the MC for the 'first order' to within one minute of arc. From this we may conclude that:

1. The Nazi chart contained the seed of World War Two and the war could therefore start only at a time which was astrologically related to the Nazi chart. When Hitler planned to start the war at an inappropriate time his plans were abortive, but when he later selected an appropriate time the astrological synchronicity was exact.

2. There are two charts for the beginning of the war, the 'first order' and the 'first shot'. Each of these charts may be taken as a 'birth chart' for the war, but on a different level. The 'first order' chart refers specifically to the intention to fight as expressed through the giving of orders; and the 'first shot' chart (Fig. 14.20 refers to the actual physical war. The second chart was a product astro-logically of the first, deriving its MC from the earlier ascendant, an illustration of the manifestation in politics of 'ideal' or psychic changes in the physical plane.

The UK and France declare war — September 1939

Following the German attack on Poland, the UK and France waited for two days before declaring war on Germany, which they did on 3 September. The significance of this two-day wait is demonstrated by the movement of the Moon during that period. When the Germans launched their invasion the Moon was in Aries, repeating the position of the aggressive Nazi Moon, but on 3 September the Moon formed a conjunction with Saturn, a conjunction which was extremely close when the UK and France announced their intention to fight. Thus the passage of the Moon over the 'birth chart' of the war had within two days of the 'birth' of the war given notice of the limit of German power, that limit being symbolized by Saturn, and the decision of the two western allies to oppose Germany.

The horoscopes for the declaration of war by these two countries then may be taken as founding charts for all the subsequent series of events in which those nations were involved as part of the war. The horoscope for the declaration of war by the UK has an ascendant of 29° 15′ in Libra. The MC of 9° 12′ Leo, is a position which as we have seen, is closely related to the immediate past of German history, and which subsequently repeats itself during the course of the war. This MC is directly opposed to the English Mars at 8° 28′ Aquarius.

In the horoscopes for the French declaration of war we find much clearer synchronicity. If we look at the operative French horoscope for the Third Republic, then we find an ascendant of 27° 11′ Capricorn exactly opposed to Mars and Uranus on the seventh house cusp, at 25° and 27° Cancer respectively. Such a volatile conjunction indicates that this republic was conceived in a war and would likely also be destroyed in a war. On the day war was declared, transiting Sun was conjunct natal Sun, a transit which appears more often at significant events than one might expect. But much more significantly than this, transiting Mars was approaching an exact opposition to the radical Mars-Uranus conjunction. In fact, at the time of the declaration Mars was rising, conjunct an ascendant of 24° 25′ Capricorn. As the Third Republic sealed its fate the Sun and the ascendant were transiting their those in the relevant UK charts, were destined to repeat themselves throughout the war.

Planetary cycles during the war

We have referred already to the 'hierarchy of astrological timing' in which the outer planets denote tension periods of one or possibly two years, within which explosions of tension are timed by transits of the inner planets and of the ascending and culminating degrees. We can examine this process in more detail during the course of the war.

Pluto

As has already been explained, this planet occupies a critical position in the Nazi chart as a signifactor of potential destruction. During

THE ASTROLOGY OF WAR AND PEACE   423

the course of the war it was by transit opposing the conjunction of the Sun-Mercury-Saturn in the Nazi chart, so it may be taken as the general signifactor, by transit of the war. We can measure the transit of Pluto more exactly, however, and if we take the winter of 1942-3 as the turning point in the war (the battles of Stalingrad and El Alamein) then we find that it was then that Pluto made, by transit, an exact opposition with natal Saturn. It was at that time that German power reached its greatest extent, after which a decline set in as Pluto moved towards its inevitable cathartic opposition to the Sun. This opposition was not reached exactly until after the end of the war, but was very close during the 'Battle of the Bulge'. At this time the Germans attempted one last offensive in the west in a campaign which saw their front line expanding like a boil until, Pluto-like, it burst and the end was in sight.

Neptune

This planet likewise moved only a little during the war, but what movement it made was critical because it moved gradually into Libra, which it entered in October 1942, from where it was to oppose the Moon, first in the chart for the war and then in the Nazi chart. By 4 November 1942 when the Germans were critically defeated in North Africa, Neptune was within 1° of opposition to the Moon in the warchart (first shot). By the end of the following January the Germans had suffered a critical defeat in Russia. Neptune therefore acted symbolically in undermining the German war effort and literally, through its rulership of oil, in denying German access to the oil of the east as a result of these battles. The planet finally came to oppose the Nazi Moon as the Third Reich disintegrated.

Uranus

Uranus, perhaps more than any other planet, was of critical importance in the beginning of the war, making in 1939 an opposition to the Sun for the 1918 Armistice and a conjunction to the Nazi ascendant, but we find it of slightly less importance during the course of the war. However, if we note that it was opposed the ascendant for the 'first order' chart we see more of the power of this planet in the fact that it reached a square with the MC for this chart when the Germans finally surrendered. At the end of the war Uranus was at 12° Gemini, a fact which assumes greater importance when we see that the ascendant was 17° Gemini when Germany invaded the USSR.

These 'transpersonal' planets therefore established a framework in which the 'personal' planets could operate in their own hierarchy, from Saturn down to Mercury. We may take an example of each of these:

Saturn, indicating added responsibility and actions of great importance for the future, was transiting the Nazi ascendant when Hitler expanded the scope of the war and guaranteed that he would lose it, by declaring war simultaneously on the USA and USSR.

Jupiter, transiting the Nazi Neptune, and the 'first order' MC in 1945, brought the creation of peace and promise of justice.

Mars, transiting the Nazi MC brought the declaration of war.

Venus, transiting the Nazi Sun at the time of the occupation of Czechoslovakia preserved the peace through an incident which could have lead to war.

Mercury, making by transit an opposition to the Nazi Sun, coincided with the signature of the Nazi-Soviet pact.

Each planet therefore has a defined role to play both in the timing of events and the nature of those events, but the most vital planet in the precise timing of events often seems to be the Moon.

Lunar cycles

There was a rumour current during the war that Hitler believed that the success or failure of military ventures depended on the phase of the Moon at their beginning. There is no astrological evidence to support this claim, but plenty to suggest that the more complicated cycles of the Moon had plenty to do with the timing of such ventures.

We have noted how transits to the natal Moon from other planets, notably Neptune, could be important, but the Moon has an active role to play in astrological timing, and this may be treated under several headings.

1. *Transits of the Moon to its own position.* The Moon in the chart for Nazi Germany was 5°02' in Aries, and we find that at certain critical times the Moon returned to this position. For example, at the invasion of Poland the Moon was 2°0' in Aries, and at the moment of final surrender in 1945, the Moon was 6°32' in Aries.

2. *Transits of the Moon to other natal positions.* For example, the Moon was conjunct the Nazi MC during the Czech occupation, and conjunct Saturn in the 'first order' chart when the UK and France declared war.

3. *Aspects of the Moon to other planets not obviously related to 'birth' charts* For example we seen the Moon-Saturn cycle prominent at various critical moments of the war. We have noted the Moon-Saturn conjunction for the declaration of war by France and the UK, but there are other instances. The Moon was conjunct Saturn when Germany invaded Scandinavia, thus bringing war to the western front; when Germany invaded the USSR, extending the war dramatically in the east; and when the last German troops in Europe surrendered, some 8 days after the formal armistice.

4. *Aspects of the progressed Moon.* These are extremely interesting for with progressions we approach a symbolic view of the flow of time which connects us to the world view of the Greeks and Babylonians. In secondary progressions one day is equivalent to one year, just as a year is equal to the Great Year of Plato of 36,000 years. We may test progressions of the Moon during the war by taking as a natal chart the horoscope for the 'first order'. We find that in October 1942, the turning-point in Germany's fortunes was symbolized by a conjunction of the progressed Moon to natal Saturn. In June 1944 Allied armies landed in Normandy, from where they began an advance into nothern Germany, and at this time we find that progressed Moon was at 22° Taurus, conjunct not only natal descendant but aspecting angles in the 'first shot' and the Nazi horoscopes.

The Sun

The whole movement of these interlocking cycles is contained within the cycle of the Sun, embodiment of the soul. It was on 31 January 1943 that the German army at Stalingrad collapsed. This day was the birthday of the Nazi State, and thus the return of the Sun to its natal position coincided with the most fateful day in the history of that State. At the Armistice on 11 November 1918, the Sun was at 18° Scorpio, and the implications of this have been discussed. Incredibly, at midnight of 8-9 May 1945, as Germany implemented the Armistice of World War Two, the Sun was at 18° Taurus, exactly opposed. Thus the entire pre-war and war period was contained within the symbolic journey of the Sun from one side of the zodiac to the other. This almost reminiscent of the Babylonian and Greek belief that, as the cycle contained the sum total of all possibilities, so the gathering of planets at opposite poles of the cycle represented the break between different cycles of existence of civilization.

The angles
The most precise timing of mundane events is given by the repetition of certain ascending and culminating degrees. In this way we find the angles in various 'founding' charts appearing in the charts for events derived from those 'founding' charts. Charts for events such as the beginning of particular campaigns produce their own angles which many continue through those campaigns. We already have the example of the Nazi ascendant of 19°26′ Taurus, which was reproduced in a host of subsequent events such as the invasion of Poland, the surrender of Denmark (22° Taurus asc.) and the Allied invasion of Normandy (MC 21° Scorpio). Then we have the case of the MC for the 'first order' chart, 12° Virgo. This was what we might call a 'second-generation chart', the MC being generated by the repitition of the ascendant-descendant of the Nazi chart. Yet that MC angle persisted throughout the war right up to the German surrender to the Americans on 7 May when 13° Pisces was rising.

Within the war individual campaigns produced their own sensitive points. Thus when the Germans invaded the Low Countries on 10 May 1940, the MC was 17° Capricorn, inherited from the Nazi MC of 21° Capricorn. This MC gave rise to an ascendant 9°8′ Taurus, an angle which then reccured throughout the western campaign, from the surrender of the Dutch (MC 9°48′ Scorpio) to the entry of German troops into France (MC 9°48′ Taurus).[8]

Thus we may describe a situation of 'cycles within cycles' in which major cycles produce secondary starting-points and sub-cycles within the greater cycle.

D-Day: 5-6 June 1944
Reference has already been made to this event and the larger cycles of the outer planets and the progressed Moon which were symbolizing Germany's decline. The events of these days are particularly instructive astrologically because the whole process of invasion took place in two countries and involved the armies of four countries, spread over not only a large area but also a long time — about eighteen hours. The invasion was ordered to proceed at 4.00am on 5 June 1944 giving an MC of 12° Capricorn and an ascendant of 0° Taurus. This chart relates directly to the UK, for it was in London that the order was given. The MC is exactly opposed to the UK MC and the

ascendant is exactly opposed to the ascendant for the declaration of war by the UK. The chart thus combines the founding chart for the UK and the chart which describes that country's involvement in the war. The fleet began to move at 6.00am, two hours later, by which time the MC was 11° Aquarius conjunct the MC for the French Armistice in 1940, and opposed the MC for the UK declaration of war. The ascendant in this chart, 16° Gemini, is close to the rising degrees for the declaration of war by Germany on the USSR, as we have already noted. The first troops landed some sixteen hours later by which time the MC was at 21° Scorpio, repeating the Taurus-Scorpio angle which seems to lie at the heart of Nazi Germany. Thus the three horoscopes combined in a striking form the horoscopes pertaining to the involvement of four major contestants.

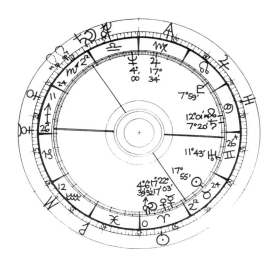

Figure 14.21 The Final Surrender of all German forces comes into effect, 24.00 MET 8 May 1945, Berlin, 13E23, 52N30. The true NN is 10CN34. NB the mean NN is exactly with the AS/MC of Fig. 14.19.

Surrender: 4-8 May 1945

Just as we have various charts for the beginning of the war, so the ending of the war was spread over four days, with German troops surrendering in accordance with a number of different agreements. These have different relationships with the countries involved. For example, when the Germans surrendered to the British on 4 May, 13° Libra was rising, conjunct the UK ascendant. However, the most interesting comparison is with the charts for the beginning of the war. It will be remembered that there was a 'first order' and a 'first shot' chart. These two charts are paralleled in the end of the war by a chart in which the Germans agreed to stop fighting, and a chart for the formal end of the war (Fig. 14.21). Thus, when the 'first order' was signed the MC-IC axis was 13° Virgo-Pisces, and when the 'last order' was signed the ascendant-descendant axis was 13° Virgo-Pisces. Furthermore when the 'first shot' was fired in 1939, the Moon (the mass will) was at 2°6′ Aries, and when the war formally ended in 1945, the Moon was at 6°32′ Aries.

Perhaps then we do not only have interlocking series of 'cycles within cycles', but cycles running in parallel operative in different planes of existence — a cycle for the world of thought, and a cycle for the world of physical action. Each cycle has its own course to run and, just as the Babylonians claimed, the operative principle is the 'eternal return of all things'.

References
Note: The data on which the material in this section is based was supplied by the archive section of the Imperial War Museum, London.

Bibliography
CAMPION, N. *The Astrology of the Second World War* London, 1983.
FIREBRACE, R. C. *Wars in the Sidereal* Moray Series No.2 (London, 1959).

15.

THE ASTROLOGY OF NATIONS

Michael Baigent, Nicholas Campion, Charles Harvey

Nations are individuals writ large and the analysis of national charts is as fully complex as that of an individual. Our problem as astrologers is that whilst we can see a national chart working out in the mass psychology, in events, and relationships with other nations, it is very difficult to begin to do anything constructive to raise the national consciousness so that potentially negative energies are put to work constructively. Perhaps one day the United Nations will not only have the ritualized psychodrama of its main assembly, but will also give time to helping belligerent nations and their leaders to sort out ways in which they can cope with their astro-psychological conflicts.

In the first part of this chapter we analyse several charts in some detail to reveal some of the characteristic ways in which nations unfold and express planetary principles. In the second part are the charts of some additional nations for the students own study. It will be seen that in several cases more than one chart has been given for a nation. This is because national charts seem to be built one upon another and even a major 'new' chart for a nation will not necessarily wipe clean the previous patternings, indeed these often seem to show through in the different 'incarnations' of a nation.

For those just testing the waters of mundane astrology it will be found that the monitoring of the transits to some of these major charts, and turning to them when these countries are in the news, will teach more than any amount of theorizing.

The horoscopes of England and the United Kingdom
— Nicholas Campion

The history of the United Kingdom presents the astrologer with an almost bewildering array of possible dates on which to base a national horoscope. There are four major possibilities:

1. The coronation of Edgar as the first king to be crowned king of all England on 11 May 973 (Fig. 15.1).
2. The coronation of William the Conqueror on Christmas Day, 1066, since when there has been no successful invasion of England by a foreign power (Fig 15.2).
3. The legal union of Great Britain and Ireland on 1 January 1801, since which time the State has borne its modern title of the 'United Kingdom' (Fig. 15.4).
4. The legal union of Great Britain and Northern Ireland at 5.28pm on 7 December 1922 in Belfast, the constitutional reformation of the United Kingdom after the independence of the Irish Free State (Fig. 15.5).

Other charts often considered are those for the constitutional union of England and Scotland on 1 May 1707 (Fig. 15.3), and the conclusion of the Battle of Hastings on 14 October 1066. Possibly the most appropriate chart should be that for English independence from the Romans, a date which may be fixed because England was the only part of the Roman Empire to receive anything like an acknowledgement of independence from the Empire. This occurred sometime in the autumn of AD 410, but unfortunately the precise date is not yet known.

Each of these charts has a character all of its own, although as we would expect, there are common themes which run through them all. The major of these is a strong emphasis on the Earth element, an emphasis which can be traced back to the conjunction of Saturn, Neptune and Pluto in Taurus in the autumn of AD 410. The earth element is again strong in the Edgar coronation chart which, set for noon, shows the Sun conjunct the MC at 23° Taurus and Virgo rising. If we take this chart as the horoscope for the Anglo-Saxon kingdom of England, then it is interesting to note that Neptune was at 24° Taurus, transiting the MC, at the time of the Norman invasion in 1066. Perhaps we may see this transit as leading to the dissolution of the old government.

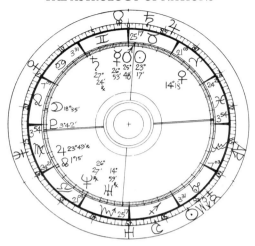

Figure 15.1   England — The Coronation of Edgar as King of the England 11 May 973, Bath, 51N22, 02W22, set for Noon as the traditionally symbolic time for such events. Edgar had in fact already been King since 959. This chart can be taken to represent the first formal and ceremonial unification of all England as we know it.

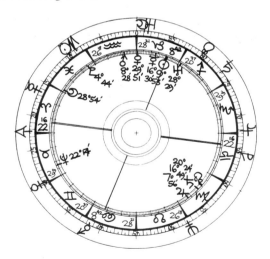

Figure 15.2   England — The Coronation of William the Conqueror, Noon, Christmas Day 1066 in Westminster Abbey, 51N30, 00W07.5. The MC/AS is 00PI29.

The chart for the coronation of William (Fig. 15.2) has the Sun at 9°53′ Capricorn, that for the union of England and Scotland has the Sun conjunct the IC at 20°29′ Taurus, and 15° Capricorn rising, while the union of Great Britain and Ireland shows the Sun at 10°11′ Capricorn, conjunct the IC. Only in the 1922 chart is the emphasis on Earth broken and indeed that chart, which has no planets or angles in Earth signs, perhaps indicates a shift in the English, or British, collective unconscious.

What meaning can we ascribe to this emphasis on the Earth element in this series of national horoscopes? Perhaps it represents the slow but persistent climb to domination by the English over their Welsh, Scottish and Irish neighbours. It in fact took about a thousand years for the strongly Capricorn-Taurus English to complete the conquest of their Celtic cousins. Unfortunately we have no effective horoscopes for the Welsh, Scots and Irish peoples before the English conquests, so no real astrological comparison is possible. However, we may allow ourselves a little speculation.

The ascendant in the 1801 chart (Fig. 15.4, opposite) is almost exactly on the mid-point of the Aquarian MC and Gemini Ascendant in the 1922 chart (Fig. 15.5). Can we therefore speculate that the Air element is particularly appropriate to the Irish portion of the United Kingdom, and perhaps to Ireland itself? Such a proposition may be tested by reference to the post-independence history of the Irish Republic. As far as the UK is concerned, can we also speculate that the absence of Earth in the 1922 chart indicates that this chart represents a phase in the break up of an empire founded on the principles of Earth? This may be the case in view of the correlation of the disintegration of the British Empire with the passage of Neptune, Uranus and Pluto over the UK ascendant in Libra since 1942. When, however, the 1922 chart is set for London, rather than Belfast, the MC moves into 29°32′ in Capricorn showing, perhaps, the tenacity with which the Ulster Protestants fought to preserve the Union.

In English history we can see the power of Earth in the country's record as a great trading nation, and as the first nation to experience both an agrarian and an industrial revolution. In terms of the English character the description of the English by Napoleon as 'a nation of shopkeepers', and images such as 'John Bull' (Taurus!) and the 'British Bulldog', come to mind. A central part of the English national mythology is that the English people 'knuckle under' and 'get on

Figure 15.3 Great Britain — The Union of Scotland and England came into force at 00.00 LT on 1 May 1707 (O.S.), 13 May N.S. This is set for Westminster, 51N30, 00W07.5, MC/AS = 18SG48, mNN 25AR03. V. E. Robinson considered this to be 'the figure for the official birth of Great Britain'. It is not generally considered to be as powerful as the 1801 chart but it is still sensitive and especially with regard to Anglo-Scottish affairs, though its precise referend remains to be determined.

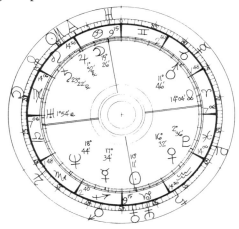

Figure 15.4 The United Kingdom — This formally came into being at 00.00 Hours on 1 January 1801. The chart is set for Westminster, 51N30, 00W07.5, MC/AS = 23LE10 -0- SA, mNN 13AR54. This specifically represents the union of Great Britain with Ireland. Despite Southern Ireland having left the Union it is undoubtedly still a very sensitive chart.

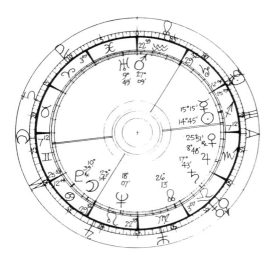

Figure 15.5   Northern Ireland — This chart, set for Belfast, for 15.28 GMT on 7 December 1922. MC/AS = 3AR08, mNN 25VI38. This is for the moment when, having been granted, with Eire, the option of Independence from the UK, as from 00.00 GMT 6 December, the Northern Ireland Senate voted N.I. back into the UK James Russell, who originally researched this precise time, has suggested this is the true chart for The Modern UK[1]

Whether or not it has significance for the UK as a whole, when set for Belfast and judged as the chart for Northern Ireland it is in some respects all too tragically appropriate. PL, and its Water Grand Trine with JU and UR, exactly configures both the UK's MC and SO and the 1066 chart's SO-MC indicating the strong, compulsive, emotional bond with the Mother Country. The elevated UR -90- AS in Gemini threatens rebellious divisions and splits within the body politic, whilst its -90-SO-ME in Sagittarius is indicative of potentially divisive religious and philosophical tensions. Likewise the elevated MA-90-VE in Scorpio is indicative of passionate feelings which could, under pressure, find violent expression along ideological (Aquarian) lines. But most particularly significant in this chart is the fact that at this precise time and place we find the all important m.p.s MC/AS 3AR08 = SO/MO 3LI59 exactly stimulated by NE 18LE07, which was also activating the mid-points MA/JU 2CN58 = PL/NN 18LE04.

Neptune is both the principle of high idealism, unitive vision, and religion, on its higher side, and of self-deception, degenerative diseases, delusions, and dissolution, on its lower side. Interpreting this planetary picture directly from COSI we find, amongst other things, 'Plans without a chance of realization. A hopeless relationship, failures,' 'Success within with the job', whatever the circumstance, and especially in adverse conditions. This is the kind of mood which led to the archetypal 'mad-dog' Englishman who goes out in the midday sun. The 'Protestant work ethic', symbolized by the trine of the Sun to Saturn and Jupiter in the sixth house in Virgo in the 1066 chart, is extremely strong in England.

A look at the other positions in the 1066 chart confirms other aspects of English character and history. Aries on the ascendant confirms the English reputation as a war-like nation, which fought its way to domination over a vast proportion of the world's surface, albeit in a slow Taurus-Capricorn fashion. Perhaps the combination of Capricorn with Aries has given rise to the famous 'spirit of Dunkirk', the concept that not only do the English work best in adverse circumstances, but that they do it best in the middle of war. It is interesting to note that in 1982 the 'spirit of Dunkirk' was reborn as the 'Falklands factor' as transiting Saturn was making a square to the natal Suns in both the 1066 and 1801 charts, and conjunctions to the 1066 Descendant and the 1801 Ascendant.

We can find intimations of English life in the other planets as well. The Moon is the twelfth house is of topical interest today (1983) as a debate rages concerning the existence of one of the largest prison

a community by means of lies and fraud,' 'The misfortune to be surrounded by deceitful or bad people,' 'Inner discontentment . . . shared suffering, mistakes, illusions or deceptions, the undermining of associations . . .' It is significant that the current apparently insoluble religious, sectarian 'civil war' began to escalate in 1966 when transit Neptune came -90-NE radical, and it really exploded towards the end of 1968 and through 1969 as UR and then JU-UR came into this highly problematic axis.

This NE axis is a configuration which could be expected to pose problems enough in an individual's chart, if they were not energizing on the highest level. How this energy can be channeled within a whole community is indeed a challenge and highlights the fact that it is easier to diagnose the problem than to offer an answer. Presumably a real solution to this seemingly endless undermining and demoralization can only come when the community as a whole is somehow able to discover the self-transcedence and idealism of the higher side of Neptune, to see their higher Brotherhood over and beyond their particular ideals and differences.

To consider this same chart from the perspective of the UK as a whole, the angles for Westminster are MC 5AQ15, AS 9GE38. Note the MC/AS 7AR27 is exactly with the UK DS.

populations in Europe. Mercury in Capricorn perhaps represents the great inventors of the eighteenth century who helped transform the English economy. Venus in Capricorn, ruler of the seventh house, shows how trade has dominated English foreign relations while Mars in the eleventh indicates the importance of war historically as a means of obtaining national objectives. Jupiter and Saturn in the sixth indicated the strength of an economy founded on the 'work ethic', while Uranus in the ninth, bringing religious independence, was highlighted by transit at the time of the Reformation. Neptune in the first house brings intimations of the seafaring nation, while Pluto in the twelfth may perhaps represent skeletons in the collective cupboard which have yet to be unlocked.

The 1801 chart provides a more detailed and additional look at more recent history and mythology. The Sun in Capricorn conjunct the IC reinforces ideas of the 'work ethic', but also represents the tremendous power of landed and industrial interests in the nation's history in the eighteenth and nineteenth centuries. Also shown here is the political stability which the United Kingdom has enjoyed more than anyother European country. Yet there are three major oppositions in the chart, one of which runs between the Sun and the Moon. Undoubtedly this is a tense chart and, although the British mainland has been very stable, the Irish connection has provided nothing but trouble for its English rulers.

In terms of national mythology, the phrase 'the Englishman's home is his castle' would seem to reflect the trine from the Sun — IC to Mars in Taurus.

The Moon itself, ruling the 'masses', is in the tenth house, bringing shades of 'parliamentary democaracy', while Mercury in Sagittarius in the third is perhaps an indication of the remarkable spread of the English language throughout the world. Venus in Aquarius opposed to Saturn definitely echoes the 'stiff upper-lip' mentality which is ashamed of public displays of emotion or affection, while Libra rising, ruled by Venus, represents the myth of 'team spirit' and the importance of 'not letting the side down'.

As far as government is concerned, Libra also represents the 'checks and balances' which are crucial to the operation of the constitution and, in foreign affairs, the obsession with maintaining the 'balance of power' which has dominated so much of English strategic thought. Mars in the eighth house is an indication of the many wars this country has fought for its international economic interests, while the opposition of Mars to Neptune in the second shows the maritime power which underlay the economic empire. Jupiter in the tenth indicates the generally high regard in which the English system of parliamentary democaracy is held, while the sextile from Jupiter to Uranus shows, perhaps, the constant process of innovation through which the natioanl constitution has evolved. Saturn in the eleventh indicates the importance of the constitutional government in maintaining national order, and Uranus conjunct the ascendant and squared to the Sun shows that innovatory spirit which underlay the agrarian and industrial revolutions. Pluto, lying in the fifth house in a quincunx to Jupiter, no doubt has an influence on the nation's cultural life, a proposition borne out by the transit of Uranus and Pluto through the opposite sign of Pisces when England, and 'swinging London', became one of the fashion centres of the world.

A natal chart of United States — Michael Baigent

This chart (Fig. 15.6) is set for the signing of the *Declaration of Independence* in Philadelphia on 4 July 1776. The time was not recorded but it is known that the acceptance and partial signing took place in the afternoon of that day. The time used, 5.10 pm local time, was given a few years afterwards, in 1787, by the London astrologer Ebenezer Sibly.[2] He was a member of a sea-captain's Masonic lodge which no doubt had good contacts with the USA, hence his information.[3]

The ascendant of a country reflects its myths, the archetypes to which the people resonate. The United States mythology shows clearly this Sagittarian quality — the cowboy who rides the vast ranges seeking freedom and justice. He is beyond the law yet imbued with a strong morality bred by the road, the path which seems to have no end. Sagittarius rising symbolizes the great enthusiasm and adventurousness of the American people — their search for meaning, for the divine, for freedom, for the valley where the grass is greener and the authorities fewer.

The Cancer Sun reflects the sentimental 'mother and apple pie' quality of US society, and its square to Saturn symbolizes, at its most positive, the strong spirit of independence amongst Americans — they will not be pushed around, they are masters of their own fate. It suggests also the great value placed upon the self-made man, who by hard work and keen ambition has achieved greatness.

A key point is Saturn falling in the tenth house — ruling

government, style of government, national honour and ambition. This placement suggests a nation with very strong ambitions *in the world,* emphasizing material rather than emotional, intellectual or spiritual values. We can see here a symbol of those early pioneers who, shunning frivolity, doggedly trekked west where they laid claim to their own piece of real estate in accordance with 'manifest destiny'. This placement further suggests a preoccupation with national honour — that the United States must at all costs be the greatest country in the world; that US values must be the standard by which all others are judged, no matter that the murder rate would seem to indicate some serious shortcomings.

The Saturnine qualities of the USA can be found right back at the very beginning of the European colony of North America in the attitudes of the Puritan founding fathers, which still remain the guiding principles of the nation. The Puritans established conservative communities where conformity based upon fear ruled. Their attitude to the feminine — to the land as well as to their wives — was that they had possession by the will of God and could do as they wished. Certain US attitudes thus long predated the signing of the *Declaration* but the chart drawn for this time in 1776 seems to have picked up some inherent qualities of the European nation of North America.

Of prime importance is the Sun square to Saturn. The positive side has been mentioned, but the negative also needs attention. This aspect suggests that a basic self-doubt, a feeling of inadequacy, runs through the nation. Curiously Soviet Russia also has this aspect, which suggests that in some way both countries are bound by the same need to prove themselves. Both need to be proved right — by the failure of the other.

The Mars trine Saturn aspect indicates a great capacity for work, for efficiency, for the utilization of all the resources of the country. No one who has worked professionally in the United States can fail to be impressed by the speed at which decisions are made, goods manufactured and delivered. By comparison, most of Europe seems to be at lunch or asleep. This aspect also reflects the great technological improvements which the United States has brought to the world, especially cost-cutting modifications such as the production line techniques pioneered by Henry Ford.

The United States, having Uranus so prominently placed in its natal chart, would seem to have reason to show a sensitivity towards this planet's transits. The truth of this is borne out by even a quick

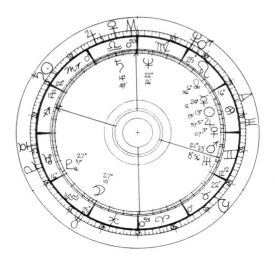

Figure 15.6 USA Declaration of Independence — Set for 5.10 pm LT, 4 July 1776, Philadelphia as per Ebenezer Sibly in 1787. This time is in close agreement with the time given by the official bulletin of the Philadelphia Historical Society.[5] MC/AS = 6SC32, mNN 7LE36. Various other charts have been suggested including three with a Gemini AS. The most popular of these, originally advocated by American astrologers about 1939, has MC 15AQ00, AS 8GE47, and MO 18AQ06. For a full discussion see 'Astrologica Americana'.[6] Another important chart is that for the USA's Declaration of War against Britain on 4 July 1775[7].

analysis. The US proves sensitive to both transits of Uranus across its natal planetary positions and to Uranus aspecting its own natal position — in other words to the Uranus cycle. An example of the former can be seen occurring during 1972. On 17 June 1972, when the break-in at the Watergate Hotel was discovered, transiting Uranus was exactly conjunct the natal Saturn in the USA chart. This aspect suggests an upset to the administration — and so events proved. At the same time, incidentally, Saturn was transiting the seventh house, symbolizing a hardening, a disillusioning, of public opinion. Additionally Pluto was conjunct the Mid-heaven, indicating a period where the hidden side of the administration would be thrust into the light of day. With both Uranus and Pluto moving through the tenth house it is little wonder that paranoia ran wild, that scandals erupted and that a president fell.

Between January 1983 and February 1984 Uranus transited the ascendant of the USA. This aspect suggested a change in the status of the nation. The Sagittarius placement indicated that the change had to do with, at the least, foreign policy and the international concerns of the American people. The transit also seems to promise the development of new and revolutionary technological discoveries which will bear fruit in the next few years.

As a guide to interpretation we should look at the events in the USA the last time that this transit occurred — between March 1899 and December 1900. This period followed the Spanish-American War at which point the USA had suddenly found itself a colonial power with control over the Philippines, Puerto Rico, Guam, Hawaii, and with troops stationed in China as part of the international force mobilized to suppress the Boxer rebellion. This then was the beginning of the USA as an international power. Secondly this period saw some important technological 'firsts': the Wright brothers flew their first full-scale glider; the mass production of cars began at the Old's Motor Company, Detroit; and the first significant oil strike was made in Texas. Uranus then, again transiting this point, bodes well for all those attempting to find their way amongst the lost hopes and false starts of alternative technology. It would seem that this current period will be firstly one of significant discoveries to be developed during the mid-eighties, and secondly a period of basic shifts in USA strategic alliances and policy. At the time of writing it is too early to see these changes clearly but certainly the traditional ties with both Israel and Europe seem to be under great strain. [4]

Natal chart of Russia — Michael Baigent

This natal chart (Fig. 15.7) is set for the moment during the meeting of the 'All Soviets Congress' in Leningrad when power was effectively taken by the Bolsheviks. The important point came when the acceptance of the *Decree of Constitution of Power* passed control into the hands of Lenin's Bolshevik Commisars. This decree was read at 2.30 am on 9 November 1917. [11] The USSR itself was not formed until 1922, but as the Soviet republic of Russia was and is the dominating force, its chart remains the basic one to use when attempting to plot the course of the USSR.

The ascendant and the Moon rule the nation and the people; in Russia's case, both are in the worker's sign, Virgo — a good symbol of the revolution as it was presented to the world. However, the twelfth-house placement of the Moon suggests a general suspicion of the intentions of others. The square to Jupiter indicates that these could easily become exaggerated to the point of over-reaction. Additionally, the ninth-house position of Jupiter symbolizes foreigners and foreign ideologies as the source of these fears. Distrust and suspicion can also be seen as arising from the chart's weakness in Fire. This can lead to a fear of all that Fire represents: the visionaries, the creators, all those who use their intuition and their imagination. It would suggest then that Russia opposes individual creative expression — a sound reflection of the reality as the countless creative people who have fled the country would attest.

There is additional symbolism to be extracted from the ninth-house Jupiter. Its square to the Moon indicates that Russia's national philosophy would be speculative and extravagant, attempting too much. This position of Jupiter can be seen as symbolic of a 'moral good' expressed in terms of ever-increasing expansion and production. Witness the constant stream of multi-year plans which, since the nation's inception, have promised much, but in common with all Jupiter afflictions, delivered little.

Perhaps the most important aspect in the chart is the *T-square* running from the third-house Sun to Saturn and Uranus — to the eleventh and fifth houses respectively. Its critical point falls on the Sun-Mercury conjunction in Scorpio. An aspect such as the T-square indicates severe internal tensions held in check by a strong centralized power. It is from this tension derived from the discordant energies which the T-square pattern symbolizes that the most serious of Russia's problems can be expected to emerge. This grouping in the third house indicates that the Russian leadership is well aware of the importance of controlling and utilizing the media and educational institutions as part of its hold on power. It can be seen, too, in the leadership's constant concern with speeches, meetings, rallys and committees all of which merely dilute the leadership rather than give the people any kind of voice. The Sun's square to Uranus expresses itself in the type of communication generally adopted by the Soviet authorities (and copied by Marxists the world over) — convoluted, polemical, intellectually revolutionary and excessively verbose.

The second square to the Sun, from Saturn in the eleventh house, suggests that a self-doubt runs through the nation. Commonly this attitude results in over-compensation — like the traditional school

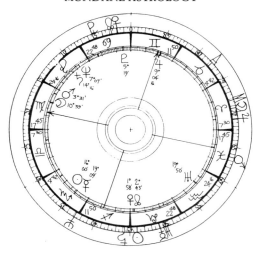

Figure 15.7   Soviet Russia — Set for the acceptance of the Decree of Constitution of Power effectively giving power to Lenin's Bolshevik Commisars at 2.30 am, 9 November 1917, Leningrad, 59N55, 30E25. The MC/AS = 29CN47, the mNN 3CP50. This is the chart suggested by the writer, MB. Charts for other times on the 7 and 8 November have also been suggested.[8]

bullies. Perhaps this is one of the factors which ensures that Russia insists on attempting to force its limited philosophy of mankind onto the rest of the world.

The last link in the T-square is the opposition from Saturn to Uranus, from the eleventh to the fifth houses. This gives additional clues as to the nation's style of government — the eleventh house ruling, among other things, the nation's goals. Tradition has it, that if this house is afflicted — which Russia's certainly is — then the people are disillusioned! Tradition apart, the eleventh house conjunction of Saturn with Neptune indicates a basic desire to combine pragmatic ambition with idealism. Certainly Marxism, as it was initially formulated, sought to do this, albeit within the context of Victorian England. The placement of this conjunction in Leo suggests the manner in which the nation's goals would best be attained: by firm central leadership — Saturn — operating in a traditionally capitalistic manner — Leo. Quite different from the Aquarian ideal but in fact the way in which the Russian leadership

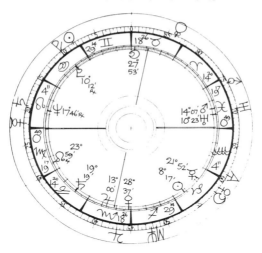

Figure 15.8   The USSR — For the proclamation of the Union of Soviet Socialist Republics,[9] 30 December 1922, 20.00 LT, Moscow, 55N45, 37E35. MC/AS 9CN37 = PL = SO; mNN 24VI24. This brought together Russia, the Ukraine, White Russia, and Transcaucasia in one federation giving central political control to Moscow through the All-Union Communist Party. NB it was formed at the SA-60-NE. The SA degree appears to be particularly sensitive.

has belatedly developed. The opposition to Uranus would emphasize the negative qualities of Saturn in Leo — the patronizing, imperious aspects. These lead to an inability to delegate authority and to subordinates who unable to make decisions for themselves, need confirmation for every act to come from above, thus involving the higher administration in a welter of petty details and reducing its efficiency of command.

These negative Saturnine qualities clash with the theoretical revolutionary attitudes suggested by the placement of Uranus in Aquarius. This chart suggests then a society torn by a desire for equality on the one hand and a desire for firm traditional leadership on the other. Unfortunately these desires are mutually exclusive, for traditional leadership does not like to share power. More critically though, just as an individual will identify with one end of an opposition while projecting the other, a nation, a collective psyche will show the same tendency. In Russia's case it would seem that it identifies with the revolutionary Uranus, supposing (erroneously) that it is in the forefront of world social development and projecting onto its opponents all the negative qualities symbolized by Saturn in Leo. The latter, as mentioned, reflects the classical capitalist, and Russia's dislike of all such people and the countries which support them is well-established. Russia cannot admit to itself that capitalism is an integral part of its own nature. Perhaps if the capitalistic sides of Russian life were given a free reign the society would become more flexible and humane. It might not of course do anything about solving the problem of human destiny, but then neither does Marxism.

This position of Saturn in Leo suggests further an administration by firm father figures who brook no criticism, who allow no interference with their rigid lines of control. This inevitably creates an over-centralized command structure which leads to profound weaknesses in the society. In Russia this tendency reaches down to all echelons of public life. Brezhnev, well aware of this, once complained that Soviet managers feared innovation 'like the Devil fears incense'.

It is possible to find certain trends for the future which are worth recording. In general, it does seem very likely that the nation will eventually disintegrate under the pressure of the strong divisive internal forces. The critical periods for Russia are reached when transiting or progressing planets pass the sensitive points of its natal T-square, especially so when they conjoin or oppose the natal Sun (leadership) thus at the same time squaring Saturn (control) and Uranus (change). I would suggest further that the conjunctions with the Sun show the times of greatest *internal* tension. Saturn transiting this point would be especially difficult since while it passes through the third house communications would be under their greatest pressure — and a centralized State must depend upon good communications to maintain control.

Saturn first transited this point from February 1925 until August 1926. This was the period immediately following the death of Lenin and was one of an internal power struggle between Stalin and Trotsky. The second transit took place from November 1954 to October 1955 — the period immediately following the death of Stalin. Again there was a power struggle between Krushchev and Malenkov. The next transit is in 1984 — presumably the effect will be much the same.

However, by far the most important transit for Russia occurs from January 1989 to November 1991 when Pluto transits the natal Sun.

At the same time Saturn, Uranus and Neptune are all opposing the natal tenth house Pluto. This latter conjunction has not happened since the early fourteenth century and so must be considered somewhat rare. The transit of Pluto across the Sun would suggest some basic reconstructing of the nation — preceded by a hardline period. It may well involve the emergence of some underground or exiled alternative leadership. The three-planet conjunction opposing the natal Pluto similarly indicates a change for the nation, again with regard to the leadership and the style of rule. It would appear possible that this period will herald some new revolution in Russia which would restructure the country dramatically. Given the activation of the energies symbolized by the T-square, then it is likely that the tight command structure will fail and that the country will collapse back into the numerous autonomous states that it once was. It is rare for an administration to survive a Pluto transit. [11]

The horoscopes of Communist China — Nicholas Campion

The People's Republic of China was officially proclaimed by Mao Tse Tung at 3.15 pm on 1 October 1949 in Peking, [10] and the horoscope for this moment, the founding of a new regime, is taken as the Chinese horoscope in preference to those for previous regimes (see Fig. 15.9, p.449). Historically this astrological assumption is demonstrated in the quite distinct course taken by Chinese history since 1949 compared to the previous years.

We find in this chart all the trademarks of collective rebellion which have made China such a fascinating country for westerners over the last thirty years. The ascendant is in Aquarius, and the ascendant ruler, Uranus, is squared to the Sun, indicating a country which, having had one revolution in 1949, was driven into further revolutionary upheaval in 1966 with the 'Cultural Revolution'. The ideology behind such revolutions is that society must operate according to collective interests (asc. Aquarius) yet the rule of the people is paramount (Moon conjunct asc.). This gives rise to a situation which democracy is simultaneously encouraged and denied, a paradox which becomes clearer when it is seen that the other ascendant ruler, Saturn, is in Virgo, a truly conservative position which indicates the subordination of ideology (Aquarius) to practical needs (Virgo). Stalinist philosophy contains the concept of 'democratic centralism', a rather confused idea which has been influential in China and may well be explained by reference to the two distinct rulers of Aquarius,

Uranus (democracy), and Saturn (centralism).

Through the action of these two planets China is seen in two quite contradictory ways. On the one hand it is seen to be revolutionary, and on the other authoritarian and conservative. The authoritarian side is very apparent to us in other countries as Saturn is in the seventh house, that which deals with projection. The seventh house also contains a conjunction of Mars and Pluto, squared to Venus in the ninth, a truly war-like pattern which is not so noticeable in the China of the 1980s, but which in the 1960s elevated the need to be ready for war with the 'paper tigers' and 'running dogs' of imperalism and revisionism almost to the level of national religion.

In November 1959, when Mars in Scorpio squared the Mars-Pluto conjunction, the Prime Minister of India, Pandit Nehru, was moved to declare that 'I doubt if there is any country which cares less for peace than China'.

During the 1960s China's beligerant rhetoric convinced many western strategists that China posed more of a military problem than the Soviet Union, but Saturn in the seventh house places limitations on her strength. On 17 February 1979 China invaded Vietnam in what was supposed to be a quick and effective campaign, but Saturn was in Virgo conjuncting its natal place and the invasion was bogged down and became a frustrating failure.

Also very noticeable in the chart is the conjunction of the Sun, Mercury and Neptune in Libra in the eighth house. This is obviously the major connection between this chart and China's past as the home of the great philosophy of balance, Taosim, and it is interesting that, even though the *I Ching* was forbidden amongst the masses, this major work of divination and change exerted a major influnce on Mao Tse Tung himself.

The eighth-house position of these planets is extremely interesting since a principal motivation behind the revolution was economic nationalism, and the desire to prevent the economic exploitation of China by foreign powers. The need for economic self-sufficiency is confirmed by the dual rulership by Venus of the eighth house (international finance) and the fourth (the land). This motivation underlies the national ideology (Neptune-Mercury) both in the radical China of Mao and the 'revisionist' China of the 1980s. Indeed the eighth-house dispute between those who were in favour of, and those who were opposed to, foreign investment, lay at the root of the power struggle which followed the death of Mao in the 1970s. The critical period of this power struggle took place from 1975-6 while transisting Pluto, ruler of the eighth, was conjunct China's natal Sun.

Economic reorganization is not always conducted in a civilized Libran fashion, and with the ruler of the IC, Venus, in Scorpio, from where it squares its dispositors, Mars and Pluto, one million peasants were executed when the communists came to power in 1950-1. There is an exact semi-sextile from Mercury to Saturn in Virgo, which may be the clue to the obsession with industrialization and the elevation of good behaviour at work to the level of national duty.

The link between economics and religion in China, which resulted in the near deification of Mao, the leader of the Marxist revolution, rests in the location of eighth-house ruler Venus in the ninth. It is notable that Mao was officially discredited under a transit of Uranus to this natal Venus.

Transits over the Chinese horoscope seem to show up the recent history of China quite well. The first Chinese President was elected on 29 December 1911 and assumed office on 1 January 1912, during which time the Sun moved from 7-10° Capricorn and the Moon moved into the latter degrees of Taurus. The declaration of the Peoples' Republic in 1949 was the final stage in the process begun in 1911, yet it overthrew the 1912 Republic. It is therefore no surprise that the 1949 Sun exactly squares the 1911 Sun and the 1949 IC picks up the 1912 Moon. It is interesting that the 1949 Saturn is exactly trine the 1912 Saturn at 13° Taurus, emphasizing the conservative aspects of the communist revolution as one which sougth to restore China to a state of justice and equality in contrast to the chaos of the early republic. It is also curious that not only the Soviet Union (Sun 10° Capricorn) but also the USA (Sun 13° Cancer) were initial supporters of the new communist regime.

There have been two further major experiments with revolution in communist China. The first was the 'Hundred Flowers' campaign of April to June 1957 during which democratic complaint against the regime was allowed, and the second was the 'Cultural Revolution' which began in mid-1966 and represented an attempt by Mao to destroy the middle class which was developing under his rule. The Hundred Flowers campaign was short-lived and coincided with a square from transiting Saturn to natal Saturn (an attempt to reconstruct the State) and an opposition from transisting Uranus to natal Moon (an experiment with democracy). The much longer Cultural Revolution began immediately following the transit of

Uranus and Pluto over natal Saturn, and under a square of transisting Saturn to its natal place. This profound upheavel in China lasted until the transit of Neptune over the MC in April 1969, and was not officially pronounced over until August 1977. By this time China was experiencing the second of its major transits through Libra. The first, that of Uranus through Libra in 1971, coincided with the struggle for supremacy between the Army and the Communist Party; while the second, that of Pluto in 1975-7, brought the protracted struggle between the Maoists and 'Revisionists' which reached its peak in 1975-7 as Pluto transited the natal Sun. In the middle of this Pluto transit, with its overtones of transformation, Mao Tse Tung died. Mao died on 9 September 1976 as Mercury, the dispositor of Saturn, was stationary retrograde, exacly conjunct China's Sun and in a conjunction with transiting Mars, Venus and Pluto. The transiting Sun itself was on that day passing over China's Saturn. On a key day for transformation in the State, the leader (the Sun) died and the power struggle entered its final phase.

The final phase of the struggle occurred with the trial of the 'Gang of Four' in the winter of 1980-1, coinciding with the transit of Uranus over the MC (the government), Much of the policy differences between the two factions centred around the role of industrialization, and Uranus is the ruler of industrialization in its innovatory capacity. As far as the Sun's rulership of the State is concerned, it is interesting to note that on the day the trial opened the transiting Sun was conjunct the MC and on the day it closed the Sun was conjunct the ascendant.

Immediately before the trial opened transiting Jupiter and Saturn entered the Chinese eighth house, where they made their periodic conjunction over the Chinese Sun. The new government, flushed from its victory over the Maoists, embarked on a programme of massive investment (Jupiter) which soon involved them in serious economic difficulties and an equally massive cancellation of contracts (Saturn).

As far as future development of government and policy is concerned, it is worth noting that in 1994 transiting Pluto will cross the MC and in 1996 transiting Uranus will pass over the ascendant.

In foreign policy China has always lived up to the proud and belligerent potential of its seventh-house conjunction of Mars and Pluto in Leo. The country has been involved in four wars; in Korea, Tibet, India and Vietnam. In the first three, issues of self-defence and legitimacy confuse the overall picture; and even in the invasion of Vietnam China's traditional view of this country as a vassal state provided it with a self-justification. However, as the clearest case of aggression the invasion of Vietnam should also provide the most suitable astrological test.

The invasion of Vietnam occurred on 17 February 1979 following a series of border clashes symbolized by transiting Uranus conjunct natal Venus and transiting Jupiter conjunct natal seventh cusp. On 10 February there had been a full Moon at 21° Leo, perilously close to China's Pluto, and seven days later, when transiting Mars reached this degree, China invaded. She did so, however, during her Saturn return and the campaign proved much more difficult than they expected and the Chinese withdrew on 19 March as transiting Venus opposed natal Pluto.

The return of Saturn to its seventh-house position was shown equally clearly in the recognition of China by the USA on 1 January 1979, as the transiting Sun squared and opposed the natal Suns of these two nations respectively. The advent of the American Saturn return in 1982, conjuncting the Chinese Sun, coincided with the first major crisis in Sino-American relations since the formation of diplomatic relations. This is a clear indication that the chart of a country cannot be taken in isolation, but must be seen as part of an unfolding global pattern.

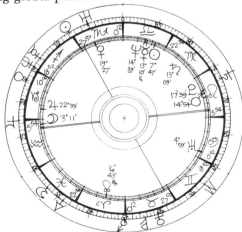

Figure 15.9 China — proclamation of the People's Republic by Mao Tse Tung at 3.15 pm LT, 1 October 1949, Peking, 39N55, 116E23. MC/AS = 1CP30, mNN 16AR59.

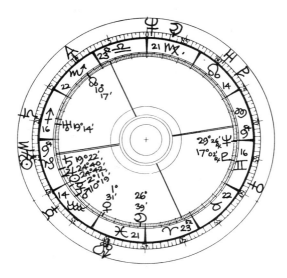

Figure 15.10   Saudi Arabia — For the moment that Ibn Saud captured
Riyadh from which dates the power of the house of Saud: 02.47 am GMT,
15 January 1902, Riyadh, 24N41, 46E42. Tyl suggests that Arabia as a whole
can be dated to the moment for the arrival of Mohammed in Medina. [12]

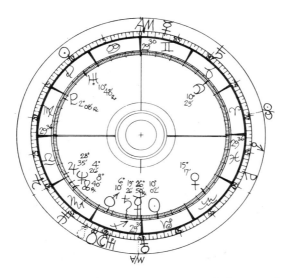

Figure 15.11   The EEC — The European Economic Community formally
came into being at 00.00 hrs MET 1 January 1958, at its official capital
of Bruxelles, 50N50, 4E21. MC/AS = 14LE. The Treaty of Rome which
brought it into being was first signed on 25 March 1957, at about 18.37
MET, in Rome, 41N53, 12E30, by the original nations France, West
Germany, Italy, Belgium, the Netherlands, and Luxembourg. Britain's
formal participation in the EEC came into force at 00.00 MET on 1 January
1973, Bruxelles. The angles are almost identical to the above: MC 29GE50,
AS 29VI52, MC/AS 14LE51, SO 10CP24, MO 00SG05, ME 24SG30, VE
16SG24, MA 00SG52, JU 17CP48, SA 15GE18R, UR 22LI45, NE 6SG14,
PL 4LI25 St R, tNN 16CP48, mNN 17CP15.

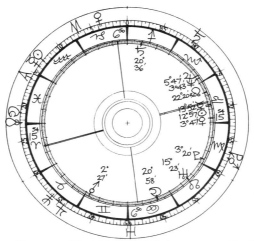

Figure 15.12   France — The Vth Republic inaugurated by De Gaulle on 5 October 1958 at MET, Paris, 48N52, 2E20, following approval of the new Constitution by popular referendum on 28 September 1958. Amongst other things the new constitution gave France's overseas possessions six months to opt for the status quo, to become integral French departments, or to become autonomous states within the French Community.

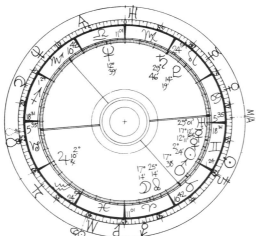

Figure 15.13   West German Federal Republic — Came into existence at 00.00 LT = 22.00 GMT, 22 May 1949, Bonn, 50N44, 7E06. MC/AS 8SG09, mNN 23AR53. There are some interesting points of contact with the earlier German charts given in Chapter 14.

Figure 15.14   Ireland — Eire — Proclamation of Independence 24 April 1916, Noon LT, Dublin, 53N20, 6W15. MC/AS 27GE30, mNN 3AQ41. This marked the start of the Easter Rebellion against the British. Though the rebellion was suppressed Irish astrologer's see this as a key chart for Eire.

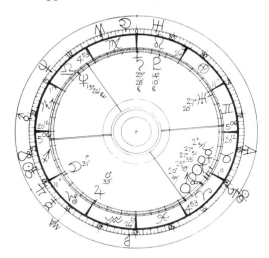

Figure 15.15   Republic of Ireland — 23.00 GMT, 17 April 1949, Dublin, 53N20, 6W15. MC/AS 4SC59, mNN 25AR46. This is for the official coming into force of the complete independence of Eire from Britain.

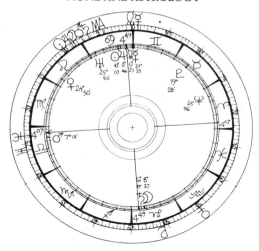

Figure 15.16 Italian Kingdom — This is for the entry of King Vittorio Emanuele II's entry into Rome which is considered by leading Italian astrologers to represent the actual coming into being of the Italian State as we now know it. The chart is normally set for 11.40 LT, 2 July 1871, Roma, 41N55, 12E28.

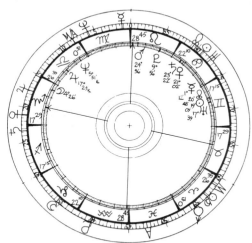

Figure 15.17 Italian Republic — Following the abdication of Vittorio Emanuele III on 9 May 1946, a referendum was held in which the monarchy was rejected by 12.7m votes to 10.7m, and the Republic was proclaimed at 18.00 LT, 16.00 GMT, 10 June 1946, Roma. The MA/AS is 8LI07, mNN 20GE59.

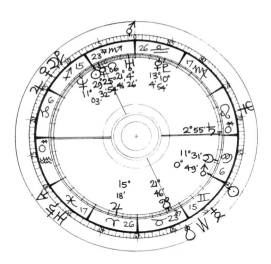

Figure 15.18 Spain — The restoration of the monarchy — This is for the Coronation of King Juan-Carlos at 12.36 LT, 22 November 1975, Madrid, 40N25, 3W45. The time taken from live TV coverage.

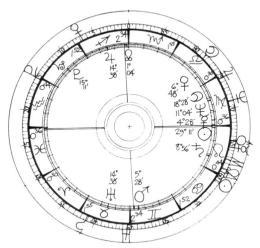

Figure 15.19 is the chart for 6 pm, 22 August 1770, the moment that Captain Cook took possession of Australia for the British Crown, at Possession Island, 142E24, 10S52. (Data from Cook's log and chart calculations by courtesy of Doris Greaves and the FAA.)

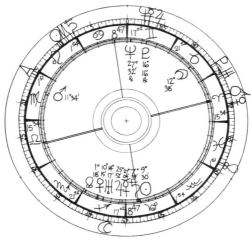

Figure 15.20 is for the coming into force of the Australian Federation or Commonwealth at 00.00 hrs LT, 1 January 1901, in Melbourne, Victoria, the provisional capital, 145E00, 37S50. The mNN is 29SC51.

A thirds chart which is of importance for Australia as a whole is the chart for the opening of Canberra Parliament on 9 May 1927, at 11.00 — 01.00 GMT, 149E08, 35S18: MC 2TA10, AS 11CN32, SO 17TA25, MO 21LE54, ME 4TA55, VE 26BE10, MA 12CN56, JU 25PI18, SA 5SG39, UR 1AR59, NE 24LE12, PL 14CN06, tNN 28GE45, mNN oCN11.

The interconnections between these three charts make very interesting reading. The strong Jupiter-Neptune contacts in each, with Jupiter in Saggitarius in the first two and Pisces in third, are certainly reflected well in Australian optimism, 'She'll be apples', her love of sport and wide open space, of drinking, gambling and speculation, and her reputation for scandal and corruption in politic, or as Nina Culotta sums it up 'they're a weird mob'. The Venus-Mars contacts in 1770 and 1901 and with Uranus in 1901 bring out the pugnacious camaraderie and strongly hedonistic orientation. The immense emphasis on Earth in all three charts, with the Grand Trines in the 1770 and 1901 charts closely interlocked, reflects not only the strongly materialistic outlook of the nation but also the fact that very literally Australia's enormous material wealth has come, and still comes, from the land, from farming and mining, with manufactured goods only contributing a very small proportion of her GNP. The 1901 chart is typical of charts connected to Britain in having a strong emphasis on 8-9 CN/CP and 28 GE/SG and last degrees of mutables. These of course are highly sensitive areas in the 1066 chart. The especial stress in these areas was reflected on 22 January 1901 in the death of Queen Victoria, just 3 weeks after the formation of the Federation.

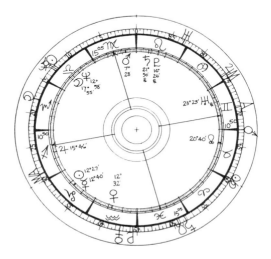

Figure 15.21 Burma — Independence — A classic example of the power that astrologers still wield in Asia the Burmese astrologers chose for the nation to become independent from Britain well before dawn at 04.20 LT, as Jupiter was about to rise in favourable aspect with Moon and Venus, on 4 January 1948, Rangoon, 16N45, 96E20. As traditional Hindu astrologers they would not have considered Neptune's position. Despite the inconvenience of the hour the annual Independence Day parade is still held every year at this same time in the morning!

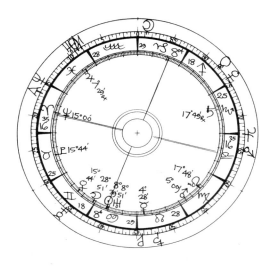

Figure 15.22   Dominion of Canada — This came into being at 00.00 LT, 1 July 1867, Ottawa, 45N27, 75W42, MC/AS 27AQ09.

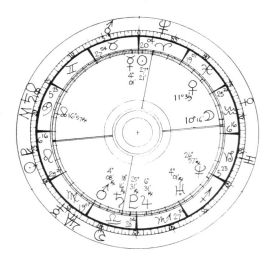

Figure 15.23   Canadian Constitution repatriated — For the signing of the Constitution by the Queen at 11.35 am, 17 April 1982, Ottawa, MC/AS 13GE20, mNN 17CN32.

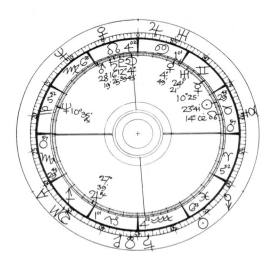

Figure 15.24 Israel declaration of Independence — 16.37 LT = 14.37
GMT, 14 May 1948, Tel Aviv 32N07, 34E45. This is for the moment at
the end of the Declaration of Independence Speech when Ben Gurion struck
the table with his gavel and said 'The State of Israel has arisen!'[13] MC/AS
17VI30, mNN 13TA42. It is also possible to argue for the movement of
the beginning of the Declination Broadcast at 16.00 L.T. = 14.00 GMT,
MC 25CN01 AS 23LI01, MC/AS 9VI01, SO 23°39′48″, MO 4°21′, ME
10°22′, VE 4°48′.

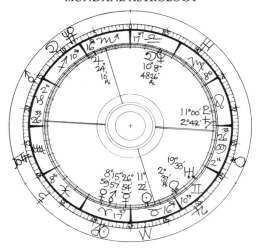

Figure 15.25   Japan new constitution — Came into effect 00.00 LT, 3 May 1947, Tokyo, 35N45, 139E45, MC/AS 21SG43, mNN 3GE47. The new Constitution was agreed 3 November 1946 and provided for a transfer of sovereignty from the emperor to the people.

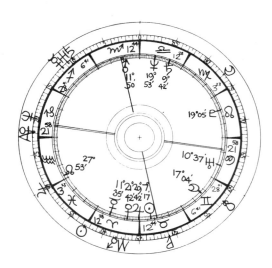

Figure 15.26   Japanese sovereignty restored — 00.00 LT, 28 April 1952, Tokyo, MC/AS 17SG21, mNN 27AQ12 = SO/MO 27TA10.

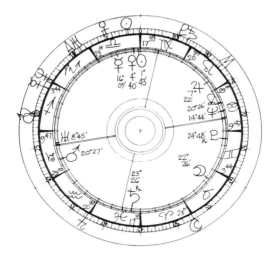

Figure 15.27 is for 11.00 LT, 26 September 1906 = 23.21 GMT on 25, Wellington, New Zealand, 174E46, 41N19, the time that the Dominion of New Zealand was proclaimed. The mNN is 19CN37. This is one of several charts for New Zealand but one which appears to be sensitive to transits. As with the Australian Commonwealth beginning we see here Uranus rising on the 1066/1801 SO and MC/IC. Also like that chart the Moon is in Taurus forming a Grand Trine with Mars and Mercury, again reflecting the very great proportion of New Zealand's wealth which comes from agriculture, forestry, and minerals. The Taurus and strong Venus indicate the natural, easy-going hedonistic materialism which predominates. The Libra emphasis encourages both social concern and love of socializing. The angular Uranus-Neptune-Mercury T-square may be related to the large number of New Zealand Prime Minister's who have died in office and the proneness to scandal and political drama. In the long run it can also be said to promise the possibility of actualizing New Age ideas in the country in a major way. The MA-NN perhaps indicates the love of individual and team sport and also the dependence of the nation on vigorous overseas trade. The Saturn in the fourth -60-MO TA, seems an appropriate reflection not only of the solid material wealth of the nation but also the tendency to be isolated both by distance and by continuing strict currency controls.

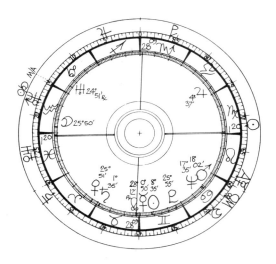

Figure 15.28 Union of South Africa — 00.00 LT, 30 May 1910, Capetown, 33S55, 18E22, MC/AS 14CP45, mNN 27TA50. This chart still appears to be sensitive but needs to be taken in conjunction with 15.

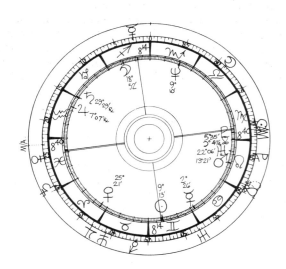

Figure 15.29 Republic of South Africa — 00.00 LT, 30 May 1961, Pretoria, 25S44, 28E12, MC/AS 23CP27, mNN 1VI24.

Figure 15.30 Turkey — Republic proclaimed at 20.30 LT, 29 October 1923, Ankara, 39N57, 32E50, MC/AS 11TA58, mNN 8VI22. This marked a major stage in Kemal Ataturk's program to completely Westernise Turkey and have it considered as an integral part of Europe rather than of the Middle East. In pursuit of this total revolution, in addition to the abolition of the Caliphate, of polygamy, of religious orders, the latinisation of the alphabet, etc., Ataturk also banned the wearing of the fez, which he considered a mark of servitude, and had it replaced with the Lancashire cloth cap. He also decreed that Members of Parliament attend all sessions in white tie and tails, even during the day, reflective perhaps of the ME-0-SA in LI in fifth house!

References

1 Russell, James, *The Horoscope of the United Kingdom*, AJ Vol. III-2.

2 Sibly was publishing an astrology text in parts. The part for 1787 contained the USA chart. All parts were collated into one book which was published as *A New and Complete Illustration of the Occult Sciences,* London, 1790. The USA chart (set for London) faces page 1054.

3 See Baigent, M. *'Ebenezer Sibly and the Time of Signing the Declaration of Independence in the USA,* ISCWA, London, 1984.

4 For a fuller analysis of the chart of the USA and the future trends see: Baigent, M. 'The Astrological Chart of the United States'

The Astrological Journal Winter, 1980-1, p. *3ff*. The Sagittarius rising chart for the USA has today found general acceptance amongst most astrologers both in Europe and the USA. Certain small variations do occur however. For example see Al H. Morrison who places the ascendant rather at 10° Sagittarius; 'Discovering our discoverer' in *CAO Times* Vol.2, no.2, p. 21*ff*, New York, summer, 1976.

 5 See *Astrologica Americana* (ref. 6 below), Appendix H — 'Our National Horoscope' by Manly P. Hall, pp.83-89, for a comprehensive study of the known historical background, which leaves no doubt that the first signature was made 'at approximately 5.00 pm, or a few minutes thereafter'. This does not of course preclude the possibility of other charts being valid for other events.

 6 *Astrologica Americana*, AFA Research Bulletin No. 3, 1949, available from the AFA, gives a most valuable and extensive coverage and discussion of all the main charts for the 'Declaration' together with the charts of key figures and moments in the history of the USA. It is essential reading for anyone wishing to join debate on the knotty issue of the correct US chart.

 7 This chart which has been put forward by Helen Boyd and strongly championed by Jim Lewis is for 11.00 am LT = 16.01 GMT, 4 July 1775, Philadelphia: MC 29GE30, AS 29VI30, SO 14CN16, MO 20LI54, ME 10LE11, VE 26LE14, MA 27VI23, JU 9GE36, SA 2LI56, UR 4GE54, NE 20VI17, PL 25CP33, mNN 27LE00.

 8 Another version of the 'Soviet Russia' chart is that most vigorously advocated by Barry Lyne's for 03.31.30 am EET, on 8 November (*rectified*) when Lunarcharsky read Lenin's proclamation of Soviet power. This chart has MC 25GE19, AS 26VI50, SO 15SC02, MO 29LE18, ME 17SC37, VE 00CP54, MA 3VI00, JU 9GE10R, SA 14LE14, UR 19AQ49, NE 7LE07R, PL 5CN20, mNN 2CP46, mNN 3CP52, Chiron 25PI47R.

 9 This time for the Proclamation of the USSR Constitution is given by Robert Sauve in *L'Astrologue* No. 15, Autumn 1971.

10 Reed, J. *Ten Days that Shook the World*, Harmondsworth: Penguin, 1977, p.138.

11 Baigent, M. 'The natal chart of Communist Russia' *The Astrological Journal* Summer, 1980, p.134*ff*.

12 Tyl, Noel, *Astrology: Mundane, Astral, Occult*, Llewellyn 1975, p.28 gives the chart for the arrival of Mohammed in Medina at sunset 16 July AD 622: MC 00SC, AS 15CP30, SO 15CN27, MO 27LE12, ME 20LE18, VE 15LE21, MA 20VI21, JU 7PI36R, SA 1LE58, UR 1VI12, NE 5VI18, PL 26AR00, NN 6LE48.

13 See *Ben Gurion*, by Michael Bar-Zohar, Weidenfeld 1978, p.163. It is alleged that a transcription of the radio broadcast times this moment as 30" later for which this chart is cast. There is a false chart in wide circulation with a 10LI Ascendant. This is based upon Carter's erroneous statement in IPA that Summer Time was in force. Some astrologers take the beginning of the broadcast at 4.00 pm LT as the significant moment which gives MC 26CN01, AS 23LI01, MC/AS 9VI01. For a full discussion of this and related charts see *Astrology of the Middle East* by Michael Baigent and Charles Harvey, ISCWA 1984.

Bibliography
Sources for National Charts
No single, reliable, source of data for national charts exists at present. ISCWA is working on such a collection and publishes and discusses such charts in its quarterly *Bulletin*. Meanwhile the most comprehensive source of background data available is that published by Robert Sauve in issues 13-28 of Barbault's *L'Astrologue*, between Spring 1971 and Autumn 1974. He unfortunately gives few of his sources and gives no charts or chart positions. The AFA has published series of national charts from time to time in their monthly Bulletin, notably in the mid-1960s. These charts are on file at the AFA HQ. Reinhold Ebertin has always had an interest in mundane and has regularly published charts in his bi-monthly Kosmischer Beobachter and more recently in MER.

Some of the main books containing data and charts of nations are:

ANDERSEN, HANS J., *Astro-Geographie und Geschichte*, Ebertin 1974, pp.400. Anderson gives the charts of the founding of some nations but emphasizes the importance of the main planetary conjunction under which a country comes into being. Thus he considers that Great Britain as an Imperial power was dominated by the UR-0-PL in 29AR35 of 22 June 1850, whilst modern Britain he places under the JU-0-UR of 11 March 1969.

CAMPION, N. 'Mundane astrology and the horoscope of England' *Transit*, 38, August, 1982.

CAMPION, N. The horoscope of the United Kingdom *Transit*, 39, November, 1982; 40, February, 1983.

CARTER, C. E. O., IPA pp.60-69 lists some data and contains a few drawn charts. This appears to be the origin of the erroneous data for Israel. Summer Time was **not** in force.

MALEC, GLENN C., *International Horoscopes*, AFA 1982. Contains the drawn charts and background commentary for 71 countries together with the charts for NATO, Warsaw Pack (no time), CIA, and KGB (no time). Contains some useful data, usually taken from the New York Times. Unfortunately the charts are often for the latest regime rather than fundamental charts for the nation, this together with the lack of adequate research and high proportion of charts without times makes this publication relatively valueless.

MOORE, MOON, *The Book of World Horoscopes*, Seek-It Publications 1980. Gives *a* chart for almost every country in the world, complete with a full two page computer print-out of details including the asteroids, helio and RA positions, complete aspectarian, planetary nodes and mid-points. A worthy attempt to fill the gap. In view of 'the long years of reclusive research' it is a pity that the author shows no familiarity with other work in the field which could have greatly reduced the number of 'time unknown' and 'time assumed' charts. A useful source for the more recently independent colonies where the time has usually been taken from the *New York Times,* but otherwise a 'delusion and a snare'. When you are certain the chart is correct the large quantity of technical data is valuable.

PENFIELD, MARC, Title not yet known, Astro-Computing Services 1984. From discussion with the ACS editor this would seem likely to be a valuable work with computer drawn charts for each nation. The quality of the background research is as yet an unknown quantity.

Data on world leaders is available for:

BARBAULT, ANDRE, *La prévision de l'avenir par l'astrologie,* Hachette 1982, pp.275-286 — This provides a listing of full data for heads of state and Prime Ministers for the past 150, or so, years for France, Germany, Britain, Austria, Belgium, Italy, Russia, Spain, and U.S.A.

APPENDIX I
ABBREVIATIONS USED IN THIS BOOK

The International Astrological Abbreviations (IAA)
For the sake of brevity the IAA has been used throughout in the type setting of this book. This is now the standard, internationally agreed system of two-letter abbreviations for the signs, planets, and angles. If you are not familiar with these you will find them valuable in your own work when glyphs are not possible such as when typing astrological studies and reports. These abbreviations are as follows:

SO	= Sun	NE	= Neptune	LE	= Leo
MO	= Moon	PL	= Pluto	VI	= Virgo
ME	= Mercury	NN	= N. Node	LI	= Libra
VE	= Venus	SN	= S. Node	SC	= Scorpio
MA	= Mars	AR	= Aries	SG	= Sagittarius
JU	= Jupiter	TA	= Taurus	CP	= Capricorn
SA	= Saturn	GE	= Gemini	AQ	= Aquarius
UR	= Uranus	CN	= Cancer	PI	= Pisces

MC = Mid-heaven	IC = Imum Coeli	AS = Descendant
VX = Vertex	EP = Eastern Point	DS = Descendant
	GC = Galactic Centre	

The Aspects are stated as degrees separated by hyphens. Thus:

-0-	= Conjunction	-135-	= Sesquiduadrate
-90-	= Square	-160-	= Quadri-novile
-51-	= Septile	-30-	= Semi-Sextile
-45-	= Semi-Square	-120-	= Trine
-80-	= Bi-Novile	-60-	= Sextile
-108-	= Tri-Decile	-154-	= Tri-Septile
-180-	= Opposition	-40-	= Novile
-72-	= Quintile	-36-	= Decile
-103-	= Bi-Septile	-150-	= Quincunx

Example: SO 2VI17 -45- JU 16CN42, -90- UR 4GE29 would be read as 'The Sun in 2 degrees 17 minutes of Virgo is semi-square Jupiter in 16 degrees 42 minutes of Cancer, and is square to Uranus in 4 degrees 29 minutes of Gemini.'

The **Mid-Point**, abbreviated m.p., between chart factors is indicated by an oblique stroke /.

Example: SO/MO means the mid-point of Sun and Moon or the Sun/Moon mid-point. MC/AS or AS/MC means the mid-point of MC and Ascendant.

When a third body is at the mid-point of another two either by conjunction or by some multiple of -45- this is indicated by an 'equals' sign: = .

Example: JU = SO/MO means that Jupiter is aspecting the mid-point of Sun and Moon either by conjunction, -45-, -90-, -135-, or -180- within an orb of 2°00′ (or 1°30′ when the personal points SO, MO, MC, and AS are not involved).

Example: ME = MA = UR/PL means that both Mercury and Mars are configured with the mid-point of Uranus and Pluto within an orb of 1°30′. Mercury and Mars themselves may be separated by -0-, -45-, -90-, -135-, or -180-. Theoretically, their mutual aspect in this case could be up to 3°00′ as they might be up to 1°30′ either side of the actual UR/PL.

Many additional examples are given in the text.

COSI: Interpretations of such mid-points are to be found in COSI (said 'cosy') = '*The Combination of Stellar Influences*' by Reinhold Ebertin, an invaluable work for mundane analysis as for natal work.

Orbs: These are not normally given but are noted in the usual way in numbers in brackets after the aspect if this is appropriate.

Abbreviations of periodicals and books cited

AJ   *The Astrological Journal,* pub. quarterly by the Astrological Association. Ed. F. S. Matthews, Oakfield, Goose Rye Road, Worplesdon, Surrey, GU3 3PU.

AFA   The American Federation of Astrologers, PO Box 22040, Tempe, Arizona 85282.

ALF   *Annuario Astrologico,* Alfonso X El Sabio, Editorial Eyras, Madrid 1982. This yearbook contains a very high proportion of articles on mundane. See also KEP below.

AQ   *The Astrologer's Quarterly,* pub. The Astrological Lodge of London. Ed. R. C. Davison, 70 Gravel Hill, Croydon, Surrey, CRO 5BE. Published since 1928 contains occasional studies on mundane and a valuable data section.

AR   *Astrological Review,* pub. quarterly by Astrologers' Guild of America. Ed. S. C. Neuschulz, 54 Mineola Boulevard, Mineola, N.Y. 11501, USA.

AS   *Astrology — The New Aquarian Agent,* pub. National Astrological Society (NASO). Ed. Barbara Somerfield, 205 Third Ave, 2A, New York, N.Y. 10003. A valuable publication featuring important articles on mundane.

CA   *Cahiers Astrologiques,* bi-monthly. Ed. Paul Rogel, 7 rue Condorcet, 75009 Paris, France. A quality periodical whose back issues are still available. Special issues devoted mainly to mundane astrology are: nos. 20. 25. 36. 86. 91, and 129.

CAOT   *CAO Times,* Ed. H. Morrison, Box 75, Old Chelsea Station, New York, N.Y. 10113. Publishes occasional studies in mundane and a wide coverage on all areas of astrology.

CEB   *Cosmecology Bulletin,* Ed. Charles A. Jayne, 5 Old Quaker Road, Monroe, N.Y. A fine research-oriented journal.

DEM   *Demain,* bi-monthly journal of the Belgian Astrological Centre.

EC   *The Ecliptic,* quarterly of the British Columbia Astrological Society, PO Box 2046, Vancouver, B.C. V6B 4A6.

IPA   *Introduction to Political Astrology* by C. E. O. Carter, L. N. Fowler, 1951.

ISCWA   Institute for the Study of Cycles in World Affairs, 48 Castle Street, Frome, Somerset BA11 3BW. Publishes monographs on mundane astrology and on the history of astrology. Issues a bulletin on current affairs and world trends, available on subscription.

KEP   *Kepler,* the tri-annual journal of the Spanish Escuela de Astrologia, Calle Union, 9-2, Madird 13, Spain. Ed. Jose Luis San Miguel de Pablos. This school places a strong emphasis on mundane astrology. See also their ALF above.

KOS   *Kosmos,* published quarterly by ISAR, the International Journal of Astrological Research, PO Box 38613, Los Angeles, Calif. 90038, U.S.A.

L'AST   *L'Astrologue,* pub. quarterly. Ed. André Barbault, 44 rue de General Brunet, 75019 Paris, France. Published since 1968, this is one of the finest journals of its kind. Every issue contains valuable studies in mundane, and a wealth of mundane data. A must for every serious mundane astrologer.

MA   *Modern Astrology,* a high quality monthly journal originally founded by Alan Leo, which was published between c.1896-1941.

MN   *Meridian,* bi-monthly. Ed. Hans Geisler, Fichtenstrasse 18, Gundelfingen über Freiberg i Br., West Germany. A high-quality periodocal which has a substantial regular section on mundane astrology by Reinhold Ebertin and others. Regular surveys and forecasts of the German and international political scene are contained in every issue together with retrospective assessments on past performance.

NCGR   National Council for Geocosmic Research, which published a newsletter and a monograph series, runs an educational programme and special library and research resource department: Secy NCGR, PO Box 825, McLean, VA 22101, USA.

QdZ   *Qualitat der Zeit,* Journal of the Austrian Astrological Society, 1030 Vienna, Untere Weissgerbestrasse 61/12, Austria. High quality — occasional studies on mundane.

SP   *Spica — A Review of Sidereal Astrology.* No longer published. Back issues available from the Astrological Association. In its day a regular source of studies in mundane astrology.

SuW   *Sein und Werden,* pub. quarterly by the Kosmobiosophische Gesellschaft. Ed. Edith Wangemann, 85 Schlieffenstrasse, 56-Wupertal-Vohwinkel, W. Germany.

APPENDIX II
NOTE ON THE CHARTS IN THIS BOOK

Some of the chart presentation used in this book may not be entirely familiar to all readers. The inner circle gives the positions on the 360° of the ecliptic in the usual way. The horizontal line always marks the Ascendant/Descendant, and the approximately vertical line the MC/IC. The other house cusps are not drawn in. However the positions of the *Placidus* intermediate cusps are marked alongside their appropriate zodiacal sign. The positions are given in the tropical zodiac unless otherwise stated. Degree and minute positions are normally written to be read from left to right and from top to bottom.

Around the outside of the usual chart is what is known as a

90°-circle, which is numbered in 5° blocks. Each main division represents 1°, which is divided into two sections for greater accuracy. This 90°-circle quite literally folds the 360° of the basic chart into 90°. Starting from 0° and round to 30° represents chart positions in any of the cardinal signs, i.e., AR, CN, LI, and CP. From 30°-60° are positions in the fixed signs, TA, LE, SC, AQR and from 60°-90° are the mutable signs, GE, VI, SG, PI. Any chart factors that appear close together on this circle will be either -0-, -90-, or -180- apart in the normal chart. Any factors which oppose each other across the circle will in fact be -45- or -135- apart in the normal chart. Thus in Fig. 14.17 on p.405 we see the Sun, Moon, Saturn, and Neptune all grouped together in the first degrees of this outer 90°-circle, reflecting the fact that they are all in a T-square in the normal 360° chart. If we look at the AS position, marked A, at nearly 60°, i.e., at the end of the fixed section of the 90°-circle we see that it is exactly 'opposed' the NN at 15°. This reflects that they are in fact closely -45- apart in the 360° chart.

Giving positions in this 90°-circle has several advantages:

1. It enables us to spot immediately groupings of planets linked by 'hard' angles, i.e., multiples of 45°. Since these are the aspects which are particularly related to 'manifestation' and 'events' these will be particularly sensitive points to watch.

2. It offers a uniform scale of presentation. Thus if a New Moon, conjunction, or some other kind of activity is occurring at 0° of a cardinal sign we can check through a large number of charts in a very few moments looking at the 0° point in the circle and see what factors in the chart, if any, are being activated. The same principle applies whatever area is being activated.

3. By extension it offers ease of chart comparison, so that we can quickly see how any two charts 'hit each other off' by activating hard angles aspects with one another.

4. It enables us to spot mid-point combinations, or 'planetary pictures' as they are often called. These have been found to be of very great importance in mundane work, as elsewhere.[1] Any factor in the 90°-circle which is equidistant from two others, either side if it, within an orb of about 1½°, or 2° for personal points Sun, Moon, MC, AS, will be activating their mid-point by an angle of -45-, -90-, -135-, or -180-. This creates a very powerful interaction and mixing of the energies symbolized.

In our example above (Fig. 14.17) we can, for example, see

that Saturn is almost equidistant from Moon and Neptune. This is written SA = MO/NE. Tracing our eye across the circle we can also see that Saturn and Neptune are within orbs of being equidistant from AS and MC, AS and Pluto, and Mars and MC. This is written SA = NE = AS/MC = AS/PL = MA/MC (the actual m.p.s are 4AR54 = 3CN59 = 18AQ20 so that SA, NE, and these points are all mutually configured by a combination of -90-, -180-, and -135-). Thus the 90°-circle throws into sharp relief this otherwise invisible, yet crucially important picture, for the interpretation of which see the text.

Accuracy
The angles of the charts presented are calculated exactly for the time given. In the case of precise astronomical cycles, such as ingresses and planetary phases, and for precise events these are valid. In the case of national charts they should not normally be taken too literally, unless the nation came into being at an official hour, as in the case of the UK.

The Moon's nodes
The question of which node to use, the Mean Node or the True Node, has not yet been resolved by students of astrology. These can vary by almost 2° from one another. The True Node is given in the charts and the position of the Mean Node is usually also added in the 90°-circle. Mundane charts because of their relative accuracy ought to be a valuable testing ground and the authors would be interested to receive readers observations on this point.

References
1   For the interpretation of mid-points, and aspects generally, read the indispensable *The Combination of Stellar Influences* by Reinhold Ebertin, abbreviated as COSI throughout this book. For a general introduction see *Applied Cosmobiology* by Reinhold Ebertin, and *An Introduction to Mid-points* by Charles Harvey.

THE START OF THE AGE OF AQUARIUS

By definition 'The Age of Aquarius' begins when the First Point of Aries precesses into either the equal 30 division of the sidereal sign of Aquarius or into the unequal sidereal constellation, morphomaton, of Aquarius. The moment this occurs will depend on exactly where we fix the boundary of this sidereal sign or constellation. The point varies considerably from author to author and school to school, as witnessed by the wide variations in Ayanamsa, i.e., difference between 0° Aries in the Tropical and Sidereal Zodiacs, in use in India and elsewhere.

The following list is a compilation of the various dates for the beginning of the Age of Aquarius either given or implied by astrologers. When the date is not taken from the text but calculated on the basis of the author's Ayanamsa or other information this may mean that the date given below will be some years different from that intended by the author. This is due to the differing rates for precession employed by different authors. The rate of precession assumed here is 50.25″ per annum. This list is by no means complete but represents those dates collected by the authors to date.

1762: Cheiro, *Book of World Predictions*, p.170.

1811, Jan.: Quoted in *Prediction Annual*, 1983, p.85.

1844: LCDR David Williams in *the Aquarian Age*, AA Journal, Vol. XX, No. 1, 1977/78.

1881: Sepharial, quoted in David Williams, *op. cit.*

1881: This year is also given by Elbert Benjamin (C. C. Zain), who on the basis that there were 1881 pyramid inches in the Grand Gallery of the Great Pyramid, concluded that the Aquarian Age began with the Sun's entry into tropical Aquarius 'at 3h48m24s pm LMT, Washington DC, on 19 January.' (See his *Astrological Lore of All Ages*). This was the date and chart favoured by the English astrologer John Addey who, in 1952/53, did considerable work on the chart set for the different capitals of Europe with results which he described,

in a letter of 27 October 1981 to CH, as 'pretty staggering'.
'1930's': Alice Bailey, *The Externalisation of the Hierarchy*, pp.3, 4, 567.
1962: 5 February: John Sturgess, *The Piscean Age and the Aquarian Age*, p.1. This date is a popular one amongst esoteric groups due to the location of all seven traditional planets (SO, MO, ME, VE, MA, JU, SA) in Aquarius on this day. It is said that the next World Teacher was born on this day. According to Jeanne Dixon, the American clairvoyant, the Teacher was born at 07.17 am, 'somewhere in the Middle East' (Sturgess, *op. cit.*, p.12). There is clearly some confusion about the nature of this teacher in esoteric circles. It is also recorded that the teacher forecast by Dixon is not the new Christ/ Buddha incarnation but rather the Anti-Christ, the child of Satan. All the prophecies so far associated with these claims have proved to be as false as other Millenarian predictions. (See A. Wolden, *op. cit.*, p.116.) The myth of an antichrist born in 1962 was first invented in the 1890's by the French hoaxer Gabriel Jogand as a deliberate fraud (see Christopher McIntosh, *Eliphas Levi and the French Occult Revival*, pp.208-211).
1975: Quoted in A. Woldben, *After Nostradamus*, p.24.
'Around 1980': Rabbi Joel Dobin in *The Astrological Secrets of the Hebrew Sages* 1983, p.65.
1980-1: W. Baron, *Astrologers' Quarterly*, Winter 1983.
1997-2200: C. G. Jung, *The Sign of the Fishes*, Collected Works, Vol. 9, pt. 2, *Aion*, Chapter 6, p.92. As Hand points out, see 2813 below, Nostradamus was part of the inspiration for Jung's thinking here.
2000: Quoted in A. Woldben, *op. cit.*, p.24.
2023: *ibid.*, p.24.
2059: Dane Rudhyar, *The Lunation Cycle*, p. 149.
2130: Quoted in A. Woldben, *op. cit.*, p.24.
2156: Quoted from *Prediction Annual*, 1983, p.85.
2159 Aug.: Robert de Luce, *Constellational Astrology according to the Hindu System*.
2160: Charles Carter, *Introduction to Political Astrology*, p.76. Vera Reid, *Towards Aquarius*, p.8. Paul Councel, *Your Stars of Destiny*, quoted by David Williams *op. cit*.
2260: Gavin Arthur, quoted in James Webb, *The Occult Establishment*, 1981, p.454.

2320: Zip Dobyns, *The Zodiac as a Key to History*, p.24.

2369: Cyril Fagan, *Zodiacs Old and New*, p.29.

2375-6: Powell and Treadgold, *The Sidereal Zodiac*, Cyril Fagan, AFA Bulletin, March 1950, quoted in David Williams, *op. cit.*

2395 June: Graha Laghav, quoted in S. Rajagopola Iyer, *Directions in New Age Astrology*, p.332.

2432 Oct.: Based on Lahiri's Ephemeris ayanamsa, quoted in Iyer, *op. cit.*, p.332.

2441 April: Based on Chitra Ayanamsa, quoted in Iyer, *op. cit.*, p.332.

2441 Dec.: Based on L. Narain Roa Ayanamsa, quoted in Iyer, *op. cit.*, p.332.

2449: Sepharial, *Why the War Will End in 1917*. Sepharial actually refers to the coming of the 'blessed Millenium' rather than directly to the Age of Aquarius, although the latter is his subject of concern.

2481: Sepharial, *The World Horoscope*.

2500: David Davidson, quoted by David Williams, *op. cit.*

2521: Quoted by B. V. raman, *A Manual of Hindu Astrology*, p.51.

2544 Feb: Based on Madras Ephemeris ayanamsa, quoted in Iyer, *op. cit.*, p.332.

2554: Quoted in B. V. Raman, *op. cit.*, p.51.

2557: *ibid.*, p.51.

2658: Max Heindel, *Simplified Scientific Astrology*, pp.134-5 and also quoted in B. V. Raman, *op. cit.*, p.51.

2719: Quoted in B. V. Raman, *op. cit.*, p.332.

2725 July: Based on Revati Ayanamsa, quoted in Iyer, *op. cit.*, p.332.

2740 Spring Equinox: *Prediction Annual 1983*, p.85, quoting R. H. Naylor.'

2813: Robert Hand, *Essays on Astrology*, Para Research 1982, Chapter 13, The Age and Constellation of Pisces. This date, like C. G. Jung's, see 1997 above, is based on the precession of the Vernal Point through the actual irregular morphamaton constellation of Pisces, and not the regular 30° sidereal sign. It marks the Aries Point's contact with the westernmost marking star of the constellation, Beta Pisces, 'The Mouth of the Western Fish'.

3000 + : Rupert Gleadow, *Origins of the Zodiac*, p.171, based on figures given in Fagan, *op. cit.*, p.21, on the basis of Langdon'd writing.

PARTICULAR CHARTS TO BE STUDIED IN ASSESSING WORLD / NATIONAL / GROUP TRENDS

Charts of	Application / Use	Comments	See
1. World powers: USA, USSR, main European nations etc.	Reflects national / international political / economic mood and trends in world	Interrelate specific with larger cyclical picture for world	Chap. 15
2. Major national groups: EEC, NATO, Wrasaw Pact, OPEC etc.	Judging possible collective attitudes and activities, initiatives, tensions etc.	Not easy to assess without clear idea of roles of participants	
3. Each specific nation: Japan, S.A., San Marino, etc.	Reliable chart the only sound basis for consistent forecasting	Several national charts may need to be interrelated	Chap. 15
4. National leaders' charts	Vital clues as to way the national trends likely to be constellated	Leaders' trends can manifest in personal not national life	Chap. 13
5. Groups, organizations, political parties, unions, societies, the C.I.A. etc.	Focusing, corroborating particular trends; studying special areas of national activity	Care needed to distinguish internal activity from that of national import	Chap. 15
6. Ideas and events, e.g. treaties, discoveries, etc.	Important background for evaluating / focussing specific trends / developments	Deserve intensive study to isolate valuable patterns	Chap. 15

The above table illustrates some of the richness of charts that are available to the mundane astrologer. Obviously many others can be added. Thus the charts of major multinational companies ought collectively to show, by inference, the overall mood of the world economy. Charts for the Dollar, Deutsch Mark, Yen or any other currency, where available, can be observed as barometers of likely economic performance.

Every chart represents in some senses a living unity, the ensoulment in time of an idea. As such it will have an inner life of its own and can therefore be progressed and directed like any personal chart. If there is time the 'inner' perspective should not be neglected. A study of the interaction between these inner and outer perspectives will often reveal the creative potential that is likely to be released as the developing idea and the world interact.

APPENDIX V
CALCULATING INGRESS AND OTHER CYCLE CHARTS FOR DIFFERENT LOCATIONS

The times for the entry of the Sun into each sign, and for the New and Full Moons and eclipses is given in most ephemerides, though Raphael's[1] annual ephemeris and the Michelsen[2] ephemerides are the most comprehensive in this respect. However for anyone seriously interested in making a systematic study of these charts the AFA[3] publishes all of these charts each year for the year two years ahead, set for the Capitol Building in Washington D.C. Thus by the end of 1983 it will already be possible to obtain the booklet of 1985 charts. Likewise the Astrocartography annual *Sourcebook of Mundane Maps*[3], described in Chapter 10, is printed a good twelve months in advance. This lists the planetary positions, in both longitude and latitude and in Right Ascension and declination, for all charts including the cardinal sidereal solar ingresses.

When using these charts to study national affairs the angles are normally calculated for the administrative capital city of the country under examination, on the basis that this is the 'heart and decision-making centre' of the nation. What happens in more remote parts of any nation will not always have consequence for the nation as a whole, but what happens at the centre usually tends to reverberate throughout the body politic. Sometimes, such as in the case of Canberra in Australia or Brasilia in Brazil, the official administrative centre is a relatively minor centre of population and there is then a case for also setting a chart for the major centre(s) of population and commerce, or at any rate noting what difference there is on the angles for these major centres. In the case of the USA for example, whilst Washington D.C. is undoubtedly the correct location for which to cast these charts for the nation as a whole, there is a good case for suggesting that charts cast for New York, Chicago, and Los Angeles will also offer additional valuable barometers to the general 'state of the nation' at any particular time. South Africa is a special case here for it has, as befits its strongly divided Sun Gemini, Sagittarius MC, and Pisces AS character, two official capitals, Pretoria, the administrative capital, and Cape Town the legislative capital. Although systematic analysis is needed to corroborate the observation, there would also seem to be a case for saying that the geographical centre of a nation has some claims to being considered as a sort of 'centre of gravity', and planets on angles in this area often seem to reflect the mood and orientation of the nation as a whole, as well as of that a particular area. As will be seen in Chapter 10 the use of Astrocartography in fact makes it possible to check the angularity of planets for differences immediately, so that many charts are not essential.

Transposing charts to other areas of the world

Method one: working in sidereal time
Given that we have the sidereal time at *Greenwich* for a particular chart it is relatively easy to transpose it to any other given longitude simply by adding or subtracting the 'longitude equivalent in time' to this sidereal time, and then taking out the new angles in a table of houses under the appropriate latitude. The 'longitude equivalent in time' is simply the degrees and minutes of longitude multiplied by 4, the answer being minutes and seconds of sidereal time. If the

longitude of the new location is east of Greenwich, we *add* the 'longitude equivalent in time', and if it is west we *subtract* it.

Example 1
The 1983 Capricorn ingress occurs on 22 December 1983 at 10h. 30m. 17s. am GMT, giving a sidereal time at Greenwich (GST) of 16h. 31m. 55s. To calculate the angles for Washington D.C., which is 77W00:

1. Multiply 77.00 by 4 = 508 minutes = 5h. 08m. 00s.
2. This is west so subtract from the Greenwich ST:GST = 16.31.55.
   Less Washington long equivalent in time: -5. 8.00
   = Sidereal time at Washington   11.23.55

A table of houses will give you the angles for Washington under the latitude of Washinton for this ST.

Example 2
To calculate the angles for Canberra, Australia, 149.0BE, 35S17

1. Multiply 149.08 by 4 = 596m. 32s. = 9h. 56m. 32s.
2. This is east so add to the Greenwich ST: GST = 16.31.55
   Add Canberra long. equivalent in time: + 9.56.32
   = Sidereal time at Canberra   26.28.27
   Less 24 hours   24.00.00
   = Sidereal time at Canberra   2.28.27

(Remember: if we are using a table of houses for northern latitudes we will need to add on twelve hours to this total and then take the opposite signs those given.)

Method Two: Working in Right Ascension
An alternative method is to calculate the Right Ascension (R A) of the chart for Greenwich and then add or subtract the actual degrees and minutes of geographical longitude from this value. This will give you the exact degrees and minutes of RA for the new location. Though at first sight rather more complicated, using a table of houses which gives the RA equivalent of the sidereal time makes this method much quicker if the intention is to transpose a chart to many different localities.

Right Ascension is another way of expressing ST and in most tables of houses it is given alongide the ST. Particularly valuable in this context are MC and AS tables (such as those of Kroencke and Lotze)[00] which give the MC for every 1 minute of ST.

Converting sidereal time to Right Ascension The equivalent RA for ST can easily be found with tables by dividing the hours of ST by 2 and the remaining minutes and seconds of ST by 4. The answer will be in signs, degrees and minutes of RA. This can then be easily translated into absolute longitude of RA.

Example 1
In Example 1 above we found that the ST at Greeenwich was 16h. 42m to the nearest minute.

1. Divide the hours by 2 = 16 divide 2 = signs = 8 × 30 degrees
                                                        = 240
2. Divide the minutes by 4 = 32 divide 4 = 8 degrees   8
    Right Ascension at Greenwich for the 1983 Capricorn ingress
                                                        = 248

Had we wanted to be more accurate we would have divided the 31m. 55s. by 4 giving 7 derees 59m. to nearest minute, which added to the 240 gives 247.59.

Once the Greenwich RA is established simply add (east) and subtract (west) the actual geographical longitude of any place and to find the RA for the new location.

References

1   Raphael's Ephemeris, W. Foulsham, published annually in summer for following year, with details of ingresses and other phenomena since 1906.
2   Michelsen, N. Produces a superb range of ephemerides of all kinds including heliocentric and sidereal. Astro Computing Services will also produce, to order, monthly ephemerides *for any period in history* with complete aspectarian.
3   Lewis, J. *Sourcebook of Mundane Maps*, published annually since 1979. Available direct from ACG, Box 22293, San Francisco, or from ISCWA, 48 Castle Street, Frome, Somerset BA11 3BW, England. Personal ACGs are available only from the US address:

·SOME SOURCES FOR THE CHRONOLOGY OF HISTORY, ANCIENT, MODERN AND CONTEMPORARY

Anyone wishing to correlate astrology with history on a systematic basis will need to have not only a good feel for the major trends of particular periods but will also want to have access to sources of systematic chronology. There are various such publications. None of them is perfect, but collectively they do provide a fairly comprehensive picture for any particular period, be it decade, year, month, week, or indeed day. You should however remember that all such works are selective and key events, such as decisions, which did not make the headlines will often go without mention. Thus care should be taken before assuming that 'nothing happened' at a particular time and place. Very few of these list the actual times of events. For this it is necessary to check with original sources, contemporary newspaper reports, the appropriate embassy, library, etc. Some useful source libraries for Britain are listed at the end of this section.

Chronologies
HAYDN, J. *Book of Dates* first published 1841, Ward Lock. This is a classic work and one of the first compilations of its kind, which went through many editions. It has the great advantage of having been set out under alphabetical headings, not only by contries but by towns and general subject matter. Thus, for example, under 'Constantinople' we find a listing of some of the major events in its history from its founding onwards, whilst under 'Elephant' there is a listing of various interesting dates in connection with this noble animal! Very considerable day-by-day detail is given of events in each of the major European countries for much of the nineteenth century. This is one of the only works of this kind which also sometimes notes the exact times of events.

LANGER, ₍W. L. *An Encyclopedia of World History, Ancient, Medieval, and Modern* chronologically arranged, Boston: Houghton Mifflin, 5th ed, 1972. This invaluable work will form an excellent foundation for astro-historical studies. It gives a detailed account of the main political events for each country of the world down to 1970. It also has some material on important cultural and scientific events, though these are by year only.

STEINBERG, S. H. *Historical Tables 50 BC-AD 1977* Macmillan 1977. Lists historical material absolutely chronologically under various areas of the world with separate sections for constitutional, ecclesiatical, economic, cultural highlights, usually carefully dated.

WILLIAMS, N. *Chronology of the Modern World, 1763-1965* London: Barrie and Rockliff, 1966. Gives straight chronology of the political and constitutional world day by day, with comprehensive index. Cultural, scientific, literary events and works of importance are listed for each year but without dates. A few births and deaths of notables are also given.

WILLIAMS, N. *Chronology of the World*   -1762, London: Barrie and Rockliff, 1970. Extends the volume above backwards in the same manner.

Atlases

For those who wish to study the longer-term trends of history, the effect of eclipse paths, and the movement of planetary, precessional and other cycles across the face of the earth, there are various historical atlases which will prove of great value. These allow us to see longer periods of history in particular geographical regions as a unity and as part of a larger process. A selection of these should be available in the reference section of your public library. Some notable ones are: *The Times Atlas of World History, The Hamlyn Atlas of World History*.

Periodical publications

In addition to newspapers and journals there are various publications that do list chronologically the major contemporary events. The most famous of these is *Whitakers Almanac* which in Britain is a valuable general reference work readily available in most public libraries. Of the publications by far the most important for astrological research purposes is:

Keesings Contemporary Archives established in 1931, pub.

MUNDANE ASTROLOGY

Longman, Fourth Avenue, Harlow, Essex. It is issued once a week, with a cumulative index appearing at the end of each year. This gives a detailed account of the major events for each day around the world arranged country by country. This is available at all major public libraries in Britain and probably in most of the English-speaking world. It is also available on subscription.

Whitakers Almanac pub. annually by Whitakers, 13 Bedford Square, London WC1. This is an invaluable quick general reference. It usually has some forty pages listing the main world events for each country for the previous year, whilst under each country it gives an account of the major events and dates in their history. It also lists details of the names of the full cabinet for each country together with the date that the government and the Head of State assumed office. The birth date of the Head of State for each country is also sometimes given. Various other publishers have spasmodically produced reference works on current chronology, and your library will no doubt have others. Under the Dewey Decimal system these are classified under section 902. A recent work of this kind which has proved helpful in analysing 1979 for Chapter 10 is:

HUNT, Sir D. *The Times Yearbook of World Affairs, 1978, and 1979/80.* This publication only ran for two years but it gives a valuable day-by-day account of the major events in every country of the world for the years 1978 and 1979.

Libraries

Most public libraries nowadays hold runs of the major daily newspapers, and files of *The Times* on microfilm are available in all central libraries in Britain. For other and more detailed information you should enquire at your local library. For Britain two primary sources are:

The British Library, Great Russell Street, London WC1. This is the primary source for all books printed in Britain and the English language. Special application for a reader's ticket is required. It is always crowded with long waits for books. This is a library for all-day work. Other libraries are often more useful for quick references. The photocopy service can take several weeks to deliver.

The Colindale Newspaper Library. This is an invaluable source for all British newspapers and an ideal starting-point for contemporary accounts of current affairs.

It is essential to check all dates in recent history in newspapers where possible as history books frequently record inaccurate dates. The historians primary task is to interpret the past rather than to record dates with precision whereas for the astrologer it is vital to know the date of an event.

The *Royal Institute of International Affairs*, 10 St James Square, London SW1Y 4LE runs a press library which lists cuttings under various subject headings, e.g., 'France, Politics, 1958'. This saves much time but unfortunately due to lack of storage facilities only the files back to 1950 are readily available. A ticket to the library costs £60 per year.

In cases where times are required for events it may be possible to search for official documents in national archives for example in the *Public Records Office* in London. The time of any Parliamentary announcement will be recorded in *Hansard,* the official transcript of Parliamentary debates. Especially useful are the *BBC's* transcripts of radio transmissions from most countries in the world, from which it is possible to time any event, such as a declaration of independence, which involved a radio broadcast. These transcripts may be obtained from the BBC for a fee or consulted free of charge in the *British Library.* In some cases the press and information services of embassies may be helpful but more often than not these will repsond to a specific question by sending out the latest propaganda brochure.

Museums and research institutions are often ready to help and in London the *Imperial War Museum* and the *Atomic Energy Agency* have both supplied exact data used by the authors.

If there is any doubt about the standard time used in a particular country then this may be checked with the *National Maritime Museum* at Greenwich or the *Science Research Council.*

If the background to a particular event is not known then there are certain recognised histories to consult. The many volumes of the *Oxford* and *Cambridge Histories* are standard works.

The Institute for the Study of Cycles in World Affairs was established by the three authors of this book in 1980, with the aim of promoting the study of mundane astrology. The Institute collates data and research and publishes its own material. It produces a quarterly magazine, the *Bulletin of Mundane Astrology*, which contains an astrological review of current affairs, data and horoscopes. For details please write to ISCWA, 48 Castle Street, Frome, Somerset BA11 3BW, United Kingdom.

INDEX

Index of Places

•

General Index